Agreement in Natural Language

Agreement in Natural Language

APPROACHES, THEORIES, DESCRIPTIONS

EDITED BY MICHAEL BARLOW & CHARLES A. FERGUSON

CSLI CENTER FOR THE STUDY
OF LANGUAGE
AND INFORMATION

CSLI was founded early in 1983 by researchers from Stanford University, SRI International, and Xerox PARC to further research and development of integrated theories of language, information, and computation. CSLI headquarters and the publication offices are located at the Stanford site.

CSLI/SRI International   **CSLI/Stanford**   **CSLI/Xerox PARC**
333 Ravenswood Avenue   Ventura Hall   3333 Coyote Hill Road
Menlo Park, CA 94025   Stanford, CA 94305   Palo Alto, CA 94304

Library of Congress Cataloging-in-Publication Data

Papers presented at a conference held at Stanford University in October 1984 and sponsored by Stanford's Dept. of Linguistics and Center for the Study of Language and Information.
Includes bibliography and indexes.
1. Grammar, Comparative and general–Agreement–Congresses. I. Barlow, Michael. II. Ferguson, Charles Albert, 1921–   III. Stanford University. Dept. of Linguistics. IV. Stanford University. Center for the Study of Language and Information.
P299.A35A35   1988   415   86-71109
ISBN 0-937073-02-4

Preface

THIS BOOK GREW out of a conference on Agreement in Natural Language, held at Stanford in October 1984, and sponsored by the Department of Linguistics and the Center for the Study of Language and Information (CSLI) at Stanford University.

The papers in this volume appear substantially in the form in which they were submitted by the authors. Thanks are due to CSLI for its generous support of the conference and the production of this volume. We also wish to thank Joan Bresnan, Lauri Karttunen, Paul Kiparsky, and Stanley Peters for their help in selecting the papers for inclusion in the volume and their support of the conference, and Suzanne Kemmer for sundry editorial assistance. Special thanks to Dikran Karagueuzian, who guided this volume through to fruition.

We would also like to thank the people who worked on the production of this book: Tom Burke for typesetting the manuscript; Emma Pease for the design of special characters using Metafont; Nancy Etchemendy for the cover design, and Dikran Karagueuzian for the book design.

M.B.

C.A.F.

September, 1987

Contributors

JUDITH L. AISSEN is Professor of Linguistics at the University of California at Santa Cruz. Her book *Tzotzil Clause Structure* was published in Spring, 1987 by Reidel.

LEONARD H. BABBY is Professor of Linguistics in the Department of Modern Languages and Linguistics at Cornell University. He is working on a book dealing with case theory in inflected languages.

SANDRA CHUNG is Professor of Linguistics at the University of California, Santa Cruz. She is the author of several articles on the grammar of Chamorro and has also written on the syntax of other Austronesian languages (notably Indonesian, Samoan, and Maori).

GREVILLE G. CORBETT is Reader in Russian at the University of Surrey. He is the author of *Hierarchies, Targets and Controllers: Agreement Patterns in Slavic* (Croom Helm 1983) and a co-author of *Computers, Language Learning and Language Teaching* (Cambridge University Press 1985). He is working on a book entitled *Gender*, to be published by Cambridge University Press.

WILLIAM CROFT is Assistant Professor in the Program in Linguistics at the University of Michigan at Ann Arbor. He is currently revising his dissertation, *Categories and Relations in Syntax: the Clause-Level Organization of Information*, and is working on a book on typological methodology.

KATHERINE A. DEMUTH is Assistant Professor of African Languages & Linguistics at Boston University. She has written *Aspects of Sesotho Language Acquisition* (IULC 1983) and several articles on African languages and acquisition. She is currently working on discourse, agreement

vii

phenomena, and argument structure in Setswana and Sesotho and is initiating work on the acquisition of Sesotho tone.

EDIT DORON is Lecturer in the English Department at the Hebrew University of Jerusalem. Her work includes a study of the semantics of predicate-nominals and the syntax of predicate-nominals in Hebrew.

ABDELKADER FASSI FEHRI is Professor of General and Arabic Linguistics at Mohamed V University in Rabat. He is the author of *Linguistique arabe: Forme et interprétation* (Publications of the Faculty of Letters and Human Sciences, Rabat 1982), *allisa:niyya:t wa lluRa l-ᶜarabiyya* (Toubgal Publishers, Casablanca 1985), and *al-muᶜjam l-ᶜarabi:, nama:dij tahli:liya jadi:da* (Toubgal Publishers, Casablanca 1986). He is writing a book entitled *Issues in Arabic Linguistics*.

CAROL GEORGOPOULOS is Clinical Assistant Professor of Linguistics, teaching syntax and semantics in the Linguistics Program at the University of Utah, Salt Lake City. Current projects include preparation of a book on Palauan syntax and organization of a program in cognitive science.

STEVEN G. LAPOINTE is Associate Professor of Linguistics in the Department of English at Wayne State University. He has written numerous articles on agreement and the interaction of syntax and morphology. He is working on a series of articles exploring autolexical associations between linguistic representations.

CHRISTIAN LEHMANN is Professor of Linguistics in the Faculty of Linguistics and Literature at the University of Bielefeld. He has written books on the Latin conditional sentence and the typology of relative clauses. He is writing a book on grammaticalization and editing a reader on the tasks of linguistics.

LYNELL MARCHESE is a translation consultant for United Bible Societies in Lome, Togo. She is the author of *Atlas linguistique des langues Kru* (Institut de Linguistique Appliquée 1979) and *Tense/Aspect and the Development of Auxiliaries in Kru Languages* (Summer Institute of Linguistics 1986) and is writing a book on Godié discourse.

EDITH A. MORAVCSIK is Associate Professor of Linguistics at the University of Wisconsin, Milwaukee. She is working on a syntax textbook which surveys a variety of contemporary approaches to syntax.

LINDA SCHWARTZ is Associate Professor of Linguistics at Indiana University. Her research interests include syntax and typology and she has written a number of papers on agreement and coordination.

SUSAN STEELE is Professor of Linguistics at the University of Arizona. Her major research interest is the place of grammatical elements of syntactic theory, which is pursued in *An Encyclopedia of AUX* and in her forthcoming book *A Syntax of Luiseño*.

ALAN TIMBERLAKE is Professor in the Department of Slavic Languages at the University of California, Berkeley. He currently has a National Endowment for the Humanities grant and is writing a book entitled *Grammar and Text*.

Contents

1 Introduction

CHARLES A. FERGUSON & MICHAEL BARLOW

THE PHENOMENA OF grammatical agreement or concord, by which a grammatical element X matches a grammatical element Y in property Z within some grammatical configuration, are widespread in human languages and must somehow be accommodated in any full-scale grammatical theory. It might be possible to construct a theory in which agreement plays the central role (perhaps "concordial grammar"?), but linguistic theorists have generally treated agreement phenomena as secondary or even marginal or incidental. The papers in this volume, however, all take agreement phenomena seriously, as presenting either a general issue in theory construction or a descriptive problem in particular types of languages. The theoretical perspectives range from purportedly theory-neutral typological frameworks to assumption of the validity of one or another current formal model. Also, the degree of generality ranges from a universalist nature-of-human-language agenda to concern with one or another aspect of grammatical agreement or with agreement in a single language or set of closely related languages.

These papers as well as others similar to them in aims and perspectives are evidence of a new interest in the phenomena of agreement which may conveniently be dated to Moravcsik (1978). Research in a number of areas since then has led to an increased interest in the possibility of giving a general account of agreement.

First, as might be expected, work on typology and universals has revealed the existence of hierarchies, detailed the range of agreement

Thanks are due to Suzanne Kemmer and Thomas Wasow for their comments on earlier versions of this introduction.

patterns, and discovered universal generalizations about agreement. A comprehensive survey of types of agreement, such as that given in Moravcsik (1978) and Lehmann (1982), reveals the extent (and limitations) of the diversity of the standard agreement constructions. The influence of typological/universal approaches is evident in this volume in the papers of Corbett, Croft, Lapointe, Lehmann, and Moravcsik.

A related area of research on agreement comes from a functional perspective on language phenomena. (See, for example, Givón 1984.) Papers in this volume that have a functional flavor are Croft, Lehmann, and Moravcsik. Lehmann, in particular, adopts a functional account in the sense that he gives an explanation of what agreement is in terms of what agreement does from a communicative perspective.

Third, interest in agreement has arisen from work within particular grammatical theories. All the major formal theories regard agreement as a part of language that should be accounted for within the theory. Naturally, work in this area has led to accounts of agreement couched in terms of specific grammatical frameworks, though many of the authors in this volume have customized the theory within which they work in order to treat agreement phenomena. Research in this area can be loosely grouped under the following theoretical perspectives:

(1) Extended Standard Theory and Government-Binding Theory: Chomsky (1981, 1982), Chung and Georgopoulos (this volume), Doron (this volume), Lapointe (1980), Lapointe (this volume).

(2) Lexical-Functional Grammar: Kaplan and Bresnan (1982), Bresnan and Mchombo (1986), Fassi Fehri (this volume).

(3) Relational Grammar (and Arc Pair Grammar): Perlmutter (1983), Aissen (this volume).

(4) Generalized Phrase Structure Grammar and Categorial Grammar: Sag and Klein (1982), Cann (1984), Gazdar et al. (1985), Pullum (1985), Zwicky (1986), Steele (this volume), Timberlake (this volume).

In addition to these approaches to agreement, there are other fields of linguistics that have contributed to research on agreement, such as historical linguistics (Givón 1976, Greenberg 1978, Naro 1981, Marchese, this volume), language acquisition research (Karmiloff-Smith 1979, Demuth, this volume) and sociolinguistic research (Corbett 1979, Poplak 1980, Guy 1987).

A representative selection of treatments of agreement was made in preparation for the conference that led to the compilation of this volume, and most of the participants made some effort to become familiar with items on the list: Anderson (1982), Chafe (1977), Corbett (1979, 1983), Fassi Fehri (1981), Givón (1976), Keenan (1974), Lapointe (1982), Lehmann (1982), Moravcsik (1978), Ostrowski (1982), Schwartz (1978). Other more recent contributions to the study of agreement include the papers of ESCOL '84 (Alvarez et al. 1985) and BLS 1985 (e.g., Nichols

1985, Fryzinger 1985). In spite of the new data provided in all these papers and the increased sophistication of analysis and metatheoretical discussions, no consensus has been reached on the limits to be set on what constitutes grammatical agreement or on the basic parameters in terms of which agreement phenomena can or should be characterized.

Descriptions of Agreement

In traditional, textbook-style descriptions of agreement the typical examples provided are adjective agreement with head noun in gender, number and case, and verb agreement with subject in person and number; and the languages typically chosen for illustration are Latin (or another highly inflected European language such as French or Old English) and Swahili (or another Bantu language); cf. Bloomfield (1933:191-194); Jespersen (1922:335-336, 348-350, 352-355); Lyons (1968:239-246, 263-265). Thus in (1) the Latin noun *virorum* 'of men' is inherently masculine in gender and is overtly marked as genitive plural; the adjectives match the noun by being overtly marked as genitive plural, and although *omnium* is not marked distinctively for gender, *bonorum* is at least marked as either masculine or neuter (i.e., not feminine).[1]

(1)   virorum   omnium   bonorum

        man.MASC.PL.GEN   all.PL.GEN   good.MASC.PL.GEN

        'of all good men'   *Latin*

In the Swahili example in (2) the subject *wa-toto* is overtly marked as animate plural (with the class 2 marker *wa*) and the verb *wa-nakula* matches the subject by being marked as animate plural.

(2)   wa-toto   wa-nakula   mkate

        CL2-child   CL2-eat   fish

        'The children are eating fish.'   *Swahili*

In moving from an account that can handle types of agreement such as (1) and (2) to a thorough study of agreement in general, it is necessary to come to grips with the following points of inquiry:

Domain. What is the domain of agreement, i.e., what kinds of elements agree with what kinds of elements in what kinds of grammatical configurations (in what kinds of languages)?

---

[1] The conventions for glossing morphemes in this volume are as follows. Hyphens are used to indicate relevant morpheme boundaries in both the example and the gloss. If no morpheme boundaries are indicated in the example, then feature specifications in the gloss are separated by periods. Finally, zero-marking is represented by enclosing the relevant feature within parentheses.

Features. In what properties may grammatical elements agree, i.e., what grammatical categories, inherent or overtly marked, are matched in agreement constructions?

Directionality. Which direction does the agreement relation go, in other words, which element is the starting point or "controller" of the matching and which is the "target" or one that matches? Alternatively, should such matching be treated as correlative and non-directional?

Strictness. How "strict" is the agreement, i.e., how exactly do the agreeing sets of categories match up? What neutralizations and syncretisms occur, and what kinds of "mismatches" are found?

Conflict. When two or more patterns of agreement are in conflict (e.g., "semantic" vs. "syntactic" agreement, different categories in coordinated series of head nouns, etc.) what kinds of "resolution rules" operate?

Variation. Under what circumstances are there alternative agreement options, i.e., when may more than one pattern of agreement be grammatical, and what sociolinguistic or pragmatic functions may be served by such options?

Function. What syntactic, semantic, or pragmatic functions may agreement serve, and under what conditions?

Change. What are the diachronic sources of systems of agreement and their various components, and what becomes of them over time?

For all these areas, it is important to identify both positive and negative generalizations, in other words, to pay attention to both the extent of existing patterns and the limitations on variation.

Domain

Once a close investigation is undertaken, several general questions immediately arise, such as:

Is there one phenomenon of agreement that covers, for example, both person agreement and number agreement (cf. Croft, this volume)? Is there one phenomenon of agreement that covers both NP-internal agreement and NP-external agreement (see Moravcsik 1978, Lehmann, this volume)?

Such questions come down to the fundamental issue of whether there is one agreement relation or many. The authors in this volume tend to describe a restricted set of agreement phenomena, suggesting perhaps that there are several distinct but related agreement processes. None of the authors attempts to provide a full characterization of agreement. Lapointe's paper is perhaps widest in scope, yet he too delimits a set of agreement phenomena that falls within his treatment.

Viewed from the perspective of grammatical description rather than language, the domain question concerns what part or parts of the grammar give the most adequate account of agreement. Proposed answers to this complex question include the following levels: morphology (Lapointe, this volume); syntax (Aissen, this volume, Doron, this volume, Gazdar et al. 1985); f-structure (Fassi Fehri, this volume); a logical or semantic representation (Lapointe, this volume, Gazdar et al. 1985); and a "discourse level" (Fassi Fehri, this volume, Bresnan and Mchombo 1986, Barlow 1988). The question of levels is further complicated if one distinguishes the selection problem (what agrees with what) from the determination problem (how are the agreement features instantiated). See Morgan (1972) for discussion.

The domain question is clearly the most basic. Agreement similar to the familiar prototypical cases appears in many other constructions, such as between verb and direct or indirect object, between non-final verb and (different) subject of final verb, or between head noun and quantifier. In fact, wherever the analyst starts to identify a particular phenomenon as agreement it seems possible to extend the notion further and further until it overlaps with phenomena that are not traditionally so labeled, and defensible boundary criteria are needed to set it off from other natural entities of universal grammar. For example, it is not a far cry from the traditional examples of agreement just cited to the kind of category matching illustrated in (3).

(3)   The old man left, didn't he?

Akmajian et al. (1984) note that in English "the pronoun in [a] tag question must agree in person, number, and gender with the subject" (p. 53) as when the *he* of (3) agrees with the grammatical categories of the noun phrase *the old man*. It does not take many steps from this to including intersentential pronominal anaphora as an example of such agreement, and it raises the question of whether agreement is with the head noun or with the whole noun phrase.

In Hebrew and Classical Greek the attributive adjective agrees with its head noun not only in gender and number (and in Greek, case) but also in definiteness, as in (4) and (5):

(4) a. isha   tov-a   axat
         woman   good-FEM.SG   oneFEM.SG

         'a good woman'

     b. ha-isha   ha-tov-a
         the-woman   the-good-FEM.SG

         'the good woman'   *Hebrew*

(5) a. gune   agath-e
         woman   good-FEM.SG

         'a good woman'

b. he   gune   he   agath-e
the.FEM.SG woman   the.FEM.SG good-FEM.SG

'the good woman'   *Classical Greek*

This same phenomenon appears in Arabic, both Classical and Colloquial:

(6) a.   rajul-u-n   kabiir-u-n
man-NOM-INDEF   big-NOM-INDEF

'a big man'

b.   ar-rajul-u   l-kabiir-u
the-man-NOM   the-big-NOM

'the big man'   *Classical Arabic*

(7) a.   rižžaal   kbiir
man   big

'a big man'

b.   r-rižžaal   l-kbiir
the-man   the-big

'the big man'   *Syrian Arabic*

Just as the adjective agrees with its head noun in definiteness, so the relative clause as a whole agrees with its head noun in definiteness, again in both Classical and Colloquial Arabic:

(8) a.   rajul-u-n   raʔay-tu-hu   ʔams
man-NOM-INDEF   saw-I-him   yesterday

'a man that I saw yesterday'

b.   ar-rajul-u   l-laðii   raʔay-tu-hu   ʔams
the-man-NOM   the-REL   saw-I-him   yesterday

'the man that I saw yesterday'   *Classical Arabic*

(9) a.   rižžaal   šuf-t-o   mbaarih
man   saw-I-him   yesterday

'a man that I saw yesterday'

b.   r-rižžaal   l-li   šuf-t-o   mbaarih
the-man   the-REL   I-saw-him   yesterday

'the man that I saw yesterday'   *Syrian Arabic*

In some varieties of Lebanese Arabic the relative *lli* is actually short-ened to *l-* 'the' so that the parallel with the adjective is complete (Feghali 1958:310). Thus the agreement in definiteness between noun and attri-butive adjective is readily extended to agreement between noun and the relative clause as a whole, thereby enlarging the domain of agreement from words to clauses; cf. other kinds of agreement between relative clause and antecedent discussed in Chung and Georgopoulos (this vol-ume).

Two other examples from Arabic will serve to suggest directions in which the domain of agreement may be extended or where a principled means of constraining the domain may be sought. One is the agreement between the 'of' preposition and the possessed noun it connects with its possessor. In Egyptian Arabic and various Maghribi dialects, and some other varieties of Arabic, the preposition 'of' has masculine singu-lar, feminine singular, and plural forms exhibiting agreement with the possessed noun (Mitchell 1962:18, 20, 25).

(10) a.   il-beet   bitaa^c   il-mudiir
           the-house.MASC.SG   of.MASC.SG   the-manager

          'the manager's house'

    b.   il-gineen-a   bita^c-t   il-beet
          the-garden-FEM.SG   of-FEM.SG   the-house

          'the garden of the house'

    c.   il-biyuut   bituu^c   iš-širka
          the-houses.PL   of.PL   the-company

          'the company's houses'   *Egyptian Arabic*

(The agreement on the preposition in (10c) may also be feminine singu-lar, since *biyuut* 'houses' is non-human plural. See below under **Varia-tion**.) This 'of' agreement falls outside the syntactic configurations of head/modifier, function/argument, and the like, in terms of which at-tempts are usually made to define the domain of agreement (cf. Keenan 1974), yet agreement of a possession marker with either possessed or possessor is well attested in the world's languages (cf. Lehmann, this volume).

A final example of matching is that of adjacency pairs in discourse. The typical case is where a conventional reply to a stock formula echoes a lexical item or grammatical category. This kind of matching may seem far from the more typical examples of agreement, but the root-echo responses of Arabic politeness exchanges come close to our prototypes. In many varieties of spoken Arabic certain initiating politeness formulas are responded to by a formula of the shape 'God do-something-to you' in which the verb 'do-something-to' agrees with the triconsonantal root morpheme of the initiating formula. Thus in Syrian Arabic, any of the formulas of (11) has (12) as its matching response. The agreeing roots are italicized.

(11) a. ma^c s-sa*laa*me
          with   the-peace
          'goodbye' (said to the one leaving)

   b. nšaalla ^{c}a-s-sa*laa*me
       if-God-wills   on-the-wellbeing
       'hope everything turns out all right' (said to someone about to undergo risk)

   c. sa*l*-li*m*li ^{c}al-ee
       greet-for-me   on-him
       'remember me to him'

   d. wa-^{c}alay-kumu   s-sa*laa*m
       and-on-you   the-peace
       'and peace be to you' (said in response to *?assalaamu* ^{c}*alaykum* 'peace be to you')

(12)   ?alla ysa*llm*ak
        'God keep you [in health, safety, peace]'   *Syrian Arabic*

Is it too extreme to suggest that the root-echo response "might be dealt with by the same formal devices used to describe concord"? (Ferguson 1983.)

Probably the two most obviously neighboring kinds of grammatical phenomena are anaphora and government. Some analysts treat anaphora and agreement as phenomena of the same general types; others treat them totally separately. Some analysts regard government and agreement as opposites; others see them as related types of the same general phenomenon. Some of the papers in this volume offer evidence or include argumentation on these points.

Intimately connected to these issues is the question of directionality, discussed below, and the determination of sources (controllers) and targets. For example, many researchers assume that in the sentence *Birds fly*, the subject, *birds*, is the source or controller of the agreement relation and *fly* is the target. But what can be said about controllers and targets in general? One common assumption is that the controller of agreement must be nominal or pronominal. This is true in the vast majority of cases; however, it has been suggested that there are examples in which a verb or other category acts as a controller of agreement. (See Lapointe, this volume, for a list of types.)

Even if we assume, for simplicity's sake, that the source of agreement is syntactic and nominal, several questions remain. For example, what projections of N can control agreement? In NP-internal agreement, is the source of agreement the category N̄ or NP? Different accounts take different positions on this issue. For example, it is assumed in Gazdar et al. (1985) that N̄ can be a controller for an attributive adjective. On the other hand, Lehmann and Babby both suggest (this volume) that in fact the NP is the controller.

Not surprisingly, the problems of determining the controller increase with greater structural complexity. Corbett (this volume) describes the difficulties in ascertaining the controller in conjoined noun phrases, comitatives, and quantified expressions. He also gives examples showing that the case of the controller is important.

Corbett also raises the problem of "missing" controllers, a topic discussed from a different perspective in Chomsky (1981) and in the Government-Binding literature in general. The GB literature is concerned primarily with the determination of properties governing the distribution of empty categories. (See Doron, this volume.) There are also examples in which two or more elements compete for one agreement slot. Corbett suggests that a predicate NP can oust a subject NP as controller. He gives the following Czech example as part of his evidence that the verb *je* is agreeing with the predicate complement, *pět*.

(13)   dvě a   tři   je   pět

       two and three is.SG five

       'Two and three are five'.   *Czech*

Pět imposes singular agreement, while the subject 'two and three' would normally produce plural agreement.

The characterization of controllers is discussed by Aissen in Relational Grammar terms in her paper on brother-in-law agreement. In the Relational Grammar literature, it has been suggested that agreement controllers are final terms and are dependent on the same node as their targets. However, the controllers in brother-in-law agreement do not have these properties. An example of brother-in-law agreement given in Aissen (this volume) is (14):

(14)   There seem to be unicorns in the garden.

Aissen notes that *seem* agrees with *unicorns*, a pattern that violates two laws of Relational Grammar because *unicorns* is not a final term, nor is it a dependent of the same node as *seem*. In her paper, Aissen formally identifies this class of controller and relates it to regular controllers.

Determining the target of agreement poses fewer problems than determining the source of agreement relations, since targets, by definition, carry the agreement markers. Lapointe (this volume) lists the possible grammatical targets of agreement. Nevertheless, the determination of targets is not always clear-cut; various problems remain, mostly concerning the determination of defaults and resolution rules, which are discussed by Corbett (this volume).

Features

One of the key questions for any kind of general definition of agreement is the identification of those grammatical properties that can match in agreement. The ideal answer would presumably be a principle or set of principles—syntactic, semantic, or other—which would neatly define a list of possible agreement properties. At the present time the best that can be done is a listing of agreement features that have been noted in descriptions of the world's languages, perhaps grouped together into some general types. A convenient such list is Pullum's "brief catalog of agreement properties" clustered under the headings of person, number, gender, and case (Pullum 1985:80-81). A truly comprehensive list would doubtless include other features and offer a different classification. For example, definiteness/indefiniteness is not mentioned by Pullum although it is well attested as an agreement feature and is a major complicating factor in Germanic agreement systems from Old English to Modern German (cf. the account of Norwegian agreement in Lapointe 1985).

Numeral classifiers, which would presumably be included under Pullum's heading of gender, offer a particularly interesting set of semantic features based on such characteristics as shape, size, and function. It can hardly be accidental that the widespread classifier systems of East Asia and the Americas, unlike the full-scale noun class systems of many African languages, are often limited to numeral plus noun combinations and anaphoric constructions with demonstratives and possessive pronouns. (See below under **Change** for discussion of diachronic trends in agreement systems.)

In many languages with rich inflectional morphology the markers of grammatical categories are often fused so that portmanteau morphs appear in common paradigms, as when Latin inflectional suffixes confound case, gender, and declensional classes. This may not complicate an abstract representation of agreement patterns, but it typically requires extensive ad hoc "spelling out" rules of allomorphy. One theoretical issue here is whether a principled account is possible which would predict which features are more likely to fuse under what conditions. Equally interesting is the question of the differential incidence of grammatical categories in the agreeing word classes. The subject-verb agreement features of Bengali illustrate both of these points (cf. Ferguson 1964). Bengali independent pronouns have distinct forms for 12 person/number/respect grading categories: 1st person; 2nd person inferior, 2nd ordinary, 2nd honorific; 3rd person ordinary, 3rd honorific; all singular vs. plural. Bengali verbs have fused tense-mode-aspect/person suffixes with extensive

homophony, but for each TMA set of forms (each "tense"), there is unambiguous marking of 5 person/respect-grade/number categories: 1st
person; 2nd INF, 2nd ORD; 3rd ORD; 2nd/3rd HON; no singular-plural
distinction. Thus, for example, (a) -*i* is the 1st person ending in the
present but the 2nd INF in the future, and -*o* is the 2nd ORD in the
present but 1st person in the future, while (b) only 5 feature-values in
the verb agree with 12 feature-values in the subject pronoun. Examination of a large number of languages might well reveal a hierarchy of
features and feature-bearers in relation to likelihood of fusion and neutralization. This question is touched on in the discussions of markedness
theory in this volume (e.g., Croft, Lapointe, Moravcsik).

Other questions arise with respect to agreement features. For example, is there one set of features that "take part" in every agreement
relation (even if not expressed) in a language? Related to this is the question of whether the agreement features are clustered in one entity (e.g.,
AGR, INFL or a pronoun). An alternative to the idea of a bundle of agreement features is that at least some of the features act independently.

These questions are not addressed directly in this volume, although
it would seem that if there are several agreement relations, then there is
less likelihood of there being one set of agreement features. In addition,
there seems to be some evidence that case, for example, is an agreement
feature that appears in some agreement relations, but not in others. For
example, in Classical Arabic the attributive adjective agrees with the
head noun in case (as well as gender, number and definiteness) as shown
in (15).

(15) a. al-mu^{c}allim-u   al-jadiid-u
         DEF-teacher(MASC.SG)-NOM   DEF-new(MASC.SG)-NOM
         'the new teacher'

     b. al-mu^{c}allim-i   al-jadiid-i
         DEF-teacher(MASC.SG)-GEN   DEF-new(MASC.SG)-GEN
         'of the new teacher'   *Classical Arabic*

The predicate adjective agrees with the subject in number and gender
as (16) shows.

(16) a. al-mu^{c}allim-u   jadiid-u-n
         DEF-teacher(MASC.SG)-NOM   new(MASC.SG)-NOM-INDEF
         'The teacher is new.'

     b. al-mu^{c}allim-at-u   jadiid-at-u-n
         DEF-teacher(SG)-FEM-NOM   new(SG)-FEM-NOM-INDEF
         'The (female) teacher is new.'   *Classical Arabic*

The predicate adjective, however, does not agree with the subject in case. Certain verbs such as *kaana*, the past tense of the copula, impose an accusative case on the predicate adjective, as shown in the following examples.

(17) a.   muḥammad-u   kabiir-un
          muḥammad-NOM   old-NOM

          'Mohammed is old.'

    b.   kaana   muḥammad-u   kabiir-an
         was   muḥammad-NOM   old-ACC

         'Mohammed was old.'

    c.   *kaana   muḥammad-u   kabiir-un
         was   muḥammad-NOM   old-NOM

         'Mohammed was old.'   *Classical Arabic*

Although the predicate adjective is usually nominative, as in (17a), in (17b), *kaana* induces accusative case on the adjective, resulting in a mismatch between the case of the subject and the case of the predicate adjective.

Directionality

For most of the examples cited in this volume the directionality of agreement is taken for granted: the controller has a certain feature inherently or by government and the target matches that feature. In many instances, however, this relation is not so obvious. For example, in a language in which a subject pronoun is not normally expressed but appears only when functioning as topic, focus, or bearer of "emphasis," the subject marking morphs on the verb that indicate person, number, and gender (or other concordial features) play a different role from similar subject markers in a language where the subject pronoun is required. It seems to make more sense to say that the verb agrees with the subject when the subject must be present in the sentence than it does to say so when the subject pronoun itself is optional and the categorial information about the subject must appear on the verb. It is almost as though the overt pronoun, when supplied, must agree with the verb rather than vice versa. From this perspective, the designation of INFL (Chomsky 1981) as the head with which the subject agrees may be more valid than the traditional view of verb agreeing with subject, expressed or not.

A more general treatment of directionality in agreement appears in Nichols (1985), where the author attempts to discover generalizations about the circumstances under which agreement goes "downward" from head to non-head (or higher head to lower head) or goes "upward" from non-head to head (cf. her discussion of head-marking vs. dependent-marking in Nichols 1986). Nichols concludes that the direction of agreement is upward in verb-subject and preposition-noun constructions, but may be in either direction within NPs. She suggests that the fact that the directionality of the agreement relation in noun-adjective constructions is overwhelmingly downward is an accidental property, due only to the lack of inherent features in adjectives. However, the more straightforward generalization might be the traditional one that the controller in agreement is typically a nominal expression, and that "all agreement refers to an NP" (Lehmann, this volume).

In any case, the question of directionality deserves further investigation. It is, incidentally, the kind of question for which acquisition data, diachronic data, and psycholinguistic experimentation may be especially suggestive.

Other approaches to agreement would try to characterize agreement without assuming *a priori* that one element is the originator and the other is the recipient of agreement features. This line is followed to some extent in grammatical theories that involve a declarative checking of features, such as GPSG and LFG. These theories have incorporated the notion of unification of features, which fits with a view in which no one category or level has a preferred status for contributing information (cf. Barlow 1986).

One advantage of non-directional accounts of agreement is that they can easily handle cases in which sources are not fully specified with respect to agreement features. For example, Greenberg (1963) noted that gender marking on pronouns conforms, with few exceptions, to an implicational hierarchy which can be stated as 1st → 2nd → 3rd. Thus it is relatively rare for the 1st person pronoun to show gender marking. However, the targets of agreement often exhibit gender marking even when it is absent from the source, as shown in the French example in (18).

(18) a.   Je suis heureux

   b.   Je suis heureuse

Data such as these may cause difficulties for directional theories of agreement.

Strictness

However the feature matching of agreement is regarded, whether as a discontinuous morpheme, some form of morpheme harmony or "long component" or is accomplished in a generative grammar by copying, percolating, projection, "spelling out," the operation of AGR, or some other formal device or set of devices, the basic notion is that the same feature appears in several places related syntactically, semantically, or functionally. Yet in many instances the matching is split, or partial, or ambiguous in ways that cause serious complications for any of these devices.

Further complications come from feature mismatches. One of the long-recognized concordial mismatches is the agreement with neuter plural nouns in Classical Greek. Determiners and adjectives show strict agreement with neuter plural head nouns in both number and gender (and also case), but verbs are regularly singular with neuter plural subjects. For example, (19) is quoted in Cann (1984:340).

(19)   kala   e:n   ta
        good.NOM.PL.NEUT   was(3.SG)   the

        sphagia
        sacrifice.NOM.PL.NEUT

        'The sacrifices were auspicious.'   *Classical Greek*

More striking is the pattern of agreement in Arabic in which [-human] noun plurals (especially the internal, "broken" plurals) typically take feminine singular adjectives, verbs, and anaphoric pronouns, although plural agreement is sometimes also possible. Even just these two examples suggest some kind of semantic/syntactic hierarchy of animacy and number, and data from other languages provide further evidence for this. (For an interesting discussion of one source of feature mismatches, see Schwartz, this volume.)

Some languages show feature shifts or even reversals in special subareas of agreement, one of the best known being the "polarity" patterns of gender reversal in Afro-Asiatic languages, typified by the Semitic pattern of the numerals '3' to '10' taking the opposite gender of the noun they are in construction with (Speiser 1938). Such systematic mismatches deserve more explanatory treatment than the ad hoc "irregular" labeling advocated by Pullum for a Somali feature reversal of this kind (Pullum 1985).

Conflict

Corbett and others have investigated the operation of synchronic resolution rules that yield preferred outcomes for conflicting patterns of agreement. Such conflicts may be associated with the following linguistic phenomena:

(20) a.   coordination

     b.   comitative phrases

     c.   marking of respect

     d.   semantic vs. syntactic agreement

e. quantifier phrases, numerals

f. lexical idiosyncrasies

g. word order

h. syntactic distance

i. case of the controller

j. attraction

The classic case of agreement conflict is the conjoined series of nouns or pronouns which belong to different agreement categories and thereby call for conflicting agreement in the predicate or in modifiers. Typical examples are conjoined pronouns of different persons and conjoined nouns of different genders or numbers. Linguistic factors associated with the resolution rules which operate in such cases include feature hierarchies, relative distance of the noun phrase from the target, and whether the controller precedes or follows the target. Pragmatic or sociolinguistic factors may also have a role in these rules.

The location of resolution rules in a grammar may raise interesting questions that vary, of course, with the theoretical model. Turning again to Syrian Arabic for an example, we find that a series of conjoined plural nouns referring to inanimate objects typically takes a feminine singular predicate adjective or verb, but if one or more singular or dual noun(s) is (or are) included in the series, plural agreement is required. In a descriptively adequate grammar of Syrian Arabic such a resolution rule would ideally fall out from the general agreement principles specified for the language. The specification of possible forms of resolution rules in general, however, remains a problem for linguistic theory, as Corbett observes.

Not all cases of agreement conflict are of the conjunct type. One kind that appears in many languages is the use of polite pronouns of address whose original person/number/gender conflicts with the person/number/gender of their referent in polite use. Thus Russian *vy* 'you' is originally plural but is used as a polite singular, and when it is so used both forms of agreement occur, depending on the word class of the target and the particular syntactic construction (Comrie 1975).

In some languages constructions with numerals offer complex agreement patterns that are hard to specify and even harder to relate to general principles or "universals." Again, it is Corbett who has done the most work on this question, since the Slavic languages have a challenging set of numeral agreement patterns. An Arabic example would be the agreement with a noun accompanying a numeral between 11 and 101. Such numerals take singular nouns and an adjective immediately following usually agrees in number (and gender) with the noun, but other targets of the noun phrase may be plural or (for inanimates) feminine singular.

Variation

The rules of agreement in a language ideally yield a single solution, but may of course result in alternative possibilities. Variation may arise from any of the sources mentioned under **Conflict** above.

In some instances alternative patterns of agreement are acceptable without apparent change in meaning. Such alternatives, as with other grammatical or phonological options, may reflect user preferences depending on social parameters of age, sex, class, etc., or may be determined by pragmatic considerations or communicative strategies. In either case, the variation in use may be a manifestation of a change in progress. Thus in Syrian Arabic the sentence 'I got some letters' may take any of the three shapes given in (21).

(21) a. ʔižaa-ni   makatiib
         came.3.MASC.SG-me letters

     b. ʔižit-ni   makatiib
         came.3.FEM.SG-me   letters

     c. ʔižuu-ni   makatiib
         came.3.PL-me letters   *Syrian Arabic*

The most common variant is probably (b): inanimate plurals generally take feminine singular agreement. The plural agreement of (c) is least likely: use of a plural verb with inanimate subject suggests an emphasis on the plurality (e.g., in contrast to receipt of a single letter), or a kind of personification (e.g., the letters viewed as deliberately coming), or an attraction to a series of plural agreements (e.g., with human subjects). The masculine singular agreement of (a) is an option available when the subject is indefinite and immediately follows the verb. This use of the unmarked 3.MASC.SG form of the verb with a subject of any gender and number is a remnant of the older general rule of verb-initial sentences in Classical Arabic (Ferguson 1984, Russell 1985).

Corbett (this volume and elsewhere) discusses many examples of variation in agreement and gives details of the effect of sociolinguistic factors (cf. esp. Corbett 1983). Variation of this kind is more often treated, however, in sociolinguistically oriented studies (cf. Naro 1981 on variation and change in Portuguese agreement).

Function

Authors interested in the grammatical or communicative functions of agreement have sometimes emphasized its apparent uselessness. Thus Jespersen (1922), who discussed the Latin example (22) as well as examples from other European and Bantu languages, regarded agreement as "superfluous" or even "cumbersome" and asserted that "concord is really a primitive trait" (p. 352-354).

(22)   opera virorum omnium bonorum veterum
        'works of all the good old men'

Recognizing that the redundant marking of categories in agreement might have the advantage of allowing word order to be freer, Jespersen apparently checked out possible ambiguities in unusual word orders in Latin verse and decided that the actual use of this disambiguating function was negligible, hence not sufficient to justify the existence of agreement. Modern authors, who generally avoid such strong value judgments on aspects of grammar, occasionally echo Jespersen's unhappiness with agreement. Haiman (1985), for example, refers to noun class systems and concord as "notoriously dysfunctional" (p. 162) and goes on to assert that "grammatical agreement seems a clear case of the victory of the indexical aspect of language over its iconic aspect" (p. 162) and that it is "not only non-iconic but meaningless" (p. 164).

As with any instances of apparent redundancy in language, at least three types of functions are possible explanations. The most obvious is the overcoming of "noise" in the system: multiple cues are better than a single cue when the latter is attenuated, missing, or masked by other material. The second possible function is that of "freeing" some other, presumed non-redundant expression to fulfill other functions. Thus agreement may license use of word order for topicalization, focusing, and other functions, or it may license the omission of case marking on nouns in certain grammatical relations. Finally, the apparent redundancy may be interpreted as not redundant at all, but as contributing to the message in a direct way. This is what is presumably intended by Lehmann's claim that the basic function of agreement is "referential," or what is quite explicit in Reid's complete abandonment of the notion of semantic redundancy in agreement (Reid 1985; see also Barlow 1988).

Givón (1976) finds multiple functions at least for subject-verb agreement, which he claims always arises from anaphoric pronoun paradigms in topical discourse contexts. The various synchronic functions of agreement systems, in this view, may be secondary and unpredictable, and the crucial explanatory fact is the "natural diachronic origin" of the phenomenon of agreement. Croft's paper (this volume), which accepts the pronominal origin of subject-verb agreement, offers a synchronic functional account. Agreement cross-indexes the most "important" referents: the most animate, the most definite, the most central to the events being reported.

It is interesting to note that all the functionalist explanations are in terms of efficiency in the referential use of language; no one seems to have considered the playful, poetic, aesthetic use of language, which is probably of considerable importance in the evolution and acquisition of language as well as contributing to the creative, system-building side of language. It might be worth exploring the possibility that agreement persists and even spreads in response to the same kind of factors at work in the conventionalization and persistence of rhymed word-pairs, prose rhythms, patterned repetitions, and the like.

Change

The claim has been made that systems of agreement arise by the route of an independent pronoun becoming cliticized to its verb as an anaphoric copy and then becoming incorporated as an agreement marker. Evidence of this kind of history has been presented for a number of languages (cf. Givón 1976), but counterevidence for some of these languages has also been offered (e.g., Russell 1985). Bresnan and Mchombo (1986), in a theoretical discussion of the relation between anaphora and agreement, suggest possible steps by which such a historical sequence might take place.

The "coalescence" theory of the origin of agreement systems is inadequate as it stands in that it does not apply to all forms of agreement (if indeed all forms of agreement are to be derived from certain general principles, cf. Green 1985) and there is in many languages insufficient evidence to reconstruct such a history or even negative evidence. Lehmann (this volume) offers some additional detail for this line of historical explanation of the origin of agreement, but there are few general treatments of how agreement systems change over time, e.g., factors accounting both for the various paths of dissolution of person/number concord in subject-verb agreement in the Germanic languages and the various paths of growing complexity of argument-predicate agreement in Iroquois-Caddoan languages (Chafe 1977). For this reason, historical studies of particular languages or groups of languages are especially valuable, such as Marchese (this volume), whose discussion includes reference to an animacy hierarchy, phonological conditioning, and non-pronominal anaphoric elements as factors in the paths of change.

Conclusion

The papers in this volume differ widely in theoretical and methodological perspectives and in the particular languages they discuss. They also differ in the extent to which they cope with the eight "points" commented on in this introduction. The authors do, however, share a serious interest in the grammatical phenomenon of agreement, and it is our hope that the papers they have written will contribute directly to the overall characterization of grammatical agreement, will aid in the solution of problems of analysis in particular languages, will stimulate grammatical theorists to deal more effectively with agreement, and in these and other ways will add to our understanding of the nature and uses of human language.

References

(Exclusive of articles in this volume.)

Akmajian, A., R. A. Demers and R. M. Harnish 1984. *Linguistics: An Introduction to Language and Communication.* 2nd ed. Cambridge, Mass.: The MIT Press.

Alvarez, G., B. Brodie and T. McCoy (Eds) 1985. *ESCOL '84: Proceedings of the First Eastern States Conference On Linguistics.* Columbus: Department of Linguistics, Ohio State University. (13 papers from the special session on agreement 1–164.)

Anderson, S. R. 1982. Where's morphology? *Linguistic Inquiry* 13:571–612.

Barlow, M. 1986. Unification and agreement. Paper presented at the Linguistic Society of America Winter Meeting, New York.

Barlow, M. 1988. *A Situated Theory of Agreement.* Doctoral dissertation, Stanford University.

Bloomfield, L. 1933. *Language.* New York: Holt, Rinehart and Winston.

Bresnan, J. and S. Mchombo 1986. Grammatical and anaphoric agreement. *Papers from the Twenty Second Regional Meeting of the Chicago Linguistic Society.*

Cann, R. 1984. *Features and Morphology in Generalized Phrase Structure Grammar.* Doctoral dissertation, University of Sussex.

Chafe, W. L. 1977. The evolution of third person verb agreement in the Iroquoian languages. In C. N. Li (Ed), *Mechanisms of Syntactic Change.* Austin: University of Texas Press.

Chomsky, N. 1981. *Lectures on Government and Binding.* Dordrecht: Foris.

Chomsky, N. 1982. *Some Concepts and Consequences of the Theory of Government and Binding.* Cambridge, Mass.: The MIT Press.

Comrie, B. 1975. Polite plurals and predicate agreement. *Language* 51:406–18.

Corbett, G. G. 1979. The agreement hierarchy. *Journal of Linguistics* 15:203–224.

Corbett, G. G. 1983. *Hierarchies, Targets and Controllers: Agreement Patterns in Slavic.* London: Croom Helm. (Also University Park: Pennsylvania State University Press.)

Fassi Fehri, A. 1981. Théorie lexicale-fonctionelle, controle et accord en arabe moderne. *Arabica* 28:299–332.

Feghali, P. 1958. *Syntaxe des Parlers Arabes Actuels du Liban.* Paris: Imprimerie Nationale; Librairie Geuthner.

Ferguson, C. A. 1964. Basic grammatical categories of Bengali. In H. Lunt (Ed), *Proceedings of the Ninth International Congress of Linguists.* The Hague: Mouton.

Ferguson, C. A. 1983. God wishes in Syrian Arabic. *Mediterranean Language Review* 1:65–83.

Ferguson, C. A. 1984. Grammatical agreement in Classical Arabic and the colloquial dialects. Paper presented at the meeting of the Middle Eastern Studies Association of North America.

Fryzinger, Z. 1985. Ergativity, number, and agreement. *Proceedings of the Eleventh Annual Meeting of the Berkeley Linguistics Society,* 96–106.

Gazdar, G., E. Klein, G. K. Pullum and I. A. Sag 1985. *Generalized Phrase Structure Grammar.* Cambridge, Mass.: Harvard University Press.

Givón, T. 1976. Topic, pronoun, and grammatical agreement. In C. N. Li (Ed), *Subject and Topic.* New York: Academic Press.

Givón, T. 1984. *Syntax: A Functional-Typological Introduction.* Vol. I. Amsterdam: John Benjamins.

Green, G. M. 1985. Why agreement must be stipulated for there-insertion. In Alvarez et al. (Eds), *ESCOL '84: Proceedings of the First Eastern States Conference On Linguistics.*

Greenberg, J. H. 1963. Some universals of grammar with particular reference to the order of meaningful elements. In J. H. Greenberg (Ed), *Universals of Language.* Cambridge, Mass.: The MIT Press.

Greenberg, J. H. 1978. How does a language acquire gender markers? In J. H. Greenberg (Ed), *Universals of Human Language* 3. Stanford: Stanford University Press.

Guy, G. 1987. Functional constraints on linguistic variation. Paper presented at Stanford University.

Haiman, J. 1985. *Natural Syntax.* Cambridge, England: Cambridge University Press.

Jespersen, O. 1922. *Language: Its Nature, Development and Origin.* New York: Macmillan.

Kaplan, R. and J. Bresnan 1982. A formal system for grammatical representation. In J. Bresnan (Ed), *The Mental Representation of Grammatical Relations.* Cambridge, Mass.: The MIT Press.

Karmiloff-Smith, A. 1979. *A Functional Approach to Child Language: A Study of Determiners and Reference.* Cambridge, England: Cambridge University Press.

Keenan, E. 1974. The functional principle: generalizing the notion 'subject of.' *Papers from the Tenth Regional Meeting of the Chicago Linguistic Society.*

Lapointe, S. G. 1980. *A Theory of Grammatical Agreement.* Doctoral dissertation, University of Massachusetts, Amherst.

Lapointe, S. G. 1982. A comparison of two recent theories of agreement. *Papers from the Parasession on the Interplay of Phonology, Morphology, and Syntax, Eighteenth Regional Meeting of the Chicago Linguistic Society,* 122–134.

Lapointe, S. G. 1985. Cooccurrence and agreement in Norwegian noun phrases. In Alvarez et al. (Eds), *ESCOL '84: Proceedings of the First Eastern States Conference On Linguistics.*

Lehmann, C. 1982. Universal and typological aspects of agreement. In H. Seiler and F. J. Stachowiak (Eds), *Apprehension: das sprachliche Erfassen von Gegenständen.* Teil II. Tübingen: Gunter Narr.

Lyons, J. 1968. *Introduction to Theoretical Linguistics.* Cambridge, England: Cambridge University Press.

Mitchell, T. F. 1962. *Colloquial Arabic.* London: English Universities Press.

Moravcsik, E. A. 1978. Agreement. In J. H. Greenberg (Ed), *Universals of Human Language* 4. Stanford: Stanford University Press.

Morgan, J. 1972. Verb agreement as a rule of English. *Papers from the Eighth Regional Meeting of the Chicago Linguistic Society.*

Naro, A. 1981. The social and structural dimensions of a syntactic change. *Language* 57:63–98.

Nichols, J. 1985. The directionality of agreement. *Proceedings of the Eleventh Annual Meeting of the Berkeley Linguistics Society.*

Nichols, J. 1986. Head-marking and dependent-marking grammar. *Language* 62:56–119.

Ostrowski, M. 1982. Zum Konzept der Kongruenz. In H. Seiler and C. Lehmann (Eds), *Apprehension: das sprachliche Erfassen von Gegenständen*. Teil I. Tübingen: Gunter Narr.

Perlmutter, D. (Ed) 1983. *Studies in Relational Grammar*. Chicago: The University of Chicago Press.

Poplack, S. 1980. Deletion and disambiguation in Puerto Rican Spanish. *Language* 56:371–85.

Pullum, G. K. 1985. How complex could an agreement system be? In Alvarez et al. (Eds), *ESCOL '84: Proceedings of the First Eastern States Conference On Linguistics*.

Reid, W. 1985. Verb agreement as a case of semantic redundancy. In Alvarez et al. (Eds), *ESCOL '84: Proceedings of the First Eastern States Conference On Linguistics*.

Russell, R. A. 1985. Historical aspects of subject-verb agreement in Arabic. In Alvarez et al. (Eds), *ESCOL '84: Proceedings of the First Eastern States Conference On Linguistics*.

Sag, I. A. and E. Klein. 1982. The syntax and semantics of English expletive pronoun constructions. In M. Barlow, D. Flickinger, and I. A. Sag (Eds), *Developments in Generalized Phrase Structure Grammar*. Stanford Working Papers in Grammatical Theory 2, 92–136. Bloomington: Indiana University Linguistics Club.

Schwartz, L. 1978. Object agreement in animacy precedence languages. Paper presented at the Fourth Annual Minnesota Regional Conference on Language and Linguistics, Minneapolis.

Speiser, E. A. 1938. The pitfalls of polarity. *Language* 14:187–202.

Zwicky, A. 1986. German adjective agreement in GPSG. *Linguistics* 24(5):957–90.

2 Agreement: A Partial Specification Based on Slavonic Data

GREVILLE G. CORBETT

THIS PAPER IS an attempt to specify what is required of that portion of linguistic theory which is concerned with agreement. The data are taken from Slavonic languages, which are a somewhat conservative group within Indo-European. Even within this limited area, there are ample difficulties; naturally, a linguistic theory must meet these and many more from beyond Slavonic for it to be considered an adequate account of agreement. The justification for a paper of this type is that theorists, after long treating agreement merely as a diagnostic (with notable exceptions such as Morgan 1972), are now increasingly viewing it as an important problem in its own right. This new approach is shared by linguists of different persuasions. There is now the danger that old problems will be 'rediscovered' and time wasted going over old ground. Therefore the range of problematic agreement data from Slavonic is set out in a form which will be accessible to other investigators, so that at least the groundwork need not be repeated. In order to make the survey of wider use, I have tried, as far as is possible, to keep it neutral relative to different theories. Of course, data which cause severe

Versions of this paper were read at the Conference on Agreement, Department of Linguistics and Center for the Study of Language and Information, Stanford University, and in the Department of Linguistics, University of Southern California, in October 1984. I am grateful to all those who made comments, especially to Professor Bernard Comrie. I also wish to thank the British Academy for a grant enabling me to attend the conference.

difficulties in one theoretical framework may be completely straightforward in another, and so some sections are likely to be of greater interest than others to individual readers.

1 Basic Requirements

At the very least, a linguistic theory should allow us to incorporate the equivalent of traditional statements such as: *in Polish, attributive adjectives agree with their head nouns in number;* or, more generally, *in a given language, X agrees with Y in Z.* The definition of *agrees with* is problematic, but need not detain us since it is intimately bound up with the particular theory adopted. We shall use agreement in the traditional sense, to refer to the matching of properties between elements in specified syntactic configurations. Whether there is any directionality involved and, if so, the way it goes, depends on the theory and so will be left open. We shall follow normal usage, whereby adjectives are said to agree with nouns, predicates with subjects, without implying more than a matching of properties.

When we state that: *X agrees with Y*, we specify the *domain* of agreement. We shall refer to the *X* element (the attributive adjective, for example) as the *target* and the *Y* element (the head noun) as the *controller*. This usage mirrors the relationship implied by *agrees with* but nothing crucial depends on the terms adopted. While any theory must be able to specify the domains of agreement, if it can predict them (as, for example, in Keenan 1974), this is clearly a considerable advantage. In addition to specifying the domain, we must indicate the agreement properties involved (agreement *in Z*). Following Moravcsik (1978) we shall refer to them as *agreement features,* whether or not they are to be handled by feature notation.

If we are to give an adequate theoretical description of agreement in Slavonic, the theory will have to enable us to include the following, in a principled way:

a. The attributive adjective normally agrees with its head noun in number, case and gender.

b. The predicate normally agrees with the subject in some combination of number, case, person and gender.

c. The relative and personal pronouns normally agree with their antecedent in number and gender.

Difficulties arise as soon as we try to make this account more precise and to leave out the occurrences of *normally*. These difficulties will be dealt with under *controller problems* (sec. 2), *target problems* (sec. 3), and *feature problems* (sec. 4), but it is important to note that several of the difficulties cut across this classification. An important set of problems involves agreement choices—situations in which alternative agreement features can be assigned. We shall note these in the appropriate section, and then consider the general questions of choices separately (sec. 5). Thus Sections 2–4 are concerned with the possibilities which occur, including the existence of options, while Section 5 concentrates on constructions which permit alternative agreement forms and on the factors which influence the choice.

2 Controller Problems

We need to be able to specify what is the controller (sec. 2.1) and what agreement features it carries (sec. 2.2). Hence there are two potential sources of difficulty. A third set of problems arises from the effect of other rules, which make the status of the controller less clear (sec. 2.3).

2.1 Identifying the Controller

Most problems of identifying the controller are structural, relating to particular constructions rather than lexical items. These are of two main types: first, those where it is clear which constituent is the *overall* controller, but where it is not clear which is the element within it whose features match those of the target; and second, instances where different constituents are potential controllers.

2.1.1 Competition within the Controller

There are three types of phrase in Slavonic which may function as the overall controller, yet present problems as to which element within them is the controller. They occur in various domains, of which we shall consider subject-predicate agreement. The first type is familiar; it consists of conjoined noun phrases. Consider the following Russian examples:

(1)   prepodavalis'   matematika   i   fizika
       taught.PL.REFL   mathematics.FEM.SG and   physics.FEM.SG
       'Mathematics and Physics were taught.'

(2)   prepodavalas'   matematika   i
       taught.FEM.SG.REFL mathematics.FEM.SG and
       fizika
       physics.FEM.SG
       'Mathematics and Physics were taught.'
                                              (Graudina et al. 1976, 31)

In (1) the predicate verb is plural, showing agreement with the conjoined noun phrases as a whole. Since neither of the conjoined noun phrases is plural, some sort of feature computation is required. Such feature computations, or *resolution rules,* pose problems for certain theories. Example (2), on the other hand, shows predicate agreement with just one of the conjoined noun phrases. Since both are of the same gender, we cannot tell which controls the agreement. We must therefore look at an example with NPs of different gender:

(3)   byla   v nej i   skromnost',   i

    was.FEM.SG in her and modesty.FEM.SG and

    izjaščestvo,   i   dostoinstvo

    elegance.NEUT.SG and dignity.NEUT.SG

    'She was modest, elegant and dignified.'

              (*Pravda,* quoted by Graudina et al. 1976, 31)

In this example it is clear that agreement is with *skromnost'* as this noun is feminine singular. Agreement with one of the other nouns would be ungrammatical. *Skromnost'* is both the first NP in the series and the nearest to the verb; it is the latter characteristic which is the more important, as is shown by comparison with examples with the subject before the predicate. It should be said that Slavonic languages are classified as SVO, but that VS order, as in the examples so far, is very common; word order depends, to a significant extent, on information structure. In examples with the subject preceding the predicate, the normal possibilities are again agreement with all the NPs or with just the nearest.[1] This appears to be the case throughout the Slavonic family.

There is, however, a further possibility, which is uncommon. It is *distant agreement,* that is to say agreement with the first conjunct, which, with subject-verb word order, is not the nearest. Examples occur in Slovenian, a South Slavonic language:

(4)   knjige   in   peresa   so   se

    book.FEM.PL and pen.NEUT.PL are selves

    podražile

    got dear.FEM.PL

    'Books and pens have become more expensive.'

              (Quoted from Lenček 1972, 59.)

Similar examples occur in Slovenian's closest relative, Serbo-Croat; the most extensive source is Megaard (1976). (It has also been claimed that

---

[1] See Corbett (1983a, 98–99) for examples. This work is referred to several times since it is in English and gives details of other sources of data. Data which are set out fully in that work are dealt with only briefly here, and certain claims made in this paper are more adequately justified there. While a proportion of the material covered has been discussed before, this paper focusses on those data which are most problematic for linguistic theory.

agreement in Čakavian dialects of the 16th–17th centuries could be with the most important conjunct, even if this were not the nearest or the first, Glavan 1927–28, 143-5; the evidence is very limited.)

The data from agreement with conjoined noun phrases require a theory to incorporate the following: resolution rules or their equivalent (to which we shall return) to cover the cases where agreement is with all the conjuncts; the ability to identify the conjunct nearest the predicate, when agreement is with one conjunct only. This information must be obtainable from that level of representation where word order dependent on information structure has been determined. For some languages there is the additional requirement that it must be possible to identify the first conjunct.[2]

In a related construction, the place of the conjoined noun phrases is taken by NPs linked with the preposition $s(o)$ or its equivalent; in this construction the NPs refer to animates. In the East Slavonic languages we again find both singular and plural agreement, as in this Russian example (Nichols et al. 1980, 375):

(5)   Fon Manštejna   čut'   bylo   ne   otpravil/otpravili
      Von Mannstein.ACC   little was   not   sent.MASC.SG/PL

      na tot   svet   Avdeev   so
      to that world   Avdeev.NOM.MASC.SG with

      svoim   vedomym
      his own.INST co-pilot.INST

      'Avdeev and his co-pilot almost sent Von Mannstein to the
      other world.'

The point of interest is that while in previous examples all the conjuncts were in the nominative case, in this construction the structure is NP(nominative) + preposition + NP(instrumental). If agreement is singular, then it is with the NP standing in the nominative; this is entirely as expected since in Slavonic subjects must stand in the nominative to control subject-verb agreement. When plural agreement is found in examples like (5), this indicates that the oblique conjunct is in some sense "taken into account".[3] Thus the agreement rules must be able to

---

[2] In certain frameworks it may matter whether one claims, in examples like (2)–(4), that agreement is with just one NP, or with all the NPs though taking the features of just one. This latter claim would be possible if there were a higher NP node which could take features from just one of the dominated NPs.

[3] Note that when the NP in the nominative is a pronoun, then this alone controls the agreement.

identify the comitative phrase as a whole as being nominative, and then include the oblique NP in the feature computations.

Similar situations arise with quantified expressions. These are particularly varied and complex in Slavonic; only the most salient difficulties will be described here. Though it is impossible to talk of a typical Slavonic numeral, we will start with the Russian numeral *pjat'* 'five' as a representative quantifier. When itself in the nominative case, it requires quantified nouns to stand in the genitive. A subject consisting of such a quantified expression may take either neuter singular or plural agreement:

(6)   vošlo   pjat'   devušek
       entered.NEUT.SG   five.NOM   girl.GEN.PL

       'Five girls came in.'

(7)   vošli   pjat'   devušek
       entered.PL   five.NOM   girl.GEN.PL

       'Five girls came in.'

Both (6) and (7) are fully acceptable. The question arises as to what exactly is the controller. One analysis of (6) is that it shows the failure of the subject to provide the required features: *pjat'* is not marked for number and gender and so the verb stands in the *default form* (sec. 2.2). Sentence (7) is more difficult. It appears that, as in the comitative construction just discussed, the fact that part of the subject is in the nominative is sufficient to allow access to the features of an NP in an oblique case. Thus the plural feature comes from the noun (see Corbett 1983a, 216–20 for justification). This position is strengthened by reference to Serbo-Croat which, unlike Russian, preserves gender distinctions in the plural:

(8)   pet   devojaka   su   došle
       five girl.GEN.PL   are.PL   come.FEM.PL

       'Five girls have come.'

Though the singular is more likely in Serbo-Croat, when the plural occurs it shows agreement in gender with the noun, as in (8). West Slavonic languages go further, in that adjectival predicates agree with the noun in case, as the following Polish example demonstrates:

(9)   pięć   piór   jest   nowych
       five.NOM   pen.GEN.PL   is.SG   new.GEN.PL

       'Five pens are new.'

Here *nowych* obviously agrees fully with the noun; it is not so clear what controls the agreement of the verb; one interpretation would be that it is the default form, as in (6), which results as the verb cannot reflect both genitive and plural. The main point is that the overall controller can be identified but that isolating the element which controls agreement is not so straightforward. It is evident that the relations are different in the three languages with this one numeral. On top of that, there are profound differences in the agreement and other syntactic behavior of numerals within individual languages. As an example, consider the Russian numeral *tysjača* 'thousand'. Like *pjat'*, it can take neuter singular or plural predicate agreement; in addition it can take feminine singular agreement:

(10) ljubaja   tysjača   načal'nikov   dannogo
      any.NOM.FEM.SG thousand.NOM   chief.GEN.PL given.GEN

      ranga   ravnocenna   ljuboj   drugoj
      rank.GEN   equivalent.FEM.SG   any.DAT   other.DAT

      togo   že   ranga
      that.GEN   same   rank.GEN

      'Any thousand chiefs of a given rank is equivalent to any other thousand of the same rank.'   (Zinov'ev)

In this example *tysjača*, which is in many respects like a feminine singular noun, controls the agreement.

Even between controllers which allow only plural or neuter singular agreement, there is great variation in the relative frequency of these options, as Table 1 illustrates.

quantifier	eighteenth century			nineteenth century			twentieth century		
	sg	pl	%pl	sg	pl	%pl	sg	pl	%pl
2–4	55	357	87	54	357	87	146	710	83
5–10	19	34	64	74	82	53	110	110	50
collectives (e.g., *dvoe* 'two')	25	41	62	23	82	78	35	255	88
complex numbers (e.g., *dvadcat'* '20')	48	26	35	71	62	47	103	65	39
compound numbers (e.g., *sorok pjat'* '45')	45	24	35	72	71	50	57	40	41
neskol'ko 'a few'	105	28	21	151	139	48	137	78	36
mnogo 'many', *skol'ko* 'how many', *stol'ko* 'so many'	42	0	0	not given			282	9	3

Table 1. Predicate agreement with quantified subjects in Russian: 18th-20th centuries

It can be seen from these data (derived from Suprun 1969, 185, 188) that plural predicate agreement is more likely with the numerals '2–4' than with '5–10' (there is, in fact, a difference between '2', '3' and '4'). *Neskol'ko* 'a few' is less likely than any of these to take plural agreement, while the plural with quantifiers like *mnogo* 'many' is quite unusual. It appears that a theory must allow a great deal of idiosyncratic information about the different quantifiers to be stored. However, it has been shown[4] that there is a correlation between the degree to which the syntactic behavior of a quantifier approximates to that of a noun and the likelihood of singular agreement (the more noun-like the numeral, the more likely is singular agreement). Furthermore, the higher the arithmetic value of simple cardinal numerals, the more noun-like they become. These correlations hold both within the Slavonic family and beyond. On the one hand, they indicate the presence of clear patterns in an apparently very confused area; on the other hand, it is not clear where in a grammar information of this type should be incorporated. This necessarily brief discussion of quantified expressions has shown that there are instances where there is genuine doubt as to which element in the subject NP controls agreement. Furthermore, there is great variation between controllers, which must be reflected in a grammar in some way.

2.1.2 Constituents Competing to be Controller

An interesting instance of competition between potential controllers arises in sentences of the form NP + copula + NP. Various grammarians state that, besides the expected agreement with the subject, agreement of the copula with the NP in the predicate also occurs. This phenomenon is sometimes called *attraction*, or *back* or *backward agreement*. Many of the examples quoted are not convincing; given the frequency of predicate-subject order in Slavonic, it is not sufficient merely to find examples of agreement with the second NP.

It may seem surprising that the problem has not been resolved. Part of the difficulty is that the proportion of sentences of the form NP + copula + NP in which the controller is clear is relatively small; in such sentences the subject and predicate NPs are almost always of the same number so that one must look for a clash in gender; in the East Slavonic languages the present tense of the verb 'to be' has the null form; and in several languages the predicate NP often stands in the instrumental case.[5]

---

[4] Corbett (1983a, 215–240); this source also gives information on the extensive literature on agreement with quantified expressions in Slavonic.

[5] For discussion of some of the Russian evidence see Revzin (1973, 129–136), Crockett (1976, 406–418, 425–428) and Nichols (1981, 48–54). Progress depends on being able to identify subject and predicate without, of course, using agreement as a test. The approach of Padučeva and Uspenskij (1979),

The following Czech sentences, however, do argue for the attraction analysis:[6]

(11) jedna a   dvě jsou   tři
      one   and two are.PL three

      'One and two are three.'

(12) jedna a   tři   jsou   čtyři
      one   and three are.PL four

      'One and three are four.'

(13) dvě a   tři   je   pět
      two and three is.SG five

      'Two and three are five.'

(14) tři a   tři   je   šest
      three and three is.SG six

      'Three and three are six.'

The regularity is that as long as the numeral to the right of the copula is 'two', 'three', or 'four', then the copula takes plural agreement, while if it is 'five' or above, then the singular is found. The numeral on the right would certainly appear to be part of the predicate, which would mean that we have an instance of agreement with the predicate. Two syntactic tests tend to confirm this. The predicate NP normally stands in the nominative in Czech, as in (15):

(15) Ivan je genius
      Ivan is genius.NOM

      'Ivan is a genius.'

However, with a different copula, the instrumental can occur:

(16) Ivan se   stane   geniem
      Ivan REFL   become   genius.INST

      'Ivan will become a genius.'

based on the denotative status of the NPs, appears promising; it seems to justify the analysis of at least some of the commonly quoted examples as showing agreement with the predicate NP. For Serbo-Croat data see Megaard (1976, 144–150).

[6] This construction is noted in Vanek (1970, 53). The sentences quoted in the text are based on the intuitions of Dr. Robert Slonek, confirmed by Mrs. Magda Newman and Professor Otto Pick. I am very grateful to them all.

We can, given a suitable context, apply this test to our numerals: In (17) *pěti* 'five' is clearly the predicate, as the instrumental case shows; furthermore, since it is in the instrumental it can no longer control agreement, and the expected plural is found.

(17)   v nové matematice, dvě a   dvě se   stanou
        in new mathematics two and two REFL become.PL

        pěti
        five.INST

        'In the new mathematics, two and two will become five.'

The second test is analogous to subject raising. Compare (18) with (15) above:

(18)   pokládám   Ivana   za   genia
        consider.1.SG Ivan.ACC   for genius.ACC

        'I consider Ivan a genius.'

The NP that would be the subject of the simple sentence is marked by the accusative, the predicate by the preposition *za* plus accusative. Sentence (19) shows the application of this test to the numeral examples (again the context of a sceptical speaker is required):

(19)   v nové matematice, pokládají   jednu a   dvě za šest
        in new mathematics consider.3.PL   one   and two for six

        'In the new mathematics, they consider one and two to be six.'

This test too suggests that in our original examples we have NP(subject) + copula + NP(predicate) and that it is the predicative NP which controls the agreement of the copula.

Much more needs to be done to specify exactly the conditions under which this type of agreement can occur in different Slavonic languages and the factors which favor it as opposed to the normal agreement with the subject. However, given its existence, linguistic theory must take it into account. Certainly in some theoretical frameworks it is difficult to accommodate the possibility of the subject being as it were overruled in determining the agreement features of the predicate.[7]

---

[7] Another example of competition between potential controllers is between the subject of a matrix verb and the postulated subject of an infinitive in determining the agreement of second predicates. This problem was raised by Comrie (1974, 136) and has since been discussed by Neidle (1982, 416) and Greenberg (1983).

2.2 Establishing the Controller's Features

There are numerous instances in which there is no problem in identifying the controller but where there are difficulties in establishing what
features it carries. Many of these, but certainly not all, relate to particular lexical items. We will begin with controllers which appear to have
insufficient features and progress to those with superfluous features.

Certain controllers do not carry the features found on ordinary NPs.
The most clear-cut examples are infinitive phrases, clauses and missing
subjects (Slavonic does not employ dummy subjects). Targets typically take third singular neuter agreements when agreeing with such
controllers, as in the following Russian examples:

(20)   kurit'   vospreščaetsja

        to smoke forbid.3.SG.REFL

        'It is forbidden to smoke.'

(21)   jasno,   čto   on pridet

        clear.NEUT.SG that he will come

        'It is clear that he will come.'

(22)   svetalo

        dawned.NEUT.SG

        'Day was dawning.'

The data demonstrate the need for a mechanism to assign default agreements when the controller does not carry the required features. It is
important to note, however, that it is insufficient merely to assign the
default features to the controllers in question, for both syntactic and
morphological reasons. The syntactic reason is that if infinitives or
clauses are conjoined in Slavonic they cannot take plural agreement,
which would be the case if they were marked as neuter singular. The
morphological reason concerns the target. While for verbs in Russian
the form found for neutral agreement is identical to the neuter singular, this is not so for adjectives. In ordinary predicates two forms may
occur—the long form and the short form. The factors which determine
the choice are complex and need not detain us. However, given a controller which is not specified for gender and number, only the short form
can be used. This is the form in (21) above; the long form *jasnoe* is
ungrammatical.

Agreement of the type under discussion has been termed *neutral agreement*. While the agreement marker on the target is often the same as
that found for a more usual set of features, this is not always the case.
In Ukrainian, predicative adjectives have a special form used for neutral
agreement: In (23) there is no subject, while in (24) it is an infinitive
phrase.

(23)   sobakam   dušno
       dogs.DAT   stifling

'It is stifling for the dogs.'

(24)   v odnij simji nam   žyti   i   lehko i   prekrasno
       in one   family us.DAT to live and easy   and wonderful

'It is both easy and wonderful for us to live in one family.'

The form in -o, which we find in these cases, cannot be used with a neuter noun as subject; the neuter agreement form is in -e, for example, *prekrasne* 'wonderful'.[8] Theory must therefore allow for neutral agreement, both in cases where a default agreement form is used and in languages where a special form is required. One interpretation of these data is that the absence of a feature must be distinguished from its negative value. Thus neuter would be [-masculine, -feminine], while neutral agreement would result from the lack of a gender feature.

A stage on from controllers with no features we find those with insufficient agreement features. Russian *kto* 'who' is marked as animate, and cannot take neuter agreement. It normally takes masculine singular agreements by default, both when used as an interrogative, and when used as a relative:

(25)   kto   prišel?
       who came.MASC.SG

'Who came?'

(26)   te,   kto prišel
       that.PL who came.MASC.SG

'those who came'

However, given a plural antecedent, as in (26), plural agreement is also possible:

(27)   te,   kto prišli
       that.PL who came.PL

'those who came'

There must therefore be provision for a target, in this case the verb *prišli* in the subordinate clause, to agree with a controller which is partially specified and which can itself gain features from elsewhere.

The next set of controllers is those with exactly the required set of features, which cause no special problems. We move on to those which have superfluous or contradictory features. Consider, for instance, the

---

[8] For a more detailed account see Corbett (1980).

honorific pronoun (*vi* or *vy* in most of the Slavonic languages). On the one hand, it is a plural pronoun, on the other, it takes a singular referent. The result is that it can take singular and plural agreement (the conditions vary from language to language). It is important to note that both agreement forms can occur in the same sentence, as in the following Slovak example:

(28)   Mama, vy   ste   taká   dobrá!

Mother you are.2.PL so.FEM.SG kind.FEM.SG

'Mother, you are so kind!'

Another common problem in Slavonic concerns names of professions. Some of these appear to be masculine but, when referring to a woman, may take both masculine and feminine agreements. The Russian word *vrač* 'doctor' is a well-studied example:

(29)   novyj   vrač   skazala ...

new.MASC.SG doctor said.FEM.SG

'the new doctor said ...'

The agreement form chosen depends to a large extent on the target, the feminine being more likely to occur in the predicate than with an attributive modifier (cf., sec. 5.2.1).[9]

A somewhat different problem arises in Serbo-Croat. Nouns like *gazda* 'master' have the appearance of feminine nouns but denote males. In the singular, masculine agreement is normal; in the plural, both masculine and feminine forms occur:

(30)   naši / naše   gazde

our.MASC.PL/FEM.PL masters

'our masters'

It is also possible for controllers of this type to occur with both types of agreement in the same sentence.[10]

The problem under discussion is similar to the familiar problem of agreement with nouns like *committee* in English (though the restrictions

---

[9] *Vrač* and similar nouns may take a feminine attributive modifier, instead of the masculine as in (29), but only when standing in the nominative case. In the oblique cases, the masculine is normal (but see Švedova 1980, 57).

[10] These nouns must be distinguished from those like Serbo-Croat *oko* 'eye', which is neuter in the singular, but has the plural *oči*, which is feminine. *Oko* and similar controllers present no choice of agreement. On the other hand, Serbo-Croat *deca* 'children' shows complexities well beyond that of *gazda* (see Corbett 1983a, 76–93).

according to gender or number are an added complication in Slavonic). In Slavonic languages it is less usual than in English to find a singular noun, with no dependent plural noun, taking plural agreement. Examples do occur, however, like the following one recorded in Russian speech by Lapteva (1976, 69):

(31)   vot   zdes' stojat   očered'
        here here stand.PL   queue.SG

        'Look, there's a queue here.'

Like the English examples, controllers of this type are nouns referring to groups of people. However, there are two more sets of examples which cannot be defined so easily. In Slovenian, and various other Slavonic languages, any noun referring to a person could take plural agreement, to indicate respect:

(32)   oče   so   šli
        father.SG are.PL gone.PL

        'Father went.'

This construction has largely died out.[11] The other construction is found in the Talitsk dialect of Russian (Bogdanov 1968). In this dialect, a plural verb can be used with a singular noun, to indicate that the noun refers to a person or persons besides the one indicated directly:

(33)   M'it'ixa dral'is'
        Mitixa   fought.PL.REFL

        'Mitixa had a fight.'

This refers to a fight between husband and wife. Once again, conflicting agreements can be found in the same sentence:

(34)   moj   brat   tam   toža žyl'i
        my.SG   brother.SG there also lived.PL

        'My brother and his family also lived there.'

We require therefore that a theory must be able to cope not only with agreement with straightforward NPs, but also with those which have no agreement features, insufficient features or a superfluity of features. The last case can give rise to conflicting agreements within a single sentence. Some of these problems can be associated with particular constructions (e.g., infinitive phrases) or particular types of lexical item (e.g., nouns of profession); however, the last two cases discussed can be restricted no further than to nouns referring to humans.

---

[11] See Corbett (1983a, 41) for sources.

2.3 'Reluctant' Controllers

Reluctant controllers are those which do not occur in surface structure in a form which matches that of the target. A familiar example occurs in pro-drop languages such as Serbo-Croat:

(35)   čitaš

       read.2.SG

       'You are reading.'

In such examples the controller *ti* 'you' is regularly omitted in surface structure.[12]

A much more complex problem occurs in Upper Sorbian, which is a West Slavonic language spoken in Lusatia in East Germany (GDR). Consider the following phrase in Upper Sorbian:[13]

(36)   mojeho   bratrowe   dźěći

       my.GEN.MASC.SG brother.POSS.NOM.PL child.NOM.PL

       'my brother's children'

The possessive adjective *bratrowe* agrees normally with *dźěći*. *Mojeho*, however, seems to have no controller. A possible source for its agreement features can be found in the synonymous phrase:

(37)   dźěći   mojeho   bratra

       child.NOM.PL my.GEN.MASC.SG brother.GEN.MASC.SG

       'children of my brother'

In (37) there is, of course, no difficulty about the agreement of *mojeho*. The next pair of examples show the same correspondence:

(38)   stareje   žonina

       old.GEN.FEM.SG woman.POSS.NOM.FEM.SG

       drasta

       dress.NOM.FEM.SG

       'old woman's dress'

(39)   drasta   stareje   žony

       dress.NOM.FEM.SG old.GEN.FEM.SG woman.GEN.FEM.SG

       'the old woman's dress'

---

[12] For another example of a missing controller, the subject of the infinitive, see Comrie (1974), especially page 108.

[13] Data from Fasske (1981, 385), Michałk (1974, 510) and Šewc-Schuster (1976, 27, 100–101), discussed in Corbett (1987), where data from other Slavonic languages can also be found.

Once again it appears that the noun which is the source of the possessive adjective is somehow available for agreement purposes. Example (40) illustrates anaphoric reference:

(40)   to   je našeho   wučerjowa
       that is our.GEN.MASC.SG   teacher.POSS.NOM.FEM.SG

       zahrodka.   Wón wjele w njej dźěła
       garden.NOM.FEM.SG He   a lot in it   works

       'That is our teacher's garden. He works in it a lot.'

The antecedent of *wón* 'he' is *naš wučer* 'our teacher', which underlies the phrase headed by *wučerjowa*. The main point, however, is that in Upper Sorbian adjectives can agree with a reluctant controller, apparently with a noun which is the source of a possessive adjective in surface structure. There is a further complication; example (41) is of the now familiar type:

(41)   w našeho   nanowej
       in our.GEN.MASC.SG father.POSS.LOC.FEM.SG

       chěži
       house.LOC.FEM.SG

       'in our father's house'

However, we also find comparable phrases which show what in Upper Sorbian grammar is termed *attraction:*

(42)   w našej   nanowej
       in our.LOC.FEM.SG father.POSS.LOC.FEM.SG

       chěži
       house.LOC.FEM.SG

       'in our father's house'

In such examples the adjective agrees with the head of the NP, rather than with the reluctant controller. This is a further instance of competing controllers, discussed in Section 2.1.2.

There is another reluctant controller to be found in Russian quantified expressions. The numerals *dva* 'two', *tri* 'three', and *četyre* 'four', when themselves in the nominative, take a noun in the genitive singular. *Dva* has the form *dve*, which occurs with feminine nouns:

(43)   dve   sosný[14]
       two.NOM.FEM   pine.GEN.FEM.SG

       'two pines'

The problem is that the numeral governs the form of the noun; if the noun were not singular, then there would be no agreement in gender since gender is not distinguished in the plural in Russian. This genitive singular noun then serves as the controller for agreement in gender of the numeral which governs it.

The noun also serves as a reluctant controller for attributive adjectives, which may stand in the nominative or genitive plural:

(44)   dve   krasivye   sosný
        two.NOM.FEM   beautiful.NOM.PL   pine.GEN.FEM.SG

        'two beautiful pines'

(45)   dve   krasivyx   sosný
        two.NOM.FEM   beautiful.GEN.PL   pine.GEN.FEM.SG

        'two beautiful pines'

One would expect the adjective to agree with the noun, but it clearly does not do so in surface structure. One analysis would have the noun as plural, prior to the imposition of the genitive singular by the numeral.

In general, the data discussed in this subsection appear less difficult for transformational grammar, than for its successors, though even there problems arose as to the place of agreement relative to other rules. The main difficulty to be faced is that elements occur in surface structure which appear to be agreement targets, yet whose controllers are either absent, or if present are not in a form which matches the features shown by the target.

3 Target Problems

We now turn to problems which center on the target, though several are closely connected to the controller problems just discussed. Target problems are of two main types: those arising from the existence of compound targets and those caused by 'reluctant' targets .

3.1 Compound Targets

Compound targets are usually predicates, as in this Serbo-Croat example:

(46)   Jovan je   došao
        Jovan is.3.SG   come.MASC.SG

        'Jovan has come/came.'

---

[14] Note that *sosný* cannot be interpreted as nominative plural, since the latter is stem stressed: *sósny*.

The commonest auxiliary in Slavonic is *biti* 'to be' or its cognate form. In (46) it shows agreement in person and number with the controller, as does any other present tense verb. It does not vary for gender. The active participle *došao*, on the other hand, does not vary for person, but does agree in number and gender. In any analysis which involves the copying of features onto the target, the problem arises as to whether person, number and gender features are to be copied onto both parts of the predicate and then the redundant feature in each case discarded, or whether the unnecessary features will not be copied.[15] Whatever the analysis, it is clear that the agreements shown in (46) depend in large measure on properties of the target .

In (46), the two parts of the predicate agree in different features, but the feature which they share (number) shows the same value. However, compound predicates may show different values of the same feature, as in the Slovak example already discussed (cf. (28)):

(47)   Mama,   vy   ste   taká   dobrá!

Mother you   are.2.PL so.FEM.SG kind.FEM.SG

'Mother, you are so kind!'

In this example with honorific *vy*, both parts of the predicate agree in number, but they show different forms.[16] (This would create problems for an analysis copying all features onto a higher node, say a VP node, and copying just those required onto the auxiliary and participle.)

3.2 Reluctant Targets

These are targets which do not occur in surface structure in a form which matches that of their controller. The phenomenon is, of course, similar to that of reluctant controllers; an example will clarify the distinction. In Russian, given the actual presence of a copula verb (i.e., not the null form of *byt'* 'to be') the predicative adjective may stand in the nominative or the instrumental:

(48)   ona   byla   krasivaja

she.NOM.FEM.SG was.FEM.SG beautiful.NOM.FEM.SG

'She was beautiful.'

---

[15] This is a comparable problem to that raised in Huddleston (1975).

[16] In this instance the clash of features is the normal case. A similar situation may arise when there is a choice of agreement forms. Though it is then usual for compound predicates to show consistent agreements, this does not always happen. For example, in agreement with conjoined noun phrases, the finite verb may be singular and the participle plural; see Corbett (1983a, 214) for examples from Czech and Old Church Slavonic.

(49)   ona   byla   krasivoj
         she.NOM.FEM.SG   was.FEM.SG   beautiful.INST.FEM.SG

'She was beautiful.'

In (49) the predicative adjective agrees with the subject in gender and number but not case.[17] Unlike the reluctant controller examples, here the controller is exactly as expected, in the normal case for subjects in Slavonic, while the target has undergone a rule which makes it match the controller less completely.[18]

The second type of reluctant target is the predicate noun. It might be thought that there is no question of the predicate noun showing agreement. Yet predicate nouns are possible agreement targets (in Tatar, for example, they can show agreement in person, Poppe 1963, 122–123). As Comrie (1975) has shown, however, they are the least likely type of predicate to show agreement. Normally in Slavonic, the form of a predicate noun is not determined by agreement. Nevertheless, agreement in number does occur, though very rarely. In Russian of the last century, the less well educated used a plural predicate noun for polite address to a single addressee, as in the following example from Chekhov:

(50)   izmenniki vy, čto li?
         traitor.PL you that INTERROG.PART

'Are you a traitor, then?'

Thus while the number of predicate nouns is normally determined solely by semantic considerations, there must be provision for them to be agreement targets.

The final type of problematic target is that which simply does not appear, because speakers avoid it. In Russian, adjectival predicates

---

[17] There is also the question as to whether the nominative predicate in examples like (48) shows agreement with the subject or whether the nominative results as the default if no other case is assigned. Russian provides no clear evidence on this point.

[18] A similar situation arises in 'subject-raising' sentences:

(a)   on sčitaet   ee   krasivoj
        he considers her.ACC.FEM.SG beautiful.INST.FEM.SG

'He considers her beautiful.'

Here again the target *krasivoj* agrees with the controller *ee* in number and gender. If we were to accept the subject-raising analysis then we would have a reluctant controller as well as a reluctant target, since neither the subject nor the predicate of the embedded clause appears in the expected nominative case.

with quantified subjects are very rare. When faced with a sentence like (51), Russian informants are uneasy; they do not correct the example, but prefer to use a different construction.

(51)   ? pjat'   mal'čikov   umnye
       five.NOM boy.GEN.PL   clever.NOM.PL

       'Five boys are clever.'

In Polish too, speakers are unhappy about certain combinations, and so avoid them (Bogusławski 1973, 31).

Thus targets require that a theory should have the ability to handle compound targets taking different features or different values of the same feature. The target may not match the controller in other features (notably case) as expected, and predicate nouns must be included as potential targets. Finally, in particular constructions some targets must be marked as unnatural though possible.

4 Feature Problems

In this section we assume that target and controller can be identified and consider problems which may arise as to the agreement categories or features they share (whether or not these are analyzed in feature notation). The main problems concern resolution rules (sec. 4.1), default values (sec. 4.2) and the number of genders (sec. 4.3).

4.1 Resolution Rules

The question as to whether agreement will be with one of a set of conjuncts or with all was raised in Section 2.1.1. A theory must also provide a mechanism (resolution rules) to specify what feature value will result from all possible combinations, when agreement is with more than one conjunct; if the theory can predict these values, so much the better. Since these problems have been considered at length elsewhere (Corbett 1983a 177-214), only the main points will be raised here. We will begin with Slovenian data (from Lenček 1972).

For person resolution, Slavonic has the usual rules in which the first person has priority over the second and the second over the third. Example (52) shows first and third persons conjoined:

(52)   jaz in   Tonček sva   prizadevna
       I   and Tonček are.1.DUAL assiduous.MASC.DUAL

       'Tonček and I are assiduous.'

The verb stands in the first person. Example (52) also illustrates the first number resolution rule required for languages which, like Slovenian, have the dual number: if there are two conjuncts only, both of which are in the singular, then dual agreement forms will be used. Other cases of agreement with more than one conjunct require the plural.

It is mainly in gender resolution that the problems occur. Slovenian has three genders, masculine, feminine and neuter; the gender resolution rules, somewhat surprisingly are as follows:

1.   If all conjuncts are feminine, then the feminine form is used;

2.   otherwise the masculine form is used.

The operation of the first rule can be seen in (53):

(53)   Marina,   Marta   in   Marjanca   so
       Marina.FEM   Marta.FEM and   Marjanca.FEM   are.PL

       prizadevne
       assiduous.FEM.PL

       'Marina, Marta and Marjanca are assiduous.'

Any other type of combination produces masculine agreement, even when there is no masculine conjunct present:

(54)   ta   streha,   okno   in   gnezdo   pod
       that.FEM   roof.FEM   window.NEUT   and   nest.NEUT   under

       njim   mi   bodo   ostali   v   spominu
       it   me.DAT   will.PL   remain.MASC.PL   in memory

       'That roof, window and the nest under it will remain in my memory.'

(55)   to   okno,   drevo   in   gnezdo
       that.NEUT   window.NEUT   tree.NEUT   and   nest.NEUT

       pod   njim   mi   bodo   ostali
       under it   me.DAT   will.PL   remain.MASC.PL

       v   spominu
       in memory

       'That window, tree and the nest under it will remain in my memory.'

Slovenian is relatively straightforward, in that the resolution rules need refer only to the syntactic gender of nouns. Cases occur, however, where the resolution rules require access to morphological or semantic information. Serbo-Croat has a similar gender system to that of Slovenian and the same resolution rules operate. In addition there must be provision for examples like (56). In this example we find masculine agreement even though both conjuncts are feminine (Serbo-Croat has lost the dual number).

(56)   Vredali   su   ga   nebriga   i
        offended.MASC.PL   are.PL him   carelessness.FEM   and

        lakomislenost   Tahir-begova   (Andrić)
        capriciousness.FEM   Tahir-beg.POSS.FEM

        'The carelessness and capriciousness of Tahir-beg offended him.'

Feminine nouns in Serbo-Croat belong to two main declensional classes: the majority are like *nebriga,* ending in -*a* in the nominative singular; there is also a sizable minority like *lakomislenost,* with no ending in the nominative singular. Provided that one of the conjuncts belongs to this second morphological class, then masculine agreement is possible.[19]

To find an example where semantic considerations apply we turn to Polish, which has a rather different gender system. The important examples are those like (57):

(57)   Hania   i   Reks   bawili   się
        Hania.FEM   and   Rex.MASC   amused.PERS.MASC.PL   REFL

        piłką
        ball.INST

        'Hania and Rex played with a ball.'

Normally for masculine personal agreement forms to result, at least one of the conjuncts must be masculine personal (the rules are quite different from those of the South Slavonic languages). In (57) *Reks* is a dog, masculine but not personal. The use of the masculine personal in (57), which is the more common choice though the non-masculine personal form also occurs, results from the combination of *Hania* being semantically human (personal) and *Reks* being syntactically masculine.

Thus Slavonic data require resolution rules to specify the values resulting from various feature combinations and there is evidence to suggest that these rules may require access not only to syntactic gender but also to morphological or semantic information.

4.2 Default Values

As has already been discussed in Section 2.2, there must be provision for assigning default values to features, particularly in the case of controllers which have no agreement features. Similarly, some controllers have insufficient features, and we noted the case of *kto,* a controller marked as

---

[19] See Corbett (1983b, 201–205) for more details.

animate, which took masculine agreement by default. While masculine is the normal default for animates in Slavonic, there is a special usage in Polish, which deserves attention:

(58) któreś   z małżonków   jest
one.NEUT.SG of spouse.GEN.PERS.MASC.PL is.SG

winne   zarzucanej   mu   zbrodni
guilty.NEUT.SG imputed.GEN it.DAT crime.GEN

'One of the spouses is guilty of the crime he or she has been accused of.'

Małżonkowie is masculine personal and means 'husband and wife'. When either the husband or the wife is potentially the referent, then Polish uses the *evasive neuter* (see Gotteri 1984 for the term and data). Thus even default choices can be language-specific.

4.3 The Number of Genders

It is not always self-evident how many genders a language has. The first complication involves sub-genders. Continuing with Polish, we may say that there are at least three genders in the singular, as agreement with nominative case forms shows:

(59)

masculine		**feminine**		**neuter**	
duż-y	stół	duż-a	książka	duż-e	okno
large	table	large	book	large	window

Within the masculine gender, different agreement forms are found with certain nouns:

(60)

	inanimate		**animate**	
nominative	duż-y	stół	duż-y	koń
accusative	duż-y	stół	duż-ego	konia
genitive	duż-ego	stołu	duż-ego	konia
	large	table	large	horse

In the accusative, *stół* takes agreement forms as for the nominative while *koń* takes forms equivalent to those of the genitive.[20]

Most nouns in the latter class refer to humans or animals and so the class is called 'animate', but there are many nouns which are treated as animate but refer to inanimates. If we restrict our attention to the

---

[20] This is not a simple case of syncretism since it extends beyond single paradigms; one solution is to adopt feature-change rules (Corbett 1981, 69–70).

singular, we find that animacy is relevant only in the accusative case. The question then arises as to whether all adjectives must agree with their head noun in the feature of animacy, even though it is relevant only for masculines and only in the accusative case.

When we turn to the nominative plural we find that targets can show only two agreement markers:

(61) **masculine personal**   **non-masculine personal**

duz-i	mnisi	duż-e	stoły	konie	książki	okna
large	monks	large	tables	horses	books	windows

The distinction is between nouns referring to male humans (masculine personal) and the rest. This situation has led some linguists to treat gender in the singular as distinct from gender in the plural. In fact, the question of the number of genders in Polish has been the subject of considerable debate; at least the following numbers have been proposed: three, five, six, seven and nine. The number decided on depends largely on one's theory of agreement; one can count either the number of different controllers to be accounted for or the number of different forms for targets. The point, then, is that agreement categories may not be straightforward; their configuration may depend on the theory adopted.

5 Agreement Choices

We have noted several constructions in which alternative agreement forms occur. We must now consider the significance of these constructions and the factors which constrain the choice.

5.1 The Significance of Agreement Choices

The first point to note about agreement choices is that they exist and are quite common. Yet they have received relatively little attention from theorists. Of the examples discussed above, conjoined noun phrases and quantified expressions frequently involve agreement choices in languages outside the Slavonic group. Furthermore, agreement choices are common in the sense that they occur frequently in language use. Some idea of their frequency can be gained from the following figures. A corpus of about 49,000 words of spoken Russian (Zemskaja and Kapandze 1978) was scanned for examples of the two choices just mentioned plus the choice of agreement with relative *kto* described in Section 2.2. There were 22 examples, in other words examples occurred more frequently than once in 2,500 words. In addition, there were other agreement choices which were not included in the count.

It should also be stressed that the familiar dichotomy of syntactic and semantic agreement is insufficient, since in some constructions in Slavonic we find three agreement options. The case of *tysjača* has already been mentioned (sec. 2.1.1). Another example is Russian *rjad* 'series, number': the following three examples[21] show that instead of talking about syntactic and semantic agreement, we should rather talk of one form having greater semantic justification than another.

(62)   rjad   čelovek   sidel
       number.MASC.SG person.GEN.PL sat.MASC.SG

(63)   rjad   čelovek   sidelo
       number.MASC.SG person.GEN.PL sat.NEUT.SG

(64)   rjad   čelovek   sideli
       number.MASC.SG person.GEN.PL sat.PL

'A number of people was/were sitting.'

Using significance in a different sense, it is worth asking whether agreement choices have semantic significance. Informants sometimes claim that there is a semantic difference between certain agreement options. In some cases it appears that they are imposing a logical interpretation on surprising and troublesome facts about their own language; they feel there ought to be a difference in meaning and so they find one. There is a need for very skilled informant work to establish whether some or all agreement choices are semantically significant.

5.2 Factors Determining the Distribution of Agreement Options

Whether or not they are semantically significant, it is certainly true to say that the distribution of agreement options is heavily constrained. The major constraints are the linguistics ones, though sociolinguistic factors, in the broadest sense, also have a role. These factors have been analyzed in detail elsewhere (Corbett 1983a), and so will be outlined very briefly here.

5.2.1 Linguistic Factors

The first obvious factor that determines choices of agreement is the controller: it must be one of those which permits a choice. A grammar must be able to include detailed information about individual controllers since, as Table 1 above shows clearly, they differ dramatically in the frequency with which they take different agreement forms. There are more general factors which relate to controllers of various different types. Controllers which refer to animates are more likely to take agreement forms with a greater degree of semantic justification than are inanimates. Similarly, controllers which precede their targets are more likely to take agreement forms with a greater degree of semantic justification than

---

[21]   For further examples see Corbett (1983a, 76–83).

are those which follow. The effect of these two factors is illustrated in Table 2, which records agreement with a set of quantifiers in a selection of Russian literary texts of the last two centuries (details in Corbett 1983a, 150–153).

	animate			inanimate		
	SG	PL	%PL	SG	PL	%PL
subject-predicate	11	48	81	21	20	49
predicate-subject	24	23	49	70	18	20

Table 2. Predicate agreement with quantified expressions in Russian

It is clear that both animacy and precedence can exert a major influence on the agreement form selected. The plural, the form with greater semantic justification, is more likely if the subject is animate and if it precedes the predicate. In addition, *real distance*—the degree of separation counted in intervening words—between controller and target has an effect.[22]

It is not, of course, sufficient merely to demonstrate that the actual quantifier involved, animacy and precedence all have an effect since they could be interconnected; it could be the case, for example, that animate subjects are more likely to precede than are inanimates. However, Table 2 establishes that both these factors have an independent effect. The data available suggest that both these factors operate independently of the quantifier involved (Akopdžanjan 1965, 113; Patton 1969, 35, 63, 148, 160; Spear, 1984, 21, 27, 34).

When we turn to target factors, we find that strong claims have been made here, constraining the distribution of agreement options in Slavonic. The agreement hierarchy consists of the following basic positions:

attributive ——— predicate ——— relative ——— personal
                                pronoun   pronoun

The original claim was that as one moved rightward along the hierarchy, so the likelihood of semantic agreement would increase monotonically.

---

[22] It has been claimed on several occasions that if the predicate is widely separated from the subject, then the form with greater semantic justification is more likely. Evidence presented by Spear (1984) suggests that this is definitely true for subject-predicate order; with predicate-subject order (for which separation is less common and so data are more difficult to obtain), then greater separation appears to make the form with greater semantic justification less likely. Thus it is not just a question of the controller preceding or following the target but also of the degree by which it does so.

In its later formulation (Corbett 1983a, 87–88) it incorporates Comrie's predicate hierarchy (Comrie 1975) and includes predictions concerning the case of the target.

A satisfactory theory must be able to handle these data and to incorporate the regularities indicated insofar as they prove justified by subsequent research. For some theories, the mere fact that the target has a major effect on the agreement form found is difficult to accommodate. More generally, the complex interaction of controller and target factors is potentially very hard to handle. On top of all this there is the important fact that most of the patterns discovered are statable not at sentence level, which is what most linguists have been concerned with in recent years, but at corpus level (cf., Johnson and Postal 1980, 20–21, 677–687). That is to say, they are statements not about individual sentences but about the whole collection of sentences of a language (or, at least, a representative sample of them). To take a specific example, in Russian the relative pronoun is more likely to show plural agreement with conjoined noun phrases than is the predicate. This regularity, demonstrated by scanning a representative sample of sentences, is in accordance with the agreement hierarchy. However, it is possible for an individual sentence in Russian to have conjoined noun phrases with a predicate showing plural agreement and a relative pronoun showing singular agreement. The problem of stating regularities of this sort has still to be faced in many theoretical frameworks.

While the regularities stated at corpus level cause obvious difficulties, sentence-level constraints on parallel and stacked targets, which complement the agreement hierarchy, are also interesting (Corbett 1983a, 69–74). Recall that Serbo-Croat nouns like *gazda* 'master', when in the plural, permit both masculine and feminine modifiers (as in (30)). Suppose that targets are stacked. Usually both take the same form, but this is not always the case, as in the following example (Marković 1954, 95):

(65)   ovi   privatne   zanatlije
        these.MASC.PL   private.FEM.PL   artisan.PL

        'these private artisans'

Both agreement possibilities are found together. However, they must be as in (65) with the form with greater semantic justification, the masculine, further from the controller (*ove privatni zanatlije* is ungrammatical). The constraint is as follows:

(66)   If stacked targets show different agreement forms, the target
        further from the controller will show the form with greater se-
        mantic justification.

To incorporate a constraint of this type means allowing the agreement shown by one target to be determined in part by that of another target.

5.2.2 Sociolinguistic Factors

Besides the various linguistic factors so far described, the choice between agreement options is influenced by a range of sociolinguistic factors. There is evidence to show that all of the following operate in Slavonic: the educational level of the speaker, occupation, region within the area of a standard language (there is also considerable variation between standard language and dialects) and the sex and age of the speaker (Corbett 1983a, 30–39). The fact that differences can be correlated with age suggests, of course, that agreement is subject to diachronic change. There is evidence for this in Table 1. It should be noted, however, that diachronic change does not always involve change in favor of forms with greater semantic justification; Table 1 illustrates change in both directions.

The fact that there are so many sociolinguistic variables, which interact with the target and controller factors described above, makes it very difficult to pin down the effect of one particular factor. Such analysis will require either extensive and careful informant work or the scanning of large corpora (or preferably both).

6 Conclusion

Agreement is an apparently simple phenomenon, the evidence for which is easily available on the surface. Yet this attempt to set out a basic specification of agreement in Slavonic has revealed numerous complications, all within a single language group, which have been spelled out at various points. A recurring theme is the interaction of the target, the controller and the agreement features. While data of this type are of potential interest to any theorist, agreement data would appear to be of particular relevance to those concerned with features and to those trying to provide a more satisfactory account of performance data within linguistic models. The problems outlined in the paper may seem daunting; that is not the effect intended. Rather it is hoped that data provided here will be of use in attempts to bring linguistic theory closer to an adequate account of agreement.

References

Akopdžanjan, A. A. 1965. O forme čisla glagola-skazuemogo v predloženijax s količestvennym podležaščim: Forma glagola-skazuemogo v predloženijax s podležaščim tipa 'tri čeloveka'. *Voprosy teorii i metodiki izučenija russkogo jazyka*, Iževsk, vyp. 4, 104–113.

Bogdanov, V. N. 1968. Osobyj slučaj dialektnogo soglasovanija skazuemogo s podležaščim po smyslu i kategorija predstavitel'nosti. *Naučnye doklady vysšej školy: filologičeskie nauki*, no. 4, 68–75.

Bogusławski, A. 1973. Nazwy pospolite przedmiotów konkretnych i niektóre właściwości ich form liczbowych i połączeń z liczebnikami w języku polskim. In Z. Topolińska and M. Grochowski (Eds), *Liczba, ilość, miara.* Wrocław: Polska Akademia Nauk.

Comrie, B. 1974. The second dative: a transformational approach. In R. D. Brecht and C. V. Chvany (Eds), *Slavic Transformational Syntax.* Ann Arbor: University of Michigan.

Comrie, B. 1975. Polite plurals and predicate agreement. *Language* 51:406–418.

Corbett, G. G. 1980. Neutral agreement. *Quinquereme—New Studies in Modern Languages* 3:164–170.

Corbett, G. G. 1981. Syntactic features. *Journal of Linguistics* 17:55–76.

Corbett, G. G. 1983a. *Hierarchies, Targets and Controllers: Agreement Patterns in Slavic.* London: Croom Helm. (Also University Park: Pennsylvania State University Press.)

Corbett, G. G. 1983b. Resolution rules: agreement in person, number and gender. In G. Gazdar, E. Klein, and G. K. Pullum (Eds), *Order, Concord and Constituency* (Linguistic Models 4). Dordrecht: Foris.

Corbett, G. G. 1987. The morphology-syntax interface: evidence from possessive adjectives in Slavonic. *Language* 63:299–345.

Crockett, D. B. 1976. *Agreement in Contemporary Standard Russian.* Cambridge, Mass.: Slavica.

Fasske, H. 1981. *Grammatik der obersorbischen Schriftsprache der Gegenwart: Morphologie.* Bautzen: VEB Domowina Verlag.

Glavan, V. 1927-28. Kongruencija u jeziku starih čakavskih pisaca. *Južnoslovenski filolog* 7:111–159.

Gotteri, N. 1984. The evasive neuter in Polish. In F. E. Knowles and J. I. Press (Eds), *Papers in Slavonic Linguistics* II. Birmingham, England: Department of Modern Languages, University of Aston in Birmingham, 1–8.

Graudina, L. K., V. A. Ickovič, and L. P. Katlinskaja. 1976. *Grammatičeskaja pravil'nost' russkoj reči: opyt častotno-stilističeskogo slovarja variantov.* Moscow: Nauka.

Greenberg, G. R. 1983. Another look at the second dative and related subjects. *Linguistic Analysis* 11:167–218.

Huddleston, R. 1975. Homonymy in the English verbal paradigm. *Lingua* 37:151–176.

Johnson, D. E. and P. M. Postal. 1980. *Arc Pair Grammar.* Princeton: Princeton University Press.

Keenan, E. L. 1974. The functional principle: generalizing the notion of 'subject of'. *Papers from the Tenth Regional Meeting of the Chicago Linguistic Society,* 298–310.

Lapteva, O. A. 1976. *Russkij razgovornyj sintaksis.* Moscow: Nauka.

Lenček, R. 1972. O zaznamovanosti in nevtralizaciji slovnične kategorije spola v slovenskem knjižnem jeziku. *Slavistična revija* 20:55–63.

Marković, S. V. 1954. O kolebljivosti slaganja u rodu kod imenica čiji se prirodni i gramatički rod ne slažu (i o rodu ovih imenica). *Pitanja književnosti i jezika* (Sarajevo) 1:87–110.

Megaard, J. 1976. *Predikatets kongruens i serbokroatisk i setninger med koordinerte subjektsnominalfraser.* Doctoral dissertation, University of Oslo.

Michałk, F. 1974. Kratkij očerk grammatiki verxnelužickogo jazyka. In K. K. Trofimovič (Ed), *Hornjoserbski-ruski słownik.* Budyšin: Ludowe nakładnistwo Domowina.

Morgan, J. L. 1972. Verb agreement as a rule of English. *Papers from the Eighth Regional Meeting of the Chicago Linguistic Society,* 278–286.

Moravcsik, E. A. 1978. Agreement. In J. H. Greenberg (Ed), *Universals of Human Language* 4. Stanford: Stanford University Press.

Neidle, C. 1982. Case agreement in Russian. In J. Bresnan (Ed), *The Mental Representation of Grammatical Relations.* Cambridge, Mass.: The MIT Press.

Nichols, J. 1981. *Predicate Nominals: A Partial Surface Syntax of Russian.* Berkeley: University of California Press.

Nichols, J., G. Rappaport, and A. Timberlake 1980. Subject, topic and control in Russian. *Proceedings of the Sixth Annual Meeting of the Berkeley Linguistics Society,* 372–386.

Padučeva, E. V. and V. A. Uspenskij 1979. Podležaščee ili skazuemoe? (Semantičeskij kriterij različenija podležaščego i skazuemogo v binominativnyx predloženijax). *Izvestija Akademii Nauk SSSR, Serija literatury i jazyka* 38:349–360.

Patton, H. 1969. *A Study of the Agreement of the Predicate with a Quantitative Subject in Contemporary Russian.* Doctoral dissertation, University of Pennsylvania. Distributed by University Microfilms, Ann Arbor, 70-7839.

Poppe, N. 1963. *Tatar Manual: Descriptive Grammar and Texts with A Tatar-English Glossary.* Bloomington: Indiana University.

Revzin, I. I. 1973. Nekotorye sredstva vyraženija protivopostavlenija po opredelennosti v sovremennom russkom jazyke. In A. A. Zaliznjak (Ed), *Problemy grammatičeskogo modelirovanija*. Moscow: Nauka.

Šewc-Schuster, H. 1976. *Gramatika hornjoserbskeje rěče, 2. zwjazk-syntaksa*. Budyšin: Ludowe nakładnistwo Domowina.

Spear, S. M. 1984. *Soglasovanie skazuemogo s količestvennym podležaščim*. Undergraduate dissertation, University of Surrey.

Suprun, A. E. 1969. *Slavjanskie čislitel'nye (stanovlenie čislitel'nyx kak osoboj časti reči)*. Minsk: Belorussian State University.

Švedova, N. Ju. 1980. Podčinitel'nye svjazi slov i slovosočetanija. In *Russkaja grammatika: II: sintaksis*. Moscow: Nauka.

Vanek, A. L. 1970. *Aspects of Subject-Verb Agreement*. (Studies in Slavic Linguistics 1). Edmonton: Department of Slavic Languages, University of Alberta. (Republished 1977 as Current Inquiry into Language and Linguistics 23. Edmonton: Linguistic Research.)

Zemskaja, E. A. and L. A. Kapanadze (Eds) 1978. *Russkaja razgovor-naja reč': teksty*. Moscow: Nauka.

3 On the Function of Agreement

CHRISTIAN LEHMANN

MY CONTRIBUTION CONCENTRATES on the role of agreement in the functioning of language. It recapitulates some of the analyses and results of (Lehmann 1982a) and adds some new points concerning the role of agreement in the expression of syntactic relations. My basic thesis is that agreement is referential in nature. It helps identify or reidentify referents. It does this by giving information on grammatical properties of its referent and, thus, of the NP representing it if one is around. The functions of agreement in the marking of syntactic relations derive from this primary function.

1 The Notion of Agreement

I will start by offering a working definition of agreement in order to preliminarily delimit the range of phenomena we are talking about.

(1)   Definition of agreement

Constituent B agrees with constituent A (in category C) if and only if the following three conditions hold true:

a. There is a syntactic or anaphoric relation between A and B.

b. A belongs to a subcategory c of a grammatical category C, and A's belonging to c is independent of the presence or nature of B.

c. c is expressed on B and forms a constituent with it.

The definition in (1) virtually succeeds in comprising all and only those grammatical phenomena that have traditionally been called agreement. Since the proposed notion of agreement is thus extensionally equivalent

---

Cordial thanks are due to Edith Moravcsik for helpful criticism.

to the traditional notion, I hope that it also makes explicit the intuition standing behind it.

The definition provides us with a decision procedure enabling us to tell whether a given phenomenon is agreement or not. This should be useful since we might entertain partially different conceptions of agreement. One thing the definition excludes from agreement is *government*. In fact, government can be one of the relations mentioned in condition (1a), and therefore agreement can appear in a government relation, namely on a governing term; but government is not subsumed under agreement.

With one possible exception, the conditions of the definitions are independent of each other, and each is quite specific. Their conjunction may thus appear to identify an arbitrary, unnatural concept. This is because the definition is a strictly static, structural one which does not tell us what agreement does and what it is for. To this question we will now turn.

2 Internal and External Agreement

At first glance, we find two radically different kinds of agreement. The first of these is illustrated in (2) through (4).[1]

(2)   illarum   duarum   bonarum
       that.GEN.PL.FEM   two.GEN.PL.FEM   good.GEN.PL.FEM

       feminarum
       woman.GEN.PL.FEM

       'of those two good women'   *Latin*

(3)   bagul   waŋal-gu   baŋul-djin-gu
       DET.DAT   boomerang-DAT   DET.GEN-∅-DAT

       yaṛa-ŋu-njdjin-gu
       man-GEN-∅-DAT

       'to the man's boomerang'   *Dyirbal*

(4)   yibi   yaṛa-ŋgu   njalŋga-ŋgu djilwal-ŋu-ru   buṛa-n.
       woman   man-ERG   [child-ERG   kick-REL-ERG]   see-REAL

       'The man whom the child had kicked saw the woman.' *Dyirbal*

Example (2) shows the familiar agreement of the determiner, numeral and adjective attribute; (3) and (4) show the less familiar agreement of other attributes, namely of the possessor NP and the relative clause. This is, indeed rare, but by no means restricted to Dyirbal. The same

---

[1] The following abbreviations are used in this paper: ANAPH anaphoric, AT attributor, CL noun class, DYN dynamic, REAL realized, REL relative marker.

kind of agreement may be found in all adnominal modifiers, including article, possessive pronoun and nominal apposition.

This kind of agreement may involve the category of case, but never the category of person, as our three examples clearly show. There are, of course, agreement phenomena of the same kind and otherwise quite similar to the ones adduced which do not involve case. What matters here is that agreement in adnominal modification may be case agreement but never person agreement.

The second kind of agreement is illustrated in examples (5) through (7) from Abkhaz.

(5)   (sarà) a-x°əc'-k°à   a-s°q°'-k°à

       I   ART-child-PL ART-book-PL

       ɸ-rə̀-s-to-yt'.

       ABS.3-DAT.3.PL-ERG.1.SG-give.DYN-FIN

       'I give the books to the children.'   *Abkhaz*

(6)   à-c'k°'ən-c°a rə-y°n-k°à

       ART-boy-PL OBL.3.PL-house-PL

       'the boys' houses'   *Abkhaz*

(7)   (sarà) s-q'ə+n+t°'

       I   OBL.1.SG-from

       'from me'   *Abkhaz*

In (5) we see the verb agreeing with the absolutive, ergative and indirect object actants. In (6) the possessum agrees with the possessor NP. Example (7) shows the agreement of the postposition with its complement. Some of these processes are relatively rare, but none is restricted to Abkhaz. Examples (5) to (7) virtually exhaust the constructions in which this type of agreement may be found. They are the constructions in which an NP depends on the agreeing term, excluding those where the NP bears a concrete semantic relation, i.e., an adverbial relation to the superordinate term so that it is not properly an NP but an adverbial.

This kind of agreement may involve the category of person, but never the category of case, as the examples again show quite clearly. Notice, in particular, that the construction of possessive attribution figures in both sets ((3) and (6)), but only the possessor may show case agreement, while only the possessum may show person agreement. Since the two sets of constructions do not otherwise overlap, one may wonder whether it is really the same construction which may show both agreement of the modifier and agreement of the head. The answer is an interesting "no" for the details of which see Lehmann (1983, sec. 3.3).

As I said, at first these two kinds of agreement appear to be radically different. In the first set of constructions, modifiers appear to agree with their heads, while in the second kind governing terms agree with their dependent NPs. What can agree in case never agrees in person, and vice versa. However, the fact that the two kinds of agreement exclude each other means that they are in a perfect complementary distribution. From what we know about complementary distributions, this points to a deeper functional unity. And in fact, in all these constructions it is the case that something agrees with an NP. While this has already been granted for the constructions of person agreement, it is an unwonted analysis of the facts of case agreement. I think it will be conceded that the facts of adnominal modifier agreement as illustrated in (2) through (4) *can* be analyzed by saying that the modifier agrees with its NP, rather than by having it agree with its head noun. There is a variety of arguments to the effect that they *must* be analyzed this way. I will present two of them, based on (8) and (9).

(8)   tri   svetlye   komnaty
       three.NOM.PL   light.NOM.PL   room.GEN.SG

       'three light rooms'   *Russian*

(9)   den   alten   Frauen
       the.DAT.PL   old.DAT.PL   woman.PL

       'to the old women'   *German*

In Russian, the lower numerals take their semantic head noun as a genitive attribute in the singular. Nevertheless such an NP is grammatically plural, as becomes evident when it includes an adjective attribute: the adjective in (8) shows nominative plural and thus agrees with its NP, not with its head noun (cf. also Babby in this volume). In German, determiners and attributes show case agreement (the morphemic glosses in (9) simplify the facts a bit). In general, case is a syntactic category of the NP, not particularly one of its head noun. In German, however, the situation is especially clear since case is not a morphological category of a whole class of nouns to which the one in (9) belongs. Thus, quite apart from the syntactic inappropriateness of an analysis which makes determiners and attributes agree in case with their head nouns, here there is simply no morphological basis for this solution since nothing can be made to agree with a constituent in a category which this constituent does not possess. We thus have to conclude that adnominal modifiers agree with their NP.[2]

This enables us to formulate the generalization that *all agreement refers to an NP*. For the sake of accuracy, we should mention here

---

[2] This conclusion was reached already in Fauconnier (1971). Keenan (1979, 16) tries to evade it by excluding case agreement from agreement; but in vain, since gender and number agreement are no different.

that for most sorts of agreement, the referent of the agreement need
not actually be expressed. However, if the constituent agreed with is
present, it is always an NP.[3] This is the basis for the terminology that
I propose. The agreement of adnominal modifiers is called NP internal
agreement, or simply *internal agreement*, and the agreement that refers
to an NP outside the agreeing term is called *external agreement*.

All agreement identifies a referent to which the carrier of agreement,
the agreeing word, is related. However, the kind of reference involved
is different in the two kinds of agreement. Internal agreement expresses
coreference of the agreeing word with other words belonging to the same
NP. External agreement expresses *reference* to an NP which specifies
the meaning of the agreeing word. More generally: the designations of
words connected by internal agreement apply to the same referent. The
designations of words connected by external agreement do not apply to
the same referent (even if the words displaying external agreement—
verbs, relational nouns and adpositions—were said to refer).

3 The Source of Agreement

The two types of reference expressed by the two kinds of agreement
correlate with the fact that person may be involved only in external
agreement, while case may be involved only in internal agreement, with
the consequence that within any one language, the morphological forms
of internal and external agreement are normally different.

This situation has definite diachronic correlates. The most important
and most regular diachronic source of agreement is pronominal anaphora
(including cataphora). More precisely, agreement markers usually stem
from pronouns. However, given the referential and morphological differences between internal and external agreement, we can anticipate that
they usually come from different kinds of pronouns. The markers of internal agreement are grammaticalized from weakly deictic demonstrative
pronouns, while the markers of external agreement are grammaticalized
from personal pronouns. Let us first look at two examples of incipient
internal agreement.

(10)   Pali Kati   almá-i-t   ette meg,
        Paul Kathy apple-PL.POSS.3.SG-ACC ate   up

        Mária pedig ti-é-i-d-et.
        Mary   and   you-POSS.ANAPH-PL-POSS.2.SG-ACC

        'Paul ate Kathy's apples, and Mary yours'   *Hungarian*

---

[3] Keenan (1979, 15) adduces the tense agreement of the adverbial with the
verb in Malagasy as a potential counterexample, but does not discuss the
role of this phenomenon in the grammar of the language.

(11)   ki-su   ch-a   Hamisi

         CL7-knife CL7-AT Hamisi

         'Hamisi's knife'   *Swahili*

In Hungarian, there is a special pronominal suffix, *-é*, which is appended to a possessor noun, possibly a possessive pronoun, as in (10); it picks up a concept in lexical anaphora and makes it a possessum. The suffix has two semantic components. One is of an anaphoric-pronominal nature and represents the categories of the possessum. In (10), we see the plural number of the possessum represented in the suffix *-i*. The second component is an attributor which makes the pronoun relational. Its meaning is, thus 'that of X,' where X is the possessor noun or pronoun to which the suffix is appended.

If such a possessive phrase with an anaphoric head comes to be used in apposition to its nominal referent, we have gone already half of the way to the agreement of the possessor. The next step of this evolution can be illustrated by the Swahili example (11). Here the two semantic components of the agreeing attributor, the first representing the categories of the possessum, the second linking it to a possessor, are represented by distinct morphemes. The spirit of the construction might be brought out by such English phrases as *the knife, that of Hamisi*, though this contains an appositive construction, while in (11) we are dealing with normal possessive attribution. The erstwhile anaphoric pronoun has ceased to be (obligatorily) anaphoric.

The final step in this evolution is the agglutination of the agreeing attributor to the possessor. This step has been carried out by languages related to Swahili, e.g., Tswana, and is exemplified in (3). Thereby, the categories of the possessum appear on the possessor, so that we have internal agreement of the possessor with the possessum. I submit this as a paradigm case for the evolution of internal agreement in general, including agreement of other attributes. The anaphoric pronoun which is the source of the internal agreement marker evidently expresses that the attribute which it attaches to is to be taken to be coreferential with something mentioned before (or yet to be mentioned, in the case of cataphoric origin). Its original syntactic function is to serve as a dummy head for an attribute which cannot stand alone.

The evolution of external agreement by grammaticalization of personal pronouns is much better known, both because much work has been done on what my colleagues call *cross-reference* and because we all witness its current development in spoken French. In (12) are some real-life examples from the *Corpus d'Orleans*. For the sake of variation, this time I have chosen examples which show cataphoric pronouns, referring to NPs yet to come. The anaphoric use of the same elements is illustrated once in (12a). I need not prove what is well known, namely that all these personal clitics derive from Proto-Romance independent personal pronouns, which in turn go back to Latin personal pronouns and weakly demonstrative pronouns. At the same time, it is obvious that in (12), these elements function in syntactic agreement. We might show that they are not yet affixes, as is sometimes claimed. But they will end up as external agreement affixes, as already illustrated by (5).

(12) a.   Moi oui, moi *je* suis d'ici moi.
          'Me yes, I'm from here.'   *French*

     b.   *Ils* ont peut-être un les gens.
          'Perhaps they have one, the people.'

     c.   C'est nous qu'on *les* fait les bateaux.
          'It's we who make the ships.'

     d.   Ils s'*en* occupent peut-être mieux des enfants.
          'Perhaps they care better for the children.'

The next example from Nahuatl shows that the less familiar agreement of the postposition may have exactly the same sort of early stage.

(13)   ii-waan   iskic   tlaaka-tl   ya   in   maaseewal-li
          him-with   all   man-ABS   go   ART   vassal-ABS

          'Every man went with his vassal'   *Nahuatl*

Again the pronominal element on the postposition cataphorically cross-references something which much later in the sentence is represented by an NP. Further grammaticalization of this construction leads to the agreement of the postposition with its nominal complement as shown in example (7).

The anaphoric personal pronoun which is the source of the external agreement marker evidently presupposes a certain syntactic relation belonging to the meaning of the element which later will carry the agreement; and it expresses that this relation extends to a certain referent which may be present in the linguistic context or in the speech situation. Its original syntactic function is to fill a syntactic position which is opened up by that syntactic relation and which may not be left unoccupied.

4 The Function of Agreement

We can now draw the conclusion from this evidence. At certain places in a discourse, reference is made to a certain referent. For logical and economic reasons,[4] the referent is not identified by fully specifying all its attributes each time it recurs in the discourse. Rather, it is identified by

---

[4] The logical reasons are of the kind known from the Bach-Peters Paradox.

mentioning some of the categories which it belongs to, especially person, number, gender/class and case. (Incidentally, here language functions in a way quite different from predicate calculus, which would employ individual constants for this purpose.) The pronouns appearing in such places signal that we are dealing—still or already—with a referent also appearing elsewhere in the discourse or in the speech situation. This function of identification or reidentification of a referent and keeping the reference to it constant is also the original function of agreement markers when they develop from such pronouns. The requirement that a referent be identified at a certain point in a discourse may be syntacticized in the sense that there may be a syntactic relation creating a syntactic position to be occupied by the entity to which the relation extends; and the rules of syntax may require this position to be filled.

The grammaticalization of the pronominal filler to a marker of agreement involves a number of things. When the referent of the pronominal filler is represented by a nominal expression in the same syntactic construction, we get syntactic agreement of the pronominal filler with the nominal expression. At the same time, the pronoun attaches to the word from which the syntactic relation extends and thus becomes an agreement affix of the latter. Given that the referent of the agreement affix is in the same construction and thus in the immediate neighborhood, the original semantic function of representing a referent becomes less imperative and is gradually changed into a grammatical function, namely that of signalling that what the presupposed syntactic relation relates to is the referent NP.

We may illustrate this by some of our examples. The case agreement affixes in (3) attach to a determiner and to a genitive attribute. Both of these imply a relation of adnominal modification, of subconstituency within an NP. The agreement markers signal that the NP looked for is one in the dative so that if there is a noun in the dative in the construction, this is taken to be the head of the modifiers. Similarly, the person agreement prefix in (7) attaches to a postposition, which implies a relation of government of an NP. The agreement marker signals that the NP looked for is in the first person singular, so that if there is such an NP in the construction, this is taken to be the complement of the postposition.

By contingency, an agreement affix may help set up and identify a certain syntactic relation. Thus the noun 'house' in (6) probably does not necessarily imply a relation to a possessor. Here the appearance of the agreement prefix helps set up this relation. Again in (5), it would be impossible to know which NP has which syntactic function vis-à-vis the verb if the agreement markers did not tell us. To be precise, the three syntactic functions in question are inherent in the verb, not set up by the agreement prefixes. They are distinguished by the fact that there is a prefix slot reserved for each of the three relations. So here agreement helps identify a syntactic relation. At the same time, it is clear that these functions of agreement are derivative and that its primary function remains the identification of the referent to which the relation extends.

5 External Agreement and Case Marking

Finally, we will come to a more precise understanding of the functioning of agreement by comparing it with a strategy whose primary function it is to identify dependency relations in which an NP is dependent. This is the strategy of case marking (in the proper, narrow sense which excludes agreement), which makes use of case affixes, adpositions and relational nouns intervening between the superordinate term and the dependent NP and combined with the latter.

A genitive affix on an NP signals that the relation of this NP to the context is to be the dependent element in a construction of adnominal modification, probably dependent on a noun, possibly in a possessive relationship. Again, the preposition *a* before an Italian NP signals that the relation of this NP to its context is to be dependent on a verb as its indirect object or directional adjunct. The case markers thus identify distinct syntactic and semantic relations.

Since in any one language, there are many such relations of NP dependency, it follows that they must be semantically distinct. In fact, general grammar lists dozens of case functions, among them quite concrete ones such as praeterlative and sublative; and there are languages, e.g., Permiak, with more than twenty case affixes to express them. Suppose now we order all these case functions on a scale, with the semantically richest, most concrete ones, the properly semantic functions, at the left end and the semantically empty, most grammaticalized ones, the properly syntactic functions, at the right end. This is the grammaticalization scale of case functions, of which I give an abbreviated and simplified version in (14) (cf. Lehmann 1982b, ch.III.4.2.).

(14)   Grammaticalization scale of case functions

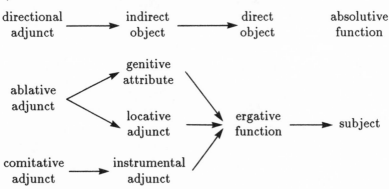

We need not go into details of this figure or the evidence for it.[5] It
suffices to see that the properly syntactic case functions are those which
are subject to the government of a word in which they are inherent, while
the properly semantic case functions are not subject to government, are
not inherent in anything and therefore have to be established.

It is against this background that we have to see the following empirical generalization: If a language has (overt) case marking at a given
vertical position of (14), it will have overt case marking for all the positions to its left. And if a language has external agreement at a given
vertical position of (14), it will have external agreement for all the positions to its right. This implies that case marking is typically used
for the semantic functions, while external agreement is typically used
for the syntactic functions. This in turn implies that case marking and
external agreement may cooccur in a language. All this is, of course,
overwhelmingly true. The typical constellation, which recurs in count-
less languages, is the presence of an agreement affix on the verb for the
subject function even if the language does not have any other external
agreement, matched with the absence of a case affix on the subject, even
if the language does have other (grammatical) cases. The reverse situation is never found. This follows naturally from our generalizations.[6]

It is not the case that external agreement and case marking are in
a strict complementary distribution, either among languages or within
every language. However, the pair of implicational generalizations formulated above make for a tendency towards such a complementary
distribution. To the degree that this is true, we may again suspect a
common functional denominator for the two complementary processes.
External agreement presupposes a dependency relation of the agreement
carrier to an NP and gives information about that NP. Case marking
gives information on a dependency relation of its carrier NP and presupposes the element on which the NP depends. Both strategies attach a
marker to one relatum (each to the opposite one), but external agreement presupposes the relation and specifies the other relatum, while
case marking specifies the relation and presupposes the other relatum.
Thus both strategies economize, but they economize on different kinds
of information. Therefore each is employed in that context where that
particular kind of information need not be given. Both are successful ways of signalling a dependency relation, but external agreement is
more successful on purely syntactic relations, while case marking is more
successful on semantic relations.

---

[5] Each arrow stands for a transition for which there is historical evidence.

[6] In Yuman and Cushitic languages, the subject, but not the direct object,
has a case suffix. This situation is not accounted for by (14). Perhaps (14)
should be weakened by putting subject and direct object in one column.

Therefore, I propose not to subsume agreement under case marking, nor vice versa, but to keep the two notions distinct. Their common denominator does not lie on the level of linguistic structure, but on that of linguistic functions: both of them share the function of signalling NP dependency relations.

References

Fauconnier, G. F. 1971. *Theoretical Implications of Some Global Phenomena in Syntax.* Doctoral dissertation, University of California, San Diego. Distributed by University Microfilms, Ann Arbor, 71-27891.

Keenan, E. L. 1979. On surface form and logical form. (Series A, No. 63.) Trier: L.A.U.T.

Lehmann, C. 1982a. Universal and typological aspects of agreement. In H. Seiler and F. J. Stachowiak (Eds), *Apprehension: das sprachliche Erfassen von Gegenständen.* Teil II, 201–267. Tübingen: Gunter Narr.

Lehmann, C. 1982b. *Thoughts on Grammaticalization.* Vol. I. (Arbeiten des Kölner Universalienprojekts 48.) Köln: Institut für Sprachwissenschaft der Universität.

Lehmann, C. 1983. Rektion und syntaktische Relationen. *Folia Linguistica* 17:339–378.

4 Toward a Unified Theory of Agreement

STEVEN G. LAPOINTE

FOR SEVERAL YEARS, I have been concerned with the question of how facts about agreement phenomena can be analyzed in terms of a fairly restricted theory of the interactions between syntax and morphology (cf. Lapointe 1980, 1981, 1983, 1984a,b). Although I still believe that the overall approach begun in the first of these works (Lapointe 1980; henceforth, TGA) remains quite interesting—I am still convinced, for example, that something like the Generalized Lexical Hypothesisis correct—I have also come to believe that that approach was partially misdirected, both in the domain of facts analyzed under the heading of agreement and in the types of theoretical analyses offered. The purpose of the present paper is therefore to outline what I now take to be a more comprehensive account of agreement and its relation to other inflectional processes. To accomplish this, I will be organizing my remarks along the following lines. After briefly considering the problems encountered by the theory presented in TGA, I will turn to a fairly large list of agreement types, from which a number of generalizations about agreement controllers, agreement controllees, and agreement features will be extracted. One result of this examination will be the suggestion that the agreement

In the presentation of the paper at the conference on Agreement in Natural Language at Stanford University, I also discussed some problems encountered by recent syntactic theories, including Government-Binding (GB; Chomsky, 1981) and Generalized Phrase Structure Grammar (GPSG; Gazdar and Pullum, 1982). Space limitations prevent me from considering those problems in detail here.

types fall into two classes, the "universally authorized" types and the rest, where the classes of authorized types is recognized as constituting the "real" agreements with the rest being analyzed in terms of various distinct and not necessarily related morphosyntactic devices. The distinction between universally authorized and other sorts of agreement will play a role in the present theory similar to that of general vs. restricted agreements in TGA and in Lapointe (1981). However, as we will also see, the two notions divide the class of morphosyntactic cooccurrences in quite distinct ways. The remainder of the paper will focus in some detail on the universally authorized type. First, I will explore the mechanisms by which agreeing elements are connected to one another in linguistic structures; the required conditions will be stated in terms of definitions in a system of logical representations (LRs) for syntactic structures (SSs) derived from recent work by Barwise and Cooper (1981). Next, I will consider the properties of the markedness system responsible for determining in part which agreement features can occur with which lexical categories. I will then point out how a theory of this sort overcomes some of the conceptual and empirical problems with the theory presented in TGA. Although I would like to be able to discuss at least some of the remaining types of agreement, space limitations prevent me from examining those matters here. Interested readers may consult Lapointe (1984a,b) for further details.

1 Problems with the TGA Account

Let us begin then by considering the problems faced by the approach taken in TGA. The proposals made there suggested that general, regular, productive agreements were divided into two classes. (a) Agreement involving case, number, and person features were handled by assuming that words with these features would have LRs marked in various ways for these essentially semantic notions; the LR for a whole sentence would be well-formed if and only if the LRs for the agreeing elements were compatible, in a sense made formal in that work. (b) Agreement involving gender features, assumed to contribute nothing semantically to a sentence, were handled entirely differently; in this case a general condition was posited which forced semantically inert elements "linked" by their LRs in a certain way to agree if they had the morphological forms to do so.

Among the problems with this approach, we may identify three major difficulties. First, it is unclear that we would want a nonunified account of general, productive agreements which treats case, number, and person agreement in a distinct way from gender agreement, especially when we consider that gender often falls together with number and case as agreeing features of the same types of categories. The second problem involves the assignment of semantic markers to the agreeing elements.

Although the assignments made were plausible, nothing in that work suggested (a) why particular kinds of semantic markers were assigned to particular categories, or (b) what the range of possible assignments of semantic markers to categories was. The problems encountered by TGA in this regard are completely parallel to those faced by theories which assume that agreement is handled in terms of the manipulation of features attached to phrasal syntactic nodes (cf. the footnote on page 67); such theories typically have little to say about why in language after language the same or similar kinds of features are assigned to the same syntactic categories, just as TGA has little to say about the same issue in the case of the semantic markers used there. The third problem with the TGA approach is that there are well-known cases in which semantically relevant features and semantically inert features behave in the opposite ways. Thus, there are cases where neutral person/number markers appear on verbs which do *not* agree with subject NPs. In such circumstances elements which are otherwise semantically relevant are acting as semantically inert, strictly formal markers, and TGA has nothing to say about this type of situation. Worse though is the case where gender agreement is determined by the semantics of the object that the noun refers to rather than by the formal gender class that the gender marker belongs to. Again, TGA has nothing to say about such cases.

Given that TGA was concerned mainly with trying to develop analyses for the classical agreements of case government, adjectival concord, and verb agreement and was *not* attempting to cover all of the known facts about agreement, in trying to rectify the problems with that approach it seems reasonable that we would start by exploring the properties of a broad range of typical agreements. However, before we do that, it will be helpful if we state a few working definitions in order to make the subsequent discussion clearer. The first such definition is given in (1).

(1)   *Definition.* The term *morphosyntactic cooccurrence* will be applied to any set of facts in which the specific morphological form of words appearing in sentences correlates with the presence, absence, or form of other words appearing in the sentences.

In TGA, I somewhat misleadingly employed the term *grammatical agreement* for this definition, but the less euphonic *morphosyntactic cooccurrence* seems more appropriate, since the class defined in (1) includes many facts which we probably would not want to include under the particular heading of agreement by itself. It should be noted that I am taking *morphological form* in (1) to include uninflected stems when these contrast paradigmatically with inflected forms of the same word. Thus, in the Norwegian NP *en stor bil* 'a big car', *stor* and *bil* are involved in morphosyntactic cooccurrences even though they are uninflected, because each contrasts with other forms of the word (i.e., *stor* vs. *stort, store; bil* vs. *biler, bilen, bilene*).

The notion of *agreement proper* can now be taken, as a first approximation, to be that in (2).

(2)   *Definition.* The term *agreement* will be applied to those morphosyntactic cooccurrences in which there is an overt controller and overt controllee and in which the form of the controllee depends on universally specified semantic categories of the controller.

This definition is, in not so many words, essentially the working definition of agreement given in Moravcsik (1978). We may need to loosen the requirements that the controller and controllee be overt in order to account for certain cases involving null categories, but I will not be concerned with that issue here. Notice that (2) commits us to the view that agreement proper involves *directionality*—semantic properties of one of the agreeing elements control morphological properties of the other element. Contrary to this position, it was claimed in TGA that semantically relevant agreements are to be handled in a nondirectional manner; agreeing elements were claimed to mutually agree, and if *either* element failed to bear the appropriate morphological form, the resulting LR for the sentence would violate the wellformedness condition alluded to above. However, the non-directional approach is, on the face of it, less plausible than the alternative since it appears that the presence of particular subject and object nouns does indeed determine the agreement forms of verbs and that verbs and prepositions in fact govern the case forms of nouns heading NPs which the verbs and prepositions subcategorize for. Furthermore, even in TGA certain general agreements, those involving gender class markers, were assumed to involve a *directional* condition on morphological forms. The theory sketched below attempts to unify the two types of agreement by generalizing the directional condition employed in TGA for agreements involving semantically inert elements to those involving semantically relevant elements as well. To do this, we will need to be concerned with the following issues in our analysis:

(3) a. Which lexical elements are universally allowed to be controllers and/or controllees?

     b. How are potential controllers and controllees linked together in structures in which they actually agree?

     c. Which semantic categories of controllers are relevant?

     d. How does the form of the controllee depend on the controller's semantic categories?

After cataloguing and categorizing a number of agreement types in the next section, we will turn in Section 3 to an analysis of questions (3a) and (3b) above, and finally in Section 4 we will consider questions (3c) and (3d).

Controllee X agrees with *Controller Y* in *features Z*

	X	Y	Z
1.	Det(dem,quant)	head N	num, gend, case (def)
2.	Adj	head N	num, gend, case (def)
3.a.	Predicate Adj	subj N	num, gend, (case) (def)
b.	Predicate Adj	subj pron	num, gend, (case) (def)
4.	Relative pron	head N	num, gend, (case) (def)
5.	Anaphoric pron	antecedent N	pers, num, gend
6.	Reflexive pron	antecedent N	pers, num, gend
7.	Possessed N/pron	possessor N	pers, num (gend)
8.	V	subj, do, N	pers, num, gend
9.	Prep	object N	pers, num, gend
10.a.	Appositive N	head N	num, case, (gend? def?)
b.	Appositive N	head pron	num, case, (gend? def?)
11.a.	Predicate nom	subj N	(case)(num? gend? def?)
b.	Predicate nom	subj pron	(case)(num? gend? def?)
12.	Embedded V	embedding V	tense, aspect (voice? mood?)
13.	Modifying V	main V	tense, aspect (voice? mood?)
14.	Adv	head V	tense, aspect, voice, mood(??)
15.a.	N/pron	V	case
b.	N/pron	Prep(Adj,N?)	case
16.	Adj	Det	declension class
17.	(Adv	Aux	conjugation class ??)
18.	Det, N mutually		def.(num? gend?)
19.	Aux, V mutually		aspect, mood, voice (tense?)
20.	Conjunct resolutions		(varies)

Table 1. Summary of some morphosyntactic cooccurrences.

2 Types of Morphosyntactic Cooccurrences

Let us now examine a range of typical morphosyntactic cooccurrences. A list of these, not intended to be exhaustive, is given in Table 1. The list is divided into major blocks so that Nos. 1–11 involve forms agreeing with nouns, Nos. 12–15, those agreeing with verbs or prepositions, and the rest something of a *potpourri* of cases.

The data in this table being somewhat diverse, let's see what sorts of generalizations we can extract from it. First, I have nothing to say about predicate nominal agreement No. 10 or about appositive NP agreement No. 11 because, as indicated by the numerous question marks, there are a number of outstanding issues related to these constructions. If we remove Nos. 10, 11 from the list then and examine the agreeing features column for the remaining types in the first block, we find an interesting division: Nos. 1–4 agree in number, gender, case, and definiteness, while Nos. 5–9 agree in number, person, gender and occasionally case and definiteness. In the case of the first group, Nos. 1–4, all of the controllees belong to the class of items traditionally described as *modifying* the head noun. What about the second group, Nos. 5–9? Here the controllees are (a) anaphoric and reflexive pronouns, (b) possessed nominals, and (c) verbs and prepositions. In the only case of possessed nominal agreement that I am at all familiar with, that of Chamorro discussed in Chung (1982), a separate, pronominal clitic element is attached to the noun. The attachment of such clitic elements is often a feature of verb agreement as well. Furthermore, in languages with verb agreement but without separable pronominal clitics, fused tense/aspect morphemes typically bear pronominal properties, and it is just these pronominal properties which appear to license the absence of explicit pronouns in so-called *pro-drop* languages.

It therefore seems reasonable to assume, following a line similar to one adopted by Chomsky (1981) in the GB framework, that Nos. 5–9 all involve agreement of a pronominal element of some sort with a noun. I hasten to add that this statement does not mean that I will be adopting the same mechanisms as GB posits in analyzing these types of agreement: on the contrary, I will be adopting a rather different sort of analysis below. Nonetheless, on this view, as in the one taken in GB, verbs and prepositions do not directly agree with nouns, but rather pronominal elements attached to the verbs and prepositions do.

There are two arguments that I am aware of which suggest that this is the correct approach in these cases. The first is that *person* is typically only a category of pronouns, *not* of full nouns or other items. By saying that verb and preposition agreement involve pronominal elements, we can capture this fact automatically. The second argument, due to Greg Carlson, who pointed it out to me in private conversation, concerns the purported fact that there are no languages in which stem-internal vowel gradation is used as the productive means of signalling person/number agreement in verbs. That is, there seem to be no languages in which verbs are productively inflected like the made-up verb in (4).[1] Assuming

---

[1] Bill Poser pointed out to me in private conversation that in the South American Indian language Tereña certain verbs inflect for 2nd person forms using internal vowel change rather than affixal elements as is found in the rest of the verb paradigm. These forms are apparently historically frozen forms, however. Furthermore, the entire general verb paradigms is not

these facts to be essentially correct, we can explain them by saying that stem-internal vowel changes typically only signal changes in inflectional categories appropriate for the stem's class. Since person and number are in general appropriate for pronouns but not for verbs, we would expect languages not to use patterns like (4) for person/number agreement; instead, we would expect markers for which these inflectional categories *are* appropriate (i.e., pronominal elements) appearing attached on the outside of verb stems.

(4)   take = 'I take'
         took = 'you (sg.) take'
         tok   = 's/he takes'
         -etc-

Moving on now to the second major block, Nos. 12–15, in Table 1, we again find two subgroups. Nos. 12–14 involve agreement in verb categories, while No. 15 involves case government of nouns by verbs and prepositions. The odd type out here is case government, to which we will return shortly. In the meantime, let us summarize the discussion so far. We have identified the three types of agreement listed in (5).

(5)   *Major Types of Agreement*

         a.   N-modifier agreement   – Nos. 1–4 in Table 1
         b.   pronominal agreement   – Nos. 5–9 in Table 1
         c.   V-modifier agreement   – Nos. 12–14 in Table 1

The terms 'N-modifier' and 'V-modifier' are being used in a rather loose way in (5a,c) and are not intended to carry any special theoretical significance with them.

The remaining block, Nos. 16–20, in Table 1 includes various other types of morphosyntactic cooccurrences with which I am familiar. No. 16 involves cases like the strong/weak markings on adjectives in Germanic and Scandinavian languages, No. 18, cases like the definiteness marking on determiners and head nouns in Scandinavian, No. 19, cases like English Aux-V form combinations, and No. 20, generalizations about the ways in which languages resolve conflicts in agreeing features in conjoined structures as discussed by Corbett (1983). I have no examples of No. 17, but there seems to be no reason by such cases cannot exist parallel to No. 16, although they may be quite rare.

What I would like to say now about Nos. 15–19 and certain aspects of No. 20 is that they involve other sorts of morphosyntactic devices from those which govern agreement proper, and that therefore only the three types of agreement listed in (5), plus perhaps certain aspects of

---

inflected in this way. These provisos lend further support to the view that this construction is indeed quite rare.

No. 20, are included in the class of universally authorized agreements proper. Under this scheme, case government would involve the system responsible for linking the LRs for NPs with verb and preposition arguments, Nos. 18, 19 would involve the system of discontinuous lexical items, as I have argued in Lapointe (1984a,b), and Nos. 16, 17 would involve a system of strictly formal agreements controlled by non-noun, non-verb lexical items (Lapointe 1984b). In adopting this classification, I wish to abandon the general vs. restricted agreement distinction of Lapointe (1981). Although that distinction may still be useful in descriptive discussions of morphosyntactic cooccurrences in general, I now take the theoretically relevant distinction to be that between the agreements proper of (5) and other sorts of cooccurrences like those listed in Nos. 15–19 in Table 1.[2]

3 Linking Controllers and Controllees

Focusing now on the universally authorized agreements in (5), let us try to formulate answers to questions (3a) and (3b) posed above. There are various approaches that we can take in analyzing the linkage between controllers and controllees; here, however, I will adopt an approach similar to the one taken in TGA in which there is a system mapping LRs from surface PS trees over which the necessary linking principles are defined. In particular, I will be assuming that the system of LR is defined in terms of a modified version of Barwise and Cooper's (1981) logic for generalized quantifiers. There are two main reasons for assuming such a system. First, there is a fairly direct correspondence between SS constituents and expressions of the LR in this type of logic, and second, it allows us to state the principles determining the linkage between controllers and controllees along with the effects of the controller on the form

---

[2] I am aware of only one counterexample to the descriptive generalizations just discussed. This is the case of Avar mentioned by Anderson (1982). In that language, adverbs apparently agree with subject nouns in absolutive case. I have not been able to study this language, since the only grammar on Avar available to me is written in Russian, which I cannot read. However, there are other possibilities for analyzing this case than the one which Anderson suggests. He notes, for instance, that verbs in Avar also agree with subject nouns in absolutive case, so one possibility is that the adverbs are agreeing with the verbs in some sort of pronominal element rather that agreeing directly with the nouns. Another possibility is that this is a case of multiple marking in which every [+V] element in the clause is marked [+ABS]. A third possibility is that this adverbial marking occurs only with subject-oriented adverbs but not with sentence-oriented ones. In any case, until a fuller analysis of the facts in this case is presented, it seems reasonable to adopt the otherwise clear-cut generalizations about agreement already discussed.

I.   *Basic Logical Expressions*

    a. *Logical symbols*

Connectives	$\vee, \wedge, \neg, \oplus, \ldots$
Variables	$x, y, z, x_o, \ldots$
Logical specifiers	**a, every, the, that**

    b. *Nonlogical symbols*

Class symbols (basic set terms)	**house, small**
Relation symbols	**run, see**
Names (basic quantifiers)	**Harry, Shirley**

II.   *Complex Logical Expressions*

a. Well-formed formula (wff)	– relation symbol plus appropriate number of variables	– $\mathbf{run}(x)$, $\mathbf{see}(x, y)$
b. Set term	– basic set term	– **house, small**
	– basic set terms joined by $\oplus$	– **house** $\oplus$ **small**
	– capped variable plus wff	– $\hat{x}[\mathbf{run}(x)]$
c. Quantifier	– basic quantifier	– **Harry, Shirley**
	– logical specifier plus set term	– **[the (house)]**
d. Wff	– quantifier plus set term	– **[the(woman)]** $\hat{x}[\mathbf{run}(x)]$

Table 2.   Types of logical and nonlogical expressions in a modified version of Barwise and Cooper's (1981) logic.

of the controllee in a single compact condition. After briefly sketching the main features of the logic, I will then define the condition required by the agreements in (6).

    The logic is assumed to contain a stock of basic logical and nonlogical symbols, as shown in (I) of Table 2. Among the logical symbols are various connectives, variables, and logical specifiers; among the nonlogical symbols are class symbols (basic set terms), relation symbols, and names (basic quantifiers). These elements can combine to form complex logical expression in the ways listed in (II) of Table 2. Here we find (a) wellformed formulas (wffs) consisting of relation symbols plus the appropriate number of variables; (b) set terms composed of (i) basic set terms (i.e., class symbols), (ii) basic set terms joined with other set terms by circled pluses, or (iii) capped variables plus wffs; (c) quantifiers made up of (i) basic quantifiers (i.e., names) or (ii) logical specifiers plus set terms; and (d) finally, wffs consisting of quantifiers plus set terms. In Lapointe (1984a) I assumed that general principles determined the mapping $m : \text{SS} \to \text{LR}$ and discussed the changes in the semantic interpretation required by the modifications made to Barwise and Cooper's original system. Rather than go through the details of m here, let us instead walk through a simple example to get an idea of how the system is supposed to work.

Suppose we have the English sentence in (6a), with the surface PS tree in (6b).

(6) a.   The girl kisses the boy.

b.

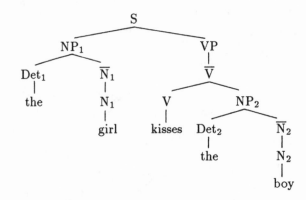

c. $m(the) = \textbf{the}$
$m(girl) = \textbf{girl}$
$m(boy) = \textbf{boy}$
$m(kiss) = \textbf{kiss}(x, y)$

d. $m(\overline{\text{N}}_1) = m(\text{N}_1) = \textbf{girl}$

e. $m(\overline{\text{N}}_2) = m(\text{N}_2) = \textbf{boy}$

f. $m(\text{NP}_1) = [\textbf{the (girl)}]; \; m(\text{NP}_2) = [\textbf{the (boy)}]$

g. $m(\text{VP}) = m(\overline{V}) = [\textbf{the (boy)}] \; \hat{y}[\textbf{kiss}(x, y)]$

h. $m(\text{S}) = [\textbf{the (girl)}] \; \hat{x}[[\textbf{the (boy)}] \; \hat{y}[\textbf{kiss}(x, y)]]$

Ignoring tense, the translation will work in the following ways. Determiners are translated as logical specifiers, nouns and adjectives as class symbols, and verbs as wffs containing relation symbols plus the appropriate number of arguments, all as in (6c). The translation conventions provide that when a node is nonbranching, the translation of the dominating node is the same as that of the dominated node; thus, the LRs for the two $\overline{\text{N}}$s of (6b) are given in (6d,e). The conventions also provide that logical specifiers combine with set terms to yield complex quantifiers as in (6f). Next, LRs for direct object NPs combine with those for verbs using capped variables, yielding the LR for $\overline{N}$ as well as the nonbranching VP in (6g). Finally, the LR for the whole sentence is produced again using capped variables as in (6h).

With this much background, we may proceed to the definitions needed to formulate the principle governing controller/controllee linkage. First, we need to define a notion parallel to x *binds* y in logics making greater use of variables than the present one does. This can be done with the definitions in (7) and (8).

(7)   *Definition.* A logical specifier **D** binds a set term τ in the following types of expressions:

   a. in a quantifier of the form $[\mathbf{D}(\tau)]$, where τ is a basic set term,

   b. in a quantifier of the form $[\mathbf{D}(\sigma)]$, where $\sigma = \tau_1 \oplus \tau_2 \oplus \ldots \oplus \tau_n$ and for some i, $\tau_i = \tau$, or

   c. in a wff of the form $[\mathbf{D}(\sigma)]\tau$.

   A name **N** binds a set term τ in a wff of the form $[\mathbf{N}] \, \tau$.

(8)   *Definition.* Let the logical specifier **D** bind the complex set term of the form $\hat{u}[\phi]$. Then **D** is also said to bind the variable u in ϕ.

The statement in (7b) is just the fancy way of saying that if the set is complex and consists of a string of set terms joined by circled pluses, then the logical specifier binds all those set terms. The definition in (8) in effect allows for a logical specifier to bind the argument of verbs. For concreteness, some examples are given in (9).

(9) a. $m(\textit{the boy}) = [\textbf{the(boy)}]$ – the binds **boy** by (7a)

   b. $m(\textit{the small boy}) = [\textbf{the(small}\oplus\textbf{boy)}]$ – the binds **small, boy** by (7b)

   c. in (6h) – $\textbf{the}_1$ binds **girl** and $\textbf{the}_2$ binds **boy** by (7a)
       $\textbf{the}_1$ binds $\hat{x} \ldots$ and $\textbf{the}_2$ binds $\hat{y} \ldots$ by (7c)
       $\textbf{the}_1$ binds x and $\textbf{the}_2$ binds y in $\textbf{kiss}(x, y)$ by (8)

Having defined the notion of binding in this kind of logical systems, we can now provide the definition of connection between controller and controllee as in (10).

(10)   *Definition.* Let $\phi = m(\sigma)$ for σ a SS. Let $\alpha', \beta' \in \phi$ be logical expressions that are *not* complex set terms. Then α', β' are said to be *logically connected* if

   a. α' is a logical specifier or a name binding β', or

   b. there is a logical specifier or a name γ which binds both α', β'.

Continuing with the examples in (9), (11) describes which of the expressions in those examples are logically connected (abbreviated here as *l-connected*).

(11) a.   in (9a) **the** and **boy** are *l*-connected by (10a);

   b.   in (9b) **the** and **small, the** and **boy** *l*-connected by (10a); **small** and **boy** *l*-connected by (10b)

   c.   in (9c) **the₁** and **girl, the₁** and **x, the₂** and **boy**, and **the₂** and **y** *l*-connected by (10a); **girl** and **x, boy** and **y** *l*-connected by (10b)

Notice that in (11c), **girl** is *not* *l*-connected to the complex set term $\hat{x}\ldots$, nor is **boy** *l*-connected to $\hat{y}\ldots$.

We now extend the notion of *l*-connectedness from logical expressions to lexical elements as in (12) and (13).

(12)   *Definition.* Let $\alpha, \beta \in \sigma$ a SS; let α, β be lexical or pronominal categories such that α corresponds to α' and β corresponds to β', where α' and β' are as described in (10). Then α, β are said to be *l*-connected whenever α', β' are.

(13)   *Definition.* Let $\gamma = \alpha$ or β in (12). Then γ corresponds to γ' whenever $m(\gamma) = \gamma'$ and

   a. γ is a lexical category or a lexical pronoun, or

   b. γ is a pronominal element of a lexical item w which determines the pronominal semantic categories of γ', an argument of $m(w)$.

We then have the extended logical connections in (14) for the preceding examples.

(14) a.   in (9a) *the* and *boy* are *l*-connected

   b.   in (9b) *the* and *boy, the* and *small*, and *small* and *boy* are *l*-connected

   c.   in (9c) (i.e., (6h)) *the₁* and *girl, the₂* and *boy*, and *girl* and *-s* are *l*-connected

Notice that given the discussion in Section 2, the 3.SG marker *-s* is being treated as the pronominal element for the *x*-argument of $kiss(x, y)$ in $m(kiss)$.

Now all that we need to do is to add the restrictions that the controller can only be a noun or a verb (cf. once again Nos. 1–14 in Table 1) and include the constraint that features of the controller determine morphological features of the controllee, and we will have the general condition in (15) and the conventions in (16).

(15)   *Universal Agreement Principle*

Let $\alpha, \beta \in \sigma$ a SS such that α is a lexical or pronominal category, β is a N or a V, and α, β are logically connected. Let α be marked for the morphological features $[F_1, \ldots, F_n]$ which are all features of β. Then for each F_i α bears the same value for F_i that β bears.

(16)   *Conventions.* Whenever (15) holds, α is said to agree with β (in $F_1, \ldots, F_n$); in symbols, $\mathrm{AGR}(\alpha, \beta(, F_1, \ldots, F_n))$. β is said to control the agreement.

Returning one last time to our examples in (14), (15) allows *the* to agree with *boy* in (14a), *the* and *small* to agree with *boy* in (14b), and *the*$_2$ to agree with *boy* and *the*$_1$ and *-s* to agree with *girl* in (14c). However, because determiners and adjectives in English are not marked for the appropriate morphological features, none but the last of these possibilities leads to an actual agreement in the language. Notice also that in (14b) neither *the* nor *boy* can agree with *small*, even though *the* and *boy* are *l*-connected to *small*, since *small* is neither a noun nor a verb and hence under (15) cannot control agreements proper.

The interaction of the logical and grammatical conditions in (15) allows for the following possible agreements: (a) determiner agreeing with head noun, No. 1 in Table 1, (b) adjective agreeing with head noun, No. 2, (c) anaphoric and reflexive pronouns with antecedents nouns, Nos. 5, 6, (d) pronominal elements of verbs or prepositions with subject, direct object, etc. nouns, Nos. 8, 9. In addition, under reasonable assumptions about the LRs of relative clauses and possessed nouns with pronominal elements, (15) should be able to accommodate Nos. 4 and 7. It should also permit predicate adjective agreement No. 3, *if* we assume that the LR of *be* is null and we continue to ignore tense; in that case, sentences with predicate adjectives will have LRs as in (17), leading to the desired agreement relation.

(17) $m(Mary\ is\ tall)$ [**Mary**] **tall** – Mary binds **tall** by (7a), *Mary* is *l*-connected to *tall* by (10, 12), so AGR(*tall, Mary*) is possible by (15).

If the LR for *be* is nonnull, we will have to do more work to get predicate adjective agreement to work out, but the extensions that would have to be made are straightforward. Nothing said so far, however, will allow V-*modifying* agreements (5c) of the sort of Nos. 12–14. In order to handle such cases, we will have to analyze the LRs that need to be assigned to embedded clauses and infinitivals within the present logical system and extend the notion of binding in (7, 8). Since these problems will take us too far afield from the present topics, we must leave them open for further study.

As noted in Section 1, the universal principle in (15) is itself a generalization of the condition in TGA which was assumed to handle just gender class agreements. It represents a formalization of the traditional notion *A modifies B* in terms of the system of LRs assumed here. As such, it also represents an extension of Avery Andrews' (1982) work on control of predicate adjective agreement in the LFG framework (Bresnan 1982), and it is the condition within the present analysis corresponding to the Control Agreement Principle in the GPSG framework (Gazdar and Pullum 1982).

4 Markedness and Morphological Features

The issues remaining to be dealt with are those raised by questions (3c) and (3d) above concerning the semantic categories of controllers and the effects of these categories on the form of controllees. Since there is a certain latitude across languages as to exactly which inflectional categories will be marked on the controller and the controllee, it seems appropriate to assume that some sort of markedness system is at work here. The approach to markedness that I will adopt and have elaborated on elsewhere follows Williams (1981) in assuming that (a) implicational universals and complexity rankings are not part of Universal Grammar (UG) proper, but (b) these instead follow from mechanisms of the language acquisition system. If we take these notions seriously, then we are committed to actually trying to formulate principles and mechanisms for the construction of grammars in acquisition which still imply these universals. Williams took a first stab at this for certain phrase structural phenomena, and I have presented several principles for learning verb markers (Lapointe, in press). For the present discussion, however, I will be treating such *variational* universals as if they *were* basic to linguistic theory and leave the job of developing the appropriate acquisition devices for future research.

Continuing in the same general vein, I take the markedness of the semantic categories which ground agreement features to be largely a matter of cognitive complexity rankings, parallel, for example, to the psychological, perceptual complexity rankings among colors. As far as linguistic morphological structure goes, there are two types of complexity, that of form and that of the semantic notions expressed. While both of these dimensions can be varied independently in the morphemes of any given language, a general principle ties the two types of complexity together; we can state this principle along the lines of (18). This condition is intended as rough way of stating what appears to be the basic idea behind the notion of a morpheme being "more (less) marked."

(18)   *Fundamental Principle of Markedness*
The formal complexity of a class of linguistic elements varies directly with the semantic complexity of the class.

A final general comment needs to be made about what I am taking the term "semantic notion" to mean. In the absence of a fully specified system of interpreted LRs for natural language, I will simply be using labels, mainly of the traditional sort for inflectional categories, as standing for whatever we ultimately decide the proper semantic representation for such objects should be. However, I will also be interpreting these notion as defining features of the usual sort in generative work which will be marked on the morphemes which express the notions. Thus, semantic complexity rankings will be peppered with familiar looking terms like *sing, 3rd person,* and so on, while inflections like the English verbal -*s* will be marked with feature bundles such as $[+SG,+3]$.[3]

Turning to nouns then, we may give the complexity rankings for N notions in Table 3. Here, as in all the rankings I will be presenting, $A < B$ means 'A is semantically less complex than B,' and a connecting line beneath a notion indicates that the lower notions are subnotions of the upper one. Some remarks about these rankings are in order. First, we observe that the rankings are not intended to be complete. Nothing is said, for instance, about the position of the mass/count distinction here, and there are no doubt further types of notions that have been omitted which a more complete analysis would want to include. Second, we may note that as stated, these rankings imply a number of well-known variational universals, including Greenberg's (1963) Universals Nos. 34, 36, 37, and in conjunction with the Fundamental Principle in (18), Nos. 35 and 38 as well. In addition, it captures a universal noted by Moravcsik (1978) that plural marking on nonhuman/inanimate nouns implies plural marking on human/animate nouns.

Taking a closer look at the individual ranking, in the case of the Card(inality) ranking, Moravcsik (1978) presents persuasive arguments

---

[3] If we were being a bit more careful about terminology, we would also want to distinguish two more kinds of universals in addition to the *variational* type, specifically, those defining the range of possible types of elements of a given category, and those defining the elements which must occur in a particular grammar. For convenience, we might refer to the first type as *range* principles and the second as *necessity* principles. Thus, in addition to providing rankings of semantic notions and morphological forms, we must also provide range universals delimiting the bounds of possible semantic notions that can be expressed by inflections of various lexical categories, plus necessity constraints compelling certain notions to be expressed where that seems appropriate. In the rest of the discussion, I will not be concerned with universals of these types, and I will simply assume that UG makes available to particular grammars at least all of the notions explicitly listed in the complexity rankings.

N Notion Rankings: CARDINALITY<ANIMACY<CASE<NEWNESS

a. CARDINALITY
   sing < plur
   └─ remaining < dual < trial < paucal
      plur

b. ANIMACY
   anim < inanim
   └─ human < nonhuman
      └─ M, F   └─ M, F

c. CASE
   direct   <   oblique
   └─ ACC   <   ERG   └─ relational < spatio-temporal
      └─ nom<acc   └─ abs<erg   └─ gen<dat   └─ abl<allative...

d. NEWNESS
   indef < def
   └─ distal < proximal ...

Pronoun Notion Ranking:

a. Anaphoric and reflexive pronouns: CARD<PERSON<ANIM<CASE
   PERS.
   3rd < discourse
        participants
        └─ 2nd < 1st
           └─ includes 2nd < excludes 2nd

b. Pronominal elements: GRAM. RELATIONS<CARD<PERS<ANIM
   GR
   SUB < DO < IO < Oblique Obj

V Notion Ranking: ATTITUDE<VOICE<ASPECT <TENSE

a. ATTITUDE
   indic < non-indic
   └─ imperative < subjunctive ...

b. VOICE
   active < passive < causative ...

c. ASPECT
   nonspecific < durative < completive ...

d. TENSE
   present < past, future

Table 3. Semantic notion rankings for Ns, Vs, and Pronouns.

that dual, etc. are to be considered subnotions of the plural and *not* notions on the same level as singular/plural. Concerning the Animacy scale, we may well ask what this category is doing here at all, since in many languages, and certainly in the familiar European ones, any semantic relations underlying gender distinctions seem hopelessly obscure. Researchers have oscillated back and forth on this issue over the years, but I believe that Greenberg (1966) basically put his finger on the appropriate way to view the problem. The idea can be captured, in a more elaborated and formal statement, as in (19).

(19) *Semantic Base for Genders*

> Whenever the following holds of a grammar, that grammar is said to have a semantic base (g_i) for gender:
>
> a. the class of Ns can be exhaustively divided into classes $G_1, \ldots, G_m$, and
> b. for some G_i (or for some union of $G_j \ldots G_k$), there is a subset g_i such that (nearly) all the nouns of the grammar referring to objects of the same real-world animacy, or referring to objects playing the same real-world social or biological role, are all members of g_i.

In the same passage in which he discusses this notion, Greenberg also notes that there are languages in which certain genders seem not to have such a semantic core, and hence could not be directly compared with genders in other languages. Given such instances, we might propose the hypothesis in (20) as the strongest one that could be put forth.

(20) *Hypothesis.* Every language exhibiting gender classes has at least one semantic base.

That we can identify such semantic cores in languages which mark gender is therefore the sense in which I take genders to be semantic. Finally, concerning Case, I am not sure what the range of possible Oblique cases is universally; it may be that UG stops about where the Case scale stops in Table 3 with individual languages allowed to fill in further notions beyond the ones given there. Similar comments apply in the rankings for Definiteness and Newness.

Turning next to the scales for Pronouns in Table 3, for anaphoric and reflexive pronouns we have the same rankings as for nouns except that there is no Newness scale and instead there is a Person scale.[4] For

---

[4] One potentially controversial aspect of the Person scale in Table 3 is that 2nd<1st. Moravcsik (1978) has argued that the complexity goes the other way around. Space limitations prevent a full discussion of the issues here, although it appears that constraints on the linearization of morphemes and politeness conditions may be interacting in the cases in which it appears that 1st<2nd. See also Schwartz (1978) for some discussion and further data.

pronominal elements, we have the same scales as for the other pronouns except that here a Grammatical Relations ranking replaces the Case scale. The reason for this difference is that pronominal elements do not really mark Case; rather they mark the arguments of predicates that they are logically linked with, and, following Dowty (1982), Marantz (1984) and others, I take linking to a predicate's arguments to be intimately related to the traditional notion of grammatical relations. As stated, the Pronoun rankings imply several variational principles, including Greenberg's UniversalsNos. 32, 33, 44, and 45.

Finally, the rankings given in Table 3 for verbs is based on previous work I have done on verb markers (Lapointe, in press). The term *Attitude* here is merely intended to indicate that these notions have to do with the speaker's attitude toward the truth of the statement; *Modality* or some other such term could instead be substituted here.

What we must do now is to connect the semantic notions of Table 3 together with the morphological elements with which they are associated in agreement; i.e., we must specify how these notions affect the form of the controllee.

(21)   *Agreement Feature Condition*

In addition to whatever semantically-grounded and ranked morphological features may be inherent to a controllee category C, if C agrees with a N (alternatively, a V), it can have as a morphological feature any of the semantically-grounded morphological features of Ns (Vs). Such features of C are called *agreement features*, and their complexity rankings are determined by the complexity scales for the corresponding N (V) semantic notions.

(22) a.   It is least complex in a grammar for the following inherent categories not to be overtly expressed:

i. Ns – animacy, countability, . . .

ii. Vs – event-type, transitivity, . . .

b.   It is least complex in a grammar for a N-modifying or V-modifying controllee (i.e., cases like (5a, c)) to have exactly the same semantically-grounded features as its controller in the grammar.

c.   Inherent features of the controllee aside, it is less complex in a grammar for a N-modifying or V-modifying controllee to have fewer semantically-grounded features than its controller.

The condition in (21) appears to be the sort of principle that we need to do this. In addition, the conditions in (22) begin to go some way toward determining the complexity of situations in which the controller and controllee bear different inflectional features. There are, of course, numerous other principles which need to be stated in this domain. Furthermore, as noted above, we would not want to leave the principles presented here in their present state, but rather we would want to try to continue on and develop explicit acquisition mechanisms from which these conditions will follow as consequences.

5 Conclusion

What I have tried to do in this paper is to present a unified theory of agreement in which (a) only nouns or verbs can be controllers of agreements proper, (b) the potential controllees in agreements can only be those elements which are logically connected to potential controllers and bear the appropriate morphological features (as in (15)), and (c) the appropriateness of those morphological features is determined by (21) and the rankings in Table 3. In the process, I have tried to overcome the problems with the proposals made in TGA described in Section 1. In the present analysis, gender is treated in an entirely parallel fashion to number, case, and person as far as agreement goes, and the assignment of semantic representations to agreeing elements, determined in part by the complexity scales relating the various semantic notions, is made in a universally defined manner. The third problem with the TGA approach—what to do when semantically relevant features do not contribute to meaning or when gender agreement is determined strictly semantically—has not been dealt with at all here. However, I believe that the present approach offers more promise in accommodating such cases than my earlier proposals did. This optimism follows from the fact that this theory expressly allows individual grammars to exploit morphosyntactic devices which lay beyond the bounds of the agreement processes discussed here in handling non-universally authorized agreements, thus making it easier for grammars to treat exceptional sorts of agreements (for example, restricted agreements where the controller is not a noun or a verb, quirky case markings, and certain aspects of conjunct agreement resolutions) in lexical or purely semantic ways. Within the earlier TGA approach, it was not at all clear what status this array of cooccurrences had. Nonetheless, to the extent that the theory presented here limits the class of possible agreement types, in the narrowed sense of (2), we will have gained a measure of explanation which we previously lacked.

References

Anderson, S. R. 1982. Where's morphology? *Linguistic Inquiry* 13:571–612.

Andrews, A. 1982. The representation of case in Modern Icelandic. In J. Bresnan (Ed), *The Mental Representation of Grammatical Relations.* Cambridge, Mass.: The MIT Press.

Barwise, J., and R. Cooper 1981. Generalized quantifiers and natural language. *Linguistics and Philosophy* 4:159–219.

Bresnan, J. (Ed) 1982. *The Mental Representation of Grammatical Relations.* Cambridge, Mass.: The MIT Press.

Chomsky, N. 1981. *Lectures on Government and Binding.* Dordrecht: Foris.

Chung, S. 1982. On extending the null-subject parameter to NPs. In D. Flickinger, M. Macken, and N. Wiegand (Eds), *Proceedings of the West Coast Conference on Formal Linguistics* 1. Stanford, Calif.: Stanford Linguistics Association.

Corbett, G. G. 1983. Resolution rules: agreement in person, number, and gender. In G. Gazdar, E. Klein, and G. K. Pullum (Eds), *Order, Concord, and Constituency.* Dordrecht: Foris.

Dowty, D. 1982. Grammatical relations in Montague Grammar. In P. Jacobson and G. K. Pullum (Eds), *The Nature of Syntactic Representation.* Dordrecht: Reidel.

Gazdar, G. and G. K. Pullum 1982. *Generalized Phrase Structure Grammar: A Theoretical Synopsis.* Bloomington: Indiana University Linguistics Club.

Greenberg, J. H. 1963. *Universals of Language.* Cambridge, Mass.: The MIT Press.

Greenberg, J. H. 1966. *Language Universals, With Special Reference to Feature Hierarchies.* (Janua Linguarum Series Minor, 59.) The Hague: Mouton.

Lapointe, S. G. 1980. *A Theory of Grammatical Agreement.* Doctoral dissertation, University of Massachusetts, Amherst.

Lapointe, S. G. 1981. General and restricted agreement phenomena. In M. Moortgat, H. v.d. Hulst and T. Hoekstra (Eds), *The Scope of Lexical Rules.* Dordrecht: Foris.

Lapointe, S. G. 1983. A comparison of two recent theories of agreement. In J. Richardson, M. Marks and A. Chukerman (Eds), *Papers from the Parasession on the Interplay of Phonology, Morphology, and Syntax, Chicago Linguistic Society.*

Lapointe, S. G. 1984a. Cooccurrence and agreement in Norwegian noun phrases. In *ESCOL '84: Proceedings of the First Eastern States Conference on Linguistics.* Columbus: Department of Linguistics, Ohio State University.

Lapointe, S. G. 1984b. Syntactic phrase-level mismatches involving grammatical markers and their semantic effects. Ms. Wayne State University.

Lapointe, S. G. In press. Markedness, the organization of linguistic information in speech production, and language acquisition. In F. Eckman, et al. (Eds), *Markedness, Proceedings of the Twelfth Annual University of Wisconsin-Milwaukee Symposium.* New York: Plenum.

Marantz, A. 1984. *On the Nature of Grammatical Relations.* Cambridge, Mass.: The MIT Press.

Moravcsik, E. 1978. Agreement. In J. H. Greenberg (Ed), *Universals of Human Language* 4. Stanford: Stanford University Press.

Schwartz, L. 1978. Object agreement in animacy precedence languages. Presented at the Fourth Annual Minnesota Regional Conference on Language and Linguistics, Minneapolis.

Williams, E. 1981. $\overline{X}$ features. In S. Tavakolian (Ed), *Language Acquisition and Linguistic Theory.* Cambridge, Mass.: The MIT Press.

5 Agreement and Markedness

EDITH A. MORAVCSIK

IN THIS PAPER, I will draw on Lehmann (1982) for a general concept of grammatical agreement as well as for a number of generalizations that are suggested in his paper. Using this framework as a take-off point, I will focus on the question of how some of the facts and generalizations that Lehmann and others have found to be true could be explained. By *explaining something* I will not mean anything more elaborate than finding an independently motivated principle from which the facts to be explained naturally follow. More specifically, I will consider a version of markedness theory and probe into the extent to which agreement phenomena are predicted by its principles.

The paper consists of two parts. First I will outline Lehmann's concept of agreement and Greenberg's markedness theory as proposed in Greenberg (1966) and I will attempt to articulate the points of contact between the two. In other words, I will consider which are the questions about agreement that markedness theory can be held accountable for answering as opposed to those that fall outside its domain. In the second part of the paper, I will evaluate the actual degree of success with which markedness theory manages to predict facts about agreement.

1 Agreement and Markedness—the Logical Fit

1.1 Agreement

Let us first consider agreement. In order to delimit this grammatical concept, I will adopt Lehmann's definition which runs as follows:

Constituent *B* agrees with constituent *A* (in category *C*) if and only if the following conditions hold true:

(i)   There is a grammatical or semantic syntagmatic relation be-
        tween A and B.

(ii)   A grammatical category C with a form paradigm of subcate-
        gories exists.

(iii) A belongs to a subcategory c of C and A's belonging to c is
        independent of the presence or nature of B.

(iv)   Subcategory c is expressed on B and forms a constituent with
        it. (Lehmann 1982)

For example, in the case of English subject-verb agreement, the verb is
B, the subject is A, and person-number is C; c is third person singular.
Although this definition is not entirely satisfactory—some of the conditions appear to me to be vague and others seem redundant—it will serve
as a useful framework within which the basic questions that need to be
answered about agreement can be enumerated.

The basic puzzle of agreement phenomena is the occurrence of what
are called agreement markers. There are three things that are puzzling
about them. First, agreement markers are, by definition, *displaced*: they
say something about a constituent other than what they are formally
associated with. For example, the person-number markers attached to
the verb reflect the person-number of the subject. Second, agreement
markers are, in the majority of their uses, *redundant*: the information
they convey is also conveyed in some form by the constituent they pertain to (such as person and number also being indicated by the subject
itself). And, third, the occurrence of agreement markers is *variable*,
both language-internally and also across languages: they show up under certain conditions but not under others. Correspondingly, the main
questions about agreement in a synchronic account are: (1) the nature
of the agreement markers—their meaning (C in Lehmann's definition),
their form, and their location in the sentence—and (2) the specification
of the conditions under which they occur. These conditions include,
first of all, the identification of the terms of agreement: what are possible A's; what are possible B's; and what are possible combinations of A's
and B's? They also include other attendant conditions for agreement
in the sentence or discourse (such as whether the sentences exhibiting
agreement are main or subordinate, declarative or interrogative, etc.)
and structural characteristics which correlate with the very occurrence
of agreement in a language to begin with.

1.2 Markedness

Let us now consider markedness theory as proposed in Greenberg (1966):
this is the system of principles to which we will look for possible explanations of agreement phenomena. Greenberg's version of markedness is,
to my knowledge, the most elaborate version of this concept and one

that is the most articulate about empirical predictions. Other formulations are, I believe, compatible with the Greenberg concept and they differ from it only in that they elaborate some subset of the markedness criteria proposed by Greenberg and in that they place the basic claim within the context of some more general framework such as Government and Binding Theory.

I will briefly summarize the theory as I see it. The domain with respect to which it makes claims is pairs of structural entities that form an opposition. It is then claimed that members of such oppositions exhibit an asymmetrical relation: the two are not on a par. The core hypothesis is that this asymmetrical relation is manifested in more than one respect and that the various tests that demonstrate this asymmetry will have converging results. That is to say, if we know how the two members of the opposition fare in one of the relevant tests, we can predict how they will fare under other relevant tests: if one test assigns a member to the so-called marked pole of the opposition, other tests will do the same.

The various tests—Greenberg identifies ten of these; more have been proposed subsequently by others—appear to me to pertain to three basic parameters: complexity of structure, complexity of paradigm, and range of use. The first, *syntagmatic complexity*, is manifested in various ways such as complexity of meaning, and complexity of syntactic, morphological, or phonetic form. Of the Greenberg criteria, zero expression and facultative expression belong to this class.

Paradigmatic complexity simply means the range of subvarieties, such as the number of case distinctions in singular or plural or the number of allomorphs or allophones. Greenberg's syncretization, defectivation, and morphological variation belong here.

Range of use has to do with distribution within a given variant of a language (such as which of two phenomena wins out in neutralization, or which of two structures is more frequent in the lexicon or in texts); with distribution across language variants—which of two structures is learned first by children or second language learners and which is lost first in aphasia or language death—and with distribution across languages: namely, which of two structures figure as the implicans in implicational universals of the type "if a language has X, it also has Y." Greenberg's remaining criteria—par excellence expression, neutralization, dominance, text frequency, and typological distribution—all fall into this third category.

Let us now look at the claims involved in more detail. What the theory proposes is, first, that there is consistency among the criteria that pertain to any one of these three general domains. Thus, if a test shows a given member of an opposition to be structurally more complex than the other, then the other syntagmatic complexity criteria will also select the same member as the more complex one of the two.

For example, the category plural is semantically more complex than the singular and it tends to be morphologically more complex as well. The same goes for the other two domains: according to the strictest formulation of the theory, all tests having to do with the range of subvarieties of a structural entity will agree in characterizing the same term as more paradigmatically differentiated than the other (e.g., nasal vowels tend to have both fewer length distinctions and also fewer height distinctions); and all tests having to do with range of use—whether language-internal or cross-language—should converge on showing one member as consistently more widely distributed than the other (e.g., sound types that "win out" in neutralization in a language should also be cross-linguistically more widespread; or if a language has more than one word order possibility, the one with the broader range of use should also be the one that is typologically implied by the other).

Secondly, and more interestingly, the theory also proposes that there is consistency across the three general parameters. For example, if a member of an opposition can be shown to be more complex in structure, a prediction is possible regarding its paradigmatic complexity and breadth of distribution. The particular correlation among the three parameters proposed is as follows: the member that is syntagmatically *less* complex will turn out to be *more* complex in its paradigm and also *more* widely distributed; and the member that is syntagmatically *more* complex is *less* differentiated in its paradigm and is *less* widely used. Or, putting it quite simply, things that are much used are simple in structure and rich in subvarieties and things that are used less are more complex in structure and less elaborated in terms of subtypes. The former are labelled *unmarked* and the latter, *marked*. For example, voiceless stops are simpler in articulation than voiced ones; they tend to show more subtypes (in English, for example, they have both aspirated and unaspirated allophones while the voiced ones do not); and they are universal while the voiced ones are not.

The empirical force of this version of markedness theory lies in the fact that the tests that are claimed to show converging results in assigning terms of opposition to the *marked* and *unmarked* poles are logically independent. Thus, for example, there is no *a priori* reason why a more widely distributed object should be simpler and, at the same time, richer in subtypes. The theory thus exhibits the basic characteristic of other significant scientific insights: where plain logic would predict no relationship among things, the theory does claim one. Or, putting it differently, it suggests that things are related which otherwise would never appear to have any relationship with each other.

What I have outlined above is the most restrictive interpretation of the theory, in that all markedness criteria are claimed to be mutually predictive of each other with respect to all oppositions in all human languages. It is not very difficult to find examples to show that this maximal claim is false. There are nonetheless two things going for the theory. First, as the examples given above illustrate, there are many cases where some of the correlations claimed do hold true. Second, there is some intuitive plausibility to the basic claim. It is plausible not only that the various criteria within each of the three domains should correlate but also that there be correlations across the three domains. For example, it appears reasonable to expect that human artifacts that are simpler in structure are more popular—more widely used—and that more subtypes of them should be developed to suit the wider range of uses to which they are put. There are examples of this in extra-linguistic domains such as in food and clothing patterns; e.g., everyday—i.e., more frequently used—foods are simpler to prepare and have more versions than festive or fancy food.

Given the partial success and intuitive plausibility of markedness theory as outlined, it recommends itself as a useful angle from which to view linguistic phenomena. I will therefore consider next the particular claims that markedness theory makes relative to agreement patterns. The hoped-for gain is in both the development of markedness theory and the understanding of agreement. While markedness may serve to explain facts about agreement, evidence from this area of grammar serves to test the theory.

1.3 Agreement and Markedness

As seen above, agreement phenomena always involve the presence of an *extra* morpheme (or morphemes) which shows that some constituent belongs to one or another subclass—such as agreement on the adjective showing that the head noun is masculine or feminine. Agreement thus always involves, by definition, two of the three basic parameters that markedness theory makes claims about: syntagmatic complexity (the presence of an extra marker) and paradigmatic complexity (providing a particular subclassification for a constituent). Since markedness theory, by definition, predicts which of two opposing terms is more syntagmatically complex and which is more paradigmatically complex, it should have some predictions to offer on what constituent types should have greater propensity for figuring as controllers and agreeing terms; what categories and subcategories should preferentially figure as agreement features; what should be preferred forms for various agreement markers; and what general conditions ought to be conducive to the occurrence of agreement within and across languages.

Let us consider some specific predictions derivable from markedness theory with respect to these questions. What does it have to say about *controllers?* Since in agreement an additional morpheme shows up as part of the total expression of the controlling constituent and since this marker is, by definition, redundant, and thus does not provide for additional subcategorization of the controller, agreement can be seen as a phenomenon that results in increased structure without any increase in subclassification—i.e., as a symptom of markedness. The prediction is, therefore, that agreements should be favored for controllers that are marked other ways as well (structurally more complex, paradigmatically less elaborate, and less widely distributed) over potential controllers that are unmarked (simpler in structure, richer in subcategories, and more widely used).

Another aspect of the agreement problem on which markedness has a prediction to make is the choice of the *agreement term*. What agreement does to the agreeing term is subcategorize it. Thus, for example, the English past tense verb which shows no agreement with the subject does not therefore have person-differentiated subtypes, whereas the present tense verb which shows some agreement with the subject does. Since increased paradigmatic complexity is the hallmark of unmarked terms, markedness theory predicts that unmarked should preferentially agree over marked ones.

Third, some prediction is derivable from markedness theory also regarding the *category* in terms of which agreement takes place. Let us, for example, consider a situation where the controller is a conjoined structure and thus there is more than one person or gender value competing for expression in the agreement marker. Since the particular person or gender value that wins out will thus acquire wider distribution, the prediction is that, in the case of competing feature values, the value that is known on other grounds to be unmarked should prevail.

Fourth, markedness theory also has something to say about the form of *agreement markers*. The prediction is that the agreement marker that represents a more marked—let us say, for instance, crosslinguistically less widespread—category or category value should have a more complex form than one that carries an unmarked or less marked value.

Finally, we may predict that agreement should preferentially occur in *construction types* that are marked over those that are unmarked. This is because a construction that exhibits agreement is more complex and thus marked over one that does not; and because, according to the theory, different markedness criteria must converge.

2 Agreement and Markedness—the Empirical Fit

2.1 Predictions Borne Out

Let us now attempt to gauge the empirical adequacy of these predictions by considering a sample of facts about agreement patterns.

For one example where markedness theory does make the right prediction concerning the choice of *controllers*, recall what is known about the kinds of objects that the verb preferentially agrees with. In general, objects that are semantically more complex in that they are definite or animate (Comrie 1981, Lehmann 1982, 237) or topicalized (Lehmann 1982, 237, 240, Corbett 1979) and objects that are morphologically more complex in that they are case-marked (Moravcsik 1978) are more prone to controlling agreement than objects that are indefinite, inanimate, non-topical, and not case-marked. In Lebanese Arabic, for instance, the verb shows agreement with the object if the object is either case-marked by *la* or preposed (topicalized?); and both of these are possible only with definite objects (Koutsoudas 1969):

(1) a. l   walad   šaaf   l   rižžaal
      the   boy   saw   the man

    b. l   walad   šaaf-*u*   la l   rižžal
       the   boy   saw-him to the man

    c. l   rižžaal   šaaf-*u*   l   walad
       the   man   saw-him the boy

    d. *l   walad   šaaf-*u*   l   rižžal
       the   boy   saw-him the man
      all: 'The boy saw the man.'

In Swahili, the verb agrees only with definite objects, as in example (2) (Givón 1976):

(2) a. ni-li-soma   kitabu
      1.SG-PAST-read book
      'I read a book.'

    b. ni-li-*ki*-soma   kitabu
      1.SG-PAST-it-read book
      'I read the book.'

Let us now turn to the choice of the *agreeing term*. One example where markedness theory's prediction that unmarked constituents should show agreement preferentially is borne out is with respect to the opposition of tensed and untensed verbs. Verb agreement in person occurs, in the overwhelming majority of cases, in the tensed verb and very rarely in untensed verb forms such as in the infinitive. In languages like Hungarian or Portuguese where the infinitive does show person agreement with the subject, the finite verb does so, too. The following is an illustration from Hungarian:

(3) a. Jancsinak   nem   szabad   dohányoz-ni-*a*.
        Johnny.DAT   not   allowed   smoke-INF-3.SG

        'Johnny is not allowed to smoke.'

    b. Jancsi   dohányz-*ik*.
        Johnny   smoke-3.SG

        'Johnny smokes.'

The prediction is borne out here in that the finite verb can be shown, on independent grounds, to be unmarked as opposed to the infinitive: it has no extra marker to show finiteness, while the infinitive generally does and it has a wider distribution both within languages and also crosslinguistically.

Another example, apparently having to do with the choice of the agreeing term, seems to run counter to the prediction. However, there is a possible alternative interpretation of the facts. As illustrated in (4), appositive postposed adjectives in Hungarian agree in case with the head noun (or the noun phrase) while attributive preposed adjectives do not (cp. Greenberg 1963, universal 40; also Lehmann 1982, 259).

(4) a. Barackot   akarok,   szép*et*.
        peaches.ACC   want.1.SG   nice-ACC

        'I want peaches, nice ones.'

    b. Szép   barackot   akarok.
        nice   peaches.ACC   want.1.SG

        'I want nice peaches.'

Since appositive adjectives are, by other criteria, marked, it would seem that in such cases marked constituents preferentially agree, which is the opposite of what we would expect on grounds of markedness theory. However, the difference between attributive and appositive adjectives may be better considered as a difference between a simpler and a more complex overall construction, rather than that between an adjective which is more simply or more complexly positioned. Under this view, the facts are in conformity with markedness theory: as stated above, we would expect that marked constructions will preferentially show agreement over unmarked ones.

There is additional evidence concerning unmarked constituents preferentially agreeing just as markedness theory predicts. In German, singular adjectives—which are known independently as unmarked as opposed to plural ones—show gender agreement with the head noun while plural ones do not:

(5) a. kein   schön-*er*   Mann
      NEG   handsome-MASC.SG man

      'no handsome man'

   b. keine   schön-*e*   Frau
      NEG   handsome-FEM.SG   woman

      'no handsome woman'

   c. kein   schön-*es*   Kind
      NEG   handsome-NEUT.SG child

      'no handsome child'

   d. keine   schön-*e*   Männer/Frauen/Kinder
      NEG   handsome-PL   man.PL/woman.PL/child.PL

      'no handsome men/women/children'

In Russian, masculine adjectives show more case agreement than feminine ones:

(6)

	'young boy'	'young girl'
Nom	molod*oj* mal'čik	molod*aja* devuška
Acc	molod*ogo* mal'čika	molod*uju* devušku
Gen	molod*ogo* mal'čika	molod*oj* devuški
Dat	molod*omu* mal'čiku	molod*oj* devuške
Ins	molod*ym* mal'čikom	molod*oj* devuškoj
Prep	molod*om* mal'čike	molod*oj* devuške

In Serbo-Croatian, numerals expressing low numbers show more agreement in gender and case than higher numbers: *jedan* 'one' has both gender and case, *dva* 'two' and *tri* 'three' have case but not gender; and most higher numbers (*pet* 'five' and above) show neither kind of agreement.

If, after having considered agreeing verbs, adjectives, and numerals, we look at agreeing adpositions, another apparent counterexample crops up. In Hungarian, postposed adpositions—those that are in their standard position and are thus unmarked—show no agreement with their complement noun phrase in person and number but some preposed (or separated) ones do:

(7) a. a   fiú   mellett
      the   boy   next:to

      'next to the boy'

   b. mellett-*e*   a   fiú-nak
      next:to-3.MASC.SG   the   boy-of

      'next to the boy'

But, again, rather than concluding that a marked term preferentially shows agreement over an unmarked one—something that would be counter to prediction—it may be more appropriate to say that agreement occurs preferentially in a marked construction—a fact in conformity with markedness theory.

Let us now turn to some data concerning competing *agreement features*. The following French data, taken from Schane (1970), bear out the prediction of markedness theory and they are in fact referred to by Greenberg in his original presentation of markedness theory under the term "agreement a potiori."

(8)   Le   garçon   et   la   fille   sont   petit-*s*

       the boy   and the girl   are   small-MASC.PL

       'The boy and the girl are small.'

Here there is an instance of conjoined subjects, one masculine and one feminine, and it is the masculine value that wins out. To the extent that masculine can be independently shown to be unmarked over feminine, this fact is in accordance with markedness theory: the unmarked category has wider distribution than the marked one.

While the above example had to do with competing values of the same feature—namely gender—the next one concerns what are essentially separate categories in competition: two different capital C's, in Lehmann's terminology, as opposed to two different lower-case c's. The case has to do with the rivalry of semantic and syntactic agreement. Corbett (1979) proposed that the prevalence of semantic agreement over syntactic agreement increases with the syntactic distance between controller and agreeing constituent. Thus, for example, anaphoric pronouns have a greater propensity for semantic agreement than modifiers or determiners within the noun phrase. More specifically, Corbett proposes that semantic agreement within the noun phrase in a language implies semantic agreement on the anaphoric pronoun in that language. This can be exemplified with Corbett's own data from Russian involving a sequence of two sentences:

(9)   Ivanova   xoroš-*ij*/xoroš-*aja*   vrač.

       Ivanova.fem   good-MASC/FEM   doctor(MASC)

       'Ivanova is a good doctor.'

       Čto   on*a*   skazala?

       what   she   say

       'What did she say?'

Is this generalization within the domain of markedness theory; and, if so, is it explained by it or is it counter to its predictions? It seems to me that this generalization *is* within the realm of markedness phenomena and it is in fact correctly predicted by the theory. What the correlation pertains to is preferential pairing of a kind of agreement feature with a kind of agreement term. Markedness theory would require that the preferred combinations should be between marked term and marked feature, on the one hand, and between unmarked term and unmarked feature, on the other. Since the facts show that pronominal agreement is preferentially correlated with agreement of the semantic type and noun phrase-internal agreement with agreement of the syntactic type, these facts will corroborate the prediction if we can show that agreement by a pronoun and agreement in a semantic feature are either both unmarked or both marked; and that agreement by noun phrase-internal constituents and agreement in non-semantic features are similarly on the same end of the unmarked-marked dimension.

I think there is evidence to show that things are as expected. Thus, by the criterion of crosslinguistic distribution, agreement by the anaphoric pronoun is more widespread than agreement within the noun phrase as pointed out by Lehmann (1982). At least to this extent, agreement by the anaphoric pronoun can be seen as unmarked over noun phrase-internal agreement. And it is quite likely—although the question would need to be systematically researched—that syntactic agreement is crosslinguistically less widespread than semantic agreement; indeed, the former may typologically imply the latter. If so, the Corbett generalization turns out to be a consequence of markedness theory.

Before we turn to facts about agreement where markedness theory becomes more problematic, let me refer to one more situation where the predictions of the theory are substantiated by facts. Evidence here has to do with the form of the *agreement marker*. As we noted above, markedness theory would predict that within an agreement paradigm, the markers that stand for the more marked value of a feature—let us say, for plural versus singular, or for definite versus indefinite—are, by some criteria, marked themselves. I believe this is so in Hungarian verb agreement.

In Hungarian, as is well known, transitive verbs have two conjugational paradigms. Each paradigm consists of six forms corresponding to the two numbers and three persons of the subject. The choice between the two paradigms depends, roughly, on the definiteness of the object. This is exemplified in (10) below by the transitive verb *hallgat* 'listen to.' According to the prediction, the definite paradigm—used with definite and thus marked objects—should be itself marked over the indefinite paradigm used with indefinite and thus unmarked objects. There is multiple indication that this is so. Notice, first, that four of the suffixes in the definite paradigm are bimorphemic (i.e., syntagmatically complex): they show the recurrent *j* marker. There is no trace of such morphological complexity in the indefinite paradigm. Second, notice that there is one person—the third singular—where the indefinite paradigm has a zero marker and thus exhibits maximal simplicity in morphological form, while the definite paradigm has an overt suffix.

(10) a. hallgat*om* (a zajt)   'I am listening (to the noise).'
         hallgat*od*   'You ... '
         hallgat*ja*   'He/she ... '
         hallgat*juk*   'We ... '
         hallgat*játok*   'You ... '
         hallgat*jak*   'They ... '

     b. hallgat*ok* (egy zajt)   'I am listening (to a noise).'
         hallgat*sz*   'You ... '
         hallgat   'He/she ... '
         hallgat*unk*   'We ... '
         hallgat*tok*   'You ... '
         hallgat*nak*   'They ... '

Whereas these two points serve to show the markedness of the definite paradigm by the criterion of *morphological* complexity, it can also be shown to be *semantically* more complex: the definite forms express an implied pronoun while the indefinite ones do not. Thus, *hallgatom* when occurring by itself means 'I am listening to it.' There is no such implied pronominal meaning for *hallgatok*, the corresponding indefinite form.

Proceeding to the criterion of *paradigmatic complexity*: the indefinite paradigm can be shown to be somewhat more complex in that there are actually two conjugation types within this paradigm. Besides the more common type there is also the so-called *ik* type (not exemplified here). This distinction is syncretized in the definite paradigm. Finally, from the point of view of *breadth of distribution*, the indefinite paradigm once again turns out to be unmarked: it is used not only with objects that have the indefinite article but also with objects that have no article (e.g., *Zajokat hallgatok.* 'I am listening to noises.'). Furthermore, it is also used when there is no object at all whether overt or understood; i.e., with intransitive or intransitively used verbs. This is shown in (11).

(11)   hallgat*ok*   'I am silent.'
         hallgat*sz*   'You ... '
         hallgat   'He/she ... '
         hallgat*unk*   'We ... '
         hallgat*tok*   'You ... '
         hallgat*nak*   'They ... '

Thus, in this instance, the agreement markers that correlate with the unmarked feature value—the indefiniteness of the object—are consistently unmarked by other criteria as well, just as the theory says they should be.

2.2 Problematic Cases

There are nonetheless facts in the domain of agreement phenomena where markedness principles make predictions that are counterfactual. Four such problematic cases will be considered below.

The first concerns competing agreement features in the controller. Let us assume that the verb agrees with the subject in person in a language and the subject is a conjoined structure where the conjuncts differ in person. Markedness theory would predict that if the competing values for person form a markedness opposition, the less marked person would win out in determining the person of the verb. There is abundant evidence to indicate that the three persons first, second, and third do constitute pairs of marked-unmarked terms. Greenberg (1966) and Givón (1976) both argued that the three persons make up a hierarchy of markedness with each occupying a different position on the resulting scale. Schwartz (1978) argued that while the markedness relation between first and second person is not universally invariant, both the first and the second person are universally marked as opposed to the third person. Assuming this to be true, it would follow from markedness theory that if the subject is a conjunction of first and third, the verb should show third person agreement; and if the subject includes both second and third person, the verb should again be third. These predictions follow from the assumption that unmarked categories—the third person, in this case—should have wider distribution than the corresponding marked ones. The facts are, however, quite different (cp. Schwartz 1978 and Corbett 1982). In actuality, it is always the lower-numbered person that prevails. Thus, verbs with mixed first and third person subjects—'I and he did such-and-such.'—show first person plural suffixes and verbs with second and third person subjects—'You and he did such-and-such.'—take second person plural suffixes.

Although the facts thus go against the predictions of markedness theory in this case, the reason why person conflicts should be resolved in this particular manner is not hard to find. As Corbett points out, what is usually called "first person plural" is not literally the plural of the first person; instead, it is a heterogeneous category as far as person is concerned which, by definition, refers to any collection of individuals that includes the speaker. Similarly, the "second person plural" is in many cases not used in reference to a group of addressees; instead, it refers to a group that includes at least one addressee and excludes the speaker. Thus, the facts appear to contradict the predictions of markedness theory only because of the somewhat misleading nature of the traditional terminology used to identify plural person forms. What really happens is that in the case of mixed-person subjects, *neither* person prevails over the other; instead, the language has a *third* category that, by its very definition, covers mixed groups. In order to accommodate situations of this kind—where a language has a marked-unmarked opposition and also a category distinct from both the marked and the unmarked serving to subsume both—the general prediction that markedness theory makes for the unmarked element winning out in case of a competition needs to be supplemented by the proviso that this is so only if the language does not also have a third category which includes in its range both of the two competing ones. That this proviso is independently necessary can be shown by simple facts. For example, while the masculine gender may very well be unmarked in English, the concepts *sons* and *daughters* cannot ordinarily be jointly referred to by *sons*—presumably because the language also has a term *children* which, by definition, includes both sons and daughters.

The next two problematic cases both have to do with the markedness hierarchy into which basic sentence constituent functions such as subject, direct object, and indirect object fit from the point of view of agreement with the verb. A number of linguists—Keenan (1974) and Lehmann (1982, 253), among others—noted that whenever the verb agrees with direct objects, it also agrees with (some) subjects in that language. I will now set aside the problem of how subjects and direct objects can be identified in ergative and other non-Standard-Average-European languages and will assume that the generalization is true. Lehmann, in a 1983 paper on agreement and government, points out that there is something very surprising about this. What struck Lehmann was that the exact opposite hierarchy obtains for subjects and direct objects when it comes to case marking. In other words, subjects tend to be morphologically marked on the verb in terms of agreement markers more than direct objects; but direct objects tend to be morphologically marked by case markers over subjects: in many languages, objects are case-marked but subjects are not. Although Lehmann does not explicitly consider these facts from the point of view of markedness theory, it is clear that this discrepancy between case marking and verb agreement hierarchies is a problem for markedness. It is a problem because the theory says that various criteria of syntagmatic complexity should converge: if some structure is syntagmatically complex in one way—let us say, it carries a case marker—it should also be syntagmatically complex in other ways: for example, it should command agreement on the verb. The facts fly squarely in the face of this conjecture.

In the same paper where Lehmann raises the problem, he also proposes an answer to it. The crucial insight that his explanation involves is that the relationship between the verb and its dependent noun phrases is two-fold: it involves both modification and also government. More specifically, both subjects and objects modify their verb and both are governed by their verb. The two differ, however, in the degree to which they partake in these relations: subjects are more extensively governed by their verbs than direct objects but the latter more strongly modify their verbs than subjects do. In order to complete the explanatory argument, one more of Lehmann's assumptions needs to be adduced. This is that, given a relationship between two constituents, this relationship will be explicitly marked on what he calls the relational member of the pair. In government of noun phrases by verb, the verb is the relational element and thus government relations will be marked on the verb. In modification of the verb by noun phrase complements, the noun phrases are the relational terms and thus they will be marked for the relationship. It now follows that, since subjects are more strongly governed by the verb than objects, the markers to show government—agreement affixes—will preferentially occur with subjects. Case markers, however, which signal modifier relations, should preferentially occur on objects since objects are higher on the modification scale than subjects.

Assuming that Lehmann's explanation is correct, the lesson to be drawn here for markedness theory is that a given structure—such as subject or object—cannot in all cases be declared globally marked or unmarked vis-à-vis another: the very same structure may be marked in one respect (e.g., in the function of a modifier) and unmarked in another respect (e.g., as a governed element).

A third case where facts do not directly follow from a blind application of markedness principles concerns agreement between verbs and direct and indirect objects. Just as subjects are higher in the hierarchy of verb agreement than direct objects, the latter are higher than indirect objects in the sense that in languages where the verb can agree with some indirect objects, it can also agree with some direct objects. The following chart illustrates this generalization.

(12)	S-V	D-V	IO-V	Example languages
Type A:	−	−	−	Japanese
Type B:	+	−	−	English
Type C:	+	+	−	Hungarian, Geez, E. Aramaic
Type D:	+	+	+	Spanish, Amharic, Swahili, L. Arabic
*Type E:	−	−	+	
*Type F:	−	+	−	
*Type G:	−	+	+	
*Type H:	+	−	+	

This generalization has actually been called into question by some linguists such as Givón (1976) and Faltz (1978): both of them suggested that the verb preferentially agrees with indirect objects over direct objects. Although the implicational universal asserting the priority of direct objects over indirect objects is I believe true to fact, there is a grain of truth in Givón's and Faltz's suggestion. Whereas the implicational universal testifies to the priority of direct objects over indirect objects in verb agreement, there is one sense in which indirect objects must be granted priority over direct objects. In some languages, ditransitive verbs are allowed to carry both the direct object agreement marker and also a marker indicating agreement with the indirect object. One example is Lebanese (Koutsoudas 1969):

(13) a. samiir   ba?at-*la*   *yeh*   la   l   walad   la   salma
         Samir   send.PAST-her   him   to   the boy   to   Salma

         'Samir sent the boy to Salma.'

     b. samiir   ba?at-*lu*   *yeha* la   salma   la   l   walad
         Samir   send.PAST-him   her   to   Salma   to   the boy

         'Samir sent Salma to the boy.'

In other languages, however, there is only a single object agreement slot on the verb. In unitransitive sentences, this is filled by the direct object agreement marker. In ditransitive sentences, however, it is the indirect object whose agreement marker ends up occupying this one available slot. This is shown in the Swahili examples below.

(14) a. a-li-*wa*-ona   wa-toto
         3.SG.SUBJ-PAST-them-see   PL-child

         'He saw his children.'

     b. a-li-*m*-pa   m-kewe   wa-toto
         3.SG.SUBJ-PAST-her-give   SG-wife PL.child

         'He gave the children to his wife.'

     c. *a-li-*wa*-pa   m-kewe   wa-toto
         3.SG.SUBJ-PAST-them-give   SG-wife PL-child

We have a situation, therefore, where verb agreement with the direct object has a wider *cross-language* distribution than agreement with the indirect object; but this distributional asymmetry is not matched by the respective distributions of the two verb-agreement types *within languages*. This mismatch between language-internal and cross-language distribution is against the prediction of markedness theory since it claims that distributional evidence of any type should consistently select one member of the opposition as marked over the other. Intuitively speaking, the priority of indirect object agreement over direct object agreement in languages that have only one object agreement marker slot on the verb is not surprising: if direct object verb agreement took precedence over indirect object verb agreement in such languages, indirect object agreement would hardly ever get a chance to make an appearance since indirect objects mostly occur in conjunction with direct objects and rarely as sole objects of verbs. It nonetheless remains to be seen how we could extrapolate from this one case and arrive at a general principle which would render this instance into a principled, rather than random, exception to markedness theory.

There is additional evidence to show that intra- and cross-language distribution is not always consistent. In a 1983 paper, Gundel, Houlihan, and Sanders examined the relationship between these two criteria of markedness in the light of various phonological and syntactic phenomena and they concluded that the correlation was not perfect between the two. More specifically, they concluded that breadth of distribution within a language is not predictive of crosslinguistic distribution, although the facts they considered were consistent with the opposite claim: that cross-language distribution is predictive of distribution within a language. What the facts about verb agreement with direct and indirect objects show is that there is lack of predictiveness in this direction, too.

This is supported by another fact about agreement noted by Lehmann. He found that if a language has "internal agreement," then it also has "external agreement" but not necessarily vice versa (Lehmann 1982, 260). In other words, there are languages where only anaphoric pronouns, verbs, adpositions, and/or the possessum agree and not determiners, attributive and appositive adjectives, relative clauses, possessors or predicate nominals. However, Lehmann found no languages which have only agreement of the latter kind without agreement of the former type. At the same time, Lehmann also noted that languages may choose to elaborate internal agreement much more richly than they elaborate external agreement. In other words, the language-internal distribution of the two agreement types does not necessarily match their cross-language distribution—a fact that is counter to what markedness theory would predict.

3 Conclusions

In sum: there are three main points that emerge from all of this. First, given the concept of agreement as proposed by Lehmann and given markedness theory as outlined by Greenberg, agreement is very much the kind of grammatical phenomenon that markedness can be held responsible for. There are points of contact between the domain of agreement and the domain of facts that markedness theory proposes to be responsible for. Second, we have seen that in many cases, the predictions of markedness theory do hold for agreement and to this extent the theory provides an explanation for these facts. And, third, we have also seen that there are other facts about agreement that are counter to markedness theory as we assumed it to be and that these facts thus call for a more refined version of the theory.

References

Comrie, B. 1981. *Language Universals and Linguistic Typology*. Chicago: The University of Chicago Press.

Corbett, G. G. 1979. The agreement hierarchy. *Journal of Linguistics* 15:203–224.

Corbett, G. G. 1982. Resolution rules for predicate agreement in the Slavonic languages. *The Slavonic and East European Review* 60(3): 347–378.

Faltz, L. M. 1978. On indirect objects in universal syntax. In D. Farkas, W. Jacobsen and K. Todrys (Eds), *Papers from the Fourteenth Regional Meeting of the Chicago Linguistic Society*, 76–87.

Givón, T. 1976. Topic, pronoun, and grammatical agreement. In C. N. Li (Ed), *Subject and Topic*. New York: Academic Press.

Greenberg, J. H. 1963. Some universals of grammar with particular reference to the order of meaningful elements. In J. H. Greenberg (Ed), *Universals of Language*, 73–113. Cambridge, Mass.: The MIT Press.

Greenberg, J. H. 1966. *Language Universals, With Special Reference to Feature Hierarchies*. (Janua Linguarum Series Minor, 59.) The Hague: Mouton.

Gundel, J. K., K. Houlihan and G. A. Sanders. To appear. Markedness and distribution in phonology and syntax. In F. R. Eckman, E. A. Moravcsik and J. R. Wirth (Eds), *Markedness*. New York: Plenum.

Keenan, E. L. 1974. The functional principle: generalizing the notion of 'subject of.' *Papers from the Tenth Regional Meeting of the Chicago Linguistic Society*, 298–309.

Koutsoudas, A. 1969. *Workbook in Syntax*. New York: McGraw Hill.

Lehmann, C. 1982. Universal and typological aspects of agreement. In H. Seiler and F. J. Stachowiak (Eds), *Apprehension: das sprachliche Erfassen von Gegenständen*. Teil II, 201–267. Tübingen: Gunter Narr.

Lehmann, C. 1983. Rektion und syntaktische Relationen. *Folia Linguistica* 17:339–378.

Moravcsik, E. A. 1978. On the case marking of objects. In J. H. Greenberg (Ed), *Universals of Human Language* 4, 249–289. Stanford: Stanford University Press.

Schane, S. A. 1970. Phonological and morphological markedness. In M. Bierwisch and K. E. Heidolph (Eds), *Progress in Linguistics*, 286–294. The Hague: Mouton.

Schwartz, L. 1978. Object agreement in animacy precedence languages. Paper presented at the Fourth Annual Minnesota Regional Conference on Language and Linguistics, Minneapolis.

6 Agreement in Arabic, Binding and Coherence

Abdelkader Fassi Fehri

Any theory of Universal Grammar is adequate only to the extent that it is able to characterize which agreement phenomena are likely to occur in natural languages, and which are not. This goal is pursued in different theories by making use of different levels of representation and appealing to very complex assumptions about the modules of grammar. This makes it difficult to compare different approaches to agreement problems, partly because the argumentation for one representation and/or analysis is highly theory internal. When comprehensive grammars of languages are written, however, it is possible to make significant cross linguistic generalizations about agreement, to postulate the principles from which they follow, and to design an appropriate evaluation metric.

The purpose of this paper is to contribute to the understanding of agreement systems in natural languages by proposing a treatment of some agreement phenomena in Standard Arabic. In doing so, we present a fragment of a conceptual framework in which agreement phenomena are naturally characterized in correlation with *grammatical functions*,

This paper was written for the most part while I was visiting CSLI (at Stanford) in April and May of 1984. A grant to support this work was provided through Joan Bresnan. This paper benefited from discussions at CSLI before and during the Conference on Agreement with Joan Bresnan, Ron Kaplan, K. P. Mohanan, Tom Wasow, Charles Ferguson, Ivan Sag, Susan Stucky and Mike Barlow. I am also grateful to the Group of Arabic Linguistics at the University of Rabat for creating the appropriate atmosphere and for stimulating discussions. Mike Barlow, Charles Ferguson and Bouchaib Idrisi have read the manuscript and suggested some improvements. Errors are my own.

and the appropriate constraints are stated on functional structure, rather than any other level of the grammar. The general framework is essentially the theory of grammatical representation assumed in Lexical Functional Grammar (LFG) where the lexical structure and the functional structure play an essential role in parametric and universal language characterizations. Our conceptual contribution is to make a number of assumptions about the set of grammatical functions, their taxonomy and how they interact in natural agreement processes. We also extend and redefine the Coherence Condition to account for the complex phenomena of government and binding from which different types of agreement follow.

The paper is organized in three parts. First, we deal with representational problems of affixes and some consequences of the affix identification for so-called *pro-drop* phenomena, doubling, as well as nesting, crossing and "avoid pronoun" effects. It will be shown throughout this section that a typology of affixes is needed, which makes a distinction between *pronominal* and *non pronominal* types, and that pronominal affixes behave in every respect like pronouns. Arguments are also provided favoring an *incorporation analysis* (where the affix is an incorporated argument in the governor) over an *agreement analysis* (where the affix has no referential function but rather agrees with the referential *pro*). Second, we raise some issues about the domain and the typology of agreement phenomena. Three types of agreement are distinguished depending on the nature of the agreeing expressions, the directionality of agreement, the features involved and the domain in which the agreeing expressions are located. It will be shown that in all these cases functional specifications play a central role. In the third part, we propose a theory to derive the descriptive statements made in the first two parts. It turns out that when agreement phenomena are considered in detail, the assumptions about rules, conditions and principles that can account for them are far from trivial.

1 The Affix Identification Problem

1.1 Pro-Drop, Doubling and Agreeing Features

Consider the following sentences:

(1) a. ja:ʔ-u:
        came-3.MASC.PL
        'They came.'

     b. ᶜud-tu
        returned-I

        'I returned.'

(2)   ja:ʔ-u: hum   la: ʔixwatu-hum
       came-3.MASC.PL they   not   brothers-their

       'They came, not their brothers.'

One of the central issues any theory of grammar should address concerns
the nature of the affix attached to the verb in such sentences. The
characterization of this affix implies, among other things, answering the
following questions:

    a.   What features is the affix made of?

    b.   What modules of the grammar are relevant for its characteri-
        zation?

    c.   Is it a possible agreeing expression taking part in an agreement
        relationship or is it merely an agreement marker?

Especially subsumed under (b) is the question whether the affix can
be a referential expression or an argument (in the sense of Chomsky
1981), or whether it can bear a grammatical function such as SUBJ,
OBJ, etc. (as in Bresnan 1982a). Assuming the latter, a lexical entry
for the subject affix in (1a), for example, could be (3), given a Lexical
Functional framework:

(3) u: SUBJ $\begin{bmatrix} \text{NB} & \text{PL} \\ \text{GEND} & \text{MASC} \\ \text{PERS} & 3 \\ \text{HUM} & + \\ \text{CASE} & \text{NOM} \\ \text{PRED} & \text{'PRO'} \end{bmatrix}$

This analysis makes use of two crucial representational assumptions:
the first one is that the affix has no corresponding syntactic category
at constituent structure (c-structure) and the second one is that it is
pronominal, i.e., it has an attribute PRED whose value is 'PRO.' Call this
the *incorporation analysis*. Equally compatible with LFG is an analysis
where (b) does not hold, that is, an analysis where u: has all the features
in (3) except the PRED feature. In such a case, the affix is not taken
to be pronominal, nor is it the subject of the verb. The subject is
rather PRO, introduced at the level of functional structure (f-structure)

to satisfy the Completeness Condition. This analysis will be termed the *non pronominal* theory of the affix.[1]

A framework like the Government Binding Theory (henceforth GB) allows different complexes of representational assumptions. One such possible complex is summarized in (4) and made more explicit in (5), following the suggestions by Chomsky (1982):[2]

(4) AGR^i ... pro^i

    ⋮

    affix

(5) AGR^i ... pro^i

$$\begin{bmatrix} \alpha\text{CASE} \\ \beta\text{NB} \\ \gamma\text{GEND} \\ \ldots \\ - \end{bmatrix} \qquad \begin{bmatrix} \alpha\text{CASE} \\ \beta\text{NB} \\ \gamma\text{GEND} \\ \ldots \\ \text{PRED 'PRO'} \end{bmatrix}$$

Here AGR and *pro* are abstract syntactic categories introduced at c-structure while the affix is just a spelling out of the category AGR (agreement). AGR is not an argument. It agrees with *pro* in the specified features, as is indicated by cosuperscripting. Call this the *agreement hypothesis*. The agreement hypothesis (henceforth AGRH) and the incorporation hypothesis (INCH) not only embody different assumptions about two components of the grammar (morphology, on one

---

[1] As things stand now in the LFG formalism, it might be difficult to distinguish between the pronominal and the non pronominal theory of the affix. Because PRO lacks its own lexical entry, it is either introduced on the lexical entry of the predicate (say the verb), or on the affix attached to the predicate. In both cases, the distinction is hardly visible, mainly because the entries are associated before the insertion of the fully inflected word in the syntactic tree.

[2] Given the projection principle (as formulated in (i)), which amounts essentially to saying that that every syntactic representation should be a projection of the thematic structure and the properties of subcategorization of lexical items, PRO should be introduced as an empty category in the c-structure:

(i)   Representations at each syntactic level (i.e., LF, D- and S-structures) are projected from the lexicon, in that they observe the subcategorization properties of lexical items

(See Chomsky 1981). No pronominal hypothesis is possible in GB, nor any incorporation hypothesis along the lines defined.

hand, and argument theory, on the other) but also make different predictions and have different consequences for other subtheories of the grammar.

Consider, for example, how the so-called *pro-drop* phenomenon is characterized given INCH. We hypothesize the existence of two types of affixes: pronominal (and/or referential) affixes and non pronominal ones. *Pro-drop* languages like Standard Arabic, Moroccan or Italian have pronominal affixes, non *pro-drop* languages like English or French do not.

The type of AGRH embodied in (4) and (5) allows a different theory. Chomsky (1982) characterizes the *pro-drop* parameter in terms of Case. Specifically, the complex of assumptions Chomsky makes are as follows:

a. AGR can have Case but no referential function.

b. *Pro* has Case and a referential function.

c. There is a strict feature matching between AGR and *pro*.

These characteristics are hypothesized to hold cross-linguistically. What is claimed to be specific is whether AGR has Case or not. If AGR has no Case, then *pro* cannot appear since there must be a strict feature matching between AGR and *pro*. This bars *pro* from non *pro-drop* languages where AGR is claimed to have no Case, and allows the occurrence of *pro* in *pro-drop* languages where AGR is assumed to bear Case.

As a consequence of INCH or AGRH and this interpretation of the *pro-drop* phenomenon, so-called pronominal (or clitic) doubling, the phenomenon that occurs in (2), for example, has to be interpreted in different ways. Under GB and AGRH, doubling is viewed as relating a non argument expression, the affix or the clitic, to an argument, the pronoun or lexical NP. These expressions are assumed to agree in all the specified features (by virtue of (iii) above). The way we view doubling in Standard Arabic, however, is different. We assume that the two expressions involved in doubling are assigned different grammatical functions: the affix is assigned one of the subcategorized functions (SUBJ, OBJ, etc...), and the strong form of the pronoun bears the FOCUS function which is not subcategorized for by the predicate (see Section 3 for details). Given INCH and our characterization of doubling we predict that there is no necessary case matching between the affix and the strong form of the pronoun. This prediction is borne out. In Modern Standard Arabic, the pronominal affix varies according to whether it bears nominative or non nominative case. The pronoun doubling the affix is invariably nominative, as shown in the following examples.[3] In (6b) and (6c), although the affix is non nominative, the pronoun is in the nominative form.

---

[3] There is a controversy in traditional grammars on whether the isolated accusative form can actually double the accusative affix or not. See Fassi Fehri (1983). In Modern Standard Arabic, the usual way to double is via the nominative form.

(6) a. rajaᶜ-a   huwa   wa   baqi:-tu   ʔana:
        returned-3.MASC.SG   he   and stayed-I   I.NOM

        'He returned and I stayed.'

    b. iltaqay-tu   bi-hi   huwa
        met-I   with-him.GEN   he.NOM

        'I met him.'

    c. nu-ba:yiᶜu-ka   ʔanta
        we-give.allegiance-you.ACC   you.NOM

        'We give allegiance to you.'

There is more reason to doubt that case agreement is involved in doubling, as will become clear when we present our typology of agreement
in Section 2, and the derivation of this typology in Section 3. Here, we
would only like to emphasize that the case matching assumption embodied in (c) above is far from trivial for any agreement theory. Moreover,
it is not supported by *prima facie* empirical evidence, as we have shown.

Also, INCH makes a specific prediction as to which features are clustered together for an affix to be pronominal in a given language. It is
no accident that the features a pronominal affix is specified for are the
ones a pronoun is specified for. Thus *hum* in (7) is specified for the same
features as the affix on the verb, i.e., PERS, NB, GEND, HUM and CASE:

(7)   hum   ja:ʔ-u:
        they   came-3.MASC.PL

        'As for them, they came.'

Under AGRH, this identity of features is assumed rather than predicted.
But we see little reason to think that this assumption is correct. For
example, when a non pronominal NP occurs as a SUBJ of a verb, the
verb agrees with it only in gender as in (8a). It cannot agree with it
in other features, as shown by the ungrammaticality of (8b) and (8c),
where the verb agrees also in number.

(8) a. ja:ʔ-ati   l-bana:tu
        came-FEM   the-girls

        'The girls came.'

    b. *jiʔ-na   l-bana:tu
        came-FEM.PL   the-girls

    c. *ja:ʔ-u: l-ʔawla:du
        came-MASC.PL   the-boys

The choice of features encoded on the verb to point to the subject seems to be somewhat arbitrary and varies from language to language. However, the features involved in *pro-drop* or pronominal doubling are not. They are all the inherent (or referential) features, including namely PERS and NB.

In sum, we have shown that one version of AGRH would run into problems essentially because the auxiliary (implicit) assumptions it makes about the clustering of agreeing features are far from desirable for a theory of agreement. There are other types of evidence internal to the grammar of Standard Arabic (and other languages as well) that favor INCH over AGRH. These matters will be discussed in the next subsections.

1.2 Interpreting the Pronominal and Affix Systems

1.2.1 A Complementary Distribution?

Arabic has two context dependent forms of pronominals: isolated pronoun forms and affixed forms which are usually incorporated in the form of their governor. The affix system is richer than the full pronoun system. It has different affixes for subjects and objects. Processes of subject affixation on the verb vary depending on its aspect. With the imperfective, there is a discontinuous affix, mainly prefixing but also suffixing. Subject affixes on the adjective are homophonous with the number and gender inflection on nouns. Non subject affixes, on the other hand, are invariably suffixes. They are not sensitive to aspect nor to the category of their governor. In Tables 1 and 2, we list the verbal subject affixes and in Table 3 the object affixes (dashes follow prefixes):[4]

PERS	GR	SG	DUAL	PL
1		tu		na:
2	MASC	ta	tuma:	tum(u:)
	FEM	ti	tuma:	tunna
3	MASC	a	a:	u:
	FEM	at	ata:	na

Table 1
(perfective)

---

[4] Obviously, there is a way of arranging this list more systematically. For example, *t* stands for feminine or second person, *n* for first, *na* for plural feminine, *a:* for dual, *u* or *u:* for plural masculine, *i* for feminine as opposed to *a*, etc. This is not our concern here, however. Note also that vowel harmony may take a place, converting the underlying *hu* to *hi*, as in (10b) and (11a) for example.

PERS	GR	SG	DUAL	PL
1		ʔ—		n—
2	MASC	t—	t—a:	t—u:
	FEM	t—i:	t—a:	t—na
3	MASC	y—	y—a:	y—u:
	FEM	t—	t—a:	t—na

Table 2
(imperfective)

PERS	GR	SG	DUAL	PL
1		i:(ia,ni:)		na:
2	MASC	ka	kuma:	kum(u:)
	FEM	ki	kuma:	kunna
3	MASC	hu	huma:	hum(u:)
	FEM	ha:	huma:	hunna

Table 3
(objects)

The following examples illustrate the essential contexts in which pronominal affixes occur:

(9)   jiʔ-na
        came-3.FEM.PL.HUM
        'They came.'

(10) a.   ntaqad-tu-hu   b.   ʔaᶜṭay-ta-ni:-hi
           criticized-I-him   gave-you-me-it/him
           'I criticized him.'   'You gave it/him to me.'

(11) a.   ltaqay-tu bi-hi   b.   ntaqad-a   muʔallifa-hu
           met-I   with-him.   criticized-he author-his
           'I met with him.'   'He criticized his author.'

     c.   zaydun ḥasanu l-wajhi wa ʔanta qabi:ḥu-hu
           Zayd   nice   the-face and you   ugly-it
           'Zayd has a nice face and you have an ugly one.'

In (9), a subject is cliticized to the verb. Constructions in (10) are examples of multiple affixation where OBJ1 and OBJ2 are cliticized. In

(11), the clitic is attached to a preposition, a noun or an adjective. It functions as a POBJ, POSS OBJ, and AOBJ. In all these instances, the object affix has one and the same form.

Isolated forms of the pronouns are of two classes, with different historical origins and different productivity. The more productive class consists of nominative forms listed in Table 4. These forms occur in ungoverned contexts as TOPICs, THEMEs, or doubling (with the pronominal affixes cited above).[5] They do not occur as objects or subjects without an affix on the governor. The class of non nominative forms is listed in Table 5. While there is a striking morphological similarity between the forms in Tables 1 and 2 and the ones in 4, there is a partial identity between the forms in Tables 3 and 5. These forms are identical apart from the fact that the isolated forms are preceded by the prefix *?iyya:*. The isolated forms occur only in accusative contexts, where the pronoun is an object of a verb. They would normally appear in contexts where the succession of affixes is more than two (sometimes only more than one). They also occur as fronted foci objects. Examples summarizing the distribution of isolated pronouns are given below, after the tables listing them:

PERS	GR	SG	DUAL	PL
1		?ana:	naḥnu	naḥnu
2	MASC	?anta	?antuma:	?antum(u:)
	FEM	?anti	?antuma:	?antunna
3	MASC	huwa	huma:	hum(u:)
	FEM	hiya	huma:	hunna

Table 4

PERS	GR	SG	DUAL	PL
1		?iyya:ya	?iyya:na:	?iyya:na:
2	MASC	?iyya:ka	?iyyakuma:	?iyya:kum(u:)
	FEM	?iyya:ki	?iyya:kuma:	?iyya:kunna
3	MASC	?iyya:hu	?iyya:huma:	?iyya:hum(u:)
	FEM	?iyya:ha:	?iyya:huma:	?iyya:hunna

Table 5

(12)   ?anta   mari:ḍun

        you   sick

'You are sick.'

---

[5] See our definition of THEME in Footnote 18.

(13)   hum   ja:ʔ-u:
       they   came-3.MASC.PL.HUM
       'As for them, they came.'

(14)   sal   ᶜan   xabari-ka   ʔanta
       ask   about   story-your   you
       'Ask about your story.'

(15) a.   ʔaᶜṭay-ta-ni: ʔiyya:hu
          gave-you-me   him/it
          'You gave it/him to me.'

    b.   ʔaᶜṭay-ta-hu   ʔiyya:ya
         gave-you-him   me
         'You gave me to him.' / 'You gave it/him to me.'

(16)   ʔiyya:ka   naᶜbudu
       you   1.PL.adore
       'You, we adore.'

In (12), the nominative pronoun is a TOPIC, in (13) it could be a
THEME, and in (14), it is doubling the affix on the nominative possessor. Other examples of doubling are also given in (6). The essential
contexts of the ʔiyya: form are given in (15) and (16). The construction
(15a) is equivalent to (10b) and preferable. The construction (15b) has
no multiple affixation equivalent to the first reading. This is because
Arabic has a constraint on the order of persons in cliticizing OBJ1 and
OBJ2. The Person Constraint can be formulated as follows:

(17)   If OBJ1 and OBJ2 are affixes, then Pers OBJ1 < Pers OBJ2

What (17) says is that given the context stated, the first person should
occur before the second person which, in turn, occurs before the third
one. This constraint rules out the following affixations:

(18) a.   *ʔaᶜṭay-tu-hu:-ka   b. *ʔaᶜṭa:-ka-ni:
          gave-I-him-you   gave-he-you-me
          'I gave you to him.'   'He gave me to you.'

    c.   *ʔaᶜṭay-ta-hu:-ni:
         gave-you-him-me
         'You gave me to him.'

Thus the ʔiyya: form occurs in the contexts where cliticization would
lead to violations of the Person Constraint. In addition, this form can

also be fronted as in (16), although the construction is not as productive as the one where the nominative form occurs. At any rate, this form appears only in governed contexts and behaves essentially like affixes for the relevant properties. Leaving aside the non relevant details and taking *ʔiyya:* to be a clitic-like form rather than a strong form of the pronoun (see Fassi Fehri 1981 for arguments as well as the historical origin of isolation), the generalization that suggests itself is that affixes and/or clitics are pronominals whose distribution is limited to governed contexts (or contexts of subcategorization in Bresnan's terms). Nominative isolated forms, on the other hand, are limited to ungoverned contexts. Such a distribution can be summarized in the following descriptive statement:

(19)   Pronouns occur for non subcategorized functions, affixes and clitic-like forms for subcategorized functions.

This generalization is compatible with INCH and it provides a simple and a natural description of the facts.

Alternatively, one might hypothesize that subcategorization is not the notion needed to describe the facts. Rather, what is needed is a distinction of two types of pronominals: overt pronouns (like the ones listed) and non overt pronominals (namely *pro*). When the pronoun is not overt, as in (1), the missing argument is *pro* rather than the affix. This is compatible with AGRH provided a further auxiliary assumption is made: that pronominal governors (say verbs) should agree with their pronominal governees (including *pro*). This assumption, while apparently correct for subjects, does not take into account the behavior of *ʔiyya:*. With *ʔiyya:*, no doubling form occurs in Modern Arabic. This would mean that the agreement rule supposedly relating the governor and the governee has to be obligatory for subjects but not for objects. We are then left with an asymmetry, and AGRH would no longer provide a unified account of the distribution of pronominals in Arabic.

Before turning to avoid pronoun, nesting and crossing effects in Subsections 1.3 and 1.4, we would like to analyze the different patterns of cooccurrence of the NP types with the verbal affix types.

1.2.2 NP Types, Affix Types, and Codistribution

Out of the lists in Tables 1–5 given above, only third person singular affixes can occur on the verb when it precedes a non pronominal subject. In such a context, the verb agrees with the subject only in gender. It cannot agree in number as shown in (20):

(20) a. ja:ʔ-a   l-ʔawla:du
         came-MASC.SG   the-boys

         'The boys came.'

b. ja:ʔ-ati   l-bana:tu
    came-FEM.SG the-girls
    'The girls came.'

c. *ja:ʔ-u: l-ʔawla:du
    came-MASC.PL the-boys

d. *jiʔ-u: l-bana:tu
    came-MASC.PL the-girls

e. *jiʔ-na   l-bana:tu
    came-FEM.PL the-girls

When the understood subject precedes the verb, the agreement in number is obligatory:

(21) a. al-bana:tu   jiʔ-na
         the-girls   came-FEM.PL
         'As for the girls, they came.'

b. *al-bana:tu   ja:ʔ-at
    the-girls   came-FEM.SG
    'As for the girls, they came.'

The agreement with the understood subject is not necessary, however, in this context. It could be with an object, object of preposition, possessive object, etc.:

(22) a. zaydun   ntaqad-tu-hu
         Zayd   criticized-I-him
         'Zayd, I criticized him.'

b. zaydun   ltaqay-tu   bi-hi
    Zayd   met-I   with-him
    'Zayd, I met him.'

c. zaydun   laqi:-tu   ʔaba:-hu
    Zayd   met-I   father-his
    'Zayd, I met his father.'

In fact, what looks like an agreement marker is actually a pronominal affix that is anaphorically related to the THEME in a left dislocated construction. It is in no way similar to the English marker on the verb, or to the feminine marker on the verb in (20b). Our claim is that there exist two different classes of affixes in Arabic: the biggest class is the one of pronominal (and/or referential) affixes. Some affixes can only be pronominal (e.g., *u:*). Others can be either pronominal or non pronominal. We assume that some affixes have two different lexical entries, depending on whether they occur with non pronominal NPs or with pronouns. The lexical entries for an affix like *at*, for example, would be the following:

(23) a. *at* SUBJ $\begin{bmatrix} \text{GEND} & \text{FEM} \\ \text{NB} & \text{SG} \\ \text{PERS} & 3 \\ \text{PRED} & \text{'PRO'} \end{bmatrix}$

   b. *at* SUBJ $\begin{bmatrix} \text{GEND} & \text{FEM} \end{bmatrix}$

In (23a), the affix is specified as being referential since it has a PRED value. Other features follow from this specification, in particular PERS and NB. The affix in (23b) is only specified for GEND. This accounts for the grammaticality judgements in (20b) and (21b). The affix entry for (20b) has to be (23b). It cannot be (23a) because SUBJ would have two PRED values, an option barred by the Uniqueness Condition.[6] Uniqueness excludes also (20c) and (20d) because there is more than one PRED value for SUBJ. The construction (21b) is ungrammatical because whatever entry is selected, the resulting f-description is barred either by Uniqueness or by Coherence (see Section 3).

The multiple entries for affixes allow also an account of the distribution in (24), where the subject is non human plural (as in (24a)), or belongs to a particular class of human broken plurals (as in (24b)):

(24) a. ja:ʔ-ati   l-kila:bu
          came-FEM.SG the-dogs
          'The dogs came.'

   b. taqu:l-u   l-fala:sifatu   ...
          say-FEM.SG   the-philosophers
          'The philosophers say ...'

---

[6] The Uniqueness or Consistency Condition requires that in a functional domain F, a particular attribute may have at most one value.

It is true of all non human plural nouns that they behave like a feminine singular. This is what is instantiated in (24a), where *kila:b,* although masculine when singular behaves as if it were feminine when plural by triggering feminine agreement on the verb. Similarly, a limited class of human broken plurals can be used in a distinguished literary style in the feminine singular. It includes *ḥukama:ʔ* 'wise men,' *fala:sifa* 'philosophers,' *furs* 'Persians,' *ru:m* 'Byzantines,' *ᶜarab* 'Arabs,' and names of peoples or ethnic groups in general. This is exemplified in (24b). Let us assume that the non human broken plural is marked as feminine (by some redundancy rule), and that the verb agrees with it when it is a subject to its right. In other words, the verb bears the affix whose lexical entry is (23b) in such cases. When the understood subject is preverbal, the verb bears apparently the same affix, as exemplified in (25):

(25) a.   al-kila:bu   ja:ʔ-at
        the-dogs   came-FEM.SG

   b.   al-fala:sifatu   taqu:l-u
        the-philosophers say-FEM.SG

We assume, however, that this is just a homophony and that the affix here is pronominal. The affix needed in (25a), for example, will have the following lexical entry:

(26)   *at*   SUBJ $\begin{bmatrix} \text{NB} & \text{PL} \\ \text{HUM} & - \\ \text{PRED} & \text{'PRO'} \end{bmatrix}$

The rule taking into account the redundancy in lexical entry specifications can be formulated as follows:

(27)   [PL, α GEND, -HUM] → [∅NB, FEM, -HUM]

This rule applied to nouns states that any plural non human noun is also feminine and has no number. Nouns like the one in (25b) would simply be marked in the lexicon as being optionally feminine and unspecified for number. The Completeness and Uniqueness Conditions would ensure the appropriate distribution in postverbal contexts, and Coherence the appropriate distribution in preverbal contexts (see Section 3).

Summarizing, we claim that most subject affixes are referential and that they are assigned the governed grammatical function SUBJ, just as non subject affixes are referential and assigned the grammatical function OBJ, etc. We assume also that there is a limited number of non referential affixes (or agreement markers) whose sole function is to encode the subject gender on the verb. These non referential affixes have homophonous referential counterparts. In other words, all affixes are referential and only a limited subset of subject affixes can be non referential as well as referential. Moreover, to allow constructions where pronominal doubling occurs such as (6), we assume that the strong form of the pronoun is not assigned a subcategorized function; rather, it is an emphatic modifier of the subject or the object, a modifying FOCUS. If this is true, then the appearance of the pronoun in such contexts would not be sanctioned by Uniqueness, the affix and the pronoun having different functions.

The pronominal type of affixes occurs either alone as in (1), or doubled by a focused pronoun as in (6). It may also occur as a resumptive pronominal in left dislocation or relativization. The non pronominal type of affixes occurs with non pronominal NPs. This codistribution of affixes with the different types of NPs provides indirect support for our typology of affixes.

1.3 Avoid Pronoun Effects

Chomsky (1981) formulates the principle (28) and interprets it as imposing a choice of PRO over an overt pronoun:

(28)   Avoid pronoun

This principle can be extended to cases where the strong form of the pronoun is undesirable and the affix retained. Such a contrast is obtained in relative clauses using the resumptive strategy, where the strong form of the pronoun would not normally occur, as exemplified in (29):

(29) a. ??ntaqad-tu   rrajula   lladi: ja:ʔ-a   huwa
        criticized-I   the man   who   came-3.MASC.SG   he
        'I criticized the man who (he) came.'

   b. ??ja:ʔa   rrajulu   lladi: ntaqad-tu-hu   huwa
        came   the man   who   criticized-I-him   he
        'The man who I criticized came.'

Obviously, there is a difference in interpretation between constructions where the pronoun appears and where it does not (see Section 3). Nothing seems grammatically wrong with these constructions except that it is difficult to imagine a situation in which they are interpretable, compared to sentences where no strong form of the pronoun occurs, as in (30). Here, the interpretation is straightforward.

(30) a.   ntaqadtu   rrajula   llaḏi: ja:ʔ-a
          criticized-I the man   who   came-3.MASC.SG
          'I criticized the man who came.'

   b.   ja:ʔa   rrajulu   llaḏi: ntaqad-tu-hu
        came   the man   who   criticized-I-him
        'The man who I criticized came.'

Leaving aside the question of what specific statements the avoid pronoun principle is supposed to entail (in particular with respect to the
distribution of empty elements and pronominals), let us assume that its
effects should be captured in the theory of grammar. Consider now the
following examples:

(31) a.   zaydun   raʔay-tu   l-fata:ta   llati: qabbal-a
          Zayd   saw-I   the-girl   who   kissed-he
          'Zayd, I saw the girl who he kissed.'

   b. ??zaydun   raʔay-tu   l-fata:ta   llati: qabbal-a-ha:
        Zayd   saw-I   the-girl   who   kissed-he-her
        'Zayd, I saw the girl who he kissed.'

   c. ?zaydun   raʔay-tu   l-fata:ta   llati: qabbal-a-ha: huwa
        Zayd   saw-I   the-girl   who   kissed-he-her   he
        *'Zayd, I saw the girl who he kissed her.'

(32) a.   ʔayyu-hum   raʔay-ta   l-fata:ta   llati: qabbal-a ?
          which-them   saw-you   the-girl   who   kissed-he
          *'Which of them did you see the girl who he kissed?'

   b. ???ʔayyu-hum   raʔay-ta   l-fata:ta   llati: qabbal-a-ha?
        which-them   saw-you   the-girl   who   kissed-he-her
        *'Zayd, I saw the girl who he kissed her.'

(33) a.   bi-ʔayyi-him   ltaqay-ta?
          with-which-them   met-you
          'With which of them did you meet?'

   b.   ʔayyu-hum   ltaqay-ta   bi-hi?
        which-them   met-you   with-him
        *'Which of them did you meet with him?'

There is a difference in acceptability between examples (a) and (b). The examples without the clitics are preferred to the ones with, although Arabic uses both the resumptive and the gap strategies for questioning and relativizing (with different syntactic conditions and different conditions on interpretation. Cf. Fassi Fehri 1978 and 1981 for detail, and also infra). The differences in acceptability seem to fall out in accordance with a principle similar to (28). However, to extend the Avoid Pronoun Principle to such cases, it is necessary to assume that the affix in (31b) and (32b) is pronominal. If it were not, but were rather an agreement marker, the contrast would remain unexplained.[7] As a matter of fact, there are reasons to think that the affix in those two examples, in particular, should be avoided: in interpreting such sentences, resumptive affixes create a non nested reading which is barred in such contexts. Crossing is allowed, however, in (31a) and (32a). This is because when a "gap" occurs, it is locally bound and the pronominal affix is not necessarily bound to the nearest antecedent. Such a behavior of affixes is predicted given the incorporation analysis, but not the agreement analysis. In the following subsection, we provide an account of how such contrasts are captured in the grammar.

1.4 Nesting, Crossing, Binding and Focusing

1.4.1 The Nesting Constraint

Nesting has been claimed to be a constraint on traces (or gaps) and their possible antecedents/chains (see Bordelois 1974, Chomsky 1977, and Fodor 1978, among others). In LFG, the biconditional for the grammaticality of a string requiring its f-description to be properly instantiated states, for one thing, that metavariable correspondences should be nearly nested. The Nested Metavariable Correspondence Constraint is a weak version of the Nesting Constraint (NC) allowing parametric variation among languages in terms of their crossing degree. For example, English allows no crossing in extraction because its crossing limit is $\emptyset$. Icelandic, however, does allow crossing, though its crossing limit is only 1 (see Kaplan and Bresnan 1982 on this matter; hereafter KB). An interesting consequence of NC is its filtering effect: where potentially multiple readings are available for a sentence, NC limits these to one.

1.4.2 Nesting and Crossing in Arabic

Consider now the case of languages where a constraint like NC is needed to characterize anaphoric rather than constituent binding. Such languages either have no gaps (like Egyptian), or use the gap strategy as

---

[7] It is difficult to see how such a contrast can be accounted for given the version of GB theory in Chomsky (1982), where the affix cannot be itself the pronominal.

124 Abdelkader Fassi Fehri

well as the resumptive strategy for extractions (this is the case in Moroccan and Standard Arabic).[8] No multiple gaps can occur, however, in these languages where the following generalizations hold:

  a. if resumptive pronominals are affixed clitics, the actual reading is the nested one;

  b. if a strong form of the pronoun occurs, crossing obtains;

  c. if a gap occurs, there is a crossed reading.

All these languages are subject *pro-drop* languages. Generalizations (a) and (b) hold for Egyptian, Moroccan and Standard Arabic. Generalization (c) holds for Standard Arabic and Moroccan.

1.4.3 Egyptian

Egyptian has been hypothesized by Eid (1977) to have an obligatory deletion rule that deletes only subject pronouns in relative clauses, provided the subject is located in the clause adjacent to the head (see Farghali 1982 for a precise formulation of such a rule as well as the conditions under which it operates). Although Egyptian is a subject *pro-drop* language, Eid claims that the relativization rule is different from the *pro-drop* rule. This is because some deletions that occur in relative clauses do not occur in normal sentences, and because subject pronoun deletion is obligatory in relatives while optional in non relatives. The contrast is exemplified in (34) and (35):

(34) a. huwa   ša:ṭir
         he   clever

         'He is clever.'

     b. *ša:ṭir
          clever

     c. (huwwa)   katab   ilgawa:b
         (he)   wrote   the letter

         'He wrote the letter.'

---

[8] I use the expressions anaphoric binding (a-binding) and constituent binding (c-binding) instead of anaphoric control and constituent control used in Bresnan (1982a). In a-binding, the bindee is not necessarily the functional subject anaphor PRO. It could be any form of a resumptive pronoun. C-binding is supposed to arise in c-structure, and is subject to conditions that refer to the mapping at c-structure like the f-precedence condition of Bresnan (1984). See Section 3 for the properties of these two types of binding.

(35) a.   ilwalad   illi   ša:ṭir   ga
      the boy   who   clever   came

      'The boy who is clever came.'

  b. *ilwalad   illi   huwwa   ša:ṭir   ga
      the boy   who   he   clever   came

      'The boy who he is clever came.'

  c.   ilwalad   illi   (*huwwa)   katab   ilgawa:b
      the boy   who   (he)   wrote   the letter

      'The boy who (he) wrote the letter ...'

The relative rule does not delete the pronoun, however, when the antecedent of the pronoun is not the nearest. Basically, the contrast is the following:

(36) a.   ilwalad   illi   šuf-t   ilra:gil   illi   huwwa   ḍarab-u
      the boy   that   saw-I   the man   who   he   hit-him

      *'The boy that I saw the man who he hit him ...'

  b.   ilwalad   illi   šuf-t   ilra:gil   illi   ḍarab-u
      the boy   that   saw-I   the man   who   hit-him

      'The boy that I saw the man who hit him.'

The readings of (36) are both potentially ambiguous for the subject and the object in the most embedded relative clause, yet they are limited to one. In (36a), the obligatory reading, according to Eid (1977), is the one where *huwwa* takes *ilwalad* as its antecedent. In (36b), the head of the relative clause is understood as the subject of the internal verb.

Leaving aside the question of whether only one reading is possible in these constructions, or whether this is the favored reading (see Farghali 1982 and Eid 1983 for discussion), let us assume that no deletion rule is at stake here, only independent principles of interpretation. In particular, let us assume that there is no relative rule deleting the subject resumptive pronoun. Such a rule would be difficult to state in optimal terms (see Farghali's formulation as an example). Consider now the contrast between (35) and (36). The resumptive pronoun in relative clauses being usually a TOPIC (or old information), it is no surprise that it takes the weak form of pronominals, i.e., the affix (as in (35c)) or even PRO (as in (35a)). When the strong form of the pronoun occurs, it is taken to be contrastive (contrastive FOCUS) and this is what prevents it from taking *ilwalad* as its antecedent in (35b) and (35c), or *ilra:gil* in (36a). The only reading left for (36a) is the one where *huwwa* does not take the nearest NP as antecedent. Crossing effects obtain. By contrast, the pronominal resumptive subject in (36b) takes the nearest NP as its antecedent, while the pronominal object takes the farthest, resulting in nesting effects. Thus, resumptive (non focused) pronominals in Egyptian seem to observe NC just as gaps in English do. There is an obvious difference between gaps and resumptives, however: violations of the usual constraints are possible with resumptive pronouns, but not with gaps. It is an open question whether, this and other differences aside, constituent binding (i.e., binding a gap to an antecedent) and anaphoric binding (i.e., binding a resumptive pronoun to its antecedent) do share common properties and are governed by common principles (see Section 3). If this were the case, NC would not be appropriate to account for nesting effects with resumptive affixes. This is because NC is supposed to apply at constituent structure, while the nesting effects do not obtain at this level.[9] It might be that NC is capturing a spurious generalization and that we need to define an interpretive constraint that would account for all these facts at once, together with the facts about crossing. Before presenting our proposal, we would like to review the facts in two other Arabic languages: Standard and Moroccan Arabic. In these languages, not only is there an interaction between pronominal affixes and pronouns in getting the appropriate readings, but there are also full gaps interacting with pronominals.

1.4.4 Moroccan

Moroccan relativizes with gaps and resumptive pronominals. With the resumptive strategy, violations of the usual constraints are possible, including the Complex Noun Phrase constraint, the Wh Island constraint and the Coordinate Structure constraint. With the gap strategy, these constraints are observed (see Fassi Fehri 1978 for detail). The pronominal in the relative clause is usually an affix on the verb, the preposition or the noun, but it can also be a strong form of the pronoun. When the strong form occurs, it is focused or contrastive. The basic facts are the following:

(37) a. ḥməd   səbb   rrajl   lli   ḍərb-u
        Hməd   insulted   the man   who   hit-him

    'Hməd insulted the man who hit him.'

   b. hməd   səbb   rrajl   lli   huwwa   ḍərb-u
       Hməd   insulted   the man   that   he   hit-him

    'Hməd insulted the man that he himself hit.'

---

[9] They might obtain at c-structure only if we assume that PROs are introduced at the level of c-structure, in accordance with AGRH.

c. ḥməd   səbb   rrajl   lli   ḍrəb
   Hməd   insulted   the man who   hit

'Hməd insulted the man that he hit.'

d. lli   taydhak   mᶜa   lli   ma   yswaš   hada   jazaʔ-u
   who   laughs   with   who   not   valued this   reward-his

'This is the reward of one who laughs with the one who does not deserve respect.'

(38) a. hada   huwwa   rrajl   lli   huwwa   maši   wə-huwwa
        this   he   the man   who   he   walking   and-he

        tayakul
        eat.PROG

        'This is the man who is always eating.'

    b. hada   rrajl   lli   ʔana   mšit   wə-huwwa   bqa
       this   the man   who   I   left   and-he   stayed

       'This is the man who stayed while I left.'

Any relevant pronominal affix in this language can be referential. Subject affixes are referential or non referential depending on whether they occur with a subject NP or not. Non subject affixes are referential only. Pronominal doubling occurs in contexts very similar to those found in Standard Arabic. The examples given above illustrate these points. In (37a), the subject affix is bound to the head of the relative clause, and the object affix to the matrix subject. This reading is not possible in (37b) and (37c). There, the focused pronoun is bound to the farthest antecedent, and the gap is bound to the relative head, forcing the crossed readings. The constructions in (38) illustrate other contexts where the strong form of the pronoun occurs inside a relative clause: in (38a), the relative clause is coordinated to an adjunct clause; in (38b), the conjoined clauses are contrastive.

1.4.5 Standard Arabic

Both Moroccan and Egyptian can be hypothesized to be of the SVO type. It is interesting to note that quite the same contrasts hold for a VSO language, namely, Standard Arabic. The examples below illustrate cases of double binding in left dislocation and relativization, or relativization inside a relative:

(39) a. zaydun   ntaqada   l-wazi:ra   llaḍi: staqbal-a-hu
        Zayd   criticized the-minister   who   received-he-him

        'Zayd criticized the minister who received him.'

   b.   zaydun   ntaqada   l-wazi:ra   lladi: staqbal-a

       Zayd   criticized   the-minister   who   received-he

       'Zayd criticized the minister who he received.'

   c.   zaydun   ntaqada   l-ᶜawna   lladi: waddaf-a-hu   huwa

       Zayd   criticized   the-aid   who   employed-he-him   he

       'Zayd criticized the aid who he himself employed.'

(40) a.   rajaᶜa   man   raʔay-tu   rrajula   lladi:

       came-back   who   saw-I   the man   who

       ntaqad-a-hu

       criticized-he-him

       'The one who I saw the man who criticized him came back.'

   b.   rajaᶜa   man   raʔay-tu   rrajula   lladi: ntaqad-a

       came-back   who   saw-I   the man   who   criticized-he

       *'Who I saw the man who he criticized came back.'

As is clear, constructions with no gap and no focused resumptive have the nested reading. Constructions with a gap or a focused pronoun have the crossed reading.

1.4.6 The Proximity Principle

Our purpose is to propose a constraint on the appropriate readings that is relevant not just for gaps or just for resumptive affixes, but for a mixture of bindees. We assume that the relevant constraint applies at f-structure. The information it uses is the relative proximity of the binder and the bindee and a hierarchy of possible bindees and their grammatical functions.

First, we need to define a superiority hierarchy for grammatical functions. This is because when multiple, non focused and resumptive pronominal NPs are bound, the resumptive subject is bound first to the nearest antecedent, then the next grammatical function (say OBJ) is bound to the farthest antecedent, giving the effect of nesting. The same seems to be true for multiple gap binding (see Kaplan and Bresnan 1982). The superiority hierarchy is stated in (41):

(41)   SUBJ < OBJ < POBJ, POSS OBJ ...

As stated, (41) characterizes homogeneous binding, i.e., when all the bindees are of the same category (a gap: e↑, Pro or Pronoun). When there is a mismatch, the following descriptive hierarchy seems to hold:

(42)   gap < resumptive < resumptive FOC

We call (42) the bindee hierarchy. A resumptive can be a pronominal affix (or pro), a clitic or a non stressed pronoun, depending on languages.

Resumptive FOC is the strong form of pronominals, usually stressed. Having these two strategies in mind, we can define a notion of a nearest possible antecedent as follows:

(43)   Nearest antecedent

An antecedent a_i of a bindee b_i is the nearest if and only if for any bindee b_j contained in F, F an f-structure that contains a_i and b_i, $b_i < b_j$.

We then formulate the following principle:

(44)   Proximity Principle:

a.   The antecedent of a bindee is the nearest one

b.   The antecedent of a focused bindee is not the nearest

The definition (43) incorporates the distinction of the three types of bindees that we hypothesize. Nesting and crossing follow from the Proximity Principle in the appropriate cases. To see how, consider again the examples given above. The Egyptian example (35b) is ungrammatical because the pronoun occurring there is interpreted as focused. By (44b), its antecedent cannot be the nearest. (36b) receives the nested reading because bindees are of the same category (both are affixes), and binding operates according to the superiority and the bindee hierarchies. Similarly, (36a) receives the crossed reading because there is a mismatch of bindees governed again by (44b). In Moroccan (37c), gap binding takes precedence over affix (PRO) binding, resulting in a crossed reading. Other Moroccan and Standard examples pattern essentially like the examples analyzed.[10]

The picture that emerges in this section is that the affix encoding the features NB and PERS, in particular, has also the feature PRED and behaves essentially like a pronominal. The affix bearing only the feature GEND is not pronominal. In the next section, we propose an agreement typology which conforms to this identification taxonomy.

2 An Agreement Typology and the Domain Problem

To start with, let us assume the following working definition of agreement:

(45)   Two expressions are said to agree if some of their features match by virtue of a linking relationship

---

[10] Turkish, Scandinavian and Japanese seem to pattern in the same way. For example, Japanese forces nested readings in double relativization when there are no overt pronouns (i.e., the arguments are PROs). It forces crossing when a realized pronoun occurs with a zero pronoun (or PRO). See Fassi Fehri (in preparation).

Any theory of agreement/disagreement phenomena should be able to place the appropriate constraints on three subcomponents of the agreement/disagreement system: the *nature* of the agreeing expressions, the *features* involved, and the *domain* in which the agreeing constituents are located. Our discussions will be limited mainly to the features GEND, NB, PERS, HUM, and marginally to CASE, MOOD, and DEF (definiteness).

2.1 Type I Agreement ("Internal" Agreement)

There are three distinct types of agreement depending on the nature of the agreeing elements and the domain in which they are found. We assume that the relevant level of representation for defining such domains is f-structure rather than c-structure, and that the nature of the functions assigned to the agreeing expressions is crucial for the definition of such domains. One class of grammatical functions is limited to "sisters" contained in a minimal functional nucleus. A mini f-nucleus can be defined using a notion of minimal containment at f-structure which, we assume, is needed independently in the theory. This notion can be defined as follows:

(46)   Minimal f-containment:

An f-structure F_i minimally contains (m-contains) α, α any grammatical function, if and only if F_i contains α, and there is no F_j such that F_i contains F_j and F_j also contains α.

A definition of a mini f-nucleus can then be provided:

(47)   Mini f-nucleus:

A mini f-nucleus is an f-structure that m-contains a predicate and the functions it is subcategorized for.

We assume that the domain of Type I agreement is the mini f-nucleus and the relationship between the agreeing expressions is that of subcategorization. The core patterns of this type of agreement in Arabic are the following:[11]

a.   verbs agree with their subjects

b.   adjectives agree with their subjects

c.   quantifiers or quantifier-like expressions agree with their objects

---

[11] One case of internal agreement in MOOD is the agreement of the complementizer with the verb heading the sentence. If we take the complementizer to be a predicator taking the S following it as an argument (as argued for in Fassi Fehri (1980)), then this pattern falls out under Type I with all its properties.

These patterns are cases of subcategorization in the LFG framework. The verb and the adjective are subcategorized to take subjects, and the quantifier to take a Q OBJ (as argued in Fassi Fehri 1981). Quantifier-like expressions are numerals or quantifying adjectives that behave exactly like quantifiers, except that their list is not as fixed as that of ordinary quantifiers. These pseudo-adjectives are distinguishable from real adjectives by their position in c-structure (they precede the quantified nominal while modifying adjectives follow it), and they do not vary for gender and number while normal adjectives do. We will see, however, how they can be thought of as agreeing with their head noun even when they don't seem to be. The following examples illustrate the essential cases of internal agreement:

(48)   ja:ʔ-ati   l-bana:tu
        came-FEM   the-girls

        'The girls came.'

(49) a.   zaydun   mari:ḍatun   ʔummu-hu
          Zayd.MASC   sick.FEM   mother-his

          'Zayd, his mother is sick.'

     b.   ltaqay-tu   bi-rajulin   mari:ḍatin
          met-I   with-a man.GEN   sick.FEM.GEN
          ʔumm-u-hu
          mother-NOM-his

          'I met a man the mother of whom is sick.'

     c.   *zaydun   mari:ḍatun
          Zayd   sick.FEM

          'Zayd is sick.'

(50) a.   ja:ʔ-a   ṭala:ṯ-at-u   rija:lin
          came-MASC   three-FEM-NOM   men.GEN

          'Three men came.'

     b.   ja:ʔ-at   ṭala:ṯ-u   nisa:ʔin
          came-FEM   three(MASC)-NOM   women.GEN

          'Three women came.'

(51) a.   jtamaᶜ-at   fi:-hi   jami:l-u   ṣṣifa:t-i
          gathered-FEM   in-him   good-NOM   qualities-GEN

          'He gathered good qualities.'

b. ḥtaraq-at   muxtalif-u   ddu:r-i
    burned-FEM   different-NOM   the houses-GEN
    'Different houses burned.'

c. jtamaᶜ-at   fi:-hi   jami:ᶜ-u   ṣṣifa:t-i
    gathered-FEM in-him   all-NOM   qualities-GEN
    'He gathered all the qualities.'

d. ja:ʔ-a   kull-u   rrija:l-i
    came-MASC   all-NOM   the men-GEN
    'All the men came.'

In (49b), the adjective agrees with its subject in GEND, and it agrees
with the head noun in CASE. In (50), the numeral agrees with the nominal complement in GEND, but in a particular way: since the cardinals
bear the feminine marker, this is analyzed as the unmarked case that
matches the masculine; the feminine is obtained by taking this marker
off, giving the impression that the numeral agrees in the opposite way
with its complement (for more on the properties of the numeral system,
see Fassi Fehri 1981). Constructions (51) are examples of QPs that trigger agreement on the verb in GEND, even though the quantifier head
of the QP is invariable for gender (and NB as well). The quantifier-like
wh-word ʔayyu being the head of the questioned NP and receiving the
appropriate case accordingly also triggers the agreement in GEND, as
(52) shows:

(52) ʔayy-at-u   ḥuku:m-at-in   qarrar-at
      which-FEM-NOM   government-FEM-GEN   decided-FEM
      ha:ḏa:
      this
      'Which government decided this?'

The gender involved in these constructions is grammatical rather than
any "semantic" gender. As illustrated in Subsection 1.2, the non human
plural is taken to be feminine with a singular number (or zero number),
while the singular non human noun can be masculine or feminine. Other
examples of this contrast are given here:

(53) a. kaṭur-at   l-ixtila:fa:t
         increased-FEM   the-divergences
         'There were many divergences.'

b. kaṭur-a   l-ixtila:fu
    increased-MASC   the-divergence
    'There was much divergence.'

c. *ka<u>t</u>ur-at   l-ixtila:fu
    increased-FEM   the-divergence

d. *ka<u>t</u>ur-a   l-ixtila:fa:t
    increased-MASC the-divergence

(54) a. ka<u>t</u>i:ratun   hiya   l-ixtila:fa:t
         many.FEM   she   the-divergences

         'The divergences are many.'

b. *ka<u>t</u>i:run   huwa   l-ixtila:fa:t
    many.MASC   he/it the-divergences

The word *ixtila:f* is masculine when singular, and feminine when plural. The verb governing it (as its subject) takes the appropriate gender marker depending on whether it is plural or singular. Likewise, the pronoun occurring in copular constructions such as (54) takes a gender value matching the grammatical gender of the noun it refers to.

There is some limited variation observed in internal agreement. The variation is limited to the feature GEND, the value of which is neutralized in some distinguished styles. Traditional grammarians claim that such a variation is limited to cases where the verb is separated from the subject, but there are enough well attested examples to show that this restriction does not hold. The motivation is sometimes the use of a "high" variety of speech. Some examples are given in (55). These are from Blachĕre and Demombynes (1952):

(55) a. daxal-a   nniswatu
         entered-MASC the women

         'The women entered.'

b. ḍahab-a   sa:ᶜatun   mina llayli
    went-MASC   an hour   of   the night

    'An hour of the night passed.'

c. quṭiᶜ-a   ʔaydi:-him
    cut.PASS-MASC   hands-their

    'Their hands were cut.'

d. ja:ʔakum   l-mu:min-a:t
    came.MASC.to.you   the-faithful-FEM.PL

    'The faithful women came to you.'

In all these constructions, the verb would normally be marked as feminine, but here it is not. There is no grammatical motivation for such

134 Abdelkader Fassi Fehri

a disagreement (or non agreement). The explanation seems to be sociolinguistic. In the same vein, some speakers tend to forget about gender
distinctions with the question word *?ayy*, assimilating it, probably, to
other invariable quantifiers. This variation seems to be lexical ("idiolec-
tic"). It is at play in sentences like the following:

(56)   ?ayya   nisa:?-in   ra?ay-ta ?
        which.MASC.ACC   women-GEN   saw-you

        'Which women did you see?'

In internal agreement, the agreeing constructions are of a different categorial nature. The source agreeing expression is an argument, and the
agreeing target is a predicator of some sort. The direction of agreement,
as far as the feature GEND is concerned, is from argument to predicator.
Included in this type of agreement, although with some particular properties, is the agreement that involves an argument with multiple heads,
rather than a uniquely headed argument, as was illustrated above. In
this situation, the agreement is with the first head, and there is no union
of properties of the head for this purpose:

(57) a. ja:?-a   zaydun   wa   hindun
         came-MASC   Zayd.MASC   and   Hind.FEM

         'Zayd and Hind came.'

     b. ja:?-at   hindun   wa   zaydun
         came-FEM   Hind.FEM   and   Zayd.MASC

         'Hind and Zayd came.'

     c. ja:?-a   fa?run   wa   hirrun   wa   kalbun
         came-MASC   a rat   and a cat   and   a dog

         'A rat, a cat, and a dog came.'

If any union of properties were at stake, the rule would have been
masculine (in 57b), and feminine (in 57c). This is because a conjunction
of a masculine and a feminine is masculine, and a conjunction of singular
non humans give rise to a plural non human which triggers feminine
agreement on the verb.

Let us now return to constructions where a quantifier-like element
occurs as the head of the agreement source which triggers the agreement
on the verb. In sentences like (50) or (52), it is easy to see that there is
an internal agreement between the quantifier and its object, or between
the verb and the subject. In all these cases, evidence can be provided
that the quantifier is the head of the NP (or the QP) containing it (see
Fassi Fehri 1981). In particular, case assignment rules can be stated
naturally if the quantifier is the head, and the nominal following it its

complement. The quantifier, being the head, receives the case that is assigned to the entire NP, according to its function in the sentence. Its nominal complement (more precisely its OBJ) which, incidentally, qualifies as the head for the purpose of selection, receives either the genitive case or the accusative case. This case sanctions its function internal to the NP. Notice that this complement does not qualify as the head of the construction for the purpose of subject verb agreement. Evidence comes from sentences like (58), where the agreement triggered on the verb shows that it agrees with the union of the properties of the numeral and its complement. The numeral is masculine and the complement is also masculine, but the verb is feminine:

(58)   xamsata   ᶜašara   kalban   rajaᶜ-at
        five.FEM   ten.MASC   dog.MASC   returned-FEM.SG

        'Fifteen dogs came back.'

Only a combination of the properties of the two constituents can make the whole NP plural non human and therefore feminine for the agreement purpose. Notice, interestingly enough, a peculiar property of the numeral agreement. Numerals do not take into consideration the number of their argument, and the numeral agrees with its argument according to the GEND it has when it is singular. In other words, there is no distinction in GEND, for the numeral agreement purpose, between the singular and the plural of the same argument. This is what (59) shows:

(59)   ḥtaraq-at   xams-atu   kutubin
        burned-FEM   five-FEM   books

        'Five books burned.'

The plural subject being non human should have triggered feminine agreement on the numeral (i.e., masculine marking) if the agreement were taking into account the number of the argument. This is not so, however. Equally interesting is the fact that the verb shows feminine agreement here. This means, among other things, that the verb does not agree with the gender on the numeral, and that the relevant agreement feature comes from its argument. That the features of the complement are relevant for verb agreement in these constructions is clear also when one looks at constructions such as (51), where the head is not inflected for gender, but the verb agrees with the subject in GEND according to the features of the complement.

In order to account for such cases, it might be tempting to assume that these NPs are doubly headed. This assumption can take care of the agreement problem, provided one adds the auxiliary hypothesis that the features of both heads percolate up, and that the agreement facts follow from their union. Such a solution, however, does not answer the question of case assignment to the quantifier and its argument. Another alternative would be to maintain the unique head hypothesis and assume that a phrase structure rule can take care of the agreement in such NPs. This rule can be formulated as follows:

(60)   NP $\longrightarrow$ Q   N'
                           $\uparrow=\downarrow$ $(\uparrow \text{OBJ}) = \downarrow$
                           $(\uparrow \text{QNB}) = (\uparrow \text{OBJNB})$

This solution makes the features of the argument available to the head where the head is a quantifier or a quantifier-like expression. Obviously, the mechanism used is descriptive, rather than explanatory. But until a better account could be developed, it has the desired effect.[12]

To sum up, the properties of Type I agreement are the following: the two agreeing expressions are a predicator and an argument, the direction is from the argument to the predicator, the feature involved is GEND and the domain is the mini f-nucleus.

2.2 Type II Agreement

The second type of agreement takes place in a larger domain that contains not only subcategorized functions (such as SUBJ, OBJ, POBJ, etc.) but also non subcategorized functions such as ADJ (adjunct) and MODIF (modifier). This domain is the f-nucleus, defined as in (61). The notion of linking we need is defined in (62).

(61)   F-nucleus:

An f-nucleus is an f-structure that m-contains a predicate and functions linked to it

---

[12] There are some problems in combining the application of the rules (27) and (60). If we assume that the verb agrees with the postverbal subject only in GR, then there is no way to get the feminine marker (or the [PL, -HUM] marker) on the verb, in example like (i), assuming that *kila:b* is [-HUM, PL, MASC]:

(i)   ja:ʔati   l-kila:bu
       came.FEM   the-dogs

If the rule (27) applies, converting [-hum, pl, α gr] to [$\emptyset$nb, -HUM, FEM], then there is no way to obtain the masculine on the numeral in (ii):

(ii)   ja:ʔat   xamsatu   kila:bin
        came.FEM   five   dogs

So, for the purpose of the verb, *kila:b* is [$\emptyset$nb, -hum, fem] and for the purpose of the numeral it is [pl, masc, -hum]. This mismatch is due to grammars taught at schools in which it is said that all non human plurals are feminine singular, which is what (60) is supposed to convey.

(62)   A grammatical function α is linked to a predicate P only if α is governed by P, or α contains a grammatical function β a-bound (anaphorically bound) to a grammatical function γ governed by P.

Thus, ADJ is not directly governed (lexically governed) by the predicate. It is indirectly linked to the predicate because it contains a pronominal controlled by an argument of P. This is what (63) illustrates:

(63) a.   laqi:-tu   zaydan   yalᶜabu

       met-I   Zayd   plays.3.MASC.SG

       'I met Zayd playing.'

    b.   laqi:-tu   zaydan   ra:kiban

       met-I   Zayd   riding.MASC.SG.ACC

       'I met Zayd riding.'

In (63a), the OBJ of the matrix verb controls the pronominal subject of the adjunct clause. More precisely, the PRO subject is anaphorically bound by the object (see Fassi Fehri (1981) for arguments that this is a case of local anaphoric binding). Similarly in (63b), the pronominal subject of the participal AP can be controlled (ambiguously) by the subject or the object of the matrix verb.

In Type II agreement, the two agreeing expressions are of the same category: they are nominal expressions (or argument expressions). The direction of agreement is from an argument having a subcategorized GF to an argument contained in a GF not subcategorized for. The features involved are all the pronominal (or referential) features including NB, PERS, HUM, and GEND. CASE is not involved.

Among the patterns of Type II agreement is the agreement between the head noun and a modifying adjective or an indefinite relative clause, or between the head noun and the relative marker in a definite relative clause. We assume that all these cases are instances of modification, where the head noun is the essential predicate of the construction (the NP) and the relative clause (or the AP) the MODIF (modifier). This MODIF patterns for the purposes of agreement essentially like ADJ does.[13] The MODIF contains a pronominal anaphorically related to the head noun, thus triggering agreement effects in some cases. Some examples follow for the sake of illustration (see Fassi Fehri (1981b) for details):

(64) a.   laqi:-tu   rajulan   ʔ-aᶜrifu   ʔuxta-hu

       met-I   a man   I-know   sister-his

       'I met a man I know his sister.'

---

[13]   We might want to distinguish languages where relative clauses are ADJ from languages where they are MODIF. See Subsection 3.3.2. Similar remarks hold for some adjectives.

b. laqi:-tu   rajul-an   mari:ḍ-at-an   ʔumm-u-hu
   met-I   a man-ACC sick-FEM-ACC mother-NOM-his

'I met a man whose mother is sick.'

c. laqi:-tu   rrajul-a   l-mari:ḍ-a
   met-I   the man-ACC   the-sick-ACC

'I met the man who is sick.'

d. laqi:-tu   rrajul-ayni   llaḍ-ayni   ntaqad-ta
   met-I   the men-DUAL.ACC who-DUAL.ACC   criticized-you

'I met the two men who you criticized.'

e. laqi:-tu   rrajul-ayni   llaḍi: ntaqad-ta   wa
   met-I   the men-DUAL.ACC who   criticized-you and

llaḍi: ntaqada   zaydun
who   criticized Zayd

'I met the two men, the one you criticized and the one
Zayd criticized.'

In (64a), the modifying S contains a pronominal linking the sentence
to the head noun. The resumptive pronominal is not necessarily the
subject, as the examples (64a) and (64c) show. When it happens to be
the subject of the adjective, the agreement effects obtain as in (64c).
Note in passing that modifying adjectives agree also in DEF and CASE
with the head noun. Likewise, the relative marker in a definite relative
construction behaves in essential ways like adjectives do: it agrees necessarily with the head noun in DEF and CASE, as examples (64d) and
(64e) show, but not necessarily in other features like GEND and NB (as
seen in (64e)). This suggests that definite relative clauses in Arabic are
MODIF, just like adjectival phrases are. On the other hand, indefinite
relative clauses and sentences occurring as complements of the relative
marker behave essentially like ADJ do (see Chapter VIII of Fassi Fehri
1981b for details). An indefinite relative clause like (64a) would have
the f-structure shown in (65a), and a definite relative clause like (64b)
would have the f-structure shown in (65b):

(65) a. laqi:-tu   rajulan   ta-ᶜrifu-hu
        met-I   a man   you-know-him

'I met a man who you know.'

    b. laqi:-tu   rrajula   llaḍi: ta-ᶜrifu
        met-I   the man   who   you-know

'I met the man who you know.'

(66) a. OBJ $\begin{bmatrix} \text{PRED} & \text{'rajul'}_i \\[2mm] \text{ADJ} & \begin{bmatrix} \text{PRED} & \text{'ta}^c\text{rif}<\text{(SUBJ)(OBJ)}>' \\[2mm] \text{TNS} & \text{PRES} \\[2mm] \text{SUBJ} & \begin{bmatrix} \text{PRED} & \text{'PRO'} \\[2mm] \text{PERS} & 2 \\[2mm] \cdots & \end{bmatrix} \\[6mm] \text{OBJ} & \begin{bmatrix} \text{PRED} & \text{'PRO'} \\[2mm] \text{PERS} & 3 \\[2mm] \cdots & \end{bmatrix}_i \end{bmatrix} \end{bmatrix}$

b. OBJ $\begin{bmatrix} \text{PRED} & \text{'rajul'}_i \\[2mm] \text{DEF} & + \\[2mm] \text{MODIF} & \begin{bmatrix} \text{PRED} & \text{'lla}\underline{d}\text{i:'} \\[2mm] \text{DEF} & + \\[2mm] \begin{matrix}\text{TOP}\\\text{OBJ}\end{matrix} & \begin{bmatrix} \text{PRED} & \text{'PRO'} \\[4mm] & \end{bmatrix}_i \\[6mm] \text{ADJ} & \begin{bmatrix} \text{PRED} & \text{'ta}^c\text{rif}<\text{(SUBJ)(OBJ)}>' \\[2mm] \text{SUBJ} & \\[2mm] \text{OBJ} & \begin{bmatrix} \ \ \end{bmatrix}_i \end{bmatrix} \end{bmatrix} \end{bmatrix}$

For justification of such structures and how the two nominal expressions are bound (here binding is represented by coindexing), see Section 3. See also this section for c-structure annotated rules that generate part of the f-description shown here (rules (88) to (90)).

Another pattern of Type II agreement is the one found in pronominal doubling constructions as in (6) above. There, the agreeing expressions are the affixed pronominal and the focused pronoun. We assume that the focused pronoun belongs to the same f-nucleus that contains the pronominal affix, though the focused pronoun does not belong to a mini f-nucleus. This is why the pronoun is linked anaphorically to the affix which is an argument governed by the predicate. The features involved are referential features, and the linking relationship is that of modification.

2.3 Type III Agreement ("External" Agreement)

Type II agreement, as we have seen, is a consequence of local anaphoric binding, the domain of binding being the f-nucleus. The domain of Type III agreement is larger than the f-nucleus, the controller of agreement being external to the f-nucleus where the agreeing target is found. This difference aside, Type III agreement shares some properties with Type II agreement. For example, it triggers agreement in all inherent or pronominal features (except CASE). The agreeing expressions are of the same category. The direction of agreement is from the argument external to the f-nucleus to the argument internal to it. The core patterns of external agreement are the following:

a.   left dislocation: agreement between the THEME and some resumptive pronominal inside the clause.

b.   relativization: agreement between the relative marker and the resumptive pronominal.

c.   equative sentences: agreement between the TOPIC NP and the predicative AP (more precisely a pronominal contained in the AP).

d.   questioning with pronominalization: agreement between the question word and the resumptive pronominal.

e.   clefting: agreement between the FOCUS and the relative marker in the adjacent clause.

This list is probably not exhaustive. In all these cases, it is only accidental that the predicator is involved in agreement. The target is, in fact, an argument expression. As illustrated above for left dislocation in (21) and (22), the verbal predicate can be affected by agreement, but not necessarily. This is so when the bindee happens to be the subject of the verb, for example, as in (21). Likewise, there is an agreement in (67) between the NP TOPIC and the adjective, not because the agreement is necessary in this construction, but rather because the resumptive pronominal contained in the predicative AP happened to be the adjective subject. Thus, agreement obtains as a consequence of anaphoric binding:

(67)   nnisa:ʔu   nabi:la:tun

        the women   generous.FEM.PL

        'Women are generous.'

We assume that *nnisa:?* in (67) is a TOPIC having no (internal) grammatical function, and that the AP is the head of the sentence. We will see in the next section what makes anaphoric binding necessary in all these patterns. For the moment, we simply emphasize the properties of this type of agreement, mentioning only in passing that some of its properties fall out from the properties of long distance anaphoric binding.

Concluding this section, we note that the typology of agreement parallels the typology of grammatical functions, and the demarcation of the domains of the agreement types parallels the demarcation of the domains in which different functions are defined. In Section 3, we will examine some well-formedness conditions on f-structures and we derive the taxonomic results reached in Sections 1 and 2.

3 Well-Formedness Conditions on F-Structure, Binding, and Agreement

In this section, we will be concerned with how to derive the typologies defended in Sections 1 and 2 and the agreement facts mentioned there. More particularly, we will be relying on two independently well motivated conditions on f-structure: Uniqueness and Coherence. These two conditions account for the agreement facts, directly or indirectly, provided Coherence is reformulated and extended the way we propose. We will show that such a reformulation is needed both conceptually and empirically. Our main contribution here is the way we view Coherence and its role in the grammar. Uniqueness will simply be adopted as it stands to account for Type I agreement, with no substantial change in its form or function. We will also make some assumptions about the taxonomy of grammatical functions, the function assignment procedure and the conditions on this assignment. Our purpose is to unify under a single condition on f-structure the treatment of phenomena that have been treated separately. In particular, different types of binding fall out under the same condition.

3.1 Uniqueness and Type 1 Agreement

In LFG, the Uniqueness Condition, the formulation of which is repeated in (68), plays an essential role in forcing cooccurrence restrictions:

(68)   In a given f-structure, a particular attribute may have at most one value.

Uniqueness has the desired filtering effect for functional descriptions where lexical functional specifications and syntactic specifications are not consistent. Thus, it is the role of Uniqueness to ensure that needed matching features in agreement expressions would merge at the appropriate f-structure.

Consider the formal mechanisms used in LFG to build the appropriate functional domain for agreement and determine language specific as well as cross-linguistic information.

First, needed feature specifications are encoded on the governor to point to the governee via lexical specifications of the affix (or the lexical word bearing the affix). This is what the lexical entry for the affix *at*, for example, given in (69) is supposed to convey:

(69)   -*at* : $[V-]_{V[Fin]}$ TNS = Past, SUBJ GR = fem

This lexical entry or the entry of the verb to which the affix is attached, i.e., the lexical entry of the agreement target (and governor), conveys information about the agreement source (and governee): it establishes a morphological as well as a syntagmatic relation between the governor and a specific governee (e.g., the subject). This information is highly language specific. The number of affixes and the features they encode may vary from language to language. For example, some languages do not show agreement between subjects and verbs (their verbs being entirely analytic) while other languages do. Furthermore, subject-verb agreeing languages differ (somewhat arbitrarily) in the features involved: in Arabic only gender is involved, in English and French it is person and number, in Jacaltec, case and person, and in Navajo, animacy and person (see Bresnan 1982b). The lexicon, therefore, characterizes parametric variation: whether an expression is an agreeing expression or not, which governees are agreeing expressions (SUBJ, OBJ, POSS OBJ...), which features are a matter of agreement, etc.

Second, functional annotations on c-structure rules may also play a role in building the appropriate f-structure for agreement (this is at least the position taken in KB 1982 and Bresnan 1982b). For example, it is the role of phrase structure annotations to tell whether a function is closed or whether it allows the internal information to be passed on. This is because, as Bresnan (*ibid*) puts it, "... governing morphemes appear either in the heads (or heads (of heads ...)) or in minor categories of the phrase whose constituents they govern." The mechanism used is the identification schema: ↑=↓. This equation is normally assigned to heads, in the sense of X-bar theory, and it allows propagation up the tree. It is this mechanism that takes care of subject verb agreement. The inflected verb inserted in the tree (say, *seems* in English) encodes already the information that the SUBJ person is 3 and the SUBJ number is singular. The feature set on the verb is propagated up the tree becoming features of the VP, and the features of the VP becoming features of S (and ultimately S'). Uniqueness guarantees that in the desired domain (say S), the subject will have the features carried by the affix.

The identification schema ↑=↓ is also assigned to minor modifying categories such as the determiner. This is how KB rule out a construction like (70), where the determiner does not agree with the head noun:

(70)   *A girl handed the baby a toys.

Here, both the determiner and the head noun bear the identification schema $\uparrow=\downarrow$ to allow the features to propagate up.[14]

While such a mechanism might do the job descriptively, it does so only if we make auxiliary assumptions that are questionable. Among these is the assumption that the VP is the head of S, and crucially the assumption that agreeing expressions find themselves in the same syntactic projection (in the sense of X' theory). This seems to run counter to a natural functional theory of agreement, and a restrictive theory.

The way agreement is handled in LFG is then either via lexical government (or subcategorization) or via stated syntactic percolation. It would be a welcome step if the second mechanism could be dispensed with, and if Bresnan's generalization as well as the propagation of features follow from something else, essentially (perhaps uniquely) from functional composition.[15]

---

[14] In order to account for the agreement in number and gender within the NP in French, in examples like (i), one may want to assign this schema to all constituents within the NP:

(i)   Ces   petites   braves   et   heureuses   filles

       these.PL small.FEM   good.FEM   and   happy.FEM   girls

This possibility is excluded, however, by Uniqueness. This is because the construction would have more than one major category as a head. Therefore, the identification schema would be assigned only to the demonstrative and the head noun, while the adjectives will be treated as adjuncts or modifiers.

[15] The two main constraining principles for agreement in Generalized Phrase Structure Grammars are the Control Agreement Principle, on the one hand, and the Head Feature Convention, on the other. A formulation and a criticism of the CAP are given in Subsection 3.3 below. The Head Feature Convention is formulated in Gazdar and Pullum (1982) as follows:

(i)   if β_i is the head of β_0 then $\mathrm{HEAD}(\alpha_i) = \mathrm{HEAD}(\alpha_0)$

(α is a category in an instantiated rule A, and β is its counterpart in a rule B which A instantiates).

What (i) does is require the coefficients of HEAD in the mother category and the head daughter to be identical. These two principles are very similar to lexical subcategorization and stated syntactic propagation, although less precise (see Section 3.3).

Our intention of reducing the mechanisms used to account for Type I agreement to functional composition is viable if we assume that the determiner is a function (or predicator) and the head noun its argument. Then the agreement follows as a natural case.

The fact that the set of agreeing expressions is limited to grammatical functions contained in a mini f-nucleus (in our terms) can be derived from the theory of affixation and, more generally, the theory of lexical rules. It is a property of lexical rules that they refer only to subcategorized functions, and cannot refer to functions like adjuncts or modifiers.[16] Moreover, lexical entries for affixes limit agreement to the appropriate cases. This is a parametric choice in languages.

Returning to Type I agreement in Arabic, we note that the affix bears a value of the feature GR as well as needed information about the agreement target: it is either SUBJ (with adjectives and verbs) or OBJ (with numerals and quantifiers = NUM OBJ, Q OBJ). Uniqueness ensures the appropriate feature matching.

3.2 Coherence and Types II and III Agreement

3.2.1 Coherence in the KB System

As proposed in KB, Coherence is a well-formedness condition on f-structures forcing compatibility requirements regarding government. Its effect is to duplicate in the syntax the information about government relations contained in the lexicon. Coherence is formulated as follows:

(71)   An f-structure is *locally coherent* if and only if all the governable grammatical functions that it contains are governed by its predicate. An f-structure is *coherent* if and only if it and all its subsidiary f-structures are locally coherent.

This condition is intended to account for the ill-formedness of strings such as (72):

(72)   *The girl fell the apple the dog

In (72), the governable functions OBJ and OBJ2 do appear in the f-description assigned to the string, yet they are not governed by the intransitive verb *fell*. By governable functions, KB mean functions that appear in the function assignment lists of lexical predicates. So Coherence, like Uniqueness, applies only to subcategorized functions. It does not extend to other functions like THEME, ADJ or MODIF. Consider the following examples:

---

[16] This is because, as mentioned in KB, a predicate imposes neither category nor feature restrictions on its adjuncts. This is why they do not obey the Uniqueness, Completeness and Coherence Conditions. Recall that in KB subcategorized and governable functions are one and the same. In our theory of Coherence, adjuncts are not lexically governed by the predicate, yet they obey internal Coherence (see Section 3).

(73) a. *John I saw Mary

    b. John I saw

    c. John I saw him

(74)   *raʔay-tu zaydan ra:kiban ᶜamrun
       saw-I   Zayd   riding   Amr
       *'I saw Zayd Amr riding.'

(75)   *ja:ʔa l-waladu l-mari:ḍu zaydun
       came the-boy   the-sick   Zayd
       *'The who is sick Zayd came.'

(76)   ja:ʔa l-waladu l-mari:ḍu
       came the-boy   the-sick
       'The boy who is sick came.'

As formulated in (71), Coherence does not, in these examples, distinguish well-formed strings from ill-formed ones. Both sets of strings could be thought of as well-formed by virtue of (71), yet they are not. Our purpose is to revise the Coherence Condition in three significant ways. First, we do not limit local cases of government to subcategorizable functions, but include also adjuncts and modifiers. Second, we conjecture that cases of long distance dependencies in left dislocation, relativization, clefting, etc., require a type of linking which does not fall under Condition (71). Third, the Coherence Condition should also be extended to account for so-called constituent binding. Such a move is argued for on conceptual as well as empirical grounds. We begin by presenting a taxonomy of functions needed to describe languages as well as a sketch of a grammatical function assignment procedure. In Subsection 3.2.3, we formulate the Coherence Principle and show how it accounts for Type II and Type III agreement, and how it extends to Constituent binding. In Subsection 3.3, we analyze some consequences of our formulation and extension of Coherence, in particular for the interpretation of left dislocation, relativization and adjuncts.

3.2.2 Functions and Grammatical Function Assignment

Two types of grammatical functions are used in the literature with terminological as well as conceptual confusion, although they are of different properties and different nature. The first type includes functions such as SUBJ, OBJ, POBJ, ADJ, etc. These functions are linked to the predicate and play a role in its semantic frame. They can be subcategorized for and/or associated with a governed case. On the whole, they contribute to build the semantics of the predication (the predicate argument structure of the functional nucleus).[17] A second type of function is of a separate nature. The list includes functions such as THEME, TOPIC, FOCUS, AFTERTHOUGHT TOPIC or TAIL, etc.[18] These functions contribute to build the discourse structure of the sentence. They are not subcategorized for, their case is not governed by the predicate, and they do not play a role in the predicate argument structure as such. Call the first list of functions *grammatical* functions or GFs, and the second *discourse functions* or DFs. Our claim is that these two types of functions are assigned at different levels of the grammar and they should not be mixed or confused.[19]

All syntactic theories we are aware of assume that GFs are assigned internal to the f-nucleus, and that a syntactic category external to the minimal domain defining the f-nucleus (say S) bears only a DF in our terms (e.g., TOP, THM, FOC ...). Moreover, some syntactic theories seem to assume that some DFs are only assigned externally. For example, Chomsky (1977) assumes that TOP is external, and Dik (1978) that THM and TAIL are always external, while TOP and FOC are internal. To our knowledge, no convincing arguments have been provided for

---

[17] Yet another distinction worth making is between lexically governed functions such as SUBJ, OBJ, POBJ, ..., and non lexically governed functions such as ADJ and MODIF. Although internal to an f-nucleus and contributing to the semantics of the predication, these functions are not directly associated to the predicate argument structure of the predication.

[18] I adopt some of these functions and their definitions from Dik (1978) with some modifications. As is clear from the presentation, the properties I attribute to these functions are not the ones attributed to them in Dik (*ibid*).

THEME: information with respect to which the predication can be relevant.

TAIL or AFTERTHOUGHT: information meant to clarify or modify what is predicated.

TOPIC: old information in the relevant discourse structure.

FOCUS: most salient information in the relevant discourse structure.

These definitions have no theoretical status but are meant simply to clarify what kinds of definitions we might need. Elaborated theories are obviously needed. On this issue, see the Prague School tradition, Systemic linguistics, Functional Sentence Perspective Grammars, Functional Grammars, etc. For the purpose of Coherence, these distinctions in functions are not needed. All what we need is a distinction between grammatical and non grammatical functions.

[19] As will become clear below, Coherence will check only whether a constituent is identified with a GF or not. Coherence will apply also to non GFs (or $\overline{\text{GF}}$s), and not really to DFs as such.

such views.[20] Let us assume, instead, that both GFs and DFs can be assigned to an argument (lexical assignment) or to a syntactic category (c-structure assignment) and that they play different roles in the grammar. The assignment procedure is essentially that of KB (1982). Possible combinations of GFs and DFs should be a matter of more elaborated theories and empirical investigation. Moreover, let us assume that GFs and DFs are assigned randomly, both internal to S and external to it. It is reasonable to think that grammatical function assignment is subject to universal as well as specific constraints. There is no reason, in principle, why all GFs should be assigned internally, just as there is no reason why all DFs should be assigned externally. Some GFs are likely to be assigned only internally, and some externally and internally, just as some DFs are assigned internally and externally, and some only externally. We claim that a functional hierarchy governs external GF assignment, some functions being easier to assign externally than others.[21]

As a result of the assignment procedure, some arguments may bear only a GF, and some only a DF. Thus, there are three possible outcomes of the assignment procedure:

a.   arguments assigned a GF and a DF

b.   arguments assigned only a DF

c.   arguments assigned only a GF

It is a question whether there exists a class of interpretable arguments such as (c). For now, we are more concerned with the existence of (a) and (b), and these classes do exist. As for (a), there are NPs to which the grammatical function OBJ is assigned, for example, and at the same time the discourse function FOC. Instances of this are given in (77):

---

[20] See De Groot (1981) for arguments that THM can be internal, Fassi Fehri (1983) for arguments that TOP and FOC can be external.

[21] For example, a prepositional adjunct is easier to locate external to its clause than an NP bearing a nuclear grammatical function. We hypothesize, thus, the following hierarchy:

(i)   GF external assignment hierarchy:
      Only a subset of the set of GFs can be assigned external to f-nuclei, subject to the following hierarchy (tentative):
      ADJ(some class) < OBJ < SUBJ < POBJ < POSS OBJECT < COBJ (or CGF)
      (Read COBJ as object of a complementizer and CGF as any grammatical function on the complementizer)

There are reasons to think that (i) is valid cross-linguistically. For example, Standard Arabic allows extraction of objects and adjuncts only. In French and Moroccan, no OBJ can be topicalized. Egyptian allows only extraction of prepositional adjuncts. Not many languages allow extraction of the object of the complementizer, etc. See Fassi Fehri (in preparation).

(77) a.   I saw Jóhn

   b.   Jóhn I saw

As regards class (b), the NP THEME in (74c) has no GF, or a $\overline{\text{GF}}$. One role of the Coherence Principle, as defined in the next subsection, is to constrain the possible outcomes of the assignment of GFs and $\overline{\text{GF}}$s.

3.2.3 Coherence, Binding and Agreement Types

There are significant ways in which so-called constituent binding differs from (long distance) anaphoric binding: Some of the properties of each type are listed in the table below (for details, see Fassi Fehri 1981 and 1982, Zaenen 1980 and 1981 among others):

C-binding:	A-binding:
a. case matching of the binder and the bindee (a consequence of strict feature matching)	a. no (necessary) case matching
b. no violation of the island constraints	b. apparent violations of the islands
c. the bindee has no PRED value (is a 'trace')	c. the bindee is pronominal (has a PRED value)

To these properties, we add (d):

d.   in c-binding, the binder and the bindee bear GFs that have necessarily the same value; in a-binding, this is not true.

As an illustration of the property (d), compare the f-structures (78) and (79) assigned to (74b) and (74c), respectively:

$$(78) \quad \begin{bmatrix} \begin{matrix} \text{FOC} \\ \text{OBJ} \end{matrix} & \begin{bmatrix} \text{PRED 'John'} \\ \cdots \end{bmatrix}_i & \\ \\ \text{ADJ} & \begin{bmatrix} \text{PRED} & \text{'see}\langle(\text{SUBJ})(\text{OBJ})\rangle\text{'} \\ \text{SUBJ} & \begin{bmatrix} \text{PRED} & \text{'PRO'} \\ \text{PERS} & 1 \\ \text{NB} & \text{SG} \end{bmatrix} \\ \text{OBJ} & [\quad]_i \end{bmatrix} \end{bmatrix}$$

(79)

$$
\begin{bmatrix}
\text{THM} & \begin{bmatrix} \text{PRED 'John'} \\ \cdots \end{bmatrix}_i \\[2em]
\text{ADJ} & \begin{bmatrix}
\text{PRED} & \text{'see } \langle(\text{SUBJ})(\text{OBJ})\rangle\text{'} \\[1em]
\text{TNS} & \text{PAST} \\[1em]
\text{SUBJ} & \begin{bmatrix} \text{PRED} & \text{'PRO'} \\ \text{PERS} & 1 \\ \text{NB} & \text{SG} \end{bmatrix} \\[3em]
\text{OBJ} & \begin{bmatrix} \text{PRED} & \text{'PRO'} \\ \text{PRES} & 3 \\ \text{NB} & \text{SG} \\ \text{GR} & \text{MASC} \end{bmatrix}_i
\end{bmatrix}
\end{bmatrix}
$$

The difference between (78) and (79) is taken into account in splitting Coherence into two subconditions. The first one is the Internal Coherence condition formulated in (80):

(80)   Internal Coherence Condition:

An f-structure F is internally coherent if and only if for every GF contained in F, GF is either contained in an f-nucleus F_i, or GF is c-bound in F_i.

The condition (80) forces any GF assigned external to the f-nucleus to be bound to a GF internal to it. The External Coherence Condition takes care of a-binding:

(81)   External Coherence Condition:

An f-structure F is externally coherent if and only if for every $\overline{\text{GF}}$ m-contained in F, $\overline{\text{GF}}$ is a-bound in F.

The General Coherence Principle associates (80) and (81):

(82)   General Coherence Principle:

An f-structure F is coherent if and only if it is both internally and externally coherent

Consider now how the Coherence Principle accounts for the appropriate judgements. There are two ways in which (73a) is ruled out by (82). It could be that *John* is assigned the GF OBJ, the same function that *Mary* is assigned: (73a) is then ruled out by (80) because the GF assigned to *John* is not c-bound. It could also be that *John* is assigned no GF, just a DF, say THM. In this case, the construction is ruled out by (81), *John* being not a-bound in the f-structure that m-contains it. As for (73b), it is good because *John* is assigned the function OBJ and is c-bound in the adjacent clause. The construction (73c) is good because *John*, being THM, is a-bound in the appropriate f-structure. Constructions (74), (75) and (76) are examples of f-structures where local a-binding is required to enable the ADJ or the MODIF to be linked to the predicate (see the definition of linking under (62)), and therefore to satisfy the Internal Coherence Condition. In the (a) examples, linking does not obtain and the adjunct or the modifier do not pertain to an f-nucleus, which is ill-formed by (80). Similarly, cases of doubling fall under the External Coherence Condition. To see how, consider the f-structure (83) assigned to a doubling construction like (6c) above:

(83)

$$
\begin{bmatrix}
\text{PRED} & \text{'nuba:yi}^c \text{ }\langle(\text{SUBJ})(\text{OBJ})\rangle\text{'} \\
\text{TNS} & \text{PRES} \\
\text{SUBJ} & \begin{bmatrix} \text{PRED} & \text{'PRO'} \\ \text{PERS} & 1 \\ \text{NB} & \text{PL} \end{bmatrix} \\
\text{OBJ} & \begin{bmatrix} \text{PRED} & \text{'PRO'} \\ \text{PERS} & 2 \\ \text{NB} & \text{SG} \end{bmatrix}_i \\
\text{FOC} & \begin{bmatrix} \text{PRED} & \text{'PRO'} \\ \text{PERS} & 2 \\ \text{NB} & \text{SG} \end{bmatrix}_i
\end{bmatrix}
$$

The pronominal affix receives the grammatical function OBJ governed by the verbal predicate. The pronoun *ʔanta* cannot receive a GF function because such a GF would not be internally governed, given our assumptions. It receives only the discourse function FOC (or MODI-FOC, a subcase of the function FOC). Being a $\overline{\text{GF}}$, it should therefore be a-bound in the f-structure that contains it. The candidate for binding is the pronominal OBJ, and this is what the interpretation actually is.

Thus, agreement types II and III would fall out as effects of local or long distance anaphoric binding in an obvious way, governed by the Principle (82).

3.3 Some Consequences

3.3.1 A Conceptual Advantage

There are at least two advantages in extending Coherence the way we have done, and making the relevant assumptions we have made. The first one is descriptive and has obvious empirical consequences. Coherence is forcing local anaphoric binding in adjuncts, relative clauses, predicative APs and modified NPs. It is also forcing long distance anaphoric binding in left dislocation, and constituent binding in topicalization, relative clauses, clefts, etc. (see below for examples of relativization).

The second advantage is conceptual in nature. KB rely on two conditions to define the grammaticality of a string or more precisely the well-formedness of the f-structure associated with it: a) Coherence and b) a condition on proper instantiation which imposes a one-to-one correspondence between metavariable controllers ($\Downarrow$) and metavariable controllees ($\Uparrow$). Clearly, this condition is not a well-formedness condition on f-structure. Rather, it is a condition on the mappings and the formal procedure building an f-description. Thus, the two conditions do not pertain to a homogeneous system of well-formedness conditions. Condition a) does not depend on the instantiation procedure. Condition b) does.

Our theory of definitions does not suffer such a deficiency. Control relations (whether local or long distance) are handled by one and the same condition. Given the two sets of grammatical functions we have postulated, the set of GFs = {SUBJ, OBJ, POBJ, ... } and the set of $\overline{\text{GF}}$s (instantiated by external DFs), the first set falls under the "internal" part of the condition and the second set under the "external" part. This condition is a well-formedness condition on f-structures and does not depend, in principle, on the formal assignment procedure.[22]

---

[22] One way to formulate the External Coherence Condition, suggested by Kaplan (personal communication) is represented in (i).

(i) $(\uparrow \text{DF}_i) = (\ldots \uparrow \text{GF}_j)$

This can be read as follows: every DF_i should find (in the internal structure) a corresponding GF_j. The point made is independent of the formalism used.

3.3.2 Relative Clause Interpretation

Let us turn now to some consequences of our theory for relative clause interpretation and also for left dislocation and adjuncts. As explained in Section 2, anaphoric binding is necessary in such constructions under the qualifications given there. It is forced in some relative clauses because these pattern like adjectival phrases in that they bear the grammatical function MODIF to the head noun. Since the head of a modifying AP agrees in Definiteness and Case with the head noun, the head of the modifying relative clause, which we assume to be the relative marker, also agrees with the head noun in the same features. By the same token, anaphoric binding is necessary for MODIF to be linked to the (predicate) head noun, MODIF being a $\overline{GF}$. The target of binding is PRO which is introduced as a part of the lexical entry of the relative marker *lla$\underline{d}$i:*. It might be that PRO is controlled by the head noun, in which case the agreement in NB and GR with the head noun follows (agreement in PERS is probably not relevant here; at any rate non pronominal NPs could be thought of as being third person). But this agreement is not necessary, as the contrast between (64d) and (64e) shows. The analogy then goes through with modifying adjectives: all that is necessary is the agreement in DEF and CASE; the agreement in GR and NB is just an effect of a coincidence, when the bindee happens to be a PRO acting as a subject of the adjective.

As for the relative marker, it does not make sense to think that the PRO attached to it is its subject. In fact, it is not. Rather, it is assigned a GF and/or a DF just like NPs external to the clause are assigned GFs and DFs. This assignment is then subject to the Coherence Principle. Suppose PRO is assigned the GF OBJ as well as probably the DF TOP. This is what happens when the deletion strategy is used to relativize (as exemplified in (84) below). In this case, the properties of c-binding obtain, and the construction is subject to the internal part of the Coherence principle:

(84)   laqi:-tu rrajula   lla$\underline{d}$i: ntaqad-ta
        met-I   the man   who   criticized-you

        'I met the man who you criticized.'

All the properties of the construction, however, are derived, as predicted. Suppose, on the other hand, that PRO is assigned only a DF, say TOPIC, but no internal GF. Then anaphoric binding is forced by the external part of Coherence. This is exactly what you get when you use the resumptive strategy, as exemplified in (85), with all the properties of a-binding:

(85)   laqi:-tu rrajula   lla$\underline{d}$i: ntaqad-ta-hu
        met-I   the man   who   criticized-you-him

        'I met the man who you criticized (him).'

Recall also that Arabic has a third strategy for relativization, where no relative marker is used. The internal structure of the clause is then different. This strategy is exemplified in (86):

(86)   laqi:-tu   rajulan   ntaqad-ta-hu

      met-I   a man   criticized-you-him

      'I met a man who you criticized (him).'

Note, interestingly, that no deletion strategy is possible here, just as no deletion is possible in ADJ clauses. If PRO insertion is limited to lexical insertion, as we assume, this fact is expected: there is no lexical item (like a relative marker) to which PRO can be attached, thus binding the eventual gap. Suppose then that these relative clauses are ADJ, just as relative clauses in English or French are. Then a typology of relative clauses (based on functional distinctions) might emerge: some relative clauses are MODIFs and some are ADJs. MODIFs do agree in DEF and CASE, ADJs do not. Although both are forced to be a-bound. For the differences in f-structure between the two, see (66) above. For the difference between the resumptive and the deletion strategies in definite relatives, compare (66b) and (87) below:[23]

(87)   MODIF   [PRED   'lladi:'

               TOP   [PRED 'PRO']$_i$

               ADJ   [PRED
                      'ntaqad ⟨(SUBJ)(OBJ)⟩'

                      SUBJ [PRED   'PRO'

                             PERS   1

                             NB   SG]

                      OBJ [PRED   'PRO'

                           PERS   2

                           NB   SG]$_i$

---

[23] We might assume that PRO is introduced on *lladi:* and assigned the DF function TOP in the lexicon. This would make *lladi:* necessarily a-bound if PRO is assigned a $\overline{\text{GF}}$ (see the resumptive strategy), and c-bound if PRO is assigned a GF.

The rules needed for generating these constructions could then be the following:

(88)   NP ⟶   N   AP

$\uparrow=\downarrow$ ($\uparrow$MODIF) $=\downarrow$

(89)   NP ⟶   N   S′

$\uparrow=\downarrow$ ($\uparrow$ADJ) $=\downarrow$

(90)   AP ⟶   A   NP

$$\uparrow=\downarrow \quad \begin{bmatrix} (\uparrow\text{SUBJ}) = \downarrow \\ \text{S}' \\ (\uparrow\text{ADJ}) = \downarrow \end{bmatrix}$$

It is worth mentioning that our theory of relative clause and adjectival phrase interpretation is typically syntactic in nature. It relies crucially on syntactic grammatical functions and functional relations, rather than logical or predicate argument relations. In this respect, it contrasts with semanticist or logicist theories of relative clause interpretation. By the same token, our theory of agreement in such constructions is equally syntactic.

As an example of semanticist theories of agreement, consider the Control Agreement Principle embodied in Generalized Phrase Structure Grammar (on this matter see Gazdar and Pullum 1982 among others; see also Barlow 1988):

(91)   Control Agreement Principle

If β_i controls β_j then AGR (α_i) = AGR(α_j)

The notion of control used here is that of Bach and Partee (1980) where the controllee is a function and the controller an argument. It could also be an argument-passing function that applies to some controller (see Klein and Sag 1982). The CAP is meant to be a generalization of Keenan's principle that functors may agree with nominal arguments (see Keenan 1974 and 1979). It requires the coefficients of AGR in the controller and the controllee to be identical. The CAP is supposed to constrain the possible dependence (semantic dependence) of the two agreeing expressions. While it does so, it is too general. It is difficult to make the appropriate distinctions between predicative adjectives, modifying adjectives and adjectives that are heads of the APs given the single notion of control. In all these cases, the adjective is the controllee (and the function), in the intended sense, and the TOP NP, the head noun or the subject NP is the controller. But then how do the differences in agreement follow?

Likewise, relative clauses whether definite or indefinite can be thought of as functions (or controllees) and their head nouns as arguments or controllers. The difference in behavior between the two is again not explained.

As a second example of logicist theories of relative clause interpretation, consider Chomsky's conjecture that relative clauses contain a relative operator (overt or abstract) and that structures such as (92) are barred ". . . by the requirement that an operator at LF [Logical Form] must bind a variable, and languages may differ as to how this variable is realized; pronouns can serve as variables because they need not have independent reference" (Chomsky 1982 p. 12):

(92) a. *the man who John saw Bill

   b. *the man who$_i$ John saw him$_j$ (i = j)

The analogy is established with questions where constructions such as (93) are also barred for the same reason:

(93)   *Who did John see Bill?

Notice that Coherence as extended takes care of all these constructions. Depending on the f-descriptions assigned, in particular depending on whether *who* receives a GF (and a DF) or only a DF, the result is barred by Internal or External Coherence.

We see no reason, however, to postulate a logical characteristic of relative clauses by which they should have a relative operator demanding a variable. We certainly agree with Chomsky that it is necessary to ". . . interpret relative clause constructions [. . .] as involving an operation of predication, the relative clause being regarded as an open sentence predicated of the head" (*ibid*, 13). This is the idea we have made precise by postulating a local binding linkage forced by Coherence. This mechanism, we assume, is appropriate for relative clause and adjunct interpretation as well as adjectival constructions because it enables us to make the appropriate syntactic distinctions. Moreover, agreement facts in these constructions follow, as different reflexes of different binding types and relations.

Conclusion

In this paper, we have provided a sketch of what a functional theory of agreement would look like. Our conjecture is that the appropriate agreement relationships are checked at functional structure. These are derivable from government and binding relations in ways we have suggested. The different government and binding relationships, we have shown, are properties of different grammatical functions. Our taxonomy of grammatical functions plays a role in sorting out these different properties. Moreover, our theory of grammatical function assignment makes it easy to distinguish and characterize different types of binding. Furthermore, our theory of well-formedness definitions improves on previous work within LFG.

Our characterization of agreement and different interpretation processes in functional terms differs from c-structure characterizations (especially the c-structure propagation assumption) and logicist characterizations. If such an approach is well founded, then support would be given for the "extra" level of representation it embodies.

References

Abdo, D. 1973. ʔabḥa:t̲ fi: lluga l-ᶜarabiyya. Beyrouth: Da:r al-kita:b al-lubna:ni:.

Anderson, S. R. 1982. Where's morphology? *Linguistic Inquiry* 13:571–612.

Bach, E. and B. Partee 1980. Anaphora and semantic structure. In J. Kreiman and A. Ojeda (Eds), *Papers from the Parasession on Pronouns and Anaphora, Chicago Linguistic Society.*

Barlow, M. 1988. *A Situated Theory of Agreement.* Doctoral dissertation, Stanford University.

Blachĕre, R. and G. Demombynes 1952. *Grammaire de l'Arabe Classique.* Paris: Adrien-Maisonneuve.

Bordelois, Y. 1974. *The Grammar of Spanish Causative Complements.* Doctoral dissertation, Massachusetts Institute of Technology.

Bresnan, J. 1982a. The passive in lexical theory. In J. Bresnan (Ed), *The Mental Representation of Grammatical Relations.* Cambridge, Mass.: The MIT Press.

Bresnan, J. 1982b. Control and complementation. *Linguistic Inquiry* 13(3).

Bresnan, J. and J. Grimshaw 1978. The syntax of free relatives in English. *Linguistic Inquiry* 9(3).

Chomsky, N. 1977. On wh-movement. In P. Culicover, T. Wasow and A. Akmajian (Eds), *Formal Syntax.* New York: Academic Press.

Chomsky, N. 1980. On the representation of form and function. Paper presented at the Royaumont conference, CNRS, Paris.

Chomsky, N. 1981. *Lectures on Government and Binding.* Dordrecht: Foris.

Chomsky, N. 1982. *Some Concepts and Consequences of the Theory of Government and Binding.* Cambridge, Mass.: The MIT Press.

Dik, S. 1978. *Functional Grammar.* Amsterdam: North Holland.

Eid, M. 1977. Arabic relativisation: shadow deletion or pronoun drop? *Minnesota Linguistic Papers* 4.

Eid, M. 1983. On the communicative function of subject pronouns in Arabic. *Journal of Linguistics* 19.

Emonds, J. 1976. *A Transformational Approach to English Syntax.* New York: Academic Press.

Farghali, A. 1982. Subject pronoun deletion rule in Egyptian Arabic. Paper presented at the Second National Symposium on Discourse Analysis, Cairo.

Fassi Fehri, A. 1978. Comparatives and free relatives in Arabic. *Recherches Linguistiques* 7.

Fassi Fehri, A. 1980. Some complement phenomena in Arabic, Lexical Grammar, the complementizer phrase hypothesis and the non-accessibility condition. *Analyses/Théorie.* Paris VIII St. Denis.

Fassi Fehri, A. 1981a. Théorie lexicale fonctionnelle, controle et marquage casuel en arabe. *Arabica* 28.

Fassi Fehri, A. 1981b. *Linguistique arabe: forme et interpretation.* Rabat: Publications de la Faculté des Lettres et des Sciences Humaines de Rabat.

Fassi Fehri, A. 1982. Note à propos de la dislocation accusative en arabe. *Zeitschrift für Arabische Linguistik,* 13–84. Wiesbaden: Otto Harrassowitz.

Fassi Fehri, A. 1983. Binding, agreement and typology. In A. Fassi Fehri and D. Serghouchni (Eds), *Issues in Grammar and Discourse.* Rabat: Publications of the Moroccan Society of Philosophy. (In Arabic.)

Fassi Fehri, A. In preparation. *Issues in Arabic Linguistics.*

Fauconnier, G. 1974. *La Coréférence: Syntaxe ou Sémantique?* Paris: Le Seuil.

Fodor, J. D. 1978. Parsing strategies and constraints on transformations. *Linguistic Inquiry* 9(4).

Gazdar, G. and G. K. Pullum 1982. *Generalized Phrase Structure Grammar: A Theoretical Synopsis.* Bloomington: Indiana University Linguistics Club.

Halliday, M. A. K. 1967. Notes on transitivity and theme in English. *Journal of Linguistics* 1.

Hoekstra, T., H. van der Hulst and M. Moortgat (Eds) 1980. *Perspectives on Functional Grammar.* Dordrecht: Foris.

Kaplan, R. and J. Bresnan 1982. A formal system for grammatical representation. In J. Bresnan (Ed), *The Mental Representation of Grammatical Relations.* Cambridge, Mass.: The MIT Press.

Keenan, E. 1974. The functional principle: generalizing the notion of 'subject of.' *Papers from the Tenth Regional Meeting of the Chicago Linguistic Society,* 298–309.

Keenan, E. 1979. On surface form and logical form. *Studies in the Linguistic Sciences* 9.

Klein, E. and I. A. Sag 1982. Semantic type and control. In M. Barlow, D. Flickinger, and I. A. Sag (Eds), *Developments in Generalized Phrase Structure Grammar.* (Stanford Working Papers in Grammatical Theory 2.) Bloomington: Indiana University Linguistics Club.

Li, C. (Ed) 1976. *Subject and Topic.* New York: Academic Press.

McCloskey, J. and K. Hale 1984. On the syntax of person-number inflection in Modern Irish. *Natural Language and Linguistic Theory* 1(4).

Mohanan, K. P. 1983. Functional and anaphoric control. *Linguistic Inquiry* 14(4).

Moravcsik, E. 1978. Agreement. In J. H. Greenberg (Ed), *Universals of Human Language* 4. Stanford: Stanford University Press.

Sgall, P. et al. 1973. *Topic, Focus, and Generative Semantics.* Kronberg Taunus: Scriptor Verlag.

Si:bawayh (8th century). *Al-kita:b.* Haru:n ed., 1966. Beyrouth.

Vachek, J. 1959. *Dictionnaire de Linguistique de l'École de Prague.* Utrecht: Spectrum.

Zaenen, A. 1980. *Extraction Rules in Icelandic.* Doctoral dissertation, Harvard University.

Zaenen, A. 1981. Characterizing syntactic binding domains. (Occasional Paper No. 17.) Cambridge, Mass.: The Center for Cognitive Science, Massachusetts Institute of Technology.

7   Agreement vs. Case Marking and Direct Objects

WILLIAM CROFT

THIS PAPER BEGINS with a problem in the characterization of the behavior of direct objects with respect to agreement and case marking across natural languages, and in the process of developing a solution to this problem I propose an analysis of the presence vs. the absence of agreement and case marking of arguments. The form of this analysis is that of universal structure–meaning (form–function) correspondences for agreement and case marking. This is a new type of constraint on possible human language types, and it implies that the cognitive processes which must account for such constraints are quite general. The analysis also unifies the three most important typological patterns that link structure and function in natural languages—markedness, hierarchies and prototypes—under a single concept, that of *relative markedness*, thereby allowing typological theory to be characterized in a more general and perspicuous manner.

I would like to thank Joseph H. Greenberg, Charles Ferguson and Elizabeth Traugott for their comments on an earlier version of this paper. I would also like to thank Carolyn Coleman for providing the Kun-parlang data, and Tony Davis for discussion of the Hausa data. The Quiché data is from materials in a course on Quiché offered by Norman McQuown at the University of Chicago in 1976-77.

The problem, which has been prominent in recent literature on grammatical relations and transitivity, is: are definite and/or animate direct objects marked or unmarked?

Hopper and Thompson (1980) and Givón (1976) suggest that they are unmarked. Hopper and Thompson propose an abstract concept of Transitivity to which a large number of properties are correlated. If one assumes that the "ideal" transitive utterance is the unmarked one, as Hopper and Thompson seem to imply, then one would predict that the animate and definite direct object will be unmarked, since it is highly individuated (Hopper and Thompson 1980:252-253). Givón is more explicit: he describes agreement as obeying a hierarchy Agent < Dative < Patient, the verb agreeing with the arguments that are higher on the hierarchy (Givón 1976:152, 160-166). Givón's hierarchy inverts two members of the standard case hierarchy (Keenan and Comrie 1977), in which the accusative precedes the dative. If Givón is right, then the concept of a universal case hierarchy is badly damaged.

In contrast to the position of Hopper and Thompson and Givón, Comrie (1979) suggests that definite/animate direct objects are marked, chiefly on the basis of the presence vs. absence of case marking on direct objects in a variety of languages. Thus, we have two conflicting hypotheses. The evidence that Comrie, Givón, and Hopper and Thompson cite is all descriptively accurate, however. It appears that in this case, marking theory provides inconclusive or conflicting evidence concerning the status of certain kinds of direct objects. This means that either there is no universal characterization of the markedness of direct objects, or that there is some deficiency in marking theory. I will argue that the problem can be solved by successive extensions to classical marking theory, as originally developed by Trubetzkoy, Jakobson and Greenberg. I will also argue that ultimately Comrie is correct, but the phenomena that Hopper and Thompson and Givón cite can also be accounted for.

1 The Markedness of Direct Objects

1.1 Classical Marking Theory

The classical theory of markedness is based on the discovery that paradigmatic members of the same grammatical category have asymmetrical linguistic properties. The classical theory of markedness is based largely on three properties: (1) unmarked values are morphosyntactically less complex than marked ones, in fact, they are usually "zero-marked"; (2) marked values are behaviorally defective compared to unmarked ones, that is, they do not inflect for as many grammatical categories (e.g., number) and/or their syntactic distribution is more restricted; and (3) unmarked values are textually more frequent than marked ones. In this paper, I will present arguments based chiefly on the first criterion and partly on the second; see Greenberg 1966 for extensive studies based on the third.[1]

Formally, we can represent the paradigmatic elements as privileged members of a single set, the set of members of a grammatical category:

$$C = \{u, m\} \qquad \text{OR} \qquad C = \{u, m_1, m_2, \ldots\}$$

$$(u, m_1, m_2, \ldots \text{ elements of a category } C)$$

In the classical theory of markedness, the solution to the problem we have posed seems quite simple: definite and/or animate direct objects are marked, because if there is a contrast between the presence of an agreement marker or a case marker and its absence in the direct object, it is always the more definite and/or more animate direct object which is marked by agreement and case. This is true across a very large number of languages and has been widely observed in the literature. We will consider some typical cross-linguistic facts.

In Swahili (Perrott 1972:38), agreement is sensitive to definiteness. The verb agrees with definite direct objects but not indefinite ones (there is evidence of interactions with animacy as well; see Givón 1976:159, Ashton 1944:58, 60):

(1)   U-   me-   leta   kitabu?
       2.SG-   PERF-   bring   book

       'Have you brought a book?'

(2)   U-   me-   ki-   leta   kitabu?
       2.SG-   PERF-   3.SG-   bring   book

       'Have you brought the book?'

Turning to case marking, Punjabi (Shackle 1972:69-70) provides an example of a language in which both animacy and definiteness interact with direct object status. First and second person direct objects, which are always animate and always definite by definition, require the dative postposition; third person direct objects require the postposition if they are definite, and do not use it when they are indefinite:

(3)   mɛ̃   tɛ   -nũ   pəṛàvaŋga
       1.SG   2.SG   -DAT   will.teach

       'I will teach you.'

---

[1] The version of the theory of markedness used in generative grammatical theory, particularly in generative phonology, is a different mechanism. The generative phonological use of markedness is related to the first criterion, namely, to represent "default" feature values to simplify abstract (phonological) representations and rules.

(4)   ó   nili   kitāb   nũ   mez   te   rakkho
       that   blue   book   to   table   on   put

'Put that blue book on the table.'

(5)   koi   kitāb   mez   te   rakkho
       some   book   table   on   put

'Put some book on the table.'

Comrie, in an extended discussion of the interaction of animacy and definiteness with case marking (Comrie 1979), also cites Persian, Hindi, Turkish, Russian, Spanish, Tagalog and Mongolian as languages in which both animacy and definiteness govern variation in case marking.

1.2 Marking Theory and Grammatical Hierarchies

While classical marking theory can account for the widespread data of the kind presented in the Swahili and Punjabi examples, there are other grammatical phenomena which are obviously quite closely related, but classical marking theory cannot handle them without modifications.

Kun-parlang, an Australian language, agreement with the direct object interacts with animacy. The probability of the verb agreeing with its direct object depends on its animacy: the verb agrees with a first or second person direct object almost always, with a third person human object often, and with a third person inanimate direct object almost never:

(6)   nga-   ngum-   kinyang
       1.SG.REAL-   2.SG-   cook.PAST

'I burned you.'

(7)   nga-   kinyang
       1.SG.REAL-   cook.PAST

'I burned it/him'

Thus, there is a gradation of "degree" of animacy that determines agreement in Kun-parlang.

Another example of gradable determination, this time with case marking, is found in Rumanian (Nandris 1945:183-185). Rumanian is still in the process of losing its last case distinction inherited from Latin (nominative vs. oblique), but has begun using prepositions for many of the grammatical functions, including using *pe* 'on' for direct objects. While the use of *pe* for direct objects is not easily described, there are certain situations in which *pe* is required, situations in which it is optional, and situations in which it is prohibited. It is required when the direct object is both human and definite (including pronouns), and with certain definite constructions (e.g., demonstrative + cardinal numeral, and ordinals); it is optional when the direct object is either human but a specific indefinite, or nonhuman but pronominal, and it is prohibited when the direct object is a nonspecific indefinite or a generic. Thus, one must use *pe* when the direct object is both human and definite, one may use it when the direct object is either human or definite but not both, and one must not use it when it is (nonspecific) indefinite or generic.

The theory of markedness can be extended to handle more data such as the Kun-parlang and Rumanian examples by relativizing the notion of markedness. The classical theory of markedness states that a member of a category is either marked or unmarked, absolutely. But in certain cases, there is a scale on which members of the category can be placed, and the scale applies to linguistic phenomena which are clearly in the domain of marking theory, such as the presence vs. absence of agreement or case marking. The solution is to redefine the markedness of a member of a category *relative to* other members of the same category. Formally, this is represented by a (partial) ordering of the elements of the category:

$$C = \{m_1 < m_2, m_3 < m_4 < \ldots\}$$

The formal description given here is in the familiar form of an implicational hierarchy. Given some grammatical phenomenon, one can convert the $<$'s to $\subset$'s and read the implications from right to left to obtain a series of implicational universals. This relationship between markedness and implicational universals is not accidental, and has been discussed by Greenberg (1966:21-22). Greenberg also appears to be the first to have observed that implicational hierarchies are related to properties of markedness, in particular, the behavioral and textual (frequency) criteria (Greenberg 1966:31-32, 42-45). In this section, we will demonstrate that hierarchies also adhere to the structural criteria of markedness.

All of the categories we are concerned with—definiteness, animacy and case or grammatical relations[2]—have been found to form hierarchies with respect to various grammatical processes. They are: the Animacy Hierarchy (Silverstein 1976; Dixon 1979),[3] the Definiteness Hierarchy (Greenberg 1978), and the Case or Accessibility Hierarchy (Keenan and Comrie 1977), usually given as follows:

> *Animacy:* 1st, 2nd < 3rd < Proper Name < Human < Animate
> < Inanimate

---

[2] The relationship between case and grammatical relations is quite controversial; I take the position that abstracting two (or more) separate levels is unnecessary (see Croft 1983). It is also true that most advocates of the "case" hierarchy have postulated only one hierarchy.

[3] The "Animacy Hierarchy" involves not only the animacy of the referent but also the speech act status (1st/2nd person versus 3rd person) and the type of referring expression (pronoun, proper name, or common noun). These factors are interdependent, however: 1st and 2nd person are always human and pronominal, and proper names are usually human. For this reason, the Animacy Hierarchy is normally treated as a unified phenomenon, and I will follow that practice here.

Definiteness: Definite < Specific/Referential Indefinite < Non-specific/Generic

Case: Subject < Direct Object < Indirect Object < Oblique

The extension of marking theory to hierarchies allows us to account for considerably more data. The presence vs. absence of agreement and case marking is to a great extent a function of the case hierarchy. Moravcsik (1974) discovered that agreement is associated with the upper end of the case hierarchy in the following way: if there is a construction in which the verb agrees with some member of the case hierarchy, then there are at least some constructions in which the verb agrees with members higher on the case hierarchy. This statement allows for the large number of languages which have variable object agreement, i.e., under certain conditions the verb agrees with indirect or oblique objects but not direct objects in a given construction, although it agrees with direct objects in other constructions. These languages themselves make up a subset which obeys the case hierarchy. An enumeration of existing types of agreement systems is given below:

1. Languages having no agreement: Lahu (Matisoff 1973), Chrau (Thomas 1971), Mandarin Chinese

2. Languages having agreement with the subject only: English, Russian, Turkish (Lewis 1967)

3. Languages having agreement with the subject and one object:

    a. patient only: Quiché, Ayacucho Quechua (Parker 1969)

    b. patient or Dat/Ben/Mal: Classical Nahuatl (A. Anderson 1973)

    c. patient, Dat/Ben/Mal, or oblique(s): Acoma (patient possessor; Miller 1965), Kun-parlang (comitative), Amharic (instrument; Moravcsik 1974:40)

4. Languages having agreement with subject, direct object, and indirect object or other oblique: Abkhaz (Hewitt 1979), Manam (Lichtenberk 1983)

5. Languages having agreement with subject, direct object, indirect object and benefactive: Kinyarwanda (Dryer 1983)

The presence of case marking, on the other hand, is associated with the lower end of the case hierarchy; that is to say, the absence of case marking is associated with the upper end of the hierarchy. Unlike agreement, there is a single simple hierarchy:

1. Languages with no zero case marking: Latvian (Ladziņa 1966), Japanese (Clark and Hamamura 1981)

2. Languages with zero subject (nominative/absolutive)[4] case marking: Hungarian (Whitney 1944), Turkish (Lewis 1967), Dyirbal (Dixon 1972)

3. Languages with zero subject and object case marking: Quiché, Persian (Mace 1962), Chrau (Thomas 1971)

4. Languages with zero subject, object and indirect object case marking: Manam (Lichtenberk 1983a), English

There are other phenomena outside the realm of agreement and case marking which supports the existence of the case hierarchy, namely relativization (Keenan and Comrie 1977) and causativization (Comrie 1976). Linking marking theory to these phenomena considerably broadens its scope of applicability.

Although the typological facts clearly require this extension of marking theory, we run into severe problems when we apply hierarchies to the phenomenon of definite/animate direct objects. Consider the introduction of animacy and definiteness as a partition of the case hierarchy, so that what we seek is an ordering within the category of "direct object" of definite/indefinite and animate/inanimate direct objects. Since agreement is associated with the upper end of the case hierarchy, presence of agreement implies that the entity is "less" marked. Hence, given the data above, definite/animate direct objects are less marked than indefinite/inanimate ones. Case marking, on the other hand, is associated with the lower end of the case hierarchy; therefore, presence of case marking implies that the entity is "more" marked. Thus, definite/animate direct objects are more marked than indefinite/inanimate ones. An anomaly not present in the classical theory has been generated by this extension of marking theory. Fortunately, there is a further extension to marking theory which allows us to resolve this anomaly and cover a still greater number of cross-linguistic phenomena.

1.3 Marking Theory and Natural Correlations

Actually, the original statement of the problem—are definite/animate direct objects marked or unmarked?—is an incoherent question in terms

---

[4] In ergative languages, the unmarked case in transitive constructions marks the direct object and in intransitive constructions, the subject. This would suggest a partial ordering Intr. Subject < Tr. Subject, Tr. Object < ... . However, all languages possessing ergative patterns display "split ergativity" (Dixon 1979), in which the transitive subject is unmarked under certain conditions and even the intransitive subject is marked under certain conditions (so-called "active" languages). This anomaly for the case hierarchy is solved by the extension of marking theory to natural correlations in Section 2.3.

of both classical marking theory and the extension to grammatical hierarchies. Markedness is defined solely in terms of relationships among members of the *same* grammatical category. However, the problem under consideration mixes three *different* categories: case (associated with whatever relational morphosyntax is used), definiteness (associated with the determiner system), and animacy (associated with nouns themselves and the gender/class system, if there is one). One must extend the concept of markedness still further, to include cross-categorial relations.

The final definition of markedness includes the concept of an element of a grammatical category being unmarked *relative to a member of another grammatical category*. This unmarked correlation is called a *natural correlation*. Formally, this can be represented as sets of ordered n-tuples of correlated members of different categories:

Category	Values	
A	a	b
B	j	k
C	x	y

$< a, j, x >$: unmarked (natural) correlation

$< a, k, y >$: marked correlation

The cases of simple markedness and hierarchies discussed in the previous sections occur when there is no such markedness relationship across categories.[5] In a given utterance, a category value such as "direct object (patient)" is unmarked in its realization only if all of its natural correlations are present also; in other words, one can be certain that the construction "normally" or "typically" associated with the patient will actually be used to indicate the patient only when the properties which naturally correlate with patienthood are also present. When one or all of the cooccurring properties are not naturally correlated with the patient, then the linguistic manifestation of the patient is more marked, and thus the patient nominal may carry a grammatical mark, e.g., a (nonaccusative) case marking.

Natural correlations themselves must be explained in terms of properties external to the structure of language, e.g., certain typical correlations of the kinds of phenomena people normally talk about, and the amount of attention directed to different aspects of the phenomena

---

[5] Again, Greenberg appears to be the first to have suggested the possibility of markedness relative to values across grammatical categories: "It should be noted that in some cases we had what might be called conditional categories for marked and unmarked. For example, whereas for obstruents, voicing seems clearly the marked characteristic, for sonants the unvoiced feature has many of the qualities of a marked category" (Greenberg 1966:24).

(for example, human actors). The same is of course true of classical markedness and hierarchies within morphosyntactic categories. The relevance of natural correlations to the structure of language, and thus to grammatical theory, is manifold. They allow one to determine the "true" meaning of surface grammatical categories like "direct object" or "agreement," by specifying the conditions under which those meanings are expected to appear (that is, when their natural correlates are also present). This in turn allows us to define what aspects of the grammar will be motivated by (external) semantic and pragmatic factors and what aspects will be partially arbitrary conventionalizations in the grammars of specific languages.

The natural correlations themselves are hypothesized to be universal, and thereby externally motivated. When the meaning of a grammatical category is conventionalized (grammaticalized) in some natural language, e.g., surface direct objects are always indefinite, the grammaticalization is predicted to always align itself with its natural correlations. The arbitrary aspect of grammar is the degree to which a language will mark "unnatural" correlations. Languages may or may not mark "unnatural" correlations with a distinct surface form, and for that reason, cross-linguistic variation in the marking of, say, direct objects (patients) is found. Even then, the implicational scales determined by the hierarchies are adhered to within individual languages. In these respects, natural correlations behave like "core uses," "prototypes," or "ideal types." The link between marking theory and prototypes allows us to integrate prototype analyses of certain grammatical categories with more traditional morphosyntactic properties of those categories.

It is clear from the evidence presented so far that agreement markers and case markers have a different set of natural correlations, that is, agreement and case marking have universal but distinct properties. So, it is possible to assign a "meaning" or significance to the presence vs. absence of agreement and case marking that would correlate in the proper way with animacy, definiteness, and case. In line with the general observation that highly "grammatical" morphosyntactic properties (e.g., grammatical relations (DeLancey 1981, Croft 1983) and syntactic categories (Croft 1984)) actually represent pragmatic—specifically, discourse-functional—properties, namely the organization of information by the speaker for presentation to the hearer, the following definitions for agreement and case marking are proposed.

1.3.1 Agreement

Agreement—i.e., person-based agreement, also called "cross-reference" or "indexing"—indexes the *important* or *salient* arguments. This concept is a pragmatic one: salience is a relationship between the speaker and a referent in the described situation—that is, the speaker's attitude or point of view towards the referent—rather than a relation between two entities in the described situation itself. Salience correlates with being high on the case, animacy and definiteness hierarchies, since the most salient entities are those most closely involved in the described event, closest in nature to the speaker, and most easily identifiable. The natural correlation predicts that where the presence vs. absence of agreement is grammaticalized, it will always align itself with high animacy, high definiteness, and core grammatical relations.

In addition to the evidence we have already presented, all of which is consistent with this definition, we can account for other typological phenomena. First, it is very frequently the case that the third person agreement "marker," which indexes the lower animacy (3rd person and nonpronominal) entities, is null for either subject or object. Among the many languages which have zero agreement in the third person are Quiché (singular direct object), Georgian (singular direct object; Comrie 1981:216), Yap (singular direct object; Jensen 1977), Gulf Arabic (masculine singular subject; Qafiseh 1977), Fula (singular subject; Arnott 1970), and Manam (some plural non-higher-animal direct and indirect object forms; Lichtenberk 1983).

Another very common phenomenon is that in languages with a two-argument agreement constraint, case roles such as recipient or experiencer which require mental capacity and therefore are occupied by humans (high in animacy and usually high in definiteness) are agreed with over case roles such as patient which are normally lower in animacy and/or definiteness. For example, in Kun-parlang, agreement is controlled by a hierarchy Recipient < Comitative < Patient. This hierarchy combines animacy and case: both recipients and comitatives are almost always humans, and the recipient (indirect object) case is higher on the case hierarchy than the comitative (oblique) case:

(8)   nga-   purrun-   marnany-   wom
       1.SG.REAL-   3.DUAL-   RECIP-   return.PAST
       'I returned to/for them (dual).'

(9)   nga-   purrum-   walki-   wom
       1.SG.SBJ-   3.DUAL-   COM-   return.PAST
       'I returned with them (dual).'

(10)   *nga-   marnany-   purrum-   walki-   wom
       1.SG.REAL-   RECIP-   3.DUAL-   COM   return.PAST
       'I returned to/for [no agreement] with them (dual)'

In Kinyarwanda (Kimenyi 1978) the verb agrees with patient possessors and benefactives even if instrumentals, locatives, manner, or directional arguments are promoted, and in most Bantu languages the dative/benefactive argument is obligatorily promoted (which triggers agreement). There are also languages with a one-argument agreement constraint in which the verb agrees with whichever of subject and object is higher in animacy, namely, Chukchee and Tangut (Comrie 1980:231, 233).

Finally, Manam (Lichtenberk 1983) has a complicated set of rules determining agreement which combines the animacy hierarchy with the typically animate cases. The verb agrees with the dative recipient and not the patient if both are present; but the verb agrees with both the patient and the benefactive/source unless the patient is 1st or 2nd person, in which case the verb agrees with the patient only. Thus, the patient can trigger agreement over the typically animate benefactive only if the patient actually is high in animacy.

1.3.2 Case Marking

Case marking, in contrast to agreement, denotes *non-obvious* grammatical relations. This concept is also pragmatic. "Obviousness" does not denote a subclass of semantic relations between two entities. Rather, it denotes a relationship between the speaker (and hearer) and a semantic relation. A semantic relation between two entities may be obvious in certain discourse contexts but not in others, and this of course depends on the knowledge and presuppositions of the speaker and the hearer rather than on some property of the described situation. Case marking correlates with being low on the case hierarchy, since the relation of more oblique arguments to the predicate are less obvious than those of the central, normally present or even obligatory, arguments. Case marking also correlates with deviation from the natural correlations associated with a case position. When the animacy/definiteness properties associated with the case position are not the "natural" and thereby "obvious" ones, then the case position tends to be marked.

On the basis of the typological evidence, this definition predicts that the natural correlation of direct objects is with low animacy, low definiteness, and highly affected objects (i.e. genuine patients), and that the natural correlation of subjects is with high animacy and high definiteness, as well as high volitionality (as is generally considered to be the case):

	Subject correlations	*Object correlations*
Animacy	Human/Animate	Inanimate
Definiteness	Definite	Indefinite
Volitionality	Volitional	Affected

We have thus affirmed Comrie's suggestion that the unmarked direct objects are indefinite and inanimate—that is, direct objecthood correlates with low animacy and definiteness. The reason that Hopper and Thompson, who examined both agreement and case marking data, considered highly individuated objects as indicators of Transitivity is that Transitivity—i.e., the morphosyntax that indicates Transitivity—correlates with a verb's having *two* distinct and highly salient arguments, not a surprising fact. Also, this analysis of the natural correlations of direct objects renders direct objects as exactly opposite to subjects, the other core argument position, and this is consistent with Rosch's contention that prototype categories tend to be as contrastive as possible with adjacent prototypes (Rosch 1978:37). In addition, by far the least marked direct objects are those which become incorporated into the verb, and those tend to be low in definiteness and in animacy (cf. Mithun 1984, especially p. 863; Sadock 1985). Finally, there is textual markedness evidence that suggests indefinite direct objects are unmarked: in an English text count, Givón (1979:51-52) found that 50% of the direct objects were indefinite and 82% of the indefinite NPs were direct objects.

In addition to the evidence presented so far, all of which is consistent with this definition, the definition will also account for a number of other typological facts. First, low animate/definite subjects as well as high animate/definite objects are sometimes case marked. This results in "classic" split animacy systems (Silverstein, 1976; the following examples are from Dixon 1979:87):

A	-∅	-ngu	-∅	[nasalization]	[nasalization]
S	-∅	-∅	-∅	-∅	-∅
O	-na	-∅	-a	-a	-∅
	1st & 2nd person pronouns	3rd person pronouns, all nouns	1st & 2nd person pronouns	3rd person pronouns	proper names, common nouns
	Dyirbal		Cashinawa		

The correlation of animacy can also extend to different classes of intransitive subjects in so-called "active" languages. For example, Northern Pomo displays a case marking system split roughly between human and non-human with an unmarked form for human agents and nonhuman patients, where both the agent and patient cases are used on a subclass of intransitives depending on the volitionality of the performer of the action (O'Connor and Caisse 1981:277-279). Thus, the unmarked case is used for human performers of volitional actions and nonhuman performers of nonvolitional actions, which are the natural correlations of animacy and volitionality.

A similar phenomenon is found with the causal opposite of volitionality, namely, affectedness. Direct objects which are less affected by the action have nonzero case marking. In the Russian examples in (11)–(12) (Moravcsik 1978:266), the bread in (12) is less affected by virtue of having only a part of it affected. In the well-known English examples in (13)–(14) (see S. Anderson 1970), the case-marked object is the less affected one.

(11)   Peredajte   mne   xleb
         pass.IMP   1.SG.DAT   bread.(NOM)
         'Pass me the bread.'

(12)   Peredajte   mne   xleb   -a
         pass.IMP   1.SG.DAT   bread   -GEN
         'Pass me some bread.'

(13)   John shot Harry.

(14)   John shot at Harry.

Finally, entities which fall into highly semantically-specific classes such as measure terms and deictic terms for places, directions and times, when used in case roles such as locative, allative, or extent which require equally specific semantic arguments, are not case-marked. This phenomenon is quite widespread, although the examples in (15)–(16) are from English:

(15)   George Washington slept here/in this bed/*this bed.

(16)   John ran five miles/across the field/*the field.

One also occasionally finds the converse phenomenon. In Malay (Dodds 1977:13), the prepositions *kě* 'to' and *dari* 'from' are used for motion to and from NPs which normally denote places. However, if the motion is to or from a person, an additional case marking is thus used for this, non-obvious, argument: the preposition *pada* 'at' must be added, so that the double prepositions *kěpada* and *daripada* are used instead of the single ones.

2 Agreement, Case Marking, and Possession

If the definitions proposed for (person-based) agreement and case marking are indeed correct, then the correlations they predict should be valid in other grammatical domains in which the two relation-indicating strategies are used. There is one other domain in which both person-based agreement and case marking are used, namely, possession, and there is some evidence that the natural correlations do apply in this domain as well. The domain shift from verbal case to possession can be accomplished by mapping animacy and definiteness into themselves, and mapping the case hierarchy into alienability of possession, in which inalienable possession is higher than alienable possession, obeying a hierarchy of: Body parts, Kinship, Part/Whole < Clothing, Tools < Other (cf. Seiler 1983).

There are some examples of properties correlating with cross-reference that control variation in the presence of cross-reference, although they are not numerous. The properties found are alienability, and animacy. For example, in Kanuri, a Nilo-Saharan language, the possessed item usually agrees with the possessor. If the possessor is postposed and the relation is alienable, however, then there is no agreement (Hutchison 1981:198-199; Moravcsik 1974:28 observed that preverbal position of objects correlates with presence of agreement, and postverbal with absence thereof):

(17)   yâ   -nzə́   álì -bè
        mother -3.SG Ali -GEN

        'Ali's mother'

(18)   álì -bè   fə̂r   -nzə́
        Ali -GEN horse -3.SG

        'Ali's horse'

(19)   fə̂r   álì -bè
        horse Ali -GEN

        'Ali's horse'

In a number of Polynesian languages, possession is mediated by a so-called possessive particle or classifier. If the possession relation is inalienable, then a cross-reference marker is used, and if it is alienable, then the cross-reference marker is absent; the examples are from Hawaiian (Lichtenberk 1983b:162):

(20)   k   -o   -na   lima
        ARTICLE -CLASS -3.SG hand

        'his hand'

(21)   nā   kānaka o   ke   ali'i
        ARTICLE people   CLASS ARTICLE chief

        'the people of the chief/the chief's people'

Finally, one finds zero third person singular possessive affixes, for example in Manam (Lichtenberk 1983a:264) and Dakota (Boas and Deloria 1941:127).

With case marking the evidence is more abundant. It is quite common to find case marking absent in inalienable possession relations and present in alienable possession relations; the following examples are from Awa, a Papuan language (McKaughan 1973:22, 32; cf. also Dixon 1980:293):

(22)   adena-   (a)hde
        2.SG-   ear
        'your ear'

(23)   se   -ne   nah
        3.PL -GEN   house
        'their house'

(24)   iya   -ne   nah
        dog   -GEN   house
        'the dog's house'

Finally, English complex nominal constructions provide additional evidence that the same concept of "obviousness" is primary in noun-noun relations. The semantic relations which can be found in complex nominal constructions appear to vary in indefinitely many ways (Downing 1977). However, the relation between the two nouns must be pragmatically obvious, either through conventionalization in the case of grammaticized complex nominals such as *fire engine*, or through contextual factors in the case of innovations such as *grove map*. If neither of these conditions apply, then one must use an [N PP] paraphrase such as *map of memorial groves*, with an explicit case marking relating the two nouns. The pragmatic status rather than the semantics of the relation determines whether or not the complex nominal construction may be used.

3   Conclusion

The combination of typological analysis and a generalized marking theory which includes the notion of *relative markedness* and unifies markedness, hierarchies and prototypes, has allowed us to propose that the presence of (person-based) agreement and case marking each have a pragmatic significance which is universal, although their use varies across languages and is often grammaticalized. The next step is to seek an explanation for the pragmatic significance: why does agreement index the important arguments and case marking indicate the non-obvious relations?

The explanation can be found in the different ways in which agreement and case marking serve the same function, namely, to express a relation between two entities. Case marking is a *relational* strategy: the case marker denotes the relation that holds between the two entities. Agreement is a *deictic* strategy: the agreement marker actually denotes the other entity that is related to the entity denoted by the agreeing constituent. This is a *semantic* characterization of the two strategies, since the definitions are based on the denotations of the morphemes involved. A semantic definition is required because the typological generalizations hold regardless of whether the morpheme involved is a particle, an affix, or even an internal morphophonemic alternation, and whether the morpheme is associated with the head or the dependent.[6] Our hypothesis is, however, that discourse-functional factors (salience and obviousness) determine the *presence* of either strategy in the surface structure; we assume that the semantics and the pragmatics interact closely.

Case marking is a complement of the strategy of simple juxtaposition of the related constituents, in which the hearer must infer the relation that holds between the two. Simple juxtaposition is only possible when the relation between the two terms is obvious enough for the hearer to easily infer it. Otherwise, the relation must be more explicitly represented in the utterance, and case marking is the strategy for doing so. This tends to be with the more peripheral and less prototypical participants. This appears to true no matter where the relation-indicating morpheme is located syntactically. In all of our examples so far, the case marker we have examined is either an affix on the constituent denoting

---

[6] The head- versus dependent-marking distinction figures importantly in a recently published paper by Johanna Nichols (Nichols 1986). Although there is no space to comment extensively on Nichols' arguments, the following remarks support the preference of the deictic/relational distinction over the head-/dependent-marking distinction. First, the head-/dependent-marking distinction cannot incorporate independent elements, which Nichols must describe as "neutral"; yet adpositions clearly fall under the same generalizations as case markers. (These generalizations apply to oblique arguments as well, which Nichols excludes from her analysis.) Second, the head-/dependent-marking distinction divides person-based verbal/possessive agreement and adjectival agreement, conflating the latter with case marking; yet adjectival agreement has much more in common with person-based agreement, both being deictic strategies, than with case marking. Finally, the basic head/dependent distribution of deictic and relational strategies can be explained on independent grounds. Verbs, adjectives, and adpositions are *inherently relational*, that is, they conceptually require additional entities (their "arguments"). Nouns are not inherently relational, except for "relational nouns" such as body parts and kinship terms, and except when they are functioning as predicates (Croft 1984). The relational lexical items must somehow point to the fillers of their "arguments" by indicating properties of the fillers (person, number, gender); hence the use of the deictic strategy on predicates (heads) in general, adjectives (dependents) and typically relational possessive heads. On the other hand, the nonrelational lexical items must indicate what their relation to the head is, since that information is not inherently present in the nonrelational item itself; hence the use of the relational strategy with nominal dependents.

the dependent entity or an adposition governing that entity. A relation-indicating morpheme may also appear on the constituent denoting the head entity, in which case it is called an applicative affix. These appear to be historically related to adpositions, and sometimes the morpheme may be associated with either the head or the dependent constituent, as in Mokilese (Harrison 1976:163-164), Abkhaz (Hewitt 1979:113-114) and Kun-parlang. Even in these cases, however, the morpheme obeys our predictions: for example, it is always an oblique relation such as benefactive, locative or instrumental which requires a nonzero applicative morpheme, not the patient (the normal direct object).

The deictic strategy appears to be a strategy of *person* deixis. As we have noted, the generalizations we have proposed do not appear to apply to agreement within NP's, normally based on *gender*, and only applies to agreement with dependent NP's. In fact, the natural correlations we have observed appear to be valid not only for "true" agreement—in which the deixis is endophoric—but also for agreement systems which appear to be fused pronominals, where the domain of agreement is exactly complementary to the domain of independent NP arguments (S. Anderson 1982:579; Mithun 1986). They even hold for pronominals not morphologically bound to the head, such as for example the object clitics in Hausa. The Hausa object clitics are optional when the direct object is specific, but prohibited when it is not (Cowan and Schuh 1976:135). They are also required with *sani* 'know' and *gani* 'see' when the direct object is a concrete, physical object and prohibited when the direct object is an abstract object or an activity, and can be used with the semantic recipient of a small set of verbs, including the verb *bā* 'give' (Cowan and Schuh 1976:135-137). All of these constraints conform with our hypothesis.

Thus the explanation for the meaning of the deictic strategy as indicating *salient* referents must be sought in the nature of personal pronominal reference. Both pronouns and agreement markers are used to identify and maintain the identity of their referents across the discourse (see DuBois 1980; Lehmann, this volume). There are certainly processing constraints on how much cross-referencing of entities can be handled at once by a person—this is manifested, for example, in the common two-argument agreement constraint discussed above. Therefore, the speaker must make a choice as to which entities will continue to be cross-referenced and which ones will not. Naturally, the most important or salient entities will continue to be cross-referenced, and those tend to be the most animate ones, the most definite ones, and the ones most central to the events being reported.

Finally, the deictic and relational strategies must be situated in the context of possible strategies for expressing relationship between entities in discourse. As we have already pointed out, the person-based strategy whose behavior we have examined is only one of at least two types of deictic strategies, and the relational strategy is the complement of the strategy of simple juxtaposition of constituents, the latter being the "null" relational strategy. The deictic and relational strategies exhaust the morphological possibilities for expressing a relation between two entities, since the morpheme involved must denote either the relation itself or one of the elements. The only other possible strategy for relating entities is the syntactic one of word order. Word order appears to be independent of the other strategies, which are defined in terms of morphemes (case vs. agreement) and morpheme denotations, and it appears to have its own organizing principles, such as "attention flow" (DeLancey 1981) or "newsworthiness" (Mithun, to appear).

In closing, we may point out that the deictic-relational distinction in morphosyntactic strategies for indicating grammatical relations is grammatically significant at all levels of syntactic structure, not just the clausal level that we have described here in detail. At the phrasal level we find the adnominal modification discussed in Section 3, and also the deictic but gender-based agreement, and the (probably relational) linking particles of Persian and Austronesian. Lichtenberk (1983b) argues for a distinction between the deictic numeral classifiers and the relational possessive classifiers. Finally, at the sentential level we find connectives and subordinators which are both deictic and relational in historical origin and, we expect, in grammatical behavior.

References

Anderson, A. 1973. *Rules of the Aztec Language.* Salt Lake City: University of Utah Press.

Anderson, S. R. 1970. A little light on the role of deep structure in semantic interpretation. NSF Report No. 26, II.1–II.13. Cambridge, Mass.: Harvard University.

Anderson, S. R. 1982. Where's morphology? *Linguistic Inquiry* 13:571–612.

Arnott, D. W. 1970. *The Nominal and Verbal Systems of Fula.* Cambridge, England: Cambridge University Press.

Ashton, E. O. 1944. *Swahili Grammar.* London: Longman.

Boas, F. and E. Deloria. *Dakota Grammar.* (Memoirs of the National Academy of Sciences, Vol. 23, 2d memoir.) Washington: U.S. Government Printing Office.

Clark, H. D. B. and M. Hamamura. 1981. *Colloquial Japanese.* London: Routledge and Kegan Paul.

Comrie, B. 1976. The syntax of causative constructions: cross-linguistic similarities and differences. In M. Shibatani (Ed), *The Syntax of*

Causative Constructions. (Syntax and Semantics, Vol. 6.) New York: Academic Press.

Comrie, B. 1979. Definite and animate direct objects: a natural class. *Linguistica Silesiana* 3:13–21.

Comrie, B. 1980. Agreement, animacy and voice. In G. Brettschneider and C. Lehmann (Eds), *Wege zur Universalienforschung*, 229–234. Tübingen: Gunter Narr.

Comrie, B. 1981. *The Languages of the Soviet Union.* Cambridge, England: Cambridge University Press.

Cowan, J. R. and R. G. Schuh. 1976. *Spoken Hausa.* Ithaca: Spoken Language Services.

Croft, W. 1983. Grammatical relations vs. thematic roles as universals. *Papers from the Nineteenth Regional Meeting of the Chicago Linguistic Society,* 76–94.

Croft, W. 1984. Semantic and pragmatic correlates to syntactic categories. *Papers from the Parasession on Lexical Semantics, Twentieth Regional Meeting of the Chicago Linguistic Society,* 53–71.

DeLancey, S. 1981. An interpretation of split ergativity and related patterns. *Language* 57:626–657.

Dixon, R. M. W. 1972. *The Dyirbal Language of North Queensland.* Cambridge, England: Cambridge University Press.

Dixon, R. M. W. 1979. Ergativity. *Language* 55:59–138.

Dixon, R. M. W. 1980. *The Languages of Australia.* Cambridge, England: Cambridge University Press.

Dodds, R. W. 1977. *Teach Yourself Malay.* Sevenoaks, Kent: Hodder and Stoughton.

Downing, P. 1977. On the creation and use of English compound nominals. *Language* 53:810–842.

Dryer, M. S. 1983. Indirect objects in Kinyarwanda revisited. In D. Perlmutter (Ed), *Studies in Relational Grammar* 1, 129–140. Chicago: The University of Chicago Press.

DuBois, J. 1980. Beyond definiteness: the trace of identity in discourse. In W. Chafe (Ed), *The Pear Stories: Cognitive, Cultural, and Linguistic Aspects of Narrative Production.* Norwood, N. J.: Ablex.

Givón, T. 1976. Topic, pronoun and grammatical agreement. In C. Li (Ed), *Subject and Topic,* 149–188. New York: Academic Press.

Givón, T. 1979. *On Understanding Grammar.* New York: Academic Press.

Greenberg, J. H. 1966. *Language Universals, With Special Reference to Feature Hierarchies.* (Janua Linguarum Series Minor, 59.) The Hague: Mouton.

Greenberg, J. H. 1978. How does a language acquire gender markers? In J. H. Greenberg (Ed), *Universals of Human Language* 3, 47–82. Stanford: Stanford University Press.

Harrison, S. P. 1976. *Mokilese Reference Grammar.* Honolulu: University Press of Hawaii.

Hewitt, B. G. 1979. *Abkhaz.* (Lingua Descriptive Series, 2.) Amsterdam: North Holland.

Hopper, P. and S. Thompson 1980. Transitivity in grammar and discourse. *Language* 56:251–299.

Hutchison, J. P. 1981. *The Kanuri Language.* Madison: African Studies Program.

Jensen, J. T. 1977. *Yapese Reference Grammar.* Honolulu: University Press of Hawaii.

Keenan, E. and B. Comrie 1977. Noun phrase accessibility and universal grammar. *Linguistic Inquiry* 8:63–99.

Kimenyi, A. 1978. *A Relational Grammar of Kinyarwanda.* (University of California Publications in Linguistics, Vol. 91.) Berkeley: University of California Press.

Ladziŋa, T. B. 1966. *Teach Yourself Latvian.* London: English Universities Press.

Lewis, G. L. 1967. *Turkish Grammar.* Oxford: Oxford University Press.

Lichtenberk, F. 1983a. *A Grammar of Manam.* (Oceanic Linguistics Special Publication No. 18.) Honolulu: University Press of Hawaii.

Lichtenberk, F. 1983b. Relational classifiers. *Lingua* 60:147–176.

Mace, J. 1962. *Teach Yourself Persian.* London: English Universities Press.

Matisoff, J. 1973. *The Grammar of Lahu.* (University of California Publications in Linguistics, Vol. 75.) Berkeley: University of California Press.

McKaughan, H. (Ed) 1973. *The Languages of the Eastern Family of the East New Guinea Highlands Stock.* Seattle: University of Washington Press.

Miller, W. R. 1965. *Acoma Grammar and Texts.* (University of California Publications in Linguistics, Vol. 40.) Berkeley: University of California Press.

Mithun, M. 1984. The evolution of noun incorporation. *Language* 60:847–894.

Mithun, M. 1986. When zero isn't there. Paper presented at the 12th Annual Meeting of the Berkeley Linguistics Society.

Mithun, M. To appear. Is basic word order universal? In R. Tomlin (Ed), *Discourse Relations and Cognitive Units.*

Moravcsik, E. 1974. Object-verb agreement. *Working Papers in Language Universals* 15:25–40. Stanford: Department of Linguistics, Stanford University.

Moravcsik, E. 1978. On the case marking of objects. In J. H. Greenberg (Ed), *Universals of Human Language* 4, 249–290. Stanford: Stanford University Press.

Nichols, J. 1986. Head-marking and dependent-marking grammar. *Language* 62:56–119.

O'Connor, C. and M. Caisse. 1981. Aspects of role-dominance in Northern Pomo. *Papers from the Seventeenth Regional Meeting of the Chicago Linguistic Society*, 277–285.

Parker, G. 1969. *Ayacucho Quechua Grammar and Dictionary.* (Janua Linguarum Series Practica, 82.) The Hague: Mouton.

Perrott, D. V. 1972. *Teach Yourself Swahili.* New York: David McKay Company, Inc.

Qafiseh, H. 1977. *A Short Reference Grammar of Gulf Arabic.* Tucson: University of Arizona Press.

Rosch, E. 1978. Principles of categorization. In E. Rosch and B. Lloyd (Eds), *Cognition and Categorization*, 27–48. Hillsdale, N. J.: Lawrence Erlbaum Associates.

Sadock, J. M. 1985. The Southern Tiwa incorporability hierarchy. *International Journal of American Linguistics* 51:568–572.

Seiler, H. 1983. *Possession as an Operational Dimension of Language.* Tübingen: Gunter Narr.

Shackle, C. 1972. *Teach Yourself Punjabi.* London: English Universities Press.

Silverstein, M. 1976. Hierarchy of features and ergativity. In R. M. W. Dixon (Ed), *Grammatical Categories in Australian Languages*, 112–171. Canberra: Australian Institute of Aboriginal Studies.

Thomas, D. D. 1971. *Chrau Grammar.* (Oceanic Linguistics Special Publication No. 7.) Honolulu: University Press of Hawaii.

Whitney, A. 1944. *Colloquial Hungarian.* London: Routledge and Kegan Paul.

8 Case Agreement in Lithuanian

ALAN TIMBERLAKE

I PRESENT HERE a partial description and analysis of case agreement of predicate complements in Lithuanian within one version of categorial grammar. Predicate complements are noun phrases, adjective phrases, and (active or passive) participial phrases used to predicate of an argument expression. Some examples of predicate complements are given in the English translations of possible Lithuanian sentences in (1), where predicate complements are underlined and arguments which they are predicated of are overlined.

The data reported here is taken from my reading of texts, work with native speakers (Mikolas Drunga, Jūratė Izokaitytė, Tomas Venclova, and Livija Lipaitė), and published studies (Nichols 1981, Jablonskis 1957). Jablonskis 1957, which is organized traditionally according to the criterion of the use of individual cases, contains virtually all the example types reported here. The analysis given here has evolved considerably from the initial presentation at the conference, thanks in part to comments and suggestions from Steve Anderson, Joan Bresnan, Sandra Chung, David Dowty, Ron Kaplan, Ed Keenan, Bill Ladusaw, and Sue Steele. As I understand it, the crucial feature of the analysis here—the distinction between the morphological features expressed by a predicate (or functor generally) and those it assigns to its complements—recapitulates the distinction between head and subcategorization features in Pollard (1984).

(1) a. $\overline{\text{John}}$ was happy/a hero.   [one-place predicate]

    b. We made $\overline{\text{John}}$ happy/a hero.   [two-place predicate]

    c. $\overline{\text{John}}$ seems (being) happy/a hero.   [raising to subject]

    d. We thought $\overline{\text{John}}$ (being) guilty/a hero   [raising to object]

    e. It is necessary (for $\overline{\text{one}}$) to/patient.   [inversion control]

    f. $\overline{\text{I}}$ want to be patient.   [subject control]

    g. He ordered $\overline{\text{me}}$ to be diligent.   [indirect object control]

    h. This made $\overline{\text{me}}$ be more careful.   [direct object control]

    i. ... $\overline{\text{his}}$ desire to be diligent.   [possessor control]

    j. By $\overline{\text{John}}$ was being happy.   [passive, one-place predicate]

    k. $\overline{\text{John}}$ was found happy.   [passive, two-place predicate]

Case agreement $(=CAgr)$ refers to the fact that the predicate complement may bear a surface morphological case identical to the case borne by the argument it is predicated of. $CAgr$ is accompanied by agreement in gender and number $(=GNAgr)$ in adjectives and participles, but not in nouns, which have inherent gender and number. $CAgr$ in Lithuanian is basically similar to $CAgr$ in Sanskrit, Ancient Greek, and Icelandic, but has some unique properties that offer special interest.

As the work of Andrews (1971, 1982a, 1982b) brings out, $CAgr$ presents two analytic challenges. The argument which the predicate complement is predicated of (and with which it shares case) is not necessarily the surface subject of the same clause that contains the predicate complement. The first problem, then, is to state the mechanism whereby the predicate complement and its argument acquire the same case. The second challenge derives from the fact that under some conditions (different in different languages) $CAgr$ evidently becomes opaque, in the sense that some fixed case is assigned to the predicate complement instead of agreeing case.

The proposal here, in brief, is that predicate complements receive case directly from their governing predicates, in the same way that arguments are assigned case by predicates. Although this is not the place to undertake a systematic comparison of different approaches to $CAgr$ (I acknowledge my debt to Andrews 1971, 1982a, 1982b in particular), the view that $CAgr$ is case assignment from the predicate contrasts with the more prevalent view that the mechanism of $CAgr$ mentions directly both the predicate complement and the argument it is predicated of.

There are in fact a few pieces of evidence in Lithuanian that argue in favor of $CAgr$ by case assignment from the predicate, but I would like to emphasize that the goal here is not to determine which theory has built the better casetrap, but to investigate the consequences for categorial grammar of describing this phenomenon. Among the consequences is that, if morphological features are stated as categories that obey functional application, predicates must carry not only their own morphological features, but also the features they impose on arguments and predicate complements.

1 Preliminaries

I adopt here the version of categorial grammar developed in such studies as Keenan 1980, 1982 and Keenan and Timberlake 1985a, 1985b, with some further idiosyncrasies. To emphasize the nondirectional character of this approach, I will write a (single) vertical line rather than a slanted line in category statements. Argument will be a cover term for the range of argument expressions N, S, $(S \mid N)$, $\ldots$ (written here for notational convenience without overlining, contrary to Keenan 1982), predicate complement, the cover term for the range of predicate complements N, $(N \mid N)$, $(S \mid N)$, $\ldots$, and complement, the cover term for both arguments and predicate complements. Consistent with the observation (Keenan 1980, Dowty 1982, Keenan and Timberlake 1985a) that many phenomena generalize across predicates with different numbers of arguments, I will refer to predicates with one, two, and eventually n (n an integer) arguments as one-place, two-place, and n-place predicates. This can be represented notationally here as $(S \mid \ldots) \mid A_n$, which is in turn equivalent to the simpler $S \mid \ldots \mid A_n$.

The appropriate categorial representation of predicate complements is in fact far from obvious. The stumbling block is that some full noun phrases can be used as predicate complements. As a result, a predicate that takes a subject argument and a nominal predicate complement (such as *become* in *I became a priest*) would have the category $S \mid N \mid N$, categorially indistinguishable from a predicate that takes a subject argument and object argument (such as *seek* in *I sought a priest*). Yet arguments and predicate arguments can be shown to be distinct semantically, syntactically, and morphologically. The variety of techniques that might be invoked to distinguish arguments from predicate complements reduce to two: one can encode the special status of a predicate complement in the category of the predicate complement itself or in the predicate (the latter suggested in Keenan and Timberlake 1985b). Here I will adopt a compromise of convenience and introduce predicate complements by a distinct metaoperator, notationally a double vertical line, which, however obeys functional application in the usual way. Thus, *become* includes the category $S \mid N \parallel N$, which is to say that is a predicate that needs a nominal predicate complement to be a one-place predicate. I abstain also from attempting to characterize the semantics of predicate complements other than to reassert the intuition that a predicate complement predicates a property of some argument expression (the approach of Partee 1985 seems like a promising possibility).

To deal with morphology, I will suggest (somewhat modifying the statement of rules as n-tuples in Montague 1974, Dowty 1982) that an expression is an ordered pair consisting of a syntactic category and a morphological category, concatenated notationally by a semicolon. (I omit the further statement in the n-tuple of linearization, the possibilities for which are nefarious in a "free word order" language like Lithuanian.) We can say that a predicate assigns case α to an argument or predicate complement if the predicate has the form in (2a) or (2b), respectively,

(2) a. $\langle S \,|\, \ldots \,|\, A; \; x \,|\, \ldots \,|\, \alpha C \rangle$

b. $\langle S \,|\, \ldots \,\|\, \mathrm{PC}; \; x \,|\, \ldots \,\|\, \alpha C \rangle$

where α is a variable ranging over the set of available cases and x is a variable for the morphological features manifested on the predicate itself. For example, *pažinoti* 'get to know' of category $\langle S \,|\, N \,|\, N; x \,|\, \mathrm{NOM} \,|\, \mathrm{ACC} \rangle$ can combine with an accusative noun *klerikǎ* 'priest' of category $\langle N; \mathrm{ACC} \rangle$ to give a one-place predicate [*pažinoti klerikǎ*] 'get to know a/the priest' of category $\langle S \,|\, N; x \,|\, \mathrm{NOM} \rangle$, and *ieškoti* 'seek' of category $\langle S \,|\, N \,|\, N; x \,|\, \mathrm{NOM} \,|\, \mathrm{GEN} \rangle$ can combine with genitive *kleriko* of category $\langle N; \mathrm{gen} \rangle$ to give a one-place predicate [*ieškoti kleriko*] 'seek a/the priest' of category $\langle S \,|\, N; x \,|\, \mathrm{NOM} \rangle$, and so on.

Person/number agreement in predicates can be stated by writing the relevant features at the head of the predicate category *and* by requiring an argument with the correct features to show up in a specified (namely, first) argument position. For example, 'seek' in *aš ieškojau kleriko* 'I sought a/the priest' will include the category

$$\langle S \,|\, N \,|\, N; \; 1.\mathrm{SG} \,|\, \mathrm{NOM.1.SG} \,|\, \mathrm{GEN.MASC.SG} \rangle.$$

In effect, agreement is stated on this view as lexical constraints on the (sub)categories of functor categories. The constraint for finite predicates would allow only entries that meet the condition in (3):

(3) $\langle S \,|\, N; \; \mathrm{fin}.\alpha PN \,|\, \mathrm{NOM}.\beta PN \rangle \in \mathrm{CAT}_{\mathrm{Lithuanian}}$ iff $\beta = \alpha$

This approach suffers from the familiar problems posed by agreement with missing arguments, agreement with internally complex arguments (quantified, conjoined, and comitative noun phrases), and agreement involving feature overlap but not feature identity, but a modification of this approach along the lines of Bach 1983 might mitigate some of these problems.

2 Predicate Complements in Lithuanian

Some notes on Lithuanian morphosyntax. A verb can be a finite form (and inflect for tense, mood, person, and number), infinitive (with no further inflection), or participle (with adjectival morphosyntax). Nouns belong to one of two genders, masculine or feminine, and vary for singular and plural; neuter gender exists as a category for adjectival and participial predicate complements in subjectless sentences and in agreement with a few genderless pronouns (*tai* 'that,' *kas* 'what'). Adjectives and participles agree in gender and number both as attributive modifiers and as predicate complements. Nominal parts of speech (nouns, adjectives, participles) occur in one of six (productive) cases. Of these, four occur as cases of arguments which, in one or another context, can have predicate complements predicated of them. The other two, locative and instrumental, are inert in the sense that there are no contexts in which arguments in these cases could have predicate complements predicated of them. Importantly, though, the instrumental is the non-agreeing case for predicate complements in Lithuanian, and competes generally with the appropriate agreeing case under semantic conditions that are difficult to define generally (see Nichols 1981). As a descriptive device I mark cases in examples by a hierarchy of [no mark]/†/?/*, which can be taken as a statement of the relative difficulty of assigning a meaningful interpretation to the case in a given context.

We can construct a basic typology of predicate complements as either *free* or *governed* (simplifying the typology of Nichols 1981), based on two criteria: free predicate complements can in principle be predicated of more than one argument of a given predicate, while governed predicate complements are predicated of a unique argument; and governed predicate complements are under the scope of the aspectual semantics of their governing predicate, while free predicate complements are not. Free predicate complements, then, are quite likely modifiers (adjuncts) of their predicates rather than complements, and after their illustration in (4) (taken from Nichols 1981) will be ignored in the subsequent discussion:

(4) a. Aš   jį   pažinojau dar   jaunas/?jaunu // vaikas/vaiku
          NOM   NOM   INS   NOM   INS
          I   him know   even young   child

          'I got to know him (when I was) young/a child.'

     b. Aš jį   jauną/ ?jaunu // vaiką/vaiku pažinojau.
             ACC ACC   INS   ACC   INS
         I   him young   child   know

         'I got to know him (when he was) young/a child.'

Governed predicate complements can be typologized into three sub-types. Generally speaking, each subtype is represented both by one-place predicates (such that the predicate complement is predicated of the subject argument) and by two-place predicates (such that the predicate complement is predicated of the object argument). Strongly governed predicate complements are (virtually) obligatory and include:

(5) a. Jis   buvo jaunas/*jaunu // klerikas/kleriku
        NOM   NOM   INS   NOM   INS
        he   be   young   priest

        'He was young/a priest.'

    b. Radau visį kambarį užverstą/*uzverstu knygomis.
                     ACC   ACC   INS
        find   all   room   filled   books

        'I found the room filled with books.'

    c. Jis   tapo   †turtingas/turtingu // *klerikas/kleriku
        NOM   NOM   INS   NOM   INS
        he   became rich   priest

        'He became rich/a priest.'

    d. Karas padarė jį   †neturtingą/neturtingu //
                             ACC   ACC   INS
        war   make   him   poor
        *luošą/   luošu.
        ACC   INS
        invalid

        'The war made him poor/an invalid.'

Raising predicate complements, probably a subcase of strongly governed predicate complements, allow optionally an overt copula with nominal or adjectival predicate complement:

(6) a. Jis   pasirodė (esąs)   laimingas/?laimingu //
        NOM   PRT.NOM NOM   INS
        he   seem   be   happy
        didvyris/didvriu.
        NOM   INS
        hero

        'He seemed/turned out (being) happy/a hero.'

b. Visi įtarė   jį   (†esantį /   esant)   kaltą/ kaltu //
                ACC   PRT.ACC Ø.PRT   ACC   INS
    all   suspect   him   be   guilty

*kleriką/ kleriku.
ACC   INS
priest

'Everyone suspected him of being guilty/a priest.'

Weakly governed predicate complements, which are not obligatory with a predicate, occur most naturally with verbs of motion and position:

(7) a. Jis   nuvažiavo   laimingas/*laimingu   //   *didvyris/didvyriu.
      NOM   NOM   INS   NOM   INS
      he   depart   happy   hero

'He left happy/a hero.'

b. Atnešė   givą/ ?givu   //   *trojėjų/trofėjumi   žvėrelį   karaliui.
           ACC   INS   ACC   INS   ACC
    carry   alive   trophy   beast   prince

'They took the animal to the prince alive/(as) a trophy.'

Before discussing the mechanism for *CAgr,* let me first dispose of the instrumental. As the examples above show, the distribution of agreeing case vs. instrumental is rather complex. What the examples do not show clearly is that when both cases are possible, they are associated with different semantics. The semantic parameters seem to reduce to two. First, agreeing case is interpreted as a pure property, while instrumental is interpreted as an attributive (in the sense of Donnellan 1966) description of an individual. For example, in (5a), the nominative of the noun suggests that the subject was priestly in character, the instrumental that the subject functioned as a priest. This is presumably the reason why nominal predicate complements are in general more likely than adjectival or participial predicate complements to occur in the instrumental. Second, agreeing case indicates a property that is temporally, aspectually, or modally unrestricted, the instrumental a property that is in some respect restricted. For example, the nominative is more natural with 'be' and 'find' in (5a, b), given that they need not involve a change of state, than with 'become' and 'make' in (5c, d), given that they do involve a change of state. What this suggests is that we should systematically allow both agreeing case and instrumental in all contexts, and entrust the rules of semantic interpretation with the task of assigning different interpretations to the two cases. The two interpretations might be more or less plausible in different contexts; in the limiting case, when only one of the two cases is a realistic option, this would mean assigning a nonsensical interpretation to one of the cases.

To describe $CAgr$ in these examples, we recall that the predicate complement is interpreted as predicating of the first (subject) argument of one-place predicates and of the second (object) argument of two-place predicates. Accordingly, we assign these predicates the categories $\langle S \mid N \parallel PC \rangle$ and $\langle S \mid N \mid N \parallel PC \rangle$, respectively. Correspondingly, the predicate complement shares case with the first argument of one-place and with the second argument of two-place predicates. To account for this, by lexical constraint we allow only predicates that assign either the same case to a predicate complement as they assign to the next argument or instrumental. Since a nominal predicate complement does not show $GNAgr$, we need only (8a) as a lexical constraint on predicates taking nominal predicate complements:

(8) a. $\langle S \mid \ldots \mid N \parallel N; \, x \mid \ldots \mid \alpha C \parallel \beta C \rangle \in \mathrm{CAT}_{\mathrm{Lithuanian}}$ iff

$\beta = \alpha$ or $\beta =$ instrumental

In adjectival predicate complements, which do show gender/number argument, we additionally require identity of gender/number between predicate complement and argument. Because an adjective has the category $N \mid N$, we write two sets of features inside an adjectival predicate complement and state separate conditions for each set, as in (8b):

(8) b. $\langle S \mid \ldots \mid N \parallel (N \mid N); \, x \mid \ldots \mid \alpha C.\delta GN \parallel (\gamma C. \, \zeta GN \mid \beta C.\varepsilon GN) \rangle$

$\in \mathrm{CAT}_{\mathrm{Lithuanian}}$ iff

i) $\beta = \alpha$ and $\varepsilon = \delta$

and ii) $\gamma = \alpha$ or $\gamma =$ instrumental and $\zeta = \delta$

Similarly, for participial predicate complements we normally require identity of case/gender/number with the next argument. For example, the one-place predicate *pasirodyti* 'seem, turn out' of (6a) would have as one subcategory

$\langle S \mid N \parallel (S \mid N); \, x \mid \mathrm{NOM}.\delta GN \parallel (\mathrm{PRT.NOM}.\delta GN \mid \mathrm{NOM}.\delta GN) \rangle$

where the first set of features are those manifested on the participle itself and the second are those assigned to its subject argument position. Assigning two sets of features naturally describes sentences where the participle is a predicate that governs a further predicate complement, as is the case in (6a). The features of the subject argument position are automatically imposed on the predicate complement; for example, *esąs* in (6a) would have the expansion

$\langle S \mid N \parallel PC; \, \mathrm{PRT.NOM}.\delta GN \mid \mathrm{NOM}.\delta GN \parallel \mathrm{NOM}.\delta GN \rangle.$

Two-place predicates present an interesting complication with respect to participial predicate complements. As shown in (6b) above, there are two options: the participle can take the expected accusative, with

GNAgr maintained, or it can preferably be a special form that is uninflected for case/gender/number (glossed here as 'PRT.ϕC.ϕGN'). At the same time, however, *CAgr* and *GNAgr* are maintained on an adjectival predicate complement within the participial phrase. This, then, *requires* that the case/gender/number features associated with the participle be distinguished from the features assigned to the participle's subject argument position. For example, the two-place *įtarti* 'suspect' will have as one subcategory

$$\langle S \mid N \mid N \| (S \mid N); x \mid y \mid \text{ACC.}\delta GN \| (\text{PRT.}\phi C.\phi GN \mid \text{ACC.}\delta GN)\rangle$$

where the correct features are imposed directly on the subject argument position, bypassing the head position; from the subject position the features will be imposed on a further predicate complement, by (8a) or (8b).

The lexical constraint on participles is summarized in (8c). Here (8c.i) guarantees that the correct case/gender/number features are assumed by the subject argument; (8c.ii) allows *C.GNAgr* in the participle, but (8c.ii') specifically allows the uninflected form if the predicate assigns a case other than nominative to the relevant argument.

(8) c. $\langle S \mid \ldots \mid N \| (S \mid N); x \mid \ldots \mid \alpha C.\delta GN \| (\gamma C.\zeta GN \mid \beta C.\varepsilon GN)\rangle$

$$\in \text{CAT}_{\text{Lithuanian}} \text{ iff}$$

i) $\beta = \alpha$ and $\varepsilon = \delta$

and ii) $\gamma = \alpha$ and $\zeta = \delta$

or ii') $\alpha \neq$ nominative and $\gamma = \phi$, $\zeta = \phi$

Recursive expansions that obey the subparts of (8) will produce sentences with multiple and superficially 'long-distance' agreement of the type illustrated in (9):

(9)   Jis   pasirodė dėjęsis esąs   politinis pabėgėlis.

         NOM   NOM   NOM   NOM

         he   turn out feign   be   political refugee

         'He turned out to have feigned being a political refugee'

3 Case Agreement in Infinitive Complements.

As a test of the analysis developed here, we can consider *CAgr* in infinitival complement constructions that contain a predicate complement. As all current syntactic theories express in one form or another, these are constructions in which a privileged argument of the governing predicate is in some informal sense understood as (corresponding to) the subject of the infinitive; correspondingly, in such constructions in Lithuanian there is the possibility of *CAgr* between the "controller" argument of the governing predicate and a predicate complement in the infinitival

complement. The strategy here will be to encode the morphological
features that correspond to those of the "controller" in the subject argument position of the infinitive, from where they will be communicated
to the predicate complement.

Descriptively we can distinguish five types of infinitive complement
constructions in Lithuanian on the basis of the argument relations of
the matrix governing predicate. As the examples below will show, the
relative naturalness of agreeing case vs. instrumental varies with each
type; since, however, the instrumental is close to obligatory for nominal predicate complements in all types, the examples are limited to
adjectives.

(i) With a dative controller and inversion predicate (in the sense of
Perlmutter 1984), agreeing case is normal:

(10) a.   Jai   reikia   būti   pasiruošusiai/?pasiruošusia.
          DAT   DAT   INS
          her   must   be   prepared

          'It is necessary for her to be prepared.'

     b.   Mūsų   darbe   reikia   būti   kantriam/?kantriu.
                                  DAT   INS
          our   work   must   be   patient

          'In our work it is necessary (for one) to be patient.'

(ii) With a nominative controller and semantically weak (auxiliary) predicate, agreeing case is normal:

(11)   Jis   norėjo   būti   pasiruošęs/?pasiruošusiu.
       NOM   NOM   INS
       he   want   be   prepared

       'He wants to be prepared.'

(iii) With a nominative controller and a semantically rich governing predicate, instrumental is slightly preferred to agreeing case:

(12) a.   Jis   prižadėjo   būti   †pasiruošęs/pasiruošusiu.
          NOM   NOM   INS
          he   promise   be   prepared

          'He promised to be prepared.'

     b.   Ji   nusprendė   būti   †kantri/kantria.
          NOM   NOM   INS
          she   decide   be   patient

          'She resolved to be patient.'

(iv) With a dative indirect object controller, instrumental is slightly preferred to agreeing case:

(13) a. Ji   pataré jam   būti †pasiruošusiam/pasiruošusiu.
         DAT   DAT   INS
         she advise him be   prepared
         'She advised him to be prepared.'

   b. Zakristijonas man liepé būti †stropesniam/stropesniu.
       DAT   DAT   INS
       deacon   me tell be   more diligent
       'The deacon ordered me to be more diligent.'

(v) Finally, with an accusative controller, agreeing case is virtually impossible:

(14) a. Tai dar labiau mane verté būti *atsargį/atsargiu.
                         ACC   ACC   INS
         this still more me   make be   careful
         'This even more made me be careful.'

   b. Vadžiomis tévas moké jį   iš pat mažystés būti
                              ACC
       whips   father teach him from childhood be

       *paklusnų/paklusniu.
       ACC   INS
       obedient
       'From his early childhood his father taught him with whips to be obedient.'

Curiously, though, agreeing case becomes normal if the controller is put in the genitive under negation of the governing predicate, a fact which suggests the difference between agreeing case and instrumental is not due to any structural difference inside the infinitive complement (contrary to Andrews 1982b).

(15)   Negali jo   priversti būti pasiruošusio/pasiruošusiu.
                 GEN   GEN   INS
         not-able him force   be   prepared
         'You can't force him to be prepared.'

   More generally, the complexity of the distribution of agreeing case and instrumental suggests that both cases should be available in principle in all constructions, with the details of preference to be sorted out by the rules of interpretation.

Following various current approaches, we can describe infinitive complements as one-place predicates used as arguments of their governing
predicates. Following Bach (1979) in particular, we can assume that
governing predicates are constructed so that the controller is the next
higher argument after the infinitive complement. This assumption works
well enough for both classes of nominative control ((ii, iii)) and for accusative object control ((v)). It is conceivable for control by an inversion
dative ((i)), although in general the special syntax and semantics of inversion predicates has not been described (as far as I know) in categorial
terms. The assumption is problematic only for control by a dative indirect object ((iv)), where one might rather be tempted to assume that
the infinitive complement is the second argument and the dative the
third argument (parallel to ordinary ditransitives like *duoti* 'give'). For
the purposes of the discussion here, however, all that is necessary is
that it be possible to identify a privileged 'controller' argument for each
governing predicate.

With this assumption in hand, to describe $CAgr$ in infinitives we need
only ensure, by lexical constraint, that the governing predicate assigns
the same case (and gender/number) to the privileged 'controller' argument and to the subject argument position of its infinitival complement.
A predicate taking an infinitive complement will then be subject to (16),
where the complement is specified morphologically as an infinitive:

(16) $\langle S\,|\ldots|\,N\,|\,(S\,|\,N);\,x\,|\ldots|\,\alpha C.\gamma GN\,|\,(\text{INF}\,|\,\beta C.\delta GN)\rangle$

$\in \text{CAT}_{\text{Lithuanian}}$ iff

$\beta = \alpha$ and $\delta = \gamma$

Like any other predicate, this infinitive can expand to include a predicate complement, and (8) will impose either the inherited case or instrumental on that predicate complement, as well as the appropriate
gender/number on an adjectival predicate complement. Recursive expansions that obey (8) and (16) will produce structures like those in
(17) with multiple and "long-distance" case agreement:

(17) a.   Jis   pradėjo jaustis esąs   nepaprastas žmogus.
          NOM   INF   PRT.NOM   NOM

          he   begin   feel   be   unusual   person

     'He began to feel that he was an unusual person.'

     b.   Jis   jautėsi pradedąs būti nepaprastas žmogus.
          NOM   PRT.NOM INF   NOM

          he   feel   begin   be   unusual   person

     'He felt (he was) beginning to be an unusual person.'

As a variation on this theme, we can look briefly at infinitival complements of head nouns like *teisė* 'right (to),' *noras* 'desire (to).' Observe
first that nominalizations of predicates governing predicate complements
take a genitive possessor (corresponding to the subject argument of the
finite predicate) and a genitive predicate complement, with the gen-
der/number of the possessor if the predicate complement is an adjective:

(18) a.   ... jo   vėlyvo   buvimas
          GEN GEN
          his   late   being
          '... his being late'

   b.   ... jų   pasirodymas didvyrių
          GEN   GEN
          their seeming   heroes
          '... their seeming (to be) heroes'

   c.   ... jo   apsimėtimas negyvo
          GEN   GEN
          his   pretending   dead
          '... his pretending (to be) dead'

But when the predicate complement is the complement of an infinitive
that is dependent on the head noun, a dative appears instead of the
expected genitive:

(19) a.   ... jo   prižadėjimas toliau   nebebūti tokiam žioplam
          GEN   DAT
          his   promise   further not-be   so   inattentive
          '... his promise not to be so inattentive anymore'

   b.   Moterys apgina savo teisę nebūti suskirstomoms į
                           GEN   DAT
          women   defend own right not-be divided   into

          ištekėjusias ir   netekėjusias.
          married   and unmarried

          'Women are defending their right not to be divided into those
          who are married and those who are not married.'

The predicate complement appears in the dative here even though the
genitive possessor of the head noun is interpreted as the subject of the

infinitive, and hence as the argument which the predicate complement is predicated of; further, an adjectival predicate complement carries the gender/number features of the possessor (MASC.SG. in (19a), FEM.PL. in (19b)).

To describe this we must specifically allow an infinitive that is dependent on a head noun to assign dative case to a predicate complement. This it can do if its subject argument position carries dative case along with the gender/number of the possessor. Leaving aside some details of the internal structure of noun phrases, we can minimally treat the possessor as the first argument of the head noun and the infinitive as the second argument, and assign the head noun the category

$$\langle N \mid N \mid (S \mid N); \; x \mid \text{GEN}.\alpha GN \mid (\text{INF} \mid \text{DAT}.\alpha GN)\rangle.$$

The infinitive can then expand to a predicate complement and, by (8), assign dative case (and the gender/number of the possessor) to this predicate complement.

To put this example in perspective, we have here a rare instance of a discrepancy in case between the predicate complement and the argument it is predicated of. This discrepancy can be described naturally if the mechanism of *CAgr* is accomplished in the complement categorizations within the predicate.

4 Passive

Passives of two-place predicates with predicate complements, as in (20), present some technical problems that derive from the fact that the passive participle itself is a predicate complement complement of a copula and undergoes *CAgr* and *GNAgr*.

(20)   Jis   buvo   rastas   negyvas
    NOM   PRT.NOM NOM
    he   be   found   dead

'He was found dead.'

In the interests of space, I pass over these real but not insurmountable problems to the more interesting fact that Lithuanian regularly forms passives of one-place predicates with predicate complements, including the copula:

(21) a.   Jo   būta   sumanaus.
       GEN.MASC.SG NOM.NEUT.SG GEN.MASC.SG
       him   been   clever

'He was clever.'

b. Tų nutikimų,   pasirodo,   būta   vienas už
    GEN.MASC.PL.   NOM.NEUT.SG
    adventures   apparently been   one   after

    kitą   keistesnių.
    GEN.MASC.PL
    other   stranger

    'Apparently these adventures were each stranger than the
    last.'

c. Jo   pasirodyta   visai   teisingo.
    GEN.MASC.SG NOM.NEUT.SG   GEN.MASC.SG
    him   seemed   rather just

    'He seemed entirely just.'

d. Jo   ilgai išdriko   gulėta
    GEN.MASC.SG   GEN.MASC.SG   NOM.NEUT.SG
    him   long unconscious   lain

    '(apparently) He lay unconscious for a long time.'

These completely productive (see Jablonskis 1957:588–9) sentences
are surface impersonal, with the passive participle of the one-place predicate in the nominative neuter singular. The predicate complement
appears in the genitive, the case of the "agent," and an adjective carries
the same gender/number as the "agent."

Because of the discrepancy in morphology between the passive participle and the predicate complement, the predicate must carry two sets
of features, one its own and the other evidently those of the "agent."
We thus assign the one-place predicates in (21) the category

$$\langle S \mid N; \text{ PASS.NOM.NEUT.SG} \mid \text{GEN}.\delta GN \rangle.$$

If Passive is understood generally as an operation on predicates that
cancels the subject argument position (Keenan and Timberlake 1985a),
in applying to a one-place predicate it will remove the argument position
and the morphological features of that position as well. We can therefore
assign Passive (of one-place predicates) the category

$$\langle S \mid (S \mid N); \ x \mid (\text{PASS.NOM.NEUT.SG} \mid \text{GEN}.\delta GN) \rangle.$$

When a one-place predicate expands to include a predicate complement,
the predicate complement will inherit the case/gender/number of the
subject argument position, by (8). An analysis tree for (21a) is given in
(22), with morphology written vertically rather than horizontally.

196   Alan Timberlake

(22)

α = NOM, β = NEUT.SG, γ = GEN

Thus, by carrying the case/gender/number features of the agent in the subject argument position of the predicate that undergoes Passive, we can ensure $C.GNAgr$ in the predicate complement. One problem is to guarantee that the case/gender/number features in the subject argument position are in fact those of the agent. If the agent is a modifier of the one-place predicate (Keenan 1982), we can write this modifier as $\langle(S\,|\,N)\,|\,(S\,|\,N);\ (\text{PASS}\,|\,\text{GEN}.\delta GN)\,|\,(\text{PASS}\,|\,\text{GEN}.\delta GN)\rangle$. Such a modifier will combine only with a one-place predicate with the specified morphological features. A reservation one might voice at this point is that predicates do not usually constrain morphological features in modifiers, but one could counter that this is perhaps what is special about agent phrases. In Lithuanian in particular one does not otherwise find genitive predicate modifiers, and it would seem appropriate to restrict their appearance exactly to passives.

A second, more serious problem is how to derive a predicate modifier of category $(S\,|\,N)\,|\,(S\,|\,N)$ from a noun phrase of category N. A predicate modifier is naturally formed from a noun phrase by means of a preposition if the preposition has the category $[(S\,|\,N)\,|\,(S\,|\,N)]\,|\,N$, but this option is less appealing for prepositionless case-marked noun phrases. It is worth mentioning that this problem is not unique to agent phrases, since it comes up as well for other prepositionless case-marked noun phrases used as predicate modifiers, such as instrumental and locative phrases. Except for this general problem, the mechanisms developed here account for $C.GNAgr$ of predicate complements with agent phrases in passives of one-place predicates. As before, the analysis revolves around the predicate.

5 Conclusion.

To recapitulate briefly, the analysis here is characterized by two properties. First, the basic analytic move is to give morphology an autonomous status by enriching category statements to include morphological features. The statement of morphology can then be treated categorially with some degree of success. Second, the specific analysis of $CAgr$ is characterized by a reliance on the predicate as the arbiter of morphological well-formedness; the predicate carries the morphological features of its complements, both arguments and complements. This, I think, is consistent with the spirit of categorial grammar, inasmuch as it places the burden of analysis on predicates or, more generally, functor categories. Since case agreement is one of the classic examples of a morphological dependency that is superficially nonlocal in character, the analysis here suggests by extension that other cases of apparently nonlocal morphological dependencies can also be described by a categorial approach to morphology, with predicate (or functor) formation as the basic analytic mechanism.

Internal to the description a few examples arose that might argue against alternative approaches to $CAgr$, depending of course on their precise formulation. There were two cases where the head predicate bears different morphological features from its dependent predicate complement (participial predicate complements with two-place predicates; passive of one-place predicates); such examples might be problematic for an approach that would attempt to account for $CAgr$ by feature percolation from the head to its dependents. Also, two cases seem to argue against an approach that would do $CAgr$ by creating a linkage between the predicate complement and the argument it predicates of: one, predicate complements in infinitive complements of head nouns do not agree with the possessor, although the possessor is almost certainly the argument which the predicate complement is predicated of; two, in participial predicate complements with two-place predicates ('raising-to-object'), the copular participle can be non-agreeing even when the dependent predicate complement agrees in case and gender/number, a fact which is problematic if the linkage between predicate complement and argument is created by a transitive operation applied recursively.

It is also appropriate to mention some consequences of this analysis that may seem unpleasant. One might object to the fact that the

198   Alan Timberlake

distribution of agreeing vs. non-agreeing (instrumental) case is entrusted
to the rules of interpretation, although this seems to me to be correct.
Next, the set of subcategories for any lexical predicate has to be en-
riched; often the new subcategories correspond to distinct inflectional
forms, but in some instances the subcategories have no distinct realization (for example, infinitives with a range of case/gender/number values
for the subject argument position). Finally, the statement of agreement
here is handled by constraints on the well-formedness of predicate categories that in effect require identity of features across different positions
in the predicate category; this technique is perhaps not strictly categorial
in nature.

References

Andrews, A. D. 1971. Case agreement of predicate modifiers in Ancient
    Greek. *Linguistic Inquiry* 2:127–151.

Andrews, A. D. 1982a. The representation of case in Modern Icelandic.
    In J. Bresnan (Ed), *The Mental Representation of Grammatical Re-
    lations*, 427–503. Cambridge, Mass.: The MIT Press.

Andrews, A. D. 1982b. Long distance agreement in Modern Icelandic.
    In P. Jacobson and G. K. Pullum (Eds), *The Nature of Syntactic
    Representation*, 1–34. Dordrecht: Reidel.

Bach, E. 1979. Control in Montague Grammar. *Linguistic Inquiry*
    10:515–531.

Bach, E. 1983. On the relationship between word-grammar and phrase-
    grammar. *Natural Language and Linguistic Theory* 1:65–90.

Donnellan, K. 1966. Reference and definite descriptions. *Philosophical
    Review* 75:281–304.

Dowty, D. 1982. Grammatical relations and Montague Grammar. In P.
    Jacobson and G. K. Pullum (Eds), *The Nature of Syntactic Repre-
    sentation*, 79–130. Dordrecht: Reidel.

Jablonskis, J. 1957. *Rinktiniai Raštai, 1.* Vilnius: Valstybinė Politinės
    ir Mokslinės Literatūros Leidykla.

Keenan, E. L. 1980. Passive is phrasal (not sentential or lexical). In
    T. Hoekstra, et al. (Eds), *Lexical Grammar*, 181–215. Dordrecht:
    Foris.

Keenan, E. L. 1982. Parametric variation in universal grammar. In
    R. Dirven and G. Radden (Eds), *Issues in the Theory of Universal
    Grammar*, 11–73. Tübingen: Gunter Narr.

Keenan, E. L. and A. Timberlake 1985a. Predicate formation rules in
    universal grammar. In M. Wescoat, et al. (Eds), *Proceedings of the*

West Coast Conference on Formal Linguistics 4. Stanford, Calif.: Stanford Linguistics Association.

Keenan, E. L. and A. Timberlake 1985b. Linguistic motivations for extending Categorial Grammar. Paper presented at the conference on Categorial Grammars and Natural Language Structures, May 31–June 2, Tucson, Arizona.

Montague, R. 1974. Universal grammar. In R. H. Thomason (Ed), *Formal Philosophy: Selected Papers of Richard Montague,* 222–246. New Haven: Yale University Press.

Nichols, J. 1981. Predicate instrumentals and agreement in Lithuanian. In B. Comrie (Ed), *Studies in the Languages of the USSR.* Carbondale, Ill.: LRI.

Partee, B. H. 1985. Syntactic categories and semantic types. Paper presented at the conference on Categorial Grammars and Natural Language Structures, May 31–June 2, Tucson, Arizona.

Perlmutter, D. M. 1984. Working *1s* and inversion in Italian, Japanese, and Quechua. In D. M. Perlmutter and C. Rosen (Eds), *Studies in Relational Grammar* 2:292–330. Chicago: The University of Chicago Press.

Pollard, C. 1984. *Generalized Phrase Structure Grammars, Head Grammars, and Natural Language.* Doctoral dissertation, Stanford University.

9 On the Complementarity of Subject and Subject-Verb Agreement

EDIT DORON

THE PRO-DROP LITERATURE within the Government and Binding framework has been concerned with formulating the *null-subject parameter*, which distinguishes languages that allow a null subject in tensed sentences from languages that require an overt subject (see Borer 1984; Chomsky 1981, 1982; Jaeggli 1982, 1984; Picallo 1984; Rizzi 1982; and others). Italian is often treated as a paradigmatic case of a null-subject language; in tensed clauses, missing subjects such as in (1a) alternate with realized subjects, pronominal as in (1b) or lexical as in (1c).

(1) a. ho telefonato
      phone.PAST.1.SG

      'I have phoned.'

    b. io ho telefonato   / ho telefonato io
       I   phone.PAST.1.SG

       'I have phoned.'

    c. Gianni ha telefonato   / ha telefonato Gianni
       Gianni phone.PAST.3.SG

       'Gianni has phoned.'

Acknowledgments: I am grateful to the following people from whose comments on this work I have greatly benefited: Stephen Anderson, Joan Bresnan, Jim McCloskey, David Perlmutter, Stanley Peters, and Peter Sells.

In the Government and Binding theory, it follows from the Extended Projection Principle that every clause has a subject. According to the view formulated in Chomsky (1982), the subject in a sentence such as (1a) is an empty category called *pro*, which has the features [+pronominal, −anaphor] and various combinations of the features [person], [gender], [number] (and possibly also [Case]):

(2)   *pro* $[_{\text{AGR}} \alpha F]$ ho telefonato
       $[\alpha F]$

Chomsky assumes a principle regulating the distribution of empty categories which states that the content of an empty category must be "identified." The content of traces for example is identified by an antecedent. The content of *pro* is identified by the AGR which governs it.[1] This is possible in a language where the inflectional system is "rich enough," which was Taraldsen's (1980) insight in formulating the *pro-drop* parameter. A variant of Chomsky's view is proposed in Borer (1986), where it is assumed that empty categories have no intrinsic agreement features at all. They must be assigned these features by other elements (such as an antecedent or AGR), so that they satisfy the requirement of identification. For example, *pro* in (2) is identified; the local AGR is rich enough to assign to *pro* the features $[\alpha F]$.

Both variants of the above account are based on characterizing the distribution of empty categories, in particular *pro*. This paper will suggest a different approach to the null-subject phenomenon: Null subjects are pronouns, but are not empty categories. At the syntactic level(s), null subjects are indistinguishable from pronouns. It is only considerations of Phonetic Form (PF) which determine what the phonological content of these pronouns is.

1 The Pro Account of Celtic

I will start by examining an attempt to extend Chomsky's *pro* account to another aspect of the null-subject phenomenon, namely the obligatoriness of null subjects in certain languages. It has long been noted that the Celtic languages impose a complementarity of inflected forms of the verb and overt subjects. The following examples, due to McCloskey and Hale (1984), are from Irish:

(3) a.   chuirfinn   isteach   ar   an phost sin
         put.COND.1.SG   in   on   that job
         'I would apply for that job.'

---

[1] For a definition of government, see Chomsky 1981.

b.   *chuirfinn   mé isteach ar   an phost sin
      put.COND.1.SG   I   in   on   that job
      'I would apply for that job.'

(4) a. *chuirfeadh   isteach ar   an phost sin
       put.COND   in   on   that job
       '...would apply for that job.'

   b. chuirfeadh   Eoghan isteach ar   an phost sin
       put.COND   Owen   in   on   that job
       'Owen would apply for that job.'

"Synthetic" forms of the verb (verb forms inflected for person and number) are used if and only if the subject is null, as in (3). "Analytic" forms of the verb (verb forms inflected for tense and mood but not for person and number) are used if and only if the subject is overt, as in (4). An additional wrinkle is the fact that synthetic forms do not exist in Irish for every person-number combination. When they do not exist, the analytic form is used together with an independent pronominal subject:

(5)   chuirfeadh   sibh   isteach ar   an phost sin
       put.COND   you.PL   in   on   that job
       'You would apply for that job.'

But when a synthetic form exists, such as *chuirfinn*, it is in general ungrammatical to use an analytic form together with a pronominal subject:

(6)   *chuirfeadh   mé isteach ar   an phost sin
       put.COND   I   in   on   that job
       'I would apply for that job.'

According to an analysis of McCloskey and Hale (1984), the (s-)structures of the null-subject sentences in (3a) and (4a) is as follows:

(7) a. [$_{V+AGR}$chuirfinn] [$_{NP}$*pro*] isteach ar an phost sin

   b. *[$_{V}$chuirfeadh] [$_{NP}$*pro*] isteach ar an phost sin

The ungrammaticality of (7b) follows from the fact that the analytic form *chuirfeadh* does not contain AGR; the empty category *pro* is not identified, unlike in (7a) and (2). But the ungrammaticality of (3b) is unaccounted for by the principle regulating the distribution of *pro*, which requires only that *pro* be identified, not that it is obligatory when identified. Something new and special to Irish has to be introduced at this point. McCloskey and Hale propose the following language specific filter:

$$*[\ldots[_{\text{AGR}}\alpha F]\ldots\text{NP}[\alpha F]\ldots]$$

where AGR governs NP and NP has phonetic content.

The basic generalization about the Irish agreement system, namely the incompatibility of person and number inflection with a lexical subject, is not predicted by the *pro* analysis but has to be stated ad-hoc. This is as it should be, according to McCloskey and Hale, since in different languages the pattern of incompatibility varies, giving rise to different language specific filters. One relevant case is Welsh. The Welsh agreement system is very similar to the Irish system. Welsh is a null-subject language (see (8a)), and synthetic forms are incompatible with lexical subjects (compare (8b) with (8c)). The examples in (8) are due to Harlow (1981).

(8) a. darllenais   y   llyfr
        read.PAST.1.SG   the   book
        'I read the book.'

    b. *darllenasant   y   dynion y   llyfr
        read.PAST.3.PL   the   men   the   book
        'The men read the book.'

    c. darllenodd   y   dynion y   llyfr
        read.PAST   the   men   the   book
        'The men read the book.'

But unlike Irish, Welsh allows a pronoun to cooccur with the synthetic form of the verb. The following example is from Jones and Thomas (1977, 195).

(9)   'r   oeddwn   i   'n   cwyno
        COMP   be.PAST.1.SG   I   in   complain
        'I was complaining.'

According to McCloskey and Hale, Welsh differs from Irish in the surface filter it has. The surface filter for Welsh is specified to exclude only non-pronominals governed by AGR:

$$*[\ldots[_{\text{AGR}}\alpha F]\ldots\text{NP}[-\text{pro}][\alpha F]\ldots]$$

where AGR governs NP and NP has phonetic content.

In other languages the pattern of complementarity is different yet again. In Chamorro, an unrelated null-subject language, the complementarity is reversed compared to Welsh. Pronouns are not allowed to cooccur with inflected verbs, whereas other overt subjects are. The following examples are from Chung (1982).

(10) a. hu-taitai   i   lepblu
         read.1.SG   the   book
         'I read the book.'

   b. *hu-taitai   yu'   i   lepblu
         read.1.SG   I   the   book

   c. ha-taitai   si   Maria   i   lepblu
         read.3.SG   CASE   Maria   the   book
         'Maria read the book.'

Chamorro therefore needs a different version of the surface filter:

$$*[\ldots[_{\text{AGR}}\alpha F]\ldots\text{NP}[+\text{pro}][\alpha F]\ldots]$$

where AGR governs NP and NP has phonetic content.

2 An Analysis of Hebrew Agreement

The pattern of the complementarity of inflection and overt subjects in Hebrew is the same as in Chamorro:

(11) a. etmol   šama't   harca'a
         yesterday   hear.PAST.2.SG.FEM   lecture
         'Yesterday you heard a lecture.'

   b. *etmol   šama't   at   harca'a
         yesterday   hear.PAST.2.SG.FEM   you.SG.FEM   lecture

   c. etmol   šam'a   rina   harca'a
         yesterday   hear.PAST.3.SG.FEM   Rina   lecture
         'Yesterday Rina heard a lecture.'

This section provides an analysis of the distribution of missing subjects in Hebrew which does not rely on a surface filter. I will show that the pattern in (11) follows from general principles.

I assume that the subject of both (11a) and (11b) is a pronoun, i.e., a bundle of features from among [person], [number], [gender]. Whether this bundle is associated with a phonetic content or not depends on whether it is assigned Case, which in turn depends on the configuration it is in. The structure of the relevant parts of both (11a,b) is as follows:[2]

(12) $\ldots V + [_{AGR}[2nd][\text{FEM}][\text{SG}]] \ [_{NP}[2nd][\text{FEM}][\text{SG}]] \ldots$

The configuration in (12) is an example of what I will call a "clitic configuration," i.e., a particular head+complement configuration where the features of the complement are all contained in the features of the head:

(13) $[_{\text{head}} \ldots [\alpha_1 F_1] \ldots [\alpha_n F_n]] \ldots [_{NP}[\alpha_1 F_1] \ldots [\alpha_n F_n]]$

In a clitic configuration, it is the features of the head which are phonetically realized, not those of the complement. A way of stating this generalization in the theory of Government and Binding is, following Jaeggli (1982), that in a clitic configuration Case is assigned to the clitic on the head and not to the complement, therefore the complement must be phonetically null or it violates the Case Filter. It is lack of Case assignment to a phonetically realized pronoun which makes (11b) ungrammatical. The AGR features themselves can be realized as verbal inflection without a Case feature, as in (11c), where there is no clitic configuration.[3]

This analysis explains null subjects in Hebrew as the outcome of clitic configurations. It predicts that a null subject in Hebrew obtains in and only in a clitic configuration. This prediction is corroborated on five counts.

First, a subject pronoun may precede the verb, as in (14).

(14) a.   at   šama't   harca'a
           you   heard.2.SG.FEM   lecture

     b. $[_{NP}[2nd][\text{FEM}][\text{SG}]] \ [_{VP} V + [_{AGR}[2nd][\text{FEM}][\text{SG}]] \ldots]$

---

[2] I am assuming that INFL, which contains AGR, is clause-initial in Hebrew. The verb may be fronted from its VP position and adjoined to INFL, as in (12). I have motivated these assumptions in Doron (1983).

[3] AGR differs therefore from clitics which are arguments, such as the object clitics of the Romance languages, which must be assigned Case, and therefore cannot appear if Case is assigned to an overt object:

    Il   l'aime   (*Marie)
    he   her-loves

    'He loves her.' (French)

There is no clitic configuration in (14), since V+AGR is dominated by VP and does not govern the subject.[4] Since that is not a clitic configuration, Case is assigned to the preverbal pronominal subject.

Second, subject pronouns may follow the verb when the former are contrastively stressed.

(15)   etmol   šama't   AT   harca'a
        yesterday   heard.2.SG.FEM   YOU   lecture

In this case the subject contains a feature not contained in AGR, call it [contrast]. The configuration now is (16), which is not a clitic configuration since the features of the subject are not contained in those of AGR:

(16)   ...V + [$_{AGR}$[2nd][FEM][SG]] [$_{NP}$[2nd][FEM][SG][contrast]] ...

Case is therefore assigned to the subject, which is realized as a stressed pronoun.

Third, a pronoun may appear as a conjunct within a subject NP. In this case neither is the pronoun governed by AGR nor is there an identity of features, since AGR agrees with the subject, not with one of its conjuncts. There is therefore no clitic configuration, and the pronoun is phonetically realized:

(17) a.   etmol   šma'tem   at   ve-dani   harca'a
           yesterday   heard.2.PL.MASC   you.SG.FEM   and Dani   lecture

           'You and Dani heard a lecture yesterday.'

     b.   ...V+[$_{AGR}$[2nd][MASC][PL]] [$_{NP}$[$_{NP}$[2nd][FEM][SG]]ve-dani] ...

Fourth, there is an interesting variation in the present tense: null subjects are not allowed. In the framework I propose, this indicates that for some reason a clitic configuration does not obtain. Accordingly, we expect a postverbal pronoun to be allowed, which is indeed the case:

(18) a.   axšav   šoma'at   at   harca'a
           now   hear.SG.FEM   you.SG.FEM   lecture

           'You are hearing a lecture now.'

     b.   *axšav   šoma'at   harca'a
           now   hear.SG.FEM   lecture

---

[4] In this case, AGR was moved from the sentence initial INFL node to a position adjoined to V in the VP. This is one way of bringing AGR and V together. Another way is described in Footnote 2.

A closer look at present tense inflection morphology reveals that it involves only the features [gender] and [number], and not [person], unlike past and future inflections, which involve all three features:

(19)   *šm'* 'hear'

Past

		MASC	FEM
	1st		šama'ti
SG	2nd	šama'ta	šama't
	3rd	šama'	šam'a
	1st		šama'nu
PL	2nd	šma'tem	šma'ten
	3rd		šam'u

Present

	MASC	FEM
SG	šome'a	šoma'at
PL	šom'im	šom'ot

The relevant part of the structure of (18) is therefore (20).

(20) $\ldots \text{V} + [_{\text{AGR}}[\text{FEM}][\text{SG}]] \; [_{\text{NP}}[2nd][\text{FEM}][\text{SG}]] \ldots$

This is not a clitic configuration, unlike (10), since the features of the complement are not contained in the features of the head. Case is therefore assigned to the subject, and *pro-drop* is impossible.

Fifth, the generalization that *pro-drop* is impossible in the present tense should be qualified. In case the subject is the expletive pronoun *ze* 'it,' as in (21a), *pro-drop* is possible in the present tense, as shown in (21b):

(21) a.   ze   margiz   oti   še   dani   meaxer
            it   annoys   me   that   Dani   is late

     b.   margiz   oti   še   dani   meaxer
            annoys   me   that   Dani   is late

     both: 'It annoys me that Dani is late.'

The explanation lies in the fact that expletive pronouns are specified for [number] and [gender] but not [person]. Whereas personal pronouns vary according to all three features, expletive pronouns vary according to two:

(22)   **personal pronouns**

		MASC	FEM
	1st		ani
SG	2nd	ata	at
	3rd	hu	hi

		MASC	FEM
	1st		anaxnu
PL	2nd	atem	aten
	3rd	hem	hen

expletive pronouns[5]

	MASC	FEM
SG	ze	zo
PL	ele	

The structure of the relevant parts of (21) is therefore (23):

(23) $V + [_{AGR}[\text{MASC}][\text{SG}]] \ [_{NP}[\text{MASC}][\text{SG}]]$

which is a manifestation of the following clitic configuration:

(24) $[_{head} \cdots [\text{gender}][\text{number}]] \ [_{NP}[\text{gender}][\text{number}]]$

Case is therefore assigned to AGR, and, as predicted, the expletive pronoun cannot follow the verb:

(25)   *margiz ze   oti še   dani   meaxer
         annoys it   me   that Dani   is-late

For the sake of completeness, note that there is a clitic configuration involving the expletive subject in other tenses as well, as shown in (26). In (26d), the features of the subject are contained in the features of AGR.

---

[5] *ze* is the unmarked form; expletive pronouns marked [FEM] or [PL] are used when the sentence has a predicate nominal with the same feature. For example:

zo   xucpa   leaxer
it[FEM]   chutzpa[FEM]   to-be-late

'It is rude to be late.'

(26) a. ze   hirgiz   oti   še   dani   exer
          it   annoyed me   that Dani   was-late

     b. hirgiz   oti   še   dani   exer
          annoyed me   that Dani   was-late

          both: 'It annoyed me that Dani was late.'

     c. *hirgiz   ze   oti   še   dani   exer
          annoyed it   me   that Dani   was-late

     d. $V + [_{AGR}[3rd][MASC][SG]] [_{NP}[MASC][SG]]$

3 An Analysis of Celtic Agreement

In the previous section I explained the phenomenon of null subjects
as depending on the possibility of assigning Case to AGR, which is
obligatory in a clitic configuration. This explanation undermines the
justification of the filter proposed by McCloskey and Hale, and assuming that this filter is needed to uphold the *pro* analysis in general, it also
undermines the *pro* analysis for null subjects.

Before turning to Celtic, I will say a few words about Italian. It seems
that AGR and pronominal subjects never stand in a clitic configuration
in Italian, since a pronominal subject may be realized with an inflected
verb, both preverbally and postverbally (see (1b)). But the possibility
of assigning Case to AGR exists, giving rise to a Caseless pronominal
subject, which must therefore be null (as in (1a)). This analysis is
similar to the one proposed in Rizzi (1982).

It is tempting to ascribe the total complementarity of inflection and
overt subjects in Irish to obligatory Case assignment to AGR features
whenever they are present. The problem is that this would force us to
look for a different account for Welsh. Recall that in Welsh, pronominal
subjects may cooccur with synthetic forms of the verb. But it would be
desirable to offer a unified account for the Celtic languages, since they
basically use the same agreement system.

An analysis that suggests itself for Celtic is the incorporation analysis,
a modification of Anderson's (1982) analysis. According to this analysis,
there is no AGR in Celtic at all. Verb forms are the result of "post-
syntactic" morphology, which integrates V and a pronominal NP, two
distinct nodes at the syntactic representation.[6] The syntactic structure

---

[6] It is also possible to formulate the equivalent of the incorporation analysis in
a theory where only "lexical" morphology is available. In the terminology of
the theory developed in Bresnan and Mchombo (1985), for example, Celtic
languages would be said to have the "pronominal incorporation property."

is transparent in cases such as (27a). In other cases, a suppletive form replaces the V+pronoun string, as in (28a). The syntactic structures are shown in (27b) and (28b) respectively.[7]

(27) a. chuirfeadh   sé   isteach   ar an phost sin
         put.COND   he   in   on that job
         'He would apply for that job.'

   b. [_Vchuirfeadh] [_{NP}sé] isteach ar an phost sin

(28) a. chuirfinn   isteach   ar an phost sin
         put.COND.1.SG   in   on that job
         'I would apply for that job.'

   b. [_Vchuirfeadh] [_{NP}mé] isteach ar an phost sin

The claim is that though the verb and the pronominal subject are two distinct phrases syntactically, they form one unit morphologically and phonologically, whether it is a synthetic verb form or an analytic verb form plus a pronominal subject. Some evidence from the Ulster dialect of Irish has been kindly suggested to me by Jim McCloskey. For the purposes of applying emphatic stress, a subject pronoun is treated in this dialect exactly on a par with the inflection part of a synthetic verb form. Emphatic stress on the verb is achieved by stressing its inflectional ending, if it has one, or by stressing the pronoun:

(29) a. A: ní   dhéanfainn   a leithéid
              NEG   do.COND.1.SG   its like
              'I wouldn't do such a thing.'

     B: dhéanFA
              do.COND.2.SG
              'You WOULD.' ('You would too.' 'You certainly would.')

---

[7] A similar phenomenon is attested (albeit rarely) in Hebrew, where there is sometimes cliticization of the subject pronoun on the verb in the present tense (remember that present tense forms are parallel to the Celtic analytic forms in that they show agreement in less features than forms in other tenses). One difference is that suppletive forms are introduced in Celtic, whereas in Hebrew the post-syntactic word formation obeys regular phonological rules: *xošešani* 'I'm afraid,' in variance with *xošeš ani; xošvani* 'I think,' in variance with *xošev ani; betuxani* 'I'm sure,' in variance with *batuax ani.*

b. A: an   dtabharfaidh   siad   an phost   dó
Q   give.FUT   they   the job   to-him

'Will they give him the job?'

B: caithfidh   SIAD
must   they

'They HAVE to.'

These examples are particularly interesting. It is quite unusual for an in-flectional ending to bear emphatic stress, as in (29a). This fact becomes less surprising if the inflectional ending is analyzed as an independent syntactic unit. It is also puzzling that a semantic emphasis of the verb is achieved by phonologically stressing a pronoun, as in (29b). This is explained if the verb and the pronoun are viewed as one phonological unit.

Additional evidence that the pronoun in (27) is not phonologically independent is that its distribution is limited. It appears only in environments where it can "lean to the left." For example, it cannot appear in elliptical utterances where the verb is missing:

(30)   cé   atá   ansin?
'Who is there?'

mise   /   *mé
I+CONTR   I

(from O'Siadhail (1980)[8])

The present analysis also accounts for puzzling data having to do with coordinated subjects. Notice first that the suffix -se as in (30) attaches to pronouns to derive contrastive forms. This suffix also attaches to inflected forms of verbs:

(31)   chuirfinn   -se
put.COND.1.SG   CONTR

'I would put'

The structure of (31) is (32):

(32)   [$_V$chuirfeadh]   [$_{NP}$mise]
put.COND   I+CONTR

---

[8] I am grateful to Susannah MacKaye for the reference.

When pronouns are conjoined, it is contrastive forms (or other emphatic forms) that are used, not the clitic forms:

(33) a. mise   agus tusa
          I+CONTR   and   you+CONTR

          'I and you'

     b. *mé   agus tú
          I   and   you

In example (34), the understood subject of the sentence is 'I and you,' but the inflection on the verb is first person singular:

(34)   da   mbeinn   -se   agus tusa ann
          if   be.COND.1.SG CONTR   and   you   there

          'if I and you were there'

The "agreement" of the verb with the first conjunct is surprising, but our analysis accounts for it. The structure of (34) is (35), where the subject is the NP 'I and you':

(35)   da   [$_V$mbeadh] [$_{NP}$[$_{NP}$mise] agus [$_{NP}$tusa]]   ann
          if   be.COND   I+CONTR and you+CONTR   there

Post-syntactic morphology replaces the string *mbeadh+mise* by *mbeinn-se*, exactly as in (31) and (32).[9]

According to McCloskey and Hale's *pro* analysis, the structure of (34) is (36):

(36)   da   [$_{V+AGR}$mbeinn] [$_{NP}$[$_{NP}$*pro*-se] agus [$_{NP}$tusa]]   ann
          if   be.COND.1.SG   and   you   there

Conjoining an empty pronoun with a lexical NP seems to me problematic. Also, notice that the structure in (36) violates both the requirement that *pro* be identified and the filter for Irish, since AGR governs the conjoined NP and not the left conjunct. McCloskey (1985) makes a strong

---

[9] The present formulation avoids a problem (pointed out by McCloskey and Hale) with Anderson's (1982) formulation of the incorporation analysis. According to Anderson's analysis, the d-structure of (34) is (35) but its s-structure is derived by a movement transformation:

da [$_{V+AGR}$mbeinn-se] [$_{NP}$[$_{NP}$t] agus [$_{NP}$tusa]] ann

The movement rule that relates these structures violates the Coordinate Structure Constraint.

case for redefining government so that AGR in (36) governs *pro* and not the conjoined NP. But a problem remains with respect to data from Old Irish. Old Irish differs from Modern Irish in that inflected forms of the verb agree with the conjoined NP as a whole, not just with the left conjunct. As a result, in cases where the left conjunct is *pro*, its features do not match those of AGR on the verb. This gives rise to an unidentified *pro*, regardless of the definition of government. The sentence (37) is an example where the features of AGR do not match those of *pro*, at least under the reading *He and Dubthach met.*

(37) a. conrancatar   ocus   Dubthach
         meet.PAST.3.PL   and   Dubthach

         'They/He and Dubthach met.'

   b. [$_{V+AGR}$conrancatar] [$_{NP}$[$_{NP}$*pro*] ocus [$_{NP}$Dubthach]]

So far I have discussed the application of the proposed analysis to Irish. We now turn to Welsh, which is different from Irish in that pronouns may follow a synthetic verb form, as in example (9), repeated below as (38):

(38)   'r   oeddwn   i   'n   cwyno
        COMP   be.PAST.1.SG   I   in   complain

        'I was complaining.'

This example presents a problem for the view that verbal inflection is an incorporated pronoun, since both inflection and a pronoun are present. But according to the traditional analysis of Welsh (see for example, Watkins 1976), the pronouns used following inflected forms of the verb are not independent pronouns but affixes which are appended only to words which already have inflectional endings. I suggest that we view these affixes as reduplicating the pronominal subject, similarly to the Irish suffix -*se* in (31) and (32). Accordingly, the syntactic structure of (38) contains a reduplicated pronoun in subject position:[10]

(39)   'r   [$_V$oedd]   [$_{NP}$myfi]   'n   cwyno
        COMP   be.PAST   I.redup   in   complain

        'I was complaining.'

A morphological rule provides the form *oeddwn-i* 'I was' to replace the string *oedd+myfi* (where the form *oeddwn* is the one which normally

---

[10] -*fi* in *myfi* is derived by mutation from -*mi*. I am grateful to Peter Sells for this information.

replaces *oedd+mi*). I will provide one independent piece of evidence for this claim. Welsh allows the topicalization of the subject; the analytic form of the verb must be used in such sentences, as is to be expected:

(40)   yfi   oedd   (*oeddwn)   yn   cwyno
      I   be.PAST   be.PAST.1.SG   in   complain

      'It was I who was complaining.' (Welsh)

The crucial point is that the pronoun *(m)yfi*, the reduplicated form of *mi*, is used in (40). Assuming that it has been moved from a postverbal position, we derive independent evidence for the structure in (39).

    The Breton system is very similar to the Welsh. Non-pronominal subjects cooccur only with analytic forms of the verb, but pronouns cooccur only with synthetic forms. See Stump (1984) for arguments that these pronouns are clitics with emphatic meaning.

(41) a.   bemdez   e   lennont   eul   levr
        every day   PRT   read.3.PL   a   book

        'They read a book every day.'

    b.   bemdez   e   lenn / *lennont   ar vugale   eul   levr
        every day   PRT   read   read.3.PL   the kids   a   book

        'The kids read a book every day.'

    c.   levriou   a   lennan-me   / *lenn-me
        books   PRT   read.1.SG I   read I

        'I read books.'

    I will conclude with the discussion of two problems for the present analysis pointed out to me by Jim McCloskey.[11] Irish has no words for *yes* or *no*. One answers in the affirmative by repeating the verb of the question, and in the negative by repeating the verb of the question preceded by the negative particle:

(42)   Q: ar   chuir   tú   isteach   ar an phost
           Q   put.PAST   you   in   on the job

           'Did you apply for the job?'

      A: chuir   / níor   chuir
           put.PAST   NEG   put.PAST

           'Yes.'   'No.'

---

[11] I am grateful to Jim McCloskey for all the data which follow in the text.

Moreover if the appropriate synthetic form of the verb exists, it must be used:

(43)   Q: an   gcuireann   tú   isteach   ar   phostannaí

             Q   put.PRES   you   in   on   jobs

         'Do you apply for jobs?'

         A: cuirim   /   *cuireann

                 put.PRES.1.SG   put.PRES

                 'Yes.'

The present analysis treats the analytic form of the verb together with the pronoun as equivalent to the synthetic form. It therefore predicts that in case the synthetic form of the verb doesn't exist, one should use the analytic form together with the pronoun. But the fact is that if only the analytic form is used, it is impossible to add the pronoun:

(44)   Q: an   gcuireann   sé   isteach   ar   phostannaí

             Q   put.PRES   he   in   on   jobs

         'Does he apply for jobs?'

         A: cuireann   /   *cuireann   sé

                 put.PRES   put.PRES   he

                 'Yes.'

It is possible that the rule for answering the question in the positive is: Repeat the first lexical item in the "verb complex." The synthetic form *cuirim* 'put.PRES.1.SG' is listed in the lexicon as the suppletive form which replaces *cuireann+mé*, the latter being a string of two separate lexical items. Therefore in the case of (43) the first lexical item is *cuirim*, but in the case of (44) it is *cuireann* and not *cuireann sé* because the latter counts as two lexical items.

Another problem has to do with West Munster dialects where there is a systematic exception to the incompatibility of synthetic forms and overt subjects. In these dialects, 3rd person plural synthetic forms of all tenses can cooccur with overt subjects. For example:

(45) a.   ithid   an   capall

           eat.PRES.3.PL   the   horse

           'They eat the horse.'

     b.   ithid   siad   an   capall

           eat.PRES.3.PL   they   the   horse

           'They eat the horse.'

c.   tuigid   na   haithreacha

understand.PRES.3.PL   the   fathers

'The fathers understand.'

It would be easy to state this exception in terms of McCloskey and Hale's filters. The filter for these West Munster dialects would be made more specific by requiring that AGR not contain the feature complex [3.PL]. In terms of our analysis, this phenomenon could be treated as a first step in introducing an agreement system into the language. It could be that the analytic forms in these dialects are marked for the feature [number]. The form *ithid* in (45b) could be an analytic form marked [PL], homophonous with the synthetic form in (45a). However, it is impossible to give a more specific analysis without further investigation of these dialects.

4 Conclusion

I have suggested in this paper that null subjects be treated as pronouns that have different phonological realizations in different environments. In Hebrew, pronouns have null phonological content in what I have called "clitic configurations." From this approach to null subjects, accurate predictions were derived about the complementarity of inflection and post verbal pronominal subjects in Hebrew. As to the Celtic languages, I have suggested they are not null-subject languages at all. Rather, the complementarity of inflection and subjects in these languages follows from inflection being an incorporated subject pronoun.

References

Anderson, S. R. 1982. Where's morphology? *Linguistic Inquiry* 13:571–612.

Borer, H. 1984. *Parametric Syntax*. Dordrecht: Foris.

Borer, H. 1986. I-Subjects. *Linguistic Inquiry* 17:375–416.

Bresnan, J. and S. A. Mchombo 1985. Agreement and pronominal incorporation in Chichewa. In M. Iida, S. Wechsler and D. Zec (Eds), *Working Papers in Grammatical Theory and Discourse Structure.* (CSLI Lecture Notes No. 11.) Stanford: Center for the Study of Language and Information, Stanford University.

Chomsky, N. 1981. *Lectures on Government and Binding.* Dordrecht: Foris.

Chomsky, N. 1982. *Some Concepts and Consequences of the Theory of Government and Binding.* Cambridge, Mass.: The MIT Press.

Chung, S. 1982. On extending the null subject parameter to NPs. *Proceedings of the West Coast Conference on Formal Linguistics* 1:125–136. Stanford, Calif.: Stanford Linguistics Association.

Doron, E. 1983. *Verbless Predicates in Hebrew.* Doctoral dissertation, University of Texas at Austin.

Harlow, S. 1981. Government and relativization in Celtic. In F. Heny (Ed), *Binding and Filtering.* Cambridge, Mass.: The MIT Press.

Jaeggli, O. 1982. *Topics in Romance Syntax.* Dordrecht: Foris.

Jaeggli, O. 1984. Subject extraction and the null subject parameter. *Proceedings of the Fourteenth Annual North Eastern Linguistic Society* 14:132–153. Amherst, Mass.: Graduate Linguistics Student Association.

Jones, M. and A. R. Thomas. 1977. *The Welsh Language—Studies in its Syntax and Semantics.* Cardiff: University of Wales Press for the Schools Council.

McCloskey, J. 1985. Inflection and conjunction in Modern Irish—An addendum. Ms.

McCloskey, J. and K. Hale 1984. On the syntax of person-number inflection in Modern Irish. *Natural Language and Linguistic Theory* 1:487–534.

O'Siadhail, M. 1980. *Learning Irish.* Dublin: Dublin Institute for Advanced Studies.

Picallo, M. C. 1984. The INFL node and the null subject parameter. *Linguistic Inquiry* 15:75–102.

Rizzi, L. 1982. WH-Movement, negation and the pro-drop parameter. In *Issues in Italian Syntax.* Dordrecht: Foris.

Stump, G. T. 1984. Agreement vs. incorporation in Breton. *Natural Language and Linguistic Theory* 2:289–348.

Taraldsen, K. T. 1980. *On the NIC, Vacuous Application and the that-trace Filter.* Bloomington: Indiana University Linguistics Club.

Watkins, T. A. 1976. The Welsh personal pronoun. *Word* 28:146–165.

10 Extensions of Brother-in-Law Agreement

JUDITH L. AISSEN

I SKETCH HERE a theory of agreement controllers which seeks to characterize the class of non-regular agreement controllers, i.e., those controllers which lie, in a sense clarified below, outside the set of regular controllers. The Relational Grammar notion of *brother-in-law* agreement (Perlmutter 1983) characterizes one such case. But brother-in-law agreement is relevant only in structures containing dummies, leaving other cases without any general account. The present paper attempts to characterize *all* non-regular controllers of predicate agreement through appropriate extensions of the brother-in-law relation.

1 Some Proposed Universals of Agreement and Counterexamples

(1) and (2), generalizations about predicate agreement controllers, are satisfied in a vast number of cases:

Discussions with William Ladusaw, David Perlmutter, and Geoffrey Pullum, and comments from Paul Postal and Johanna Nichols on an earlier version have helped clarify several points. Saarin Schwartz provided technical assistance. This research was supported by the Syntax Research Center at UC Santa Cruz, and by a Faculty Research Grant from the Academic Senate at UC Santa Cruz. The ideas sketched in this paper are developed in somewhat different terms and in greater detail in subsequent work (Aissen 1987, to appear).

(1)   If *a* controls agreement, then *a* is a final term (subject, direct object, or indirect object).

(2)   If *b* agrees with *a*, then *a* and *b* are dependents of the same node.

Cases which satisfy (1) and (2), and any further language-particular conditions, involve *regular* controllers. All other cases involve *non-regular* controllers. Attested cases of non-regular control include the following.

Agreement in English existential sentences appears to violate both (1) and (2):

(3)   There seem to be unicorns in the garden.

Here *seem* agrees with *unicorns*, which is neither a final term nor a dependent of the same node.

Tzotzil number agreement violates (1). Only final subjects and direct objects control person agreement. But in structures involving possessor ascension, a nominal which is final chomeur controls number agreement. See Aissen (1987) and below.

The agreement system in Southern Tiwa, as analyzed in Allen and Frantz (1983) and Allen, Gardiner, and Frantz (1984) violates principle (1). Agreement in Southern Tiwa is controlled by the final subject and direct object, and by any nominal which is initial absolutive and final chomeur. Control by a nominal which is initial absolutive and final chomeur violates (1). No less than five constructions exhibit such control.

Other cases which violate (1) include agreement in Achenese passives (Lawler 1977),[1] agreement in Tzotzil conjunct union (Aissen 1987 and below), agreement in Navajo conjunct union (Hale 1975 and below), and agreement in reflexive passive constructions in Italian (Perlmutter 1983).

2 Primary vs. Secondary Agreement Controllers

An early insight of Relational Grammar was that *unicorns* in (3) controls agreement of *seem* by virtue of its connection to *there*, a nominal whose final grammatical relation in the main clause entitles it to control agreement of *seem* as a regular controller. The relation between *unicorns* and the dummy was termed the *brother-in-law* relation. Consider the structure of (3), represented in (4a) by a stratal diagram, and in (4b) by a relational network:

---

[1] Under Lawler's analysis, a passive verb agrees with its underlying subject instead of its final subject. These cases are relevant only if they are passives, of course. Durie (1984) (brought to my attention by G.K.Pullum) claims they are not, analyzing the clauses in question as active and transitive. Under Durie's analysis, the final subject controls agreement, in accord with (1).

(4) a.

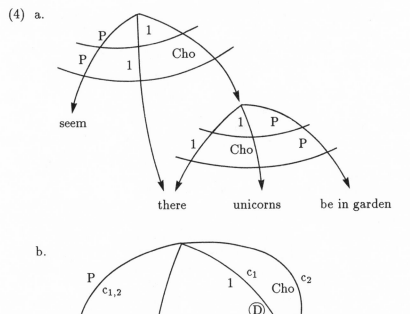

b.

Focusing on (4b), A, the complement arc headed by *there, overruns* B, the c_1 arc headed by *unicorns*. In general, an arc A overruns B if and only if A and B have the same R-Sign, A's first stratum is +1 of B's last stratum, and the R-Sign shared by A and B is a Term R-Sign (1, 2, or 3). The brother-in-law relation holds between a nominal and a dummy when the arc headed by the nominal is overrun by the earliest arc headed by the dummy in the lowest clause in which the dummy occurs (cf. Perlmutter 1983:161).[2] The idea of brother-in-law agreement is that

---

[2] Hence while C overruns D in (4), the heads of C and D are not brother-in-laws since *there* heads an arc in a lower clause than that containing C.

a nominal which is not a regular controller may control agreement by virtue of its relation as brother-in-law of a (potential) regular controller. Of the cases cited, only English and Italian involve dummies. The brother-in-law relation is irrelevant to the rest. But, the idea that underlies brother-in-law agreement—that non-regular controllers are systematically related to potential regular controllers—forms the basis for the following account of non-regular controllers. The brother-in-law relation involves a special case of *overrun*, the case when, among other things, the overrunning arc is headed by a dummy. The cases cited above have this in common: an arc headed by the non-regular controller is overrun by an arc headed by a (potential) regular controller. My proposal is that all non-regular controllers bear this relation to *some* potential regular controller. To state this condition precisely, it will be useful to define the terms *potential primary agreement controller* and *primary agreement controller*. The latter reconstructs the notion *regular controller*.

Intuitively, the set of primary agreement controllers (PAC's) in a language is determined by the set which controls agreement in the simplest clauses, i.e., in clauses which involve no changes in grammatical relations. I term such clauses *kernel clauses*. In English, only subjects are PAC's because only subjects control agreement in kernel clauses. In Tzotzil and Southern Tiwa, only subjects and direct objects are PAC's because only these control agreement in kernel clauses. With this in mind, I define the notion *Potential Primary Agreement Controller of b in a language L*.

(5)   Potential Primary Agreement Controller (a, b) in L:
       a is a P-PAC for b in L iff
       (i) a heads an arc A in the final stratum of the clause whose predicate is b AND
       (ii) the R-Sign associated with A is identical to the R-Sign of some arc headed by a kernel clause agreement controller in L.

By this definition, *there* in (4) is a P-PAC for *seem* because it heads a final 1 arc in the clause containing *seem*, and the heads of 1 arcs control agreement in kernel clauses. However, *there* is not a Primary Agreement Controller (PAC) for *seem* because it does not actually control agreement. Only those P-PAC's which actually control agreement are PAC's:

(6)   Primary Agreement Controller (a, b):
       a is a PAC for b iff
       (i) a is a P-PAC for b AND
       (ii) a controls agreement of b.

The definition of PAC incorporates what I take to be correct in (1) and (2). Like (1), (6) requires that a PAC be in the final stratum of the clause containing the agreeing predicate. Unlike (1), (6) does *not* require that PAC's be terms. If in some language benefactives control agreement in kernel clauses, then final benefactives may be PAC's in that language. (Choctaw may be such a language, Davies 1986.) Final chomeurs, however, can never be P-PAC's, and hence never PAC's, because no kernel clause contains a chomeur. Chomeurs occur only in clauses involving some change in grammatical relations (Relational Grammar Motivated Chomage Law, Perlmutter and Postal 1983a).

A Secondary Agreement Controller is any controller which is not a PAC:

(7)   Secondary Agreement Controller (a, b):
       a is a SAC for b iff
       (i) a controls agreement of b AND
       (ii) a is not a Primary Agreement Controller for b.

It is SAC's which are subject to the overrun condition:

(8)   Secondary Agreement Controller Law:
       If a is a SAC for b, then a heads an arc which is overrun by an arc headed by a PAC for b.

3 Secondary Controllers

All the cases cited in Section 2 satisfy (8).

3.1 English

In English, only final subjects are P-PAC's. Since *unicorns* in (4) is not a final subject, it must control agreement as a SAC. By (8), then, it must head an arc which is overrun by a P-PAC for *seem*. It heads B, B is overrun by A, and A is headed by a P-PAC for *seem*, namely, *there*. *There* is a P-PAC for *seem* because it heads a final 1 arc (C) in the clause whose predicate is *seem*. Hence (4) satisfies (8).

3.2 Tzotzil Possessor Ascension

In Tzotzil, subjects and objects are P-PACs. Example (9) illustrates control of person agreement by both in a kernel clause (agreement is morphologically ergative in Tzotzil):

(9)   L-i-s-k'el.
       ASP-ABS.1-ERG.3-watch
       'He/she/they watched me.'

Consider now (10) which involves possessor ascension. The predicate is plural, though both the final subject and direct object are singular:

(10)   L-i-s-k'el-be-ik   j-ch'amaltak   li   Xune.
       ASP-ABS.1-ERG.3-watch-IO-3.PL ERG.1-children the John
       'John watched my children.'

The final subject is *li Xune* which controls ergative agreement. The initial direct object is *j-ch'amaltak* 'my children'[3] but the final direct object is the first person singular pronoun, which controls absolutive agreement. In Aissen (1979), I argued that the possessor of the direct object ascends into the clause as indirect object. All indirect objects in Tzotzil advance to direct object (Aissen 1987), an advancement marked on the predicate by the suffix *-be*. The structure of (10) is (H=head):

(11) a.

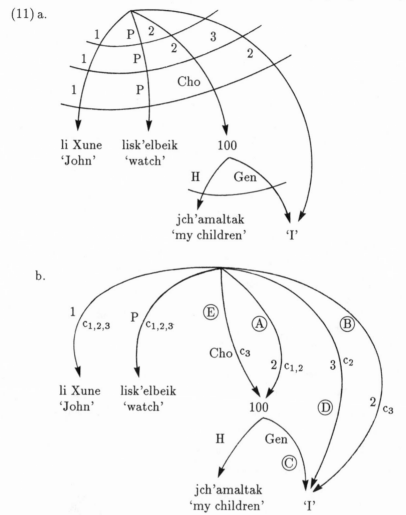

The first person pronoun heads the Genitive arc C in the nominal labelled 100. Its ascension to indirect object is represented by the c_2 3 arc, D, and its subsequent advancement to direct object by the c_3 2 arc, B. Note that B overruns A, the initial 2 arc and the arc whose head (100) hosts the ascension. The initial direct object heads a final Cho arc, E.

The plural suffix in (10) cross-references j-ch'$amaltak$ the initial direct object and final chomeur, in violation of (1). Hence, jch'$amaltak$ is a SAC, and must satisfy (8), which it does. It heads A in (11), and A is overrun by B, an arc whose head is a P-PAC (in fact, a PAC).

The head of an overrun 2 arc does not in general control number agreement in Tzotzil. It does so only when it also hosts the ascension of the nominal which heads the overrunning arc. In (11), structure of (10), 100 hosts the ascension of the first person pronoun. Compare (10) to a sentence which involves indirect object advancement, but no ascension:

(12)   Ch-a-k-ak'-be-ik

ASP-ABS.2-ERG.1-give-IO-PL

'I'll give them/her/him/it to you (PL).'

Here, ik can only cross-reference the final direct object. The number of the initial direct object/final chomeur is unconstrained. See Aissen (1987) and below for more details.

3.3 Southern Tiwa

Southern Tiwa is of particular interest because the head of *every* absolutive arc which is overrun by an arc headed by a P-PAC controls agreement as a SAC. (Final) subjects and direct objects are P-PAC's in Southern Tiwa. As they inevitably control agreement, they are also PAC's. Several grammatical categories are marked in Southern Tiwa agreement affixes. These include the person, number, and noun class of the controllers. The most striking characteristic of the Southern Tiwa agreement system is the conflation into a single affix of all determining categories. In transitive clauses, not only is it not possible, for example, to analyze the affix into morphemes corresponding to person and number, it is equally impossible to distinguish morphemes corresponding to subject and direct object.

Examples (13) and (14) show agreement with PAC's in kernel intransitive and transitive clauses:[4]

(13)   Te-ʔaru-we

1.SG-cry-PRES

'I'm crying.'

---

[4] Examples 13–17, and 19 are from Allen and Frantz (1983 1–48). Examples 23–25 are from Allen, Gardiner, and Frantz (1984 96–109). In the glosses, *3i* and *3ii* designate third person noun classes.

(14) a. Ti-mu-ban
  1.SG:3i.SG-see-PAST
  'I saw him.'

  b. I-mu-ban
  1.SG:2.SG-see-PAST
  'I saw you.'

That a third nominal may control agreement is clear in clauses involving indirect object advancement (IOA). Consider first (15), which is a kernel transitive clause with an agreement pattern like (14):[5]

(15)   Ti-khwien-wia-ban   ʔĩ-ʔay
  1.SG:3i.SG-dog-give-PAST you-to
  'I gave the dog to you.'

The verb agrees with the final subject and direct object; the second person pronoun is the indirect object. (16), in contrast, involves IOA:

(16)   Ka-khwien-wia-ban
  1.SG:2.SG/3i.SG-dog-give-PAST
  'I gave you the dog.'

That three nominals determine *ka-*, glossed in the format *S:DO/Overrun Abs*, is suggested by the fact that it is distinct both from *ti-* (1.SG:3i.SG) and from *i-* (1.SG:2.SG). Furthermore, changing the number of the initial absolutive requires a change in the affix:

(17) a. Ka-ʔuʔu-wia-ban
  1.SG:2.SG/3i.SG-baby-give-PAST
  'I gave you the baby.'

  b. Kam-ʔuʔu-wia-ban
  1.SG:2.SG/3i.PL-baby-give-PAST
  'I gave you the babies.'

(16) has the following (partial) RN. Agreement is controlled by the final subject, the final direct object, and *khwien* 'the dog,' which is initial absolutive and final chomeur. *Khwien* is a SAC, and it satisfies (8): it heads an arc (A) which is overrun by an arc (B) whose head is a P-PAC (a PAC, in fact).

---

[5] Southern Tiwa makes extensive use of noun incorporation, as in (15) below. See Allen, Gardiner, and Frantz (1984).

(18) a.

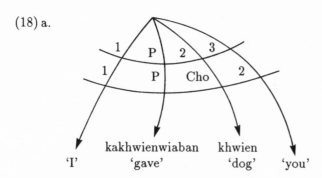

kakhwienwiaban   khwien
'I'   'gave'   'dog'   'you'

b.

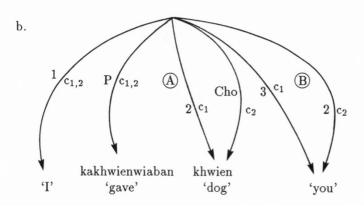

kakhwienwiaban   khwien
'I'   'gave'   'dog'   'you'

In the passive versions of clauses involving indirect object advancement, agreement is controlled by the final subject, 'I,' and the initial absolutive/final chomeur, 'the child/children':

(19) a.   In-ʔuʔu-wia-che-ban   seuanide-ba
          1.SG/3i.SG-child-give-PASS-PAST   man-by
          'I was given the child by the man.'

     b.   Im-ʔuʔu-wia-che-ban   seuanide-ba
          1.SG/3ii.PL-child-give-PASS-PAST   man-by
          'I was given the children by the man.'

The structure of (19a) is (20). Advancement of the first person pronoun to direct object puts the initial direct object in chomage; its advancement to subject puts the initial subject in chomage.

(20) a.

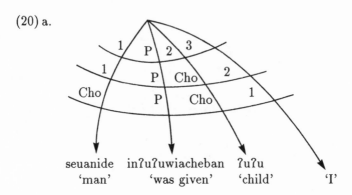

seuanide   inʔuʔuwiacheban   ʔuʔu
'man'   'was given'   'child'   'I'

b.

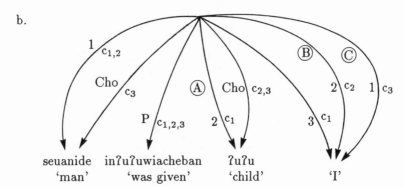

seuanide   inʔuʔuwiacheban   ʔuʔu
'man'   'was given'   'child'   'I'

The first person pronoun heads the final 1 arc, C, and hence controls agreement as a PAC.

'The child' controls agreement as a SAC, and it satisfies (8). It heads A, A is overrun by B, and B is headed by a P-PAC. B's head is a P-PAC because it heads C, the final 1 arc.

In the cases discussed above, the absolutive arc is overrun in *advancement* constructions. The affixes illustrated in those examples are summarized below:

(21)   a. Final 1   b. Final 1 / Initial Absolutive

            1.SG   te-   1.SG/3i.SG   in-
                                        1.SG/3i.PL   im-

        c. Final 1:Final 2   d. Final 1:Final 2 / Initial Absolutive

            1.SG:2.SG   i-   1.SG:2.SG/3i.SG   ka-
            1.SG:3i.SG ti-   1.SG:2.SG/3i.PL   kam-

The (b) and (d) sets are used *whenever* an absolutive arc is overrun, not only in advancement constructions, but also in ascension constructions. Possessors of initial absolutives ascend in Southern Tiwa, assuming the grammatical relation of the host nominal. (22a) represents ascension from an intransitive subject; (22b) represents ascension from a direct object:

(22) a.

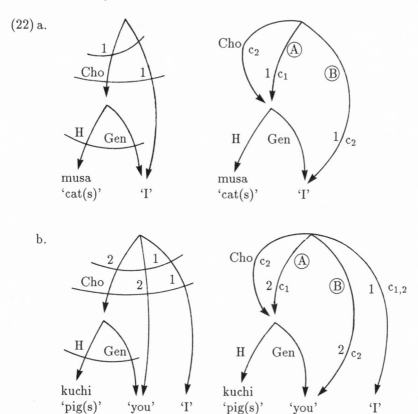

b.

In each case, A, the initial absolutive arc, is overrun by B, the arc headed by the ascending nominal. In sentences with the (a) structure, agreement is controlled jointly by the final subject (ascendee) and the initial absolutive (host). The affix is taken from the (b) set in (21):

(23) a.   In-musa-ʔĩ-hĩ
          1.SG/3i.SG-cat-come-FUT
          'My cat is coming.'

    b.   Im-musa-ʔĩ-hĩ
          1.SG/3i.PL-cat-come-FUT
          'My cats are coming.'

Here, 'I' controls agreement as a PAC, whereas *musa* 'my cat(s)' controls agreement as a SAC .

In sentences with the (b) structure, agreement is determined by three nominals: the final subject, the final direct object (ascendee) and the initial absolutive/final chomeur. The affix is taken from the (d) set in (21):

(24) a.   Ka-kuchi-thã-ban
           1.SG:2.SG/3i.SG-pig-find-PAST
           'I found your pig.'

     b.   Kam-kuchi-thã-ban
           1.SG:2.SG/3i.PL-pig-find-PAST
           'I found your pigs.'

Here, 'I' and 'you' control agreement as PAC's, *kuchi* 'your pig(s)' controls agreement as a SAC. This is licit under (22b): *kuchi* heads an arc (A) which is overrun by B, and B is headed by a P-PAC.[6]

3.4 Causatives

The failure of certain absolutives in clause union structures to control agreement in Southern Tiwa confirms the overall analysis presented here. Following Gibson and Raposo (1986) and the work they build on, I assume that clause union involves the reduction of two initial clauses to one final clause, a reduction which is accomplished by the ascension of all final dependents of the lower clause into the upper clause. Gibson & Raposo's proposal is that the assignment of grammatical relations to the raised nominals is governed by the following principle: the complement subject must raise as an object, either direct or indirect. All other nominals either inherit the grammatical relation borne in the complement, or raise as chomeurs. The latter is possible only when inheritance of the earlier grammatical relation would result in a violation of stratal uniqueness. So, if the complement subject in a transitive clause raises as a direct object, the direct object in that clause must raise as a chomeur, since to raise as direct object would violate stratal uniqueness.

In Southern Tiwa clause union, it appears that the complement subject always raises as direct object.[7] Hence, when the complement is

---

[6] The heads of overrun absolutive arcs also control agreement in Goal-to-1 advancement structures. This case also satisfies (8). See Allen, Gardiner, and Frantz (1984).

[7] Allen, Gardiner, and Frantz (1984) suggest (fn. 26) that Southern Tiwa has a version of clause union in which the complement subject raises as

transitive, the complement direct object must raise as chomeur. Consider the RN for Southern Tiwa 'I made you hold the baby' under this proposal:

(25) a.

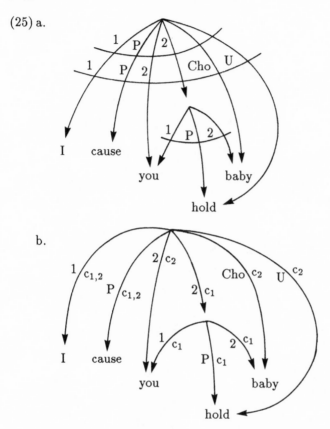

b.

The complement 1 raises as a 2, the complement 2 as chomeur. The heads of the P(redicate) and U(nion) arcs combine morphologically to form a single verb. Which nominals control agreement in the main clause? As final subject and direct object, the first and second person pronouns control agreement as PAC's. 'baby' heads an absolutive arc in the complement clause and a Cho arc in the main clause. But neither relation makes 'baby' a possible agreement controller in the main clause. To control agreement as a PAC, 'baby' would have to head a final 1 or 2 arc in the main clause, which it does not. To control agreement as a SAC, it would have to head *some* arc which is overrun, but it heads no such arc. Therefore, if (25) is well-formed in Southern Tiwa, it will be

---

indirect object. However, according to Frantz (personal communication), there is no clear evidence for a productive construction of this type.

instantiated by a sentence where only the final subject and direct object in the main clause control agreement and the agreement affix will be drawn from set c:

(26)   I-ʔuʔu-kur-ʔam-ban   (1984:96)
        1.SG:2.SG-baby-hold-cause-PAST

        'I made you hold the baby.'

Example (26) is grammatical. Further, 'baby' cannot control agreement: substituting *ka* from set d for *i* yields an ungrammatical sentence (D. Frantz, personal communication).

This case is of particular interest because it appears to be the one case in Southern Tiwa where a nominal which is an initial absolutive and final chomeur *fails* to control agreement. (8) predicts this under the analysis assumed here, for it is just in this construction that the absolutive arc is not overrun.

3.5 Conjunct Union

A construction I term *conjunct union* has been described for a number of languages, including Navajo (Hale 1975) and Tzotzil (Aissen 1987) (see also Schwartz (this volume)). The relevant feature of the construction is that the predicate is plural, but the expected controller is syntactically singular. While the 'controller' is singular, such sentences entail that several individuals satisfy the predicate. The 'controller' names one of them; the others may be named in comitative phrases. Examples from Tzotzil and Navajo are shown in (27) and (28):

(27)   ʔi-bat-ik   xchiʔuk y-ajnil   li   Xune.
        ASP-go-PL   with   his-wife the John

        'John went with his wife.'

(28)   (shí) ashiiké bił   ndaashnish.
        I   boys   with we-work

        'I am working with the boys.'   (Hale 1975)

The final subject in (27) is *li Xune*. The phrase *xchiʔuk yajnil* is a prepositional phrase, understood as comitative. The plural suffix -*ik* marks the cardinality of the set of goers, a set containing John and his wife. In (28), the final subject is the first person pronoun, with *ashiiké bił* a postpositional phrase understood as comitative. The verb can be analyzed into *na-da-sh-l-nish*, where -*sh*- cross-references a first person *singular* subject, and -*da*- a *plural* subject. The affix -*da*- entails that the number of workers is greater than one.

One might regard these as cases of semantically-driven agreement, but a syntactic account in line with the proposals of this paper is possible as well. Under this proposal, the initial subject in (27) is the coordinate nominal corresponding to 'John and his wife.' One of the conjuncts, here *li Xune*, ascends out of that coordinate nominal and assumes the subject relation. The other conjunct, the one corresponding to 'his wife,' cannot remain a conjunct, and also ascends, taking on, I propose, the dead relation in the clause (a relation characterized in Johnson and Postal 1980). This proposal is sketched below (Con = conjunct relation):

(29) a.

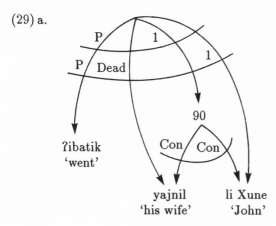

?ibatik 'went'   Con / Con   yajnil 'his wife'   li Xune 'John'

b.

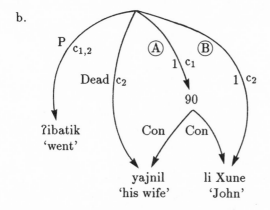

?ibatik 'went'   Con / Con   yajnil 'his wife'   li Xune 'John'

Conjunct union, then, refers to structures in which an earlier coordinate structure is dissolved, with the original conjuncts assuming grammatical relations in the clause. One assumes the grammatical relation of the host (per the Relational Succession Law (Perlmutter and Postal 1983b)), all others assume the dead relation. In Tzotzil, the dead nominal in this construction is flagged with *xchi?uk*, in Navajo, with *bił*.

As far as the agreement is concerned, the verb agrees in number with the coordinate nominal, i.e., with 90, the initial subject. But if the initial subject controls agreement, it must do so as a SAC, for it bears no grammatical relation in the final stratum at all. Then it must satisfy (8), which it does. It heads A, which is overrun by the final 1 arc, B.

In Navajo and Tzotzil, clauses containing reciprocal nominals provide additional evidence for the conjunct union analysis. In both languages, the reciprocal requires a plural antecedent, but in both languages, it can occur in sentences whose *surface structure* contains no plural antecedent. These are sentences involving conjunct union, where the antecedent is split between the surface subject and a comitative phrase. Under the present analysis, there is a level of syntactic structure in which the reciprocal has a plural antecedent, namely the initial stratum (see Hale 1975 and Aissen 1987 for details).[8]

Conjunct union in Tzotzil satisfies the Tzotzil condition on SAC's mentioned earlier. Tzotzil restricts the class of SAC's to those which host the ascension of P-PAC's. The initial subject in conjunct union hosts the ascension of the final subject, a P-PAC. Conjunct union is also possible in clauses containing coordinate initial stratum direct objects. The host may control agreement here as well, as predicted. Such structures satisfy (8), as well as the Tzotzil condition on SAC's.

4 Conclusion

For any predicate it is possible to identify a set of potential agreement controllers. This set contains all those nominals which are in the final stratum of the clause containing the predicate which have R-Signs = those of agreement controllers in kernel clauses, plus all those which head arcs that are overrun by arcs headed by P-PAC's. Language-particular rules select actual controllers from this set.

Secondary control of agreement is attested in dummy constructions (English, Italian), advancement constructions (Southern Tiwa, Tzotzil, perhaps Achenese), as well as ascension constructions (Southern Tiwa, Tzotzil, Navajo).

The present account maintains versions of (1) and (2), restricting them to PAC's. Further, it characterizes the class of agreement controllers which are not PAC's broadly enough to allow for agreement in Achenese, Tzotzil, Navajo, Southern Tiwa, English and Italian. This paper has focussed on cases where secondary agreement is possible, but (8) also rules out cases of secondary agreement (e.g., it predicts the absence of secondary agreement control in Southern Tiwa clause union). Finally, it reduces the anomalous agreement in conjunct union structures to general principles.

---

[8] Another possibility, also consistent with (8), is that the coordinate nominal bears the Chomeur relation in the final stratum, i.e., that it is put in chomage by the ascension of the conjunct *li Xune*.

References

Aissen, J. 1979. Possessor ascension in Tzotzil. In L. Martin (Ed), *Papers in Mayan Linguistics*. Columbia, Missouri: Lucas Bros.

Aissen, J. 1987. *Tzotzil Clause Structure*. Dordrecht: Reidel.

Aissen, J. To appear. Toward a theory of agreement controllers. In B. Joseph and P. Postal (Eds), *Studies in Relational Grammar* 3.

Allen, B. J. and D. G. Frantz 1983. Advancements and verb agreement in Southern Tiwa. In D. Perlmutter (Ed), *Studies in Relational Grammar* 1. Chicago: The University of Chicago Press.

Allen, B. J., D. B. Gardiner and D. G. Frantz 1984. Noun incorporation in Southern Tiwa. *International Journal of American Linguistics* 50(3):292–311.

Davies, W. 1986. *Choctaw Verb Agreement and Universal Grammar*. Dordrecht: Reidel.

Durie, M. 1984. *A Grammar of Acehnese*. Doctoral dissertation, Australian National University.

Gibson, J. and E. Raposo 1986. Clause union, the Stratal Uniqueness Law, and the chômeur relation. *Natural Language and Linguistic Theory* 4(3):295–331.

Hale, K. 1975. Counterexamples and explanations in Navajo linguistics: syntax. *Navajo Language Review* 2.1. Washington, D.C.: Center for Applied Linguistics.

Johnson, D. and P. Postal 1980. *Arc Pair Grammar*. Princeton, N. J.: Princeton University Press.

Lawler, J. 1977. A agrees with B in Achenese: a problem for Relational Grammar. In P. Cole and J. Sadock (Eds), *Syntax and Semantics* 8. New York: Academic Press.

Perlmutter, D. 1983. Personal vs. impersonal constructions. *Natural Language and Linguistic Theory* 1(1):141–200.

Perlmutter, D. and P. Postal 1983a. Some proposed laws of basic clause structure. In D. Perlmutter (Ed), *Studies in Relational Grammar* 1. Chicago: The University of Chicago Press.

Perlmutter, D. and P. Postal 1983b. The Relational Succession Law. In D. Perlmutter (Ed), *Studies in Relational Grammar* 1. Chicago: The University of Chicago Press.

11 Asymmetric Feature Distribution in Pronominal 'Coordinations'

LINDA SCHWARTZ

THIS PAPER WILL examine two asymmetric syntactic constructions that are assigned a symmetric interpretation in that they are interpreted as having two participants in the same thematic relation to the predicate. I will refer to this as a "coordinate interpretation" or "thematic coordination" and to the participants as being "thematically coordinate." The constructions are schematized in (2a) and (3a) and exemplified in (2b) and (3b) for Yapese, an Austronesian language. Person/Number abbreviations are given in (1).

In the Plural Pronoun Construction in (2), the initial pronoun is necessarily non-singular: dual in this case and others like it, or plural in other languages which have the construction but do not have a dual/plural distinction. In other contexts, a pronoun of this form would be interpreted as necessarily referring to more than one individual. However, in the Plural Pronoun Construction, the dual or plural form of the initial pronoun doesn't entail that the pronoun has a plural referent by

---

The following people have shared with me their knowledge about some of the languages used in the samples of Plural Pronoun Constructions and Verb-Coded Coordinations discussed here: Marie DeCora (Dakota), Magda Gera (Hungarian), John Hutchison (Kanuri), Judy Leidy (Diola-Fogny, Mende), Marshall Lewis (Ewe), Dzidra Liepens (Latvian), Edith Moravcsik (Hungarian, Polish), Paul Newman (Tera), Catherine Rudin (Bulgarian), Firmad Sabimana (Kirundi).

itself. Rather, what is significant about the Plural Pronoun Construction is that the pronoun can be interpreted as having a singular referent, or, in cases like Yapese, must be so interpreted.

(1)   *Person/Number Abbreviations*

1.SG	1st pers. sing.	2.SG	2nd pers. sing., etc.
1.DUAL	1st pers. dual.	3.SG	3rd pers. sing., etc.
1.DUAL(inc)	1st dual inclusive		
1.DUAL(exc)	1st dual exclusive		
1.TRIAL	1st trial		
1.PL	1st plural		
1.PO	1st pers. possessive		

(2)   *Plural Pronoun Construction*

a. [$_{NP}$ PRONOUN (&)^1 NP]
       [+PLURAL]

b. [timeew   Wag]
      2.DUAL W

    'you (SG) and Wag'   *Yapese* (Jensen 1977)

(3)   *Verb-Coded Coordination*

a. [$_S$ [$_V$ V, PRONOUN, X], NP,   Y]
              [+PLURAL]   [-PLURAL]

b. [$_S$ [$_V$ ka   ra   bow   ] Tamag]
              T/A   3.DUAL/PL   come.DUAL   T

    'he and Tamag came'   *Yapese*

In Verb-Coded Coordination, as in (3), there is no independent syntactic constituent corresponding to one of the members of the thematic coordination. Rather, the coordinate interpretation is realized syntactically in the information about person and number of participants encoded in the verbal complex[2] and information about independent noncoordinate noun phrases elsewhere in the clause.

My discussion of these structures will be asymmetrical as well, as I feel that I can say more about Plural Pronoun Constructions than Verb-Coded Coordinations at this point.[3]

---

[1] The "connector" symbolized by "&" in (2a) may or may not appear overtly in Plural Pronoun Constructions; for example, no connector appears in Yapese. More on the meaning of overt connectors later.

[2] The verbal complex is bracketed in (3b).

[3] See Schwartz (1985a) for a fuller account of the characteristics of Verb-Coded Constructions; a larger sample of languages is also presented there.

1 Plural Pronoun Constructions

1.1 Examples

Some sample Plural Pronoun Constructions (PPCs) are given in the examples in (4)–(6). I'll first briefly examine each instance and then make some general comments about the construction.

(4) a. koah   mwehuki kang rais
      2.SG   like   eat   rice

      'You (SG) like to eat rice.'   *Mokilese* (Harrison 1976)

   b. kamwa   mwehuki kang rais
      2.DUAL like   eat   rice

      'You two like to eat rice.'

   c. [kamwa   Davy] inla duhdu
      2.DUAL D   go   swim

      'You (SG) and Davy went swimming.'

(5) a. ŋà pá
      I   come

      'I have come.'   *Kpelle* (Westermann 1930, Welmers 1973)

   b. kwà pá
      1.PL come

      'We have come.'

   c. [kwà yá]   kú   pá
      1.PL 2.SG 1.PL come

      'You (SG) and I / We and you (SG) have come.'

(6) a. es   gāju   mājās
      1.SG went.1.SG home

      'I went home.'   *Latvian*

   b. mēs gājām   mājās
      1.PL went.1.PL home

      'We went home.'

   c. [mēs ar Jāni] gājām   mājās
      1.PL &   J   went.1.PL home

      'John and I / we and John went home.'

In Mokilese, the second person pronoun *kamwa* is dual, contrasting with singular *koah*, as shown in (4a) and (4b), but in (4c) it occurs in a construction in which the second person referent must be interpreted as singular. Thus, the interpretation of the whole construction is that there is a thematic coordination of two: the hearer and Davy. If more than two people are involved, the initial pronoun would have to be in the plural form *kamwai* rather than in the dual.

In Kpelle, a similar pattern occurs, but with some differences of interpretation due to lack of a dual/plural contrast. In (5b), *kwà* is interpreted as having a plural referent, contrasting with *ŋà* in (5a), which is interpreted as having a singular referent. In (5c), however, the first person referent can be understood to be either singular or plural, though *kwà* is formally plural. Latvian in (6) is parallel to Kpelle in its interpretation. It differs from the others in having an overt connector morpheme and case inflection, to be discussed later.

In (7) are listed some languages in which some version of the PPC is in general use.[4]

(7)		Language	Language Family
	a.	Latvian	Indo-European: Baltic
		Polish	Indo-European: Slavic: West
		Russian	Indo-European: Slavic: East
		Bulgarian	Indo-European: Slavic: South
	b.	Hungarian	Uralic: Finno-Ugric: Ugric
	c.	Kpelle	Niger-Kordofanian: Mande
		Mende	Niger-Kordofanian: Mande
		Temne	Niger-Kordofanian: W. Atlantic
		Diola-Fogny	Niger-Kordofanian: W. Atlantic
		Ewe	Niger-Kordofanian: Niger-Congo: Kwa
		Kirundi	Niger-Kordofanian: Niger-Congo: Bantu
	d.	Tera	Afro-Asiatic: Chadic
	e.	Tagalog	Austronesian: Indonesian
		Mokilese	Austronesian: E. Oceanic: Micronesian
		Yapese	Austronesian: E. Oceanic: Micronesian
		Hawaiian	Austronesian: E. Oceanic: Polynesian
		Fijian	Austronesian: E. Oceanic: Polynesian

---

[4] By general use, I mean that grammars give it as the only, usual or preferred form for expressing thematic coordination, or that native speakers do the same.

Now, I'll briefly summarize the findings presented in Schwartz (1985b) on the meaning of this form, some constraints on its usage and the range of syntactic forms it takes.

1.2 Meaning of Plural Pronoun Constructions

Although the precise meaning and range of meaning of this construction is not entirely clear, the follow points are salient. Sentences given to illustrate the use of PPCs typically denote activities in which more than one individual can or must participate ('unitary interpretation'). When an overt, non-reduced connector morpheme occurs in the PPC, in all cases it has a range of meaning in its other uses including accompaniment or comitativity, and the connector is generally not used for other expressions of phrasal or sentential coordination (except, in some cases, NP coordination). While this kind of of evidence would indicate that PPCs express thematic coordination with a unitary interpretation, some languages at least allow independent interpretation as well. This is true for Kirundi, Latvian and Hungarian, although a unitary interpretation is evidently preferred. In these languages, PPCs can also appropriately be used with predicates like 'be tall,' which force an independent interpretation. Thus, whatever their structure may be, PPCs seem to serve the general function served in other languages by phrasal coordinations, with the possible restriction in some, but not all, languages to an interpretation of unitary action.

1.3 Constraints on Usage of Plural Pronoun Constructions

The full range of usage of PPCs and the range of possible limitations are not explicitly discussed in many of the descriptions of these constructions. There are, however, a few clear cases which indicate that two factors may limit the use of PPCs: grammatical function and person.

It seems that in the languages where the PPCs are limited in grammatical function, they are always preferred (Kirundi) or obligatory (Ewe, Tera, Hungarian) as subjects while they may be dispreferred or disallowed in other functions.[5]

In Tagalog, first and second person pronouns are used in PPCs but third person pronouns are not. In Latvian, PPCs are strongly preferred for expressing thematic coordination involving first and second person but less strongly preferred for third. Examples of PPCs involving no apparent person restrictions or preferences are found in Hungarian, Polish, Kpelle, Temne, Ewe, Acholi, Bari, Logbara, Tera, Hawaiian, and Yapese. Associated with this, I have a strong general impression that this

---

[5] In Tagalog, PPCs are obligatory for NG phrases but not for ANG and SA-marked phrases. It's unclear how this falls under the generalization about grammatical relations given here.

construction is used preferably/exclusively with humans; Hungarian and Polish are claimed to have such a restriction (Edith Moravcsik, p.c.).

1.4 Case Government in Plural Pronoun Constructions

In the case languages with PPCs, in NP coordination, all members of a coordinate structure derive their case from the same source: that category which governs the mother node of the conjunction. In Russian, Polish, Bulgarian and Latvian, the first member of a PPC receives its case in this manner, but the second member would seem to be governed by the connector, as if the connector were functioning as a case-assigning preposition, instrumental in Russian and Polish, accusative in Latvian. This is illustrated in (8) and (9) for Russian and Latvian.[6]

(8) a. [Petja i   tovarišč]   pogibli na vojne   *Russian*
          P   & comrade.NOM perish in   war   (Crockett 1976)

          'Peter and his comrade perished in the war.'

     b. [my   s   Petej]   poedem segodnja za   gorod
          1.PL.NOM & P.INST will go today   beyond city

          'Peter and I will go to the country today.'

(9) a. [Anna   un   Jānis] gāja mājās
          A.NOM &   J.NOM went home

          'Anna and John went home.'   *Latvian*

     b. [mēs   ar Jani] gājām mājās
          1.PL.NOM & J.ACC went   home

          'John and I went home.'

In the (a) examples, both NPs of NP coordination appear in the nominative case, which is what would be expected for subject function in these constructions. However, in the (b) examples, the initial pronoun of the PPC appears in nominative case but the NP which is the second member of the construction is instrumental in Russian, accusative in Latvian. In all instances, the case of the member of the construction following the connector is exactly the one which the connector morpheme governs in its other, prepositional, uses.

Similarly, in Tagalog, the case of each NP in NP coordination is governed by the function of the whole coordination in the sentence, while

---

[6] Beginning with these examples, only the PPC interpretations will be given, not ones in which the initial pronoun may be independently interpreted as plural. See Schwartz (1985b) for a discussion of some other mechanisms found in the individual languages which prevent a dual/plural contrast from being neutralized in PPCs.

in the PPC, the case of the initial pronoun is governed in this manner, while the case of the second member is invariably the NG case. This is shown in (10).

(10) a. nakita   ko   [[si   Juan] at [si   Ben]]
         saw.OF   1.SG.NG   ANG J   & ANG B   *Tagalog*

         'I saw Juan and Ben'   (Schachter & Otanes 1972)

     b. nakita   ko   [sila   [ni   Juan]]
         saw.OF   1.SG.NG   3.PL.ANG NG   J

         'I saw him and Juan'

In (10), both members of the NP coordination in (a) are marked with ANG case-markers due to their grammatical function in the sentences as undergoers of an Object-Focus (OF) verb construction, while in (b), only the initial pronoun of the PPC is in ANG form, and the second NP is necessarily preceded by the NG marker. However, Tagalog differs from Russian, Bulgarian, Polish, and Latvian in that there is no overt constituent present in the Tagalog PPC which can be construed as governing the second member, so that construction-internal government must be considered a property of the PPC rather than an independent property of an overt, preposition-like governing morpheme.

1.5 Asymmetrical Number and Case in Plural Pronoun Constructions

PPCs, then, manifest two kinds of displaced marking, where a property marked on a given constituent is a property of the construction rather than of that constituent: obligatory duality/plurality of the initial pronoun and construction-internal case government. We might raise the question of why such a symmetry occurs in PPCs rather than in NP coordination. The answer may have to do with the universal nature and function of first and second person plural pronouns. These pronouns specify heterogeneous groups, including a speech act participant and one or more members not of the same status. For example, first person plural indicates a group including speaker and others, second person dual indicates a group including addressee and one other but excluding speaker, etc. This is significantly different from the function of plural nouns, which refer to groups of homogeneous members, in both their specific and generic uses. Thus, the plural marking on the initial pronoun of the PPC is not just a feature of the construction attached in only one (arbitrary) location within the construction. Rather, the plural pronouns already represent a nonhomogeneous group and thus are "sitting ducks" for this kind of marking. If, as suggested here, the meaning of the discourse participant pronouns is a significant factor in providing the basis for the PPC, it would then seem reasonable that some languages might limit the PPC to first and second person, as Tagalog does, or might exhibit a stronger preference for PPCs for these persons but not for third person, as Latvian does. This may also account in part for their apparent restriction to expressions of thematic coordination of humans/animates.

I would like to suggest further that the initial pronoun of the PPC should perhaps be considered to be the single head of the construction as opposed to the initial member of a multiheaded syntactic coordination. I take the externally-governed case marking of this constituent as evidence of this, and I think that the plural number marking on this constituent can be viewed in the same way: that is, these constructions can be viewed as ones in which case and number of the dominating node are morphologically marked on the head of the construction. One kind of evidence which perhaps supports this hypothesis is the general higher cohesiveness of PPCs relative to NP coordinations discussed in Schwartz (1985b). Additionally, in at least some languages, such as Kirundi and Temne, noun phrases and pronouns in NP coordination structures are interchangeable (i.e., both 'I and Sam' and 'Sam and I' are possible), while the corresponding constituents of PPCs in these languages are not interchangeable: a pronoun must always precede a noun phrase, and a $1 > 2 > 3$ person hierarchy determines the order of pronominal members. The person hierarchy in linearization of PPCs, as far as I can tell from the data so far, is invariably $1 > 2 > 3$, though as noted in Schwartz (1978), this is only one of four attested hierarchies out of six logical possibilities. This specific hierarchy can be derived from the requirement that person/number be morphologically marked on the head of the construction and from the general person hierarchy which apparently obtains universally in coordinations, such that if a coordination contains a first person member, then the person of the coordination is first; if the coordination contains a second person but no first, then the person is second, with third person being the default value (as stated, for example, in Corbett 1983 and Zwicky 1977). Furthermore, this hypothesis is consistent with the general linearization principles of the languages, in that nominal heads generally precede complex non-heads within their phrases. Also, in those languages where an overt connector morpheme of the PPC has other modifying or prepositional functions, the specific order of phrases introduced by this connector relative to its head is also consistent with this analysis. That is, in all of the languages, the general order of HEAD>NON-HEAD holds, and in languages with overt connectors in PPCs, the order HEAD>& X holds.[7]

---

[7] An implication of this hypothesis would seem to be that the same analysis (i.e., of a single-headed construction) would have to be extended to NP coordination in Type 4 languages discussed in Schwartz (1985b).

Even granting that PPCs are single-headed constructions with the initial plural pronoun as head, there remains some anomaly within the structures, in that the principles for specifying number of the mother node would seem to be of the type used for syntactic coordination so that the plurality of the mother node is warranted by a conjunction of singular daughters, while the principles for specifying number and case manifestation would be of the type used for single-headed constructions rather than multiheaded syntactic coordinations.

2 Verb-Coded Constructions

Some examples of Verb-Coded Coordinations are given in (11)–(14).

(11)   otidohme [s majka   mi]   na paza
        went.1.PL & mother 1.PO to market

        'My mother and I went to the market.'   *Bulgarian*

(12)   [tádà -nzé   -a]   káshò
        child -3.SG.PO -ASSOC   came.3.PL

        'He and his son came.'   *Kanuri* (Hutchison 1980)

(13)   [niye kići] Tim oūkiyakte
        2.SG   &   T   help.3.SG→1.DUAL(inc).FUT

        'Tim will help you and me.'   *Dakota*

(14)   Kea   guyrow [Tamag]
        3.SG.saw   3.DUAL   T

        'He saw him and Tamag.'   *Yapese*

In Bulgarian, as shown in (11), the verb is marked for first person plural, though there is no independent first person pronoun in the clause and the third person referent is manifested syntactically by the bracketed prepositional phrase. A similar pattern is found in Kanuri in (12), except that the independent NPs which are members of the thematic coordination are marked postpositionally. Dakota in (13) differs from the others in that it distinguishes a first person dual inclusive from first person plural, so the verb form clearly indicates that the thematic coordination consists precisely of speaker and hearer. Yapese in (3) and (14) differs from the others in that the independent NP member of the thematic coordination is unmarked, as it would be in the corresponding PPC as shown in (2).

Some of the languages in the sample considered in this paper which have PPCs also have VCCs: these are Bulgarian, Hungarian and Yapese.

Kanuri and Dakota, to my knowledge, have VCCs but not PPCs. At this point, I won't pursue the issue of whether there is a systematic correlation between the presence or absence of these two structures relative to each other.

In languages which have an overt connector, the preposition or postposition which marks the independent member is again of the comitative type: in Bulgarian and Hungarian it is the same as the connector in PPCs. However, the absence of an overt connector in Yapese indicates that this is not a necessary feature of the construction, just as Tagalog and Yapese demonstrate the same for PPCs. It follows from the nature of the VCC that the grammatical function of VCCs will be limited to those functions encoded on the verbal complex. There is some evidence of person restrictions, which, like the evidence of PPCs, would indicate that first person or the speech act participants are preferentially encoded in these constructions as opposed to third person; see the discussion in Schwartz (1985a).

We can identify the "missing" element from the independent NP constituent for Bulgarian, Hungarian and Dakota by the order of the connector, which would in a full coordination appear with the second member but not the first. This procedure is inconclusive for Kanuri, however, because the associative morpheme would ordinarily be attached to both members of a coordination. Of course, this would be inconclusive for Yapese as well, since there is no overt connector morpheme.[8]

I will make a few informal comments now about what could be done to deal with VCCs in a grammatical framework where agreement is accounted for by constraints on feature compatibility in specified relations. At the level of the clause, the problem arises of feature compatibility between those NPs which control verb agreement and the person/number markings on the verb. For example, the Control Agreement Principle of Generalized Phrase Structure Grammar, as stated in Gazdar and Pullum (1982) requires identity of feature coefficients for controller and controllee. The fact that in languages with an overt connector, the independent NP member of the thematic coordination looks like it has a "gap" in it would perhaps suggest an analysis using a "slash" category. However, there is no overt "displaced" NP at the clausal level to warrant this, though it might be possible to somehow allow the agreement features on the verbal complex to match up with the "slash" and provide the features of the missing NP. Alternatively, it may be that the requirement of control agreement should be stated in terms of feature compatibility rather than feature identity, in such a way that controller agreement

---

[8] In fact, in structures like (14), it isn't even clear which independent NP will be involved in a thematic coordinate interpretation. Given the fact that any participant may apparently be manifested as null within the clause, (14) could also have the interpretation 'Tamag saw those two.'

features and feature coefficients must be in an inclusion relation to controllee features—that is, that controllee features may equal or properly include controller features. The case of inclusion but not proper inclusion corresponds to the requirement of the Control Agreement Principle and is probably the unmarked case of feature compatibility universally. The case of proper inclusion of controller features by the controllee corresponds to the special case of VCC constructions.[9]

3 Conclusion

I had hoped to be able to make some general statements about feature distribution that would apply to both of these constructions. Impressionistically, it seems that the heads of these constructions bear a heavier responsibility than any member of a "standard," multiheaded coordinate structure. In the PPC, the initial pronoun, hypothesized to be the head, carries person, number and case for the full construction, though plural number is warranted only additively, by virtue of the construction expressing a thematic coordination. In the VCC, the verb as head of the clause must have all person and number information for its controller, though the controller is free to be less than fully manifested as an independent constituent. Structurally, there seems to be a very direct correspondence between VCCs and PPCs. Specifically, if the agreement features for the relation in question are taken off the verb of a VCC and added to the "gap" in the syntax of the independent member of the thematic coordination, the result would be a PPC. This should raise questions about the possible correlation of these construction which I haven't explored here, and I think that it is also suggestive of a common or similar formal treatment of these constructions. Lastly, I don't think that these constructions can be considered to be particularly rare or unusual: the PPC, at least, seems to have a wide distribution, with possible genetic and areal factors, and I suspect that the same is true of the VCC (besides the languages mentioned here, see Aissen (this volume) regarding VCCs in Tzotzil; other languages which have been suggested to me as possibly having VCCs include Hausa and Cherokee). Furthermore, the information for semantic interpretation is all there, though not distributed in a way that corresponds to a symmetrical mapping of syntax to interpretation, but such asymmetry is not surprising if we consider it to arise from the basic syntactic distinction between HEAD and NON-HEAD of a construction.

---

[9] There may be other instances where features marked on the controllee are in a proper inclusion relation to features marked on the controller, as in the cases of covert agreement discussed in Lehmann (1983) and Moravcsik (1978), where the agreeing category is not a morphological category of the controller.

References

Aissen, J. 1987. Extensions of brother-in-law agreement. *Agreement in Natural Language: Approaches, Theories, Descriptions.* Stanford: Center for the Study of Language and Information, Stanford University.

Corbett, G. G. 1983. *Hierarchies, Targets and Controllers: Agreement Patterns in Slavic.* London, Croom Helm. (Also University Park: Pennsylvania State University Press.)

Crockett, D. 1976. *Agreement in Contemporary Standard Russian.* Cambridge, Mass.: Slavica Publishers.

Gazdar, G. and G. K. Pullum 1982. *Generalized Phrase Structure Grammar: A Theoretical Synopsis.* Bloomington: Indiana University Linguistics Club.

Harrison, S. P. 1976. *Mokilese Reference Grammar.* Honolulu: University Press of Hawaii.

Hutchison, J. 1980. The Kanuri associative postposition. *Studies in African Linguistics* 11:321–354.

Jensen, J. T. 1977. *Yapese Reference Grammar.* Honolulu: University Press of Hawaii.

Lehmann, C. 1982. Universal and typological aspects of agreement. In H. Seiler and F. J. Stachowiak (Eds), *Apprehension: das sprachliche Erfassen von Gegenständen.* Teil II. Tübingen: Gunter Narr.

Moravcsik, E. 1978. Agreement. In J. H. Greenberg (Ed), *Universals of Human Language* 4. Stanford: Stanford University Press.

Schachter, P. and F. Otanes 1972. *Tagalog Reference Grammar.* Berkeley: University of California Press.

Schwartz, L. 1978. Person hierarchies in activity precedence languages. Paper presented at the Fourth Minnesota Regional Conference on Language and Linguistics, Minneapolis.

Schwartz, L. 1985a. Conditions on verb-coded coordinations. Paper presented at the Fourteenth Annual University of Wisconsin-Milwaukee Linguistics Symposium. To appear in H. Hammond, E. Moravcsik, and E. Wirth (Eds), *Studies in Syntactic Typology.* Amsterdam: John Benjamins.

Schwartz, L. 1985b. Plural pronouns, coordination and inclusion. In N. Stenson (Ed), *Papers from the Tenth Minnesota Regional Conference on Language and Linguistics,* 152–184. Minneapolis: Department of Linguistics, University of Minnesota.

Welmers, W. 1973. *African Language Structures.* Berkeley: University of California Press.

Westermann, D. 1930. *The Kpelle Language in Liberia.* Berlin: Reimer.

Zwicky, A. 1977. Hierarchies of person. *Papers from the Thirteenth Regional Meeting of the Chicago Linguistic Society,* 714–733.

12 Agreement with Gaps in Chamorro and Palauan

SANDRA CHUNG & CAROL GEORGOPOULOS

CURRENT RESEARCH IN agreement is directed not only toward describing the agreement systems we know about, but also toward constraining the types of agreement that grammatical theory allows in principle. The particular constraints one imposes are, of course, dictated largely by the theoretical perspective one adopts. For instance, Keenan (1974), in exploring the relevance of function-argument structure to morphosyntax, advances the claim that functions may agree with their arguments. Such a claim allows for the possibility that a relative clause may agree with its head NP, and a constituent question may agree with its displaced interrogative phrase. On the other hand, Zaenen (1983), working within Lexical-Functional Grammar, develops a view of unbounded dependencies in which agreement (in number, case, grammatical function, and so on) is banned between a relative clause and its head NP, or between a constituent question and its interrogative phrase. The ban follows from Zaenen's claim that the morphosyntax of unbounded dependencies is defined exclusively on constituent structures, plus the assumption that number, case, and grammatical function are encoded only in functional structures (see Zaenen 1983: 470 and Kaplan and Bresnan 1982).

This paper is distilled from other papers we have written; see, for example, Chung (1982) and Georgopoulos (1985). Our acknowledgements to Chamorro and Palauan consultants in those papers carry over to this one. The research reported here was supported in part by NSF grants BNS78-13018, BNS84-05596, and BNS84-10542 to UCSD.

We show here that two Austronesian languages, Chamorro and Palauan, exhibit a type of agreement that is not predicted by Zaenen's proposal but is (in spirit, at least) predicted by Keenan's. In these languages, the verb of a relative clause or a constituent question agrees in
grammatical function with the *gap* controlled by the head NP or the
displaced interrogative phrase. This agreement contrasts strikingly with
subject-verb agreement, modifier-head agreement, and the other types
of agreement usually discussed in the literature.

Our goal is to describe this WH-Agreement at the same time as we
demonstrate two points. First, WH-Agreement satisfies the informal expectations that one might have of an agreement system; and second, it
is consistent with Zaenen's informal characterization of the morphosyntax of unbounded dependencies, *except* for the fact that it is a kind of
agreement. The overall thrust of these observations is that the theory of
agreement must be rich enough to admit WH-Agreement as a possible
type. We conclude by exploring the issues that a Keenanesque approach
would have to address in order for the Chamorro and Palauan facts to
fall out directly.

We begin with a bare-bones description of WH-Agreement in Chamorro, then move to Palauan, and finally discuss the two agreement systems
together.

1 WH-Agreement in Chamorro

Chamorro is a VSO language with a rudimentary case marking system
and a system of subject-verb agreement. There are three morphological
cases: unmarked, oblique, and local. Subject-verb agreement is realized by one of three sets of verbal prefixes that also encode mood and
transitivity. The agreement prefixes are glossed 'realis transitive' (RT),
'realis intransitive' (RI), and 'irrealis' (IR) in our examples:

(1) a. Ha-fa'gasi   si   Henry i   kareta
         AGR(3.SG.RT)-wash UNM   Henry the   car

         ni   häpbun.
         OBL   soap

         'Henry washed the car with soap.'

     b. Pära u-fa'gasi   si   Henry i   kareta
         will   AGR(3.SG.IR)-wash UNM   Henry the   car

         ni   häpbun.
         OBL   soap

         'Henry will wash the car with soap.'

While a finite verb normally has the morphology shown in (1), its realization is different if it occurs inside a relative clause, a constituent question, or one of the other familiar unbounded dependency constructions (Chung 1982). In that case its realization is determined by the grammatical function that the gap bears to it, a point that we illustrate here with constituent questions.

If the gap is a subject and the subject-verb agreement that it normally triggers is chosen from the RT set, then the infix -*um*- occurs instead of the normal agreement prefix. This infix is italicized in (2):

(2)   Hayi   f*um*a'gasi   _   i   kareta?
       who?   AGR(WH.SBJ).wash   the car

       'Who washed the car?'

If the gap is a direct object, or the second object of a double object construction, then the verb is optionally nominalized with the infix -*in*-. Nominalized verbs agree with their subjects in the same way that lexical N's agree with their possessors: this agreement is realized as a suffix. Further, any overtly realized direct object appears in the oblique case. The infix -*in*-, and the suffix that signals possessor agreement, are italicized in (3):

(3)   Hafa   f*ina*'gase-*nña*   si   Henry   _   pära hagu?
       what?   AGR(WH.OBJ).wash-3.SG UNM   for you

       'What did Henry wash for you?'

Finally, if the gap is an instrument or the oblique object of an intransitive verb, the verb is obligatorily nominalized, but the -*in*- infix does not appear:

(4)   Hafa   fa'gase-*nña*   si   Henry ni   kareta _ ?
       what?   AGR(WH.OBL).wash-3.SG UNM   OBL car

       'What did Henry wash the car with?'

If the gap bears some grammatical function besides those just mentioned, the verb assumes its ordinary finite form.

A comparison of (2-4) confirms that the realization of the verb varies according to the grammatical function of the gap. We analyze this as the result of WH-Agreement. The WH-Agreement rule is given informally in (5), and its morphological consequences in Chamorro are described in (6):

(5)   *WH-Agreement* (first version):
       A verb agrees in grammatical function with a gap dependent on it.

(6)   *Consequences in Chamorro:*
  a. WH-Agreement with a subject gap is realized as -*um*- if the verb is realis transitive.
  b. WH-Agreement with an object is realized (optionally) as nominalization plus -*in*-.
  c. WH-Agreement with an oblique gap is realized as nominalization.

The chart in (7) reveals why we treat this agreement as reflecting the grammatical function of the gap, rather that its morphological case marking: each grammatical function determines a single form of WH-Agreement, whereas the same cannot be said for particular morphological cases.

(7) | Type of WH-Agreement | Grammatical Function of the Gap | Case Marking of the Gap |
|---|---|---|
| (6a) | subject | unmarked |
| (6b) | direct object | unmarked |
| (6b) | second object | oblique |
| (6c) | oblique | oblique |

2 WH-Agreement in Palauan

The WH-Agreement found in Palauan also conforms to (5), although its morphological realization is rather different. Palauan is a VOS language that lacks case marking, but does have subject-verb agreement. The two sets of agreement prefixes also encode realis versus irrealis mood:

(8) a.   Ak-mesa   a kekeriei el box.
          AGR(1.SG)-see.R   small

          'I see the small box.'

    b.   Ngdiak ku-sa   a kakerous.
          not   AGR(1.SG)-see.IR   difference

          'I don't see the difference.'

In addition, mood is indicated elsewhere in the verb morphology, in a way too complicated to describe here (see Josephs 1975). All that matters for our purposes is that a verb is morphologically inflected for mood even when its agreement prefix is missing—a fact that is reflected in our word-for-word glosses.

Realis and irrealis verb forms in Palauan have a distribution that is, overall, unremarkable: irrealis verbs appear in negated clauses, conditional clauses, and imperatives, while realis verbs are found elsewhere.

The situation alters, however, if the verb occurs inside an unbounded dependency. Then what we have been calling 'mood' morphology not only indicates mood but also reflects the grammatical function of the gap (see Georgopoulos 1984). We illustrate this with relative clauses.

If the gap is a subject and the semantic mood of the clause is realis, then the verb displays realis morphology but does not exhibit an agreement prefix. The relevant verb form is italicized in (9):

(9) [a 'ad [el *mil'erar*   tia el buk   _]]
     man that AGR(WH.SBJ).bought.R that   book

'the man that bought that book'

On the other hand, if the gap is a non-subject and the semantic mood of the clause is realis, then the verb displays *irrealis* morphology:

(10) [a buk [el l-*ul'erar*   _ a 'ad   ]]
      book that AGR(WH.NONSBJ).3-bought.IR   man

'the book that the man bought'

It should be emphasized that there is no difference in *semantic* mood between the relative clauses in (9) and (10). The morphological differences that we see in these examples are serving merely to register the grammatical function of the gap—they are the Palauan manifestation of WH-Agreement. We state the morphological consequences of WH-Agreement in Palauan in (11):

(11) *Consequences in Palauan:*
      a. WH-Agreement with a subject gap is realized via realis morphology if the semantic mood is realis.
      b. WH-Agreement with a non-subject gap is realized via irrealis morphology.

3 WH-Agreement and Domains

The Chamorro and Palauan versions of WH-Agreement have an important characteristic in common, namely, they demarcate the domain of an unbounded dependency, in Zaenen's sense. This can be seen from the fact that WH-Agreement appears in all and only the clauses that dominate the gap, and do not dominate its antecedent, in constituent structure. Compare Figure 1 with the Chamorro (12a). WH-Agreement cannot extend *above* the antecedent, as can be seen from (12b), nor can it extend *below* the gap, as shown in (12c). Comparable examples could be cited from Palauan.

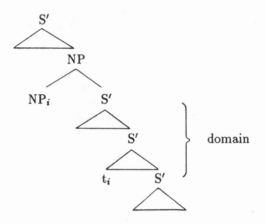

Figure 1

(12) a. Hayi   duda-*mu*   [ni
       who? AGR(WH.OBL).doubt-2.SG   that

       malagu'-*ñiha*   [pära
       AGR(WH.OBL).want-3.PL   will

       akuentuse-*nña*   i   haga-nñiha   _]]?
       AGR(WH.OBL).speak.to-3.SG   the   daughter-their

       'Who do you doubt that they want their daughter to speak to?'

    b. Kao un-sangani   si   Juan [hayi
       Q   AGR(2.SG.RT)-tell   UNM   who?

       *ni*li'e'-*mu*   _]?
       AGR(WH.OBJ).see-2.SG

       'Did you tell Juan who you saw?' (*with s*i*nangane*mmu* 'you
       tell (WH)')

    c. Hafa   bida-*ña*   _ [na
       what? AGR(WH.OBJ).do-3.SG   that

       ha-na'mänman   si   Jose]?
       AGR(3.SG.RT)-surprise   UNM

       'What did he do such that he surprised Jose?' (*with n*i*na'man-
       män*ña* 'he surprised (WH)')

Now, according to Zaenen, the morphosyntax that characterizes unbounded dependencies is defined exclusively on constituent structures,
whereas grammatical functions are encoded only in functional structures. It follows then that the morphology characteristic of unbounded

dependencies ought never involve agreement in grammatical function—a claim that is evidently contradicted by WH-Agreement.

Such a contradiction acquires significance to the extent that we can show that WH-Agreement is well-behaved in other respects. In a sense, one might be justified in closing one's eyes to WH-Agreement if it turned out to be a totally strange agreement system in other ways, or if it failed to meet our intuitive expectations of what the morphology of unbounded dependencies (abstracting away from the agreement issue) ought to be like. On the other hand, to the extent that WH-Agreement meets our expectations in these areas, its strength as a counterexample to Zaenen's proposal increases. It is for this reason that we now turn, first, to the properties of agreement systems in general, and second, to the properties that Zaenen informally attributes to the morphology of unbounded dependencies.

4 Agreement Systems

There are two properties that we believe to hold of agreement systems in general. First, agreement is disjunctive: if two morphological realizations are possible for a certain agreement, then the more specific or lexically restricted realization will take precedence over the less specific one. This is the property that Anderson's (1982) theory of inflectional morphology explains in terms of the Elsewhere Condition. Second, agreement is local. Even cases of apparent long-distance agreement involve a local controller, defined either semantically or syntactically, through which the control of agreement is mediated. In the French example (13), for instance, the local controller of gender and number agreement in *intelligentes* is the subject of the infinitive.

(13)   Elles ont essayé d'être intelligentes.
       They(FEM.PL) tried to be intelligent(FEM.PL).

Crucially for us, disjunction and locality are also properties of WH-Agreement. WH-Agreement displays the disjunctive behavior that is accommodated by the Elsewhere Condition, as can be seen in two ways. First, in both Chamorro and Palauan, WH-Agreement with a subject gap itself takes precedence over normal subject-verb agreement. This is presumably because the rule that authorizes agreement with a subject gap is more specific than the rule that authorizes agreement with a subject. Second, particular verbs whose WH-Agreement forms are idiosyncratic always employ these forms instead of the usual pattern. For example, the Chamorro verb *bida* 'do' has an idiosyncratic form for WH-Agreement with an object gap: the verb is nominalized, but the infix -*in*- exceptionally does not appear, as shown in (14a). This special realization takes precedence over the normal realization of WH-Agreement

with an object gap. So (14b), in which the ordinary morphology occurs
on top of the special morphology, is ungrammatical:

(14) a.   Hafa   bida-*mu*   –   nigap?
          what? AGR(WH.OBJ).do-2.SG   yesterday
          'What did you do yesterday?'

     b. *Hafa   b*i*nida-*mu*   –   nigap?
          what? AGR(WH.OBJ).do-2.SG   yesterday
          (What did you do yesterday?)

The local character of WH-Agreement is clearly revealed in 'long'
unbounded dependencies—unbounded dependencies whose gap is several clauses removed from its antecedent. In these, it is not the case
that every verb in the domain of the unbounded dependency agrees in
grammatical function with the gap (see Fig. 2). Instead, the verb that
takes the gap as its argument agrees in grammatical function with it;
higher verbs agree in grammatical function with whichever one of their
clausal arguments *contains* the gap. The system is so organized that
every agreeing verb has a local controller, as shown in Figure 3.

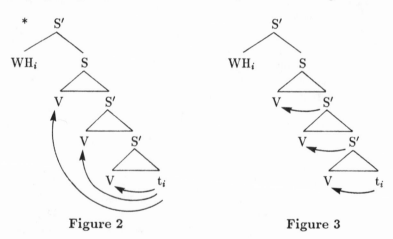

Figure 2   Figure 3

As a concrete illustration of this locality, consider the Chamorro sentences (15), in which verbs select various types of clausal arguments.
Istotba 'disturb' selects a clausal subject, *sangani* 'tell' selects a clausal
second object, and *duda* 'doubt' selects a clausal oblique. If we form
a long dependency from each of these sentences, taking the gap to be
the embedded oblique, then the embedded verb exhibits WH-Agreement
with the gap. The higher verb agrees with the clausal argument that
contains the gap; so, in (16a), *istotba* displays WH-Agreement with its

clausal subject; in (16b), *sangani* agrees with its clausal second object; and in (16c), *duda* agrees with its clausal oblique (see Chung 1982).

(15) a. Ha-istotba   yu' [na   malägu'
       AGR(3.SG.RT)-disturb   me   that   AGR(SG.RI).want

       i   lahi-hu   kareta].
       the son-my   car

       '[That my son wants a car] disturbs me.'

     b. Ha-sangani   yu' i   chi'lu-hu [na
       AGR(3.SG.RT)-tell   me   the   sister-my   that

       malägu'   gui' kareta].
       AGR(SG.RI).want   she   car

       'My sister told me [that she wants a car].'

     c. Man-duda   siha [na   malägu'
       AGR(PL.RI)-doubt   they   that   AGR(SG.RI).want

       si   Maria   kareta].
       UNM   car

       'They doubt [that Maria wants a car].'

(16) a. Hafa   *u*m*i*stotba   hao [ni
       what? AGR(WH.SBJ).disturb   you   that

       malago'-*ña*   i   lahi-mu _]?
       AGR(WH.OBL).want-3.SG   the son-your

       'What does it disturb you that your son wants?'

     b. Hafa   s*i*n*a*ngane-*nña*   i   chi'lu-mu
       what? AGR(WH.OBJ).tell-3.SG   the   sister-your

       [malago'-*ña*   _]?
       AGR(WH.OBL).want-3.SG

       'What did your sister tell (you) she wants?'

     c. Hafa   duda-*nñiha*   [ni
       what? AGR(WH.OBL).doubt-3.PL   that

       malago'-*ña*   si   Miguel _]?
       AGR(WH.OBL).want-3.SG   UNM

       'What do they doubt that Miguel wants?'

Consider also the Palauan sentences (17), in which *mengesireng* 'surprising' selects a clausal subject and *oumerang* 'believe' selects a clausal object:

(17) a. Ng-mengesireng   [el   mle   pas
     AGR(3.SG)-surprising.R   that   has.R pass.R

     er   a test a Roy].
     of

     '[That Roy passed the test] is surprising.'

   b. Ak-oumerang   [el   mo   obail   a
     AGR(1.SG)-believe.R   that   will.R wear.R

     bilir-a-redil a Mary].
     dress

     'I believe [that Mary will wear a dress].'

Once again, if a long dependency is formed from each of these types of examples, the embedded verb agrees with the gap, while the higher verb agrees with the clausal argument containing the gap. Thus 'surprising' displays WH-Agreement with its clausal subject in (18a), but 'think' agrees with its clausal non-subject in (18b):

(18) a. [a test [el   *mengesireng*
                that   AGR(WH.SBJ).surprising.R

     [el   *ble*
     that   AGR(WH.NONSBJ).have.IR

     le*pas*   _ a Roy]]]
     AGR(WH.NONSBJ).3.pass.IR

     'the test that it is surprising that Roy passed'

   b. [a bung [el   l-*ulemdasu*   a
        flower   that   AGR(WH.NONSBJ).3-thought.IR

     delak   [el   l-*omekeroul*   _ a Remy]]]
     mother   that   AGR(WH.NONSBJ).3-grow.IR

     'the flowers that my mother thought that Remy was growing'

These facts suggest that the original WH-Agreement rule in (5) should be reformulated as:

(19) *WH-Agreement* (revised): A verb agrees in grammatical function with a constituent that is dependent on it and contains a gap.

At the moment, however, this revision is less important to us than the observation that even 'long' WH-Agreement is locally controlled. Both in its locality and its disjunctive behavior, WH-Agreement satisfies our informal criteria for what an agreement system ought to be like.

5 Morphology of Unbounded Dependencies

We now turn to the extent to which WH-Agreement resembles the special morphology found in unbounded dependencies in other languages.

Aside from lack of agreement, Zaenen identifies two further characteristics of the morphosyntax of unbounded dependencies (or, as she calls it, syntactic binding). First, verbs and complementizers are the only elements in the domain of the unbounded dependency to exhibit any special marking. Second, the special marking is not a byproduct of successive cyclic WH-Movement, but rather can be found even in unbounded dependencies for which a successive cyclic derivation is implausible.

These characteristics turn out to be exhibited by WH-Agreement, and here the data match Zaenen's predictions closely. To begin with, consider the question of affected elements. WH-Agreement is, of course, realized on the verb, but there is some evidence that the complementizer of the clause is indirectly affected, as well. In Chamorro, WH-Agreement dictates the form of the complementizer: if the agreement is overtly realized, the finite complementizer *na* cannot appear. Compare (20a), where the agreement is overtly realized, with (20b), where it is not:

(20) a. Hayi *si*nangane-*nña*   si   Juan as   Maria
         who? AGR(WH.OBJ).tell-3.SG UNM   OBL

    [(*na) *u*mistótotba   _ gui']?
    that   AGR(WH.SBJ).disturbing   him

    'Who did Juan tell Maria (*that) was disturbing him?'

    b. Hayi *si*nangane-*nña*   si   Juan as   Maria
        who? AGR(WH.OBJ).tell-3.SG UNM   OBL

    [na   trinik   _ as Miguel]?
    that AGR(WH.SBJ).trick.PASS OBL

    'Who did Juan tell Maria (that) was tricked by Miguel?'

(Note, incidentally, that the grammaticality of (20b) suggests that no that-trace effect is involved in (20a).) In Palauan, particular complementizers can dictate how WH-Agreement is realized. For instance, the complementizer *el kmo,* which heads the clausal arguments of communication verbs, requires the verb immediately beneath it to have realis morphology. This requirement takes precedence over the normal realization of WH-Agreement, so that the verb is realis even when it ought to be agreeing with a non-subject gap. Compare (21a), which has *el kmo*, with (21b), which does not:

(21) a.   [a buk   [el   le-*dilu*   a Cathy
            book   that   AGR(WH.NONSBJ).3-said.IR

[el kmo *ng-'iliuii*   _ a Susan]]]
that   AGR(3.SG)-read.R

'the book that Cathy said that Susan was reading'

  b.   [a buk   [el   l-*ilsa*   a Cathy
         book   that   AGR(WH.NONSBJ).3-saw.IR

[el   *le-'iliuii*   _ a Susan]]]
that   AGR(WH.NONSBJ).3-read.IR

'the book that Cathy saw that Susan was reading'

These facts reveal an interaction between verb and complementizer that would make sense if WH-Agreement were viewed as extending to both. At the same time, neither Chamorro nor Palauan gives evidence of any other elements in the binding domain being affected, directly or indirectly, by WH-Agreement, a situation that is entirely consistent with what Zaenen describes.

As far as successive cyclicity goes, WH-Agreement can be found in several constructions for which a derivation via successive cyclic movement would be awkward, at best. The most striking example of this involves unbounded dependencies formed with resumptive pronouns in Palauan (Georgopoulos 1985).

In Palauan, the gap of an unbounded dependency may be phonetically null, or else it may be occupied by a resumptive pronoun. Resumptive pronouns appear as the object of the preposition *er*, which happens to be Palauan's only preposition; gaps appear elsewhere. Compare:

(22) a.   [a ngikel [el   ku-*lnga*   er ngii]]
            fish   that   AGR(WH.NONSBJ).1.SG-ate.IR of it

'the fish that I was eating (it)'

  b.   [a rum   [el
         room   that

le-kiltmeklii   _ a Miriam]]
AGR(WH.NONSBJ).3-clean.IR

'the room that Miriam cleaned'

If one adopts the EST assumption that transformations do not insert lexical material, including pronouns, then unbounded dependencies of the type (22a) are unlikely to be derived by a movement transformation. Nevertheless, they do exhibit WH-Agreement. The resumptive pronoun triggers WH-Agreement on the verb of which it is an argument, as shown in (22a). Further, the resumptive pronoun indirectly licenses WH-Agreement on the higher verbs in a long dependency, as can be seen from:

(23) a.   [a blai   [el   *bleketakl*   [el
          house that AGR(WH.SBJ).obvious.R   that

      l-*ongiil*   er   ngii]]]
      AGR(WH.NONSBJ).3-wait.IR for it

      'the house that it is obvious that they are waiting for (it)'

  b.   Ngngera a 'om-*ulemdasu*   [el
       what?   AGR(WH.NONSBJ).2.SG-thought.IR   that

       l-*ulengiil*   er   ngak [el
       AGR(WH.NONSBJ).3-waited.IR for me   that

       bo   ku-*ruul*
       AGR(WH.NONSBJ).will.IR AGR(WH.NONSBJ).1.SG-do.IR

       er ngii]]?
       of it

       'What did you think that they were waiting for me to do (it)?'

In these examples, the local controller of the agreement on the higher verb is the clause containing the resumptive pronoun, exactly as (19) predicts.

While these facts can be accommodated in several ways, the relevant point here is that Palauan unbounded dependencies show WH-Agreement even though they are not derived by WH-Movement. In this respect, too, WH-Agreement is consistent with Zaenen's informal description.

6 Conclusion

To sum up, we have suggested that WH-Agreement is morphologically well behaved, both as an agreement system and as an indicator of the domain of an unbounded dependency. This being the case, the fact that it is an agreement in grammatical function argues against Zaenen's claim that functional characteristics are irrelevant to the special morphosyntax of unbounded dependencies. We submit that any theory of agreement must be well developed enough to recognize WH-Agreement as a possible system. Though we will not champion any particular theory here, we would like to conclude by identifying two issues that a Keenanesque approach will have to resolve in order for the WH-Agreement facts to fall out directly.

First, and most obviously, Keenan's claim that a function may agree with its argument allows for a relative clause to agree with its head NP, or a constituent question to agree with its displaced interrogative phrase. But in WH-Agreement, the agreement is not with the head NP or the interrogative phrase, but rather with the gap controlled by these constituents. This is especially clear in relative clauses.

One may object that WH-Agreement nonetheless falls under Keenan's stipulation, given that the gap (or the clause containing it) is an argument of the agreeing verb in all the examples we have seen so far. However, the gap that controls WH-Agreement need not be an argument. Manner phrases, for instance, are modifiers—they map verb phrases into verb phrases—and so are presumably functions rather than arguments (Gazdar et al 1985). In Chamorro, manner phrases are among the obliques that control WH-Agreement, as can be seen from:

(24)   Taimänu sangan-*ña*   si   Juan _ ?

        how?   AGR(WH.OBL).say-3.SG   UNM

        'How did Juan say it?'

Examples like this suggest that, in order for WH-Agreement to be accommodated by Keenan's approach, the agreement must be viewed as ultimately controlled by the antecedent of the gap, even though it is the grammatical function of the gap, not its antecedent, that is registered on the verb. Such a view will have to lean heavily on the fact that the gap is connected to its antecedent via a binding relation.

Second, a Keenanesque approach must somehow allow for the fact that WH-Agreement may be sensitive to the larger syntactic structure in which an unbounded dependency occurs. We show this with Chamorro relative clauses.

Chamorro WH-Agreement allows a choice of two patterns in long relative clauses—relative clauses whose gap is several clauses removed from the head NP. In the first pattern, agreement is manifested on every verb in the domain of the unbounded dependency, exactly as we saw for constituent questions. This pattern, which is illustrated in (25), is available for all relative clauses. (In these examples the WH-Agreement with the object gap is not overtly realized, an option consistent with (6b).) In the second pattern, WH-Agreement appears only on the verb that has the gap as its dependent, as shown in Figure 4. This pattern is not produced by the version of the WH-Agreement rule in (19), but rather by our original rule (5).

(25) a.   Ti   in-bäba   [i   kähun [ni
          not   AGR(1.PL.RT)-open   the   box   that

          malago'*ña*   i   taotao
          AGR(WH.OBL).want.3.SG   the   person

          [pära in-bäba   –]]].
          will   AGR(WH.OBJ).1.PL-open

          'We didn't open the box that the man wanted us to open.'

     b.   Taya'   [kariñosu na   taotao
          AGR(SG.RI).not.exist   friendly   person

          [ma'a'ñao-*ña*   si   Carmen
          AGR(WH.OBL).afraid-3.SG   UNM

          [pära u-kuentusi   –]]].
          will   AGR(WH.OBJ).3.SG-talk.to

          'There doesn't exist a friendly person that Carmen is afraid to
          talk to.'

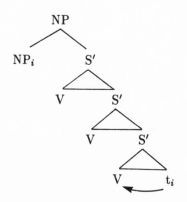

Figure 4

What interests us is that the second pattern is the preferred pattern for most types of relative clauses, but is not allowed at all for relative clauses in the existential construction (see Chung, to appear). Compare the (a) and (b) examples in (26) and (27). Nor is the second pattern allowed for constituent questions, a point that we do not illustrate here.

However one explains the presence of two WH-Agreement patterns in long dependencies, it seems clear that a description of their distribution must be able to refer to the larger syntactic structure in which a relative clause occurs. Otherwise, it would be difficult to separate the grammatical (26a) from the ungrammatical (26b).

(26) a.   In-nisisita   [lahi [ni   ti   ma'a'ñao
           AGR(1.PL.RT)-need   man   that   not   AGR(SG.RI).afraid

           si   Carmen [pära   u-kuentusi   –]]].
           UNM   will   AGR(WH.OBJ).3.SG-talk.to

           'We need a man that Carmen is not afraid to talk to.'

     b. *Taya'   [kariñosu na taotao
           AGR(SG.RI).not.exist   friendly   person

           [ma'a'ñao si Carmen
           UNM   AGR(SG.RI).afraid

           [pära u-kuentusi   –]]].
           will AGR(WH.OBJ).3.SG-talk.to

           (There doesn't exist a friendly person that Carmen is afraid to
           talk to.)

(27) a.   [Edyu i   [ma'a'ñao   yu' [na
           that the AGR(SG.RI).afraid   I   that

           u-bäba   –]]], gófdangkulu.
           AGR(WH.OBJ).1.SG-open   AGR(SG.RI).big

           'The (thing) that I'm afraid to open is very big.'

     b. *Taya'   [[ma'a'ñao   si   Carmen
           AGR(SG.RI).not.exist   AGR(SG.RI).afraid   UNM

           [pära u-kuentusi   –]]].
           will AGR(WH.OBJ).3.SG-talk.to

           (There doesn't exist (anyone) that Carmen is afraid to talk to.)

Although we have not yet investigated the matter thoroughly, we suspect that not all theories of agreement will be able to take the larger
syntactic structure into account in the way that we have in mind. In particular, Anderson's theory of morphology appears to be powerful enough
to allow WH-Agreement access to the larger context of an unbounded
dependency. However, theories in which agreement is accomplished entirely locally—and long-distance agreement is decomposed into a series
of local, and essentially disconnected steps—will have trouble describing
Chamorro WH-Agreement in a non-ad hoc way.

References

Anderson, S. R. 1982. Where's morphology? *Linguistic Inquiry* 13:571–612.

Chung, S. 1982. Unbounded dependencies in Chamorro grammar. *Linguistic Inquiry* 13:39–77.

Chung, S. To appear. The syntax of Chamorro existential sentences. In E. Reuland and A. ter Meulen (Eds), *The Representation of (In)definiteness.* Cambridge, Mass.: The MIT Press.

Gazdar, G., E. Klein, G. K. Pullum and I. A. Sag 1985. *Generalized Phrase Structure Grammar.* Cambridge, Mass.: Harvard University Press.

Georgopoulos, C. 1984. On Belauan islands: a study in agreement morphology. *Proceedings of the Tenth Annual Meeting of the Berkeley Linguistics Society.*

Georgopoulos, C. 1985. Variables in Palauan syntax. *Natural Language and Linguistic Theory* 3(1):59–94.

Josephs, L. S. 1975. *Palauan Reference Grammar.* Honolulu: University Press of Hawaii.

Kaplan, R. M. and J. Bresnan 1982. Lexical-Functional Grammar: A formal system for grammatical representation. In J. Bresnan (Ed), *The Mental Representation of Grammatical Relations,* 173–281. Cambridge, Mass.: The MIT Press.

Keenan, E. L. 1974. The functional principle: generalizing the notion of 'subject of.' *Papers from the Tenth Regional Meeting of the Chicago Linguistic Society.*

Zaenen, A. 1983. On syntactic binding. *Linguistic Inquiry* 14:469–504.

13 'Agreement' and Syntactic Composition: The Luiseño Single-Possessive Condition

Susan Steele

THIS PAPER ATTEMPTS an explanation of why the third sentence in the following triples is bad.[1]

(1) a. heelaq   up   noyaax
         is.singing   PRT.CMPLX   I.try

    'I am trying to sing.'

    b. noheelax   up
        I.good.at.singing   PRT.CMPLX

    'I am good at singing.'

    c. *noheelax   up   noyaax
         I.good.at.singing   PRT.CMPLX   I.try

    (but cf.: 'I am trying to be good at singing.')

---

[1] The source of the Luiseño data is Mrs. Villiana Hyde, a native speaker of the language. Examples are written in the orthography introduced in Hyde (1971). One abbreviation is used in the literal gloss—PRT.CMPLX for particle complex (the Luiseño instantiation of the category AUX).

(2) a. noo p   no'aash   'aw'q
        I   PRT.CMPLX   my.pet   is.sitting
        'I have a pet.'

    b. noo p   noheelaxvotaq
        I   PRT.CMPLX   I.can.sing
        'I can sing.'

    c. *noo p   no'aash   no'aw'votaq
        I   PRT.CMPLX   my.pet   I.can.sit
        (but cf.: 'I can have a pet.')

I propose a very simple, if somewhat surprising, explanation: The starred sentences are unacceptable because they contain two Possessives.[2] So, in (1a) we find *no-yaax*, in (1b) *no-heelax*, and in (1c) both *no-yaax* and *no-heelax*. Similarly, in (2a) we find *no-'aash*, in (2b) *no-heelaxvotaq*, and in (2c) *no-'aash* and *no-'aw'votaq*. The body of this paper is concerned with offering an analysis of Luiseño sentences, so that the extent of the single Possessive condition is clear. But, an explanation for the condition is in order and this too is attempted.

1 Background

We begin with an extremely abbreviated analysis of Luiseño words. I define a Luiseño word as a (compatible) combination of *Left-Occurring String* and *Right Boundary Effect*. Consider the words in (3).

(3)   Left-Occurring String—Right Boundary Effect

       a. heyi-quṣ   'was digging'
       b. taana-yk   'to the blanket'
       c. muuta-m   'owls'
       d. hengeemal-i   'boy (object)'

The Right Boundary Effect in (3a) is one of a set of Tense/Aspect suffixes, in (3b) it is one of a set of Postpositional Suffixes, and in (3c) it is the Plural Suffix, which I will say with its absence comprises a set of Number Right Boundary Effects.

(4)   muuta-NUM   'owl'   muuta-m   'owls'
       paa'ila-NUM   'turtle'   paa'ila-m   'turtles'
       hunwut-NUM   'bear'   hunwut-um   'bears'

---

[2] The Luiseño Possessives are *no* '1.SG,' *'o* '2.SG,' *po* '3.SG,' *cham* '1.PL,' *'om* '2.PL,' and *pom* '3.PL.'

And, the Right Boundary Effect in (3d) is the Object Suffix. There are other Right Boundary Effects and complications to these, but this brief introduction will do for now.

Left-Occurring Strings may have an internal analysis. Most important for this paper is the fact that some Left-Occurring Strings contain a Possessive Prefix—and some don't.

(5) a. taana-yk   'to the blanket'
    b. po-taana-yk 'to his blanket'

(6) a. po-ꞩwaamay-i   'his daughter (object)'
       po-'aach-um   'his pets'

    b. hengeemal-i   'boy (object)'
       muuta-m   'owls'

Because it will be necessary to know both the Right Boundary Effect of a word *and* whether the Left-Occurring String contains a Possessive or not, I will adopt the notation in (7) for words:

(7)   ⟨Possessive|Number⟩   ⟨—|Number⟩
        ⟨Possessive|Object⟩   ⟨—|Object⟩
        ⟨Possessive|Postposition⟩   ⟨—|Postposition⟩
                                    ⟨—|Tense/Aspect⟩

where the specification to the right of the vertical line identifies the character of the Right Boundary Effect and that to its left identifies the presence or absence of the Possessive in the Left-Occurring String.

This notation for words also applies to strings of two or more words which have a single syntactic function. Example (8) contains illustrative examples.

(8) a. ⟨Possessive|Number⟩

       po-puuch-um   konoknich-um
       HIS-eye-PL   green-PL

       'his green eyes'

       ⟨Possessive|Object⟩

       po-ꞩwaamay-i   'alaxwuch-i
       HIS-daughter-OBJ ugly-OBJ

       'his ugly daughter'

b. ⟨—|
    Number⟩

    muuta-m   yuvaataant-um
    owl-PL   black-PL

    'black owls'

    ⟨—|Object⟩

    hengeemal-i   tavulvich-i
    boy-OBJ   tall-OBJ

    'tall boy'

The examples in (8) are meant to indicate that words which share a syntactic function also share a Right Boundary Effect—hence such a collection of words can be identified, like a word, by the (shared) Right Boundary Effect. Further, it is not the case that every such collection contains a word with a Possessive, but some do. (Cf. (8a).) And, if two words in such a collection have a Possessive, the two must be compatible.

(9)   no-ma   no-mlu
         1.SG-father 1.SG-strong

         'my strong father'

Hence, a collection of words sharing a single syntactic function can be identified, like a word, as having a Possessive or not.

In short, the notation suggested above for words is actually a notation for constituents—i.e., a collection of one or more words sharing a single syntactic function. The analysis in Section 2 below is based on constituents, as represented in this notation.

2 The Analysis

Given this very abbreviated discussion of words and constituents, we are ready to consider an analysis of Luiseño sentences as it reveals the single Possessive condition.

I propose an analysis of Luiseño sentences within the framework of categorial grammar as represented in (10).[3]

---

[3] The analysis in (10) is entirely consistent with the programmatic statement of Ajdukiewicz (1967). The names *Propositional Radical, Proposition,* and *Sentence* in (10) are applied essentially as in Steele et al. (1981) Chapter Four. The term *Argument-Categorizing Element* is a category-neutral term for the element which controls the number and form of the Arguments in a sentence.

(10)   Sentence-Defining Element:

Proposition → Sentence

Propositional Function:

Propositional Radical → Proposition $\curvearrowleft$ Z

Argument-Categorizing Element:

Argument Structure → Propositional Radical $\curvearrowleft$ X

That is, a sentence is divided into two parts, a functor (the Sentence-Defining Element) and its argument (the Proposition); the Proposition is similarly divided into two parts, a functor (the Propositional Function) and its argument (the Propositional Radical); and the Propositional Radical is also divided into two parts, a functor (the Argument-Categorizing Element) and its Argument (the Argument Structure). Consider, for example, the sentence in (11).

(11)   chaqalaqi-quʂ   nil   nawitmal-i
        tickle-TENSE/ASPECT   PRT.CMPLX   girl-OBJ

'I was tickling the girl.'

The Sentence-Defining Element in (11) is *nil*; removing the Sentence-Defining Element leaves the Proposition.

(12)   nil: chaqalaqiquʂ nawitmali → chaqalaqiquʂ nil nawitmali

The Propositional Function is a condition across the Propositional Radical, the result of which is the assignment to the Proposition of a temporal value. I will simplify the analysis here by allowing the Tense/Aspect Suffix -*quʂ* in (11) to be identified with the Propositional Function. Thus, removing the Propositional Function leaves the Propositional Radical.

(13)   quʂ: chaqalaqi nawitmali → chaqalaqiquʂ nawitmali

The Argument-Categorizing Element (hereafter ACE) is *chaqalaqi*; removing the ACE leaves the Argument Structure.

(14)   chaqalaqi: nawitmali → chaqalaqi nawitmali

In addition, a Propositional Radical can be mapped, by the function labelled simply X in (10), into a Propositional Radical, and a Proposition, into a Proposition by what is labelled Z in (10). (15) is an example of the former; (16), of the latter.

(15)   noyaax: chaqalaqi nawitmali → noyaax chaqalaqi nawitmali

        as in: chaqalaqiquʂ nil   noyaax   nawitmali
                 was.tickling PRT.CMPLX   I.try   girl.OBJ

        'I was trying to tickle the girl.'

(16)   noo: chaqalaqiquʂ nawitmali → noo chaqalaqiquʂ nawitmali

as in: noo   nil   chaqalaqiquʂ   nawitmali
         I   PRT.CMPLX   was.tickling   girl.OBJ

'I was tickling the girl.'

I will have little to say here about many aspects of this analysis. I focus on the ACE, the Argument Structure, and the function X—that is, on the Propositional Radical—with a briefer consideration of the Proposition. The elements of the Propositional Radical are all involved in the single-Possessive condition; the Proposition, in the explanation.

3 The Condition

Against this sketch of the analysis it is easy to show the extent of the single-Possessive condition. I begin with the character of the Argument Structure, the ACE, and X; I conclude with the conditions on their combinations in a Propositional Radical.

3.1 The Argument Structure

An adequate account of the Argument Structure depends on three properties. First, the specification which is the Argument Structure is drawn from the character of the *obligatory* elements accompanying the ACE. The constituent types in (17) form the core of such elements.

(17) a.   ⟨Possessive|Number⟩   d.   ⟨—|Number⟩
     b.   ⟨Possessive|Object⟩   e.   ⟨—|Object⟩
     c.   ⟨Possessive|Postposition⟩ f.   ⟨—|Postposition⟩

Accompanying the ACE in (11) is a word as in (17e); accompanying the ACE in (18) is a word as in (17d).

(18)   yawaywich-um   mil   miyquʂ
        beautiful-PL   PRT.CMPLX   was

'They were beautiful.'

Note the emphasis on *obligatory*. An ACE must be associated with a number of "slots," indicating the number of arguments semantically required. So, *chaqalaqi* in (11) semantically requires two arguments (a tickler and a ticklee). But the number of elements in the Argument Structure is always one less than the number of argument slots. That is, *chaqalaqi* is accompanied only by *nawitmali*. Second, there can be no more than three elements in an Argument Structure and there can be as few as zero, which is to say that there is no ACE in Luiseño which takes more than four (semantic) arguments and fewer than one. (19) is an example of the former and (20) of the latter.

(19)   hengeemal-i   nil   potoonav-i
       boy-OBJ   PRT.CMPLX   his.basket-OBJ

       po-yk   'oovininax
       her-POSTPOSITION   made.give
       'I made the boy give his basket to her.'

(20)   tooyaquŝ   nil
       was.laughing PRT.CMPLX
       'I was laughing.'

Third, some ACEs are sensitive to the presence of a Possessive internal
to the element accompanying them and some are not. The contrast
between 'ari in (21a) and yaw in (21b) is instructive in this regard. 'ari
is clearly not sensitive to the presence or absence of a Possessive in the
form accompanying it, while yaw clearly is.

(21) a. po-toonav-i   pil   'ari-quŝ
         POSS-basket-OBJ   PRT.CMPLX   kick-TENSE/ASPECT
         'She was kicking his basket.'

     b. po-toonav-i   pil   yaw-quŝ
         POSS-basket-OBJ   PRT.CMPLX   have-TENSE/ASPECT
         'She had his basket.'

(22) a. paa'ila-y   pil   'ari-quŝ
         turtle-OBJ   PRT.CMPLX   kick-TENSE/ASPECT
         'She was kicking the turtle.'

     b. *paa'ila-y   pil   yaw-quŝ
         turtle-OBJ   PRT.CMPLX   have-TENSE/ASPECT

Thus, a constituent (instantiating an Argument) may have a Possessive whose presence is ignored by the ACE—and if this is the case, the
Argument Structure will be without a Possessive specification.

With this background, the logically possible Argument Structures
are quite clear. For example, it is logically possible to have three con-
stituents accompanying an ACE all of which are of the form ⟨—|Number⟩;
or two, one of which has the form ⟨Possessive|Number⟩ and the other
⟨—|Object⟩, and so forth. In fact, only a few of the logical possibilities
are instantiated—and the core of these is listed in (23).

(23) a.   No-element Argument Structure
          (   )

  b.   Single-element Argument Structure
        i. $(\langle-|Object\rangle)$
        ii. $(\langle Possessive|Object\rangle)$
        iii. $(\langle-|Number\rangle)$
        iv. $(\langle Possessive|Number\rangle)$
        v. $(\langle-|Postposition\rangle)$

  c.   Double-element Argument Structure
        i. $(\langle-|Object\rangle \langle-|Object\rangle)$
        ii. $(\langle-|Object\rangle \langle-|Postposition\rangle)$
        iii. $(\langle-|Number\rangle \langle Possessive|Postposition\rangle)$

  d.   Triple-element Argument Structure
        $(\langle-|Object\rangle \langle-|Object\rangle \langle-|Postposition\rangle)$

(11) is an example of (23bi); (21b), of (23bii); (18), of (23biii); and (19), of (23d). Examples of some of the others will be found in the discussion to follow.

This relatively small number of Argument Structures among the logical possibilities suggests the existence of a number of combinatorial conditions. For our immediate purposes, only one is important: There is never more than a single obligatorily Possessive-marked element per Argument Structure. Crucially, there is no such restriction when the Possessive is not specified as a critical part of the Argument Structure. So, the sentence in (24), an example of (23ci), is fine.

(24)   huu'unax   nil   po-ṣwaamay-i
        taught   PRT.CMPLX   POSS-daughter-OBJ

        no-teela-y
        POSS-language-OBJ

        'I taught his daughter my language.'

3.2 The Argument-Categorizing Element

An ACE is found in the constituent upon which the Propositional Function depends for the temporal assignment in the Proposition. The temporal properties depend on the Right Boundary Effect of the words in such a constituent—the part to the right of the slash in our notation. Hence, the ACE itself is represented in the left part. This suggests a primary division among ACEs: Some include a Possessive (i.e., occur in constituents of the type Possessive|...) and some do not (i.e., occur in

constituents of the type —|...). All of the potential ACEs in (25a) are
of the first type and those in (25b) are of the second.

(25) a. po-ma'max   'he likes'
         po-chaqalaqax   'he is good at tickling'
         no-puush   'my eyes'

     b. heyi   'dig'
         tooya   'laugh'
         yawaywish   'beautiful'

And, the pair of sentences in (26) is illustrative.

(26) a. nawitmali   up   po-chaqalaqax
         girl.OBJ   PRT.CMPLX   POSS-good.at.tickling

         'He is good at tickling girls.'

     b. heyi   xumpo
         dig   PRT.CMPLX

         'They should dig.'

As with the forms instantiating Arguments, not all such Possessives are
syntactically relevant. Compare, for example, the two sentences in (27).

(27) a. ya'ash   up   no-na'
         man   PRT.CMPLX   POSS-father

         'The man is my father.'

     b. ya'ash   up   'alaxwush
         man   PRT.CMPLX   ugly

         'The man is ugly.'

The ACE in (27a) contains a Possessive, just as the ACE in (26a) does.
However, in (27a), as the contrast with (27b) suggests, the presence of
the Possessive is not crucial. So, (27a) and (27b) are of the same semantic type—what might be called a copular sentence. On the other hand,
(26a)—what might be called a "good at" sentence—crucially contains
an ACE with a Possessive.

As suggested above, an ACE which crucially contains a Possessive is
represented as in (28a) and one which does not as in (28b). The latter
includes Left-Occurring Strings with a Possessive, as long as its presence
is syntactically irrelevant.

(28) a. Possessive|...

     b. —|...

3.3 The Function X

Finally, X, the function that takes a Propositional Radical and yields a Propositional Radical. There are two different types of elements which may perform this function. The first type—a form *Possessive-yaax*—is illustrated in (29).

(29) a. heyi   xupo   po-yaax
         dig   PRT.CMPLX   POSS-yaax
         'He should try to dig.'

     b. heyi   xupo   no-yaax
         dig   PRT.CMPLX   POSS-yaax
         'I should try to dig.'

(The argument that *po-yaax* and *no-yaax* in (29) are not in the Argument Structure would take us far afield, so I will simply stipulate it here. But, note the contrast between (27b) and the sentences in (29).) The second type appears as a morphological addition to the ACE. So, in (30) it is the form *Possessive...vota* which surrounds the ACE.

(30) a. po-heyi-vota-q   up
         POSS-ACE-vota-TENSE/ASPECT   PRT.CMPLX
         'He can dig.'

     b. no-heyi-vota-q   up
         POSS-ACE-vota-TENSE/ASPECT   PRT.CMPLX
         'I can dig.'

Although there are two different types of Possessive-marked elements which may function to map a Propositional Radical to a Propositional Radical, they may not cooccur.

(31)   *poheyivotaq up poyaax

This is clearly not a semantic restriction, since it is perfectly possible to say 'He can try to dig.' But in Luiseño this way of expressing it is impossible.

Once again, then, we have a piece of the sentence which can include a Possessive-marked element—but only one. This is represented in (32) in the now-familiar notation:

(32)   Possessive|...
        —|...

3.4 Combinations

We have now three parts that can contain a Possessive—but only one apiece. These three parts combine in the Propositional Radical, according to the sketch of an analysis in (10). Below, (33) refines the relevant part of this to show the presence of the Possessive in all three parts.

(33) $ACE_{Possessive|-}$:

$\bigwedge X_{Possessive|-}$

Argument Structure$_{Possessive|-}$ → Propositional Radical

The combinations of these parts show the same restriction, with one complication. That is, although it is logically possible, according to (33), to have a Propositional Radical with three Possessive-marked parts, with one complication a Propositional Radical may contain exactly one. The sentences with which we began exhibit this restriction.

(1) a. heelaq   up   noyaax
         is.singing   PRT.CMPLX   I.try

         'I am trying to sing.'

     b. noheelax   up
         I.good.at.singing PRT.CMPLX

         'I am good at singing.'

     c. *noheelax   up   noyaax
         I.good.at.singing PRT.CMPLX   I.try

         (but cf.: 'I am trying to be good at singing.')

(2) a. noo p   no'aash   'aw'q
         I   PRT.CMPLX   my.pet   is.sitting

         'I have a pet.'

     b. noo p   noheelaxvotaq
         I   PRT.CMPLX   I.can.sing

         'I can sing.'

     c. *noo p   no'aash   no'aw'votaq
         I   PRT.CMPLX   my.pet   I.can.sit

         (but cf.: 'I can have a pet.')

In (1a) and (2b), the element which is the function X is Possessive| ....
In (1b), the ACE is Possessive|—. And in (2a), the Argument Structure

is ($\langle$Possessive|Number$\rangle$). (1c) which contains a Possessive in both the ACE and the function X is bad, as in (2c) which contains a Possessive in both the Argument Structure and the function X.

Hence, the part of the analysis in (10) with which we are concerned can be further modified as in (34).

(34)   ACE$_{\text{Possessive}|-}$:

$\qquad\qquad\qquad\qquad\qquad\qquad$ $\bigwedge$ X$_{\text{Possessive}|-}$

$\qquad$ Argument Structure$_{\text{Possessive}|-}$ $\rightarrow$ Propositional Radical

$\qquad\qquad$ Condition: *...Possessive   ...Possessive

(34) accounts for the unacceptable sentences in (1c) and (2c) with which we began, while allowing the perfectly fine sentences in (35).

(35) a. no-toonav-i   up   no-yaax
         POSS-basket-OBJ   PRT.CMPLX   POSS-"try"

         'ariq
         is.kicking

         'I'm trying to kick my basket.'

   b. no-$waamay   up   no-ma'max
         POSS-daughter   PRT.CMPLX   POSS-like

         'I like my daughter.'

Only one of the two Possessives in each sentence in (35)—*noyaax* in (35a) and *noma'max* in (35b)—will be coded as Possessives in the analysis in (34).

I noted above the existence of a complication to the single-Possessive condition. The Argument Structure ($\langle$Possessive|Object$\rangle$) can occur with another Possessive.

(36) no-toonav-i   up   po-yaax   yawq
       POSS-basket-OBJ   PRT.CMPLX   POSS-"try"   has

       'He is trying to hold my basket.'

The difference between this Possessive-marked Argument Structure and the other two is clear upon minimal consideration. I noted above that an Argument Structure contained at most a single Possessive-marked element, but it also contains at most a single Number-marked element. So, cross-cutting the presence of the Possessive in an Argument Structure is the presence of Number.

(37) a. Possessive

    i. with Number

       $(\langle$Possessive$|$Number$\rangle)$
       $(\langle$—$|$Number$\rangle\ \langle$Possessive$|$Postposition$\rangle)$

    ii. without Number

       $(\langle$Possessive$|$Object$\rangle)$

  b. No Possessive

    i. with Number

       $(\langle$—$|$Number$\rangle)$

    ii. without Number

       $(\langle$—$|$Object$\rangle)$
       $(\langle$—$|$Postposition$\rangle)$
       $(\langle$—$|$Object$\rangle\ \langle$—$|$Object$\rangle)$
       $(\langle$—$|$Object$\rangle\ \langle$—$|$Object$\rangle\ \langle$—$|$Postposition$\rangle)$

Only the Argument Structure which does not contain Number occurs with a Possessive-marked ACE. That is, it appears that the absence of Number in the Argument Structure renders any Possessive-marked element "syntactically inert." Thus, the condition on the combination of parts in (34) must be modified as in (38).

(38)   Condition: *...Possessive ...Possessive
                  unless Possessive is $(\langle$Possessive$|$Object$\rangle)$

4 Explanation

I've offered an analysis of Luiseño sentences (main clauses, in particular) which makes abundantly clear the existence of the single-Possessive condition—and which distinguishes among those Possessives which participate in it and those which don't. It is reasonable at this point to ask why such a condition should exist.

4.1 Arguments

The first part of the explanation requires looking once again at the Argument Structure. I propose that the Argument slots associated with the Argument-Categorizing Element are filled by the Argument Structure even though the number of obligatory constituents is always one less than Argument slots. So, *chaqalaqi* has a tickler and a ticklee, is associated with two arguments, but is obligatorily accompanied by a single constituent only $(\langle$—$|$Object$\rangle)$. (Cf. (11).) The "missing" Argument is a value given by the morphological properties of obligatory constituents. In (37) Argument Structures were divided into four basic types—those which have both Possessive and Number (37a.i), those which have Possessive and no Number (37a.ii), those which have Number and No Possessive (37b.i), and those which have neither Number nor Possessive (37b.ii). In the first type the value of the Possessive supplies the value that is the missing Argument; hence, any such Argument will be 1.SG, 2.SG, 3.SG, 1.PL, 2.PL, or 3.PL.[4]

(39)   no-toonav   up   qala
        POSS-basket-number   PRT.CMPLX   is.setting
        'I have a basket.'

(40)   qala   ____   ____
                $(\langle \text{Possessive}|\text{Number}\rangle) = 1.\text{SG}$

Similarly, in the third the value of the Number specification can supply the value that is the missing Argument.

(41)   yawaywich-um   mil   miyquṣ
        beautiful-NUMBER   PRT.CMPLX   was
        'They were beautiful.'

(42)   miy   ____   ____
                $(\langle -|\text{Number}\rangle) = \text{P.PL}$

Hence, any such Argument will be P(for open person).SG or P.PL. Finally, when the Argument Structure is of either of the remaining two types, the value of the missing Argument can be simply open for Person and open for Number—i.e., can be P.N.

(43)   chaqalaqiquṣ   nil   nawitmal-i
        was.tickling   PRT.CMPLX   girl-OBJ
        'I was tickling the girl.'

(44)   chaqalaqi   ____   ____
                $(\langle -|\text{Object}\rangle) = \text{P.N}$

There is one important modification to the values available to the cases in (37bii). I ignored the Luiseño reflexive in the preceding discussion.

---

[4] This proposal will have to be supplemented with an identification of the thematic roles associated with the various Argument slots, as well as with a procedure by which the elements of the Argument Structure are connected to these. Note, in addition, that the sketch of the Person/Number values is not complete.

(45)   notaax   nil   chaqalaqiqu$

         myself   PRT.CMPLX   was.tickling

'I was tickling myself.'

I don't have time to cover all the niceties of this construction. The critical points for our purposes are two. Any ACE which can take an Object-marked Argument can also take a reflexive, so the presence of the Possessive in the reflexive form is not a critical property of such Argument Structures; however, the reflexive does, in fact, supply the value of the "missing" Argument. A representation of such Argument Structures as in (46) will allow all of these facts to be captured. So, (47) represents (45).

(46) $(\langle$—|Person and Object$\rangle)$

(47)   chaqalaqi   ____   ____

                     $(\langle$—|Person and Object$\rangle)$ = 1.SG

One question that (46) raises is the possibility of reflexives and Possessive-marked elements cooccurring. This is not possible in the Argument Structure, obviously, just as it is not possible to have two reflexives, since it would lead to there being more Arguments specified in the Argument structure than available slots. However, it is possible for a reflexive to cooccur with a Possessive on the ACE or in X.

(48) a.   notaax   up   no-chaqalaqax

          MYSELF   PRT.CMPLX   POSS-good.at.tickling

          'I'm good at tickling myself.'

     b.   notaax   up   chaqalaqiq   no-yaax

          MYSELF   PRT.CMPLX   is.tickling   POSS-"try"

          'I'm trying to tickle myself.'

The existence of such sentences rules out one possible explanation for the single-Possessive condition: It does not devolve to a condition that there can be only a single fully specified person value, as e.g., 1.SG.

4.2 The Proposition

The second part of the explanation has to do with the character of the Proposition.

The non-lexically specified Argument in the Argument Structure can be elaborated by the value of the ACE or the function X. Consider the sentences in (49), for example.

(49) a. chaqalaqiquɕ nil   noyaax   nawitmal-i

        was.tickling PRT.CMPLX   I.try   girl-OBJ

        'I was trying to tickle the girl.'

    b. 'o-y   up   chamma'max

        you-OBJ   PRT.CMPLX   we.like

        'We like you.'

In both, the value of the "missing" Argument in the Argument Structure
is P.N, but in (49a) the value of the function X modifies this value to
1.SG and in (49b) the value of the ACE modifies this value to 1.PL, as
the English glosses indicate.

This possibility suggests that a Person/Number value must be associated with some unit in addition to that in the Argument Structure.
I hypothesize that the Proposition is the unit at issue. Support for
this position is found in the function Z. In many of the example sentences above, the Argument which is a value in the Argument Structure
has no lexical instantiation. The sentences in (49) are examples. The
function Z, which takes a Proposition and yields a Proposition, is the
(non-obligatory) lexical instantiation of this Argument. So, corresponding to (49a) is (50).

(50)   noo nil   noyaax   nawitmali   chaqalaqiquɕ

        Z   PRT.CMPLX   I.try   girl.OBJ   was.tickling

        'I was tickling the girl.'

Z is compatible not with the value associated with the Argument Structure, but with the final value of the Proposition. So, the Proposition in
(50), which has the value *1.SG,* is compatible with *noo* 'I' but not with
wunaalum 'they'; the Argument Structure has the value P.N and, thus,
does not preclude the latter.[5]

4.3 The Possessive.

The third part of the explanation has to do with the properties of constituents and, in conjunction with the two other proposals just made,
accounts for the single-Possessive condition.

A constituent including a Possessive prefix in the specification to the
left of the slash like the Proposition allows the addition of a constituent
compatible with its value.

---

[5] For reasons beyond the scope of this discussion, some sentences are glossed
with more particular Person/Number values than this generalization about
the Proposition permits.

(51)   xwaan [po-puush yawaywish]   'John's beautiful face'
        noo   [no-toonav 'alaxwush]   'my ugly basket'

Now, suppose we say that the additional element compatible with a Possessive is addable at the point in the analysis when the Possessive is not—or is no longer—syntactically accessible. So, if a constituent instantiates an Argument to an ACE which does not require a Possessive, the Possessive is not syntactically accessible in the Argument Structure and an additional element can be added to the constituent at issue.

(52)   'ariquꞩ   nil   (hengeemal)   po-toonav-i
        was.kicking PRT.CMPLX   (BOY)   POSS-basket-OBJ

        'I was kicking (the boy's) his basket.'

In contrast, if a word is an Argument to an ACE which requires the Possessive, the Possessive is always syntactically accessible *internal to the Argument Structure* and, thus, no compatible element is possible in the Argument Structure. If such a Possessive occurs in an Argument Structure of the type ($\langle$Possessive|Object$\rangle$), an additional element can be added at the Argument Structure level, because this Possessive is not syntactically accessible in the Propositional Radical as we have seen. (Note in this regard that such Argument Structures never include more than one Argument.)

(53)   yawq up   (hengeemal)   po-toonav-i
        has   PRT.CMPLX   (boy)   [POSS-basket-OBJ]

        'He has (the boy's) his basket.'

Any other Possessive (as e.g., those in (40) or (49)) must allow an additional element at the Proposition.

But, the Proposition (having a single Person/Number value) is like a constituent or the Argument Structure in allowing a single additional element. If there were two accessible Possessive in the Proposition, one would be left without the possibility of a *supplementary* form; or conversely two such Possessives create the possibility of two *supplementary* forms where other conditions stipulate one. In sum, the single-Possessive condition follows automatically from the hypothesis that a Possessive allows the presence of a *supplementary* form as long as the Possessive is not syntactically accessible, if we also hypothesize that a Proposition can be *supplemented* by a single form compatible with its associated value. In fact, this latter hypothesis is already represented directly in the analysis in the function which takes a Proposition and yields a Proposition.

5 Conclusion

The analysis of Luiseño proposed here can be compared to the not uncommon (but, by no means, universal) assumption that bound elements marking number and person *agree* with and are a function of an overt expression. Taking this position in regard to the Possessives of Luiseño leaves the single-Possessive condition without obvious explanation. One such alternative might propose that what I have called the Proposition in Luiseño is always accompanied by an element (which may have a zero-instantiation). This element would control the person and number values syntactically available at various points in the Proposition. And, such an element could be represented in something like the slash notation in GPSG (cf. Gazdar 1982) which would require that if it found a syntactically accessible Possessive, it could search no further. But, this is simply a stipulation of the single-Possessive condition; the analysis proposed here is an attempt at an explanation.

References

Ajdukiewicz, K. 1967. Syntactic connexion. In S. McCall (Ed), *Polish Logic 1920–39*. Oxford: Clarendon Press.

Gazdar, G. 1982. Phrase structure grammar. In P. Jacobson and G. K. Pullum (Eds), *The Nature of Syntactic Representation*. Dordrecht: Reidel.

Hyde, V. 1971. *An Introduction to the Luiseño Language*. (Edited by R. W. Langacker et al.) Banning: Malki Museum Press.

Steele, S., A. Akmajian, R. Demers, E. Jelinek, C. Kitagawa, R. T. Oehrle and T. Wasow 1981. *An Encyclopedia of AUX: A Study in Cross-Linguistic Equivalence*. (Linguistic Inquiry Monograph 5.) Cambridge, Mass.: The MIT Press.

14 Noun Phrase Internal Case Agreement in Russian

LEONARD H. BABBY

IT IS GENERALLY assumed that attributive adjectives agree in gender, number, and case with the head of the noun phrase (NP) in which they occur (Anderson 1982). I will argue on the basis of Russian quantified NPs that while the head noun does in fact control the number and gender agreement of its modifiers, it does not control their case marking. My major hypothesis is that case is assigned to the head noun's maximal projection (N^m), and then percolates down to all the NP's available lexical and phrasal categories. NP-internal case agreement is therefore the direct result of percolation (cf. Muysken 1983); there is no exchange of case features among lexical items. Case should be thought of as a property of the NP as a whole, not of the head noun. Russian quantified NPs therefore provide overwhelming support for the hypothesis that the distribution of case in a NP is determined by structural relations defined on X-bar structures (cf. Chomsky 1981).

This article is the most recent in a series devoted case distribution and quantifiers in Russian (see References).

1 Some Basic Notions

A NP consists of a head noun, modifiers, and subcategorized complements to the head and to its modifiers. Only the head noun and its modifiers, the NP internally unsubcategorized constituents, are in the *path of percolation* of the case assigned to N^m (cf. Bowers 1984). A complement's case marking is exhaustively determined by its head, and is therefore totally independent of the case assigned to the NP as a whole. For example, adnominal complements in Russian normally have genitive (GEN) case marking, which is independent of the case assigned to the head noun, its modifiers, and the phrasal categories that dominate them (e.g., see *vina* (GEN) 'wine,' the complement of the head noun in (1) and (2)). When we speak below of case agreement and distribution, we will therefore be speaking about categories in the path of percolation only.

An oblique case in Russian is characterized as a *lexical case* if it is assigned to N^m by a particular lexical item. For example, the preposition *s* 'with' is a lexical case assigner since the prepositional phrase (PP) it heads is well-formed only if its complement has instrumental (INST) case marking (e.g., see (1)).

Nominative (NOM) and accusative (ACC) are *structural cases*: they are assigned to N^m in accordance with the NP's overall structural environment (see Belletti and Rizzi 1981). N^m is assigned accusative case in Russian when it is governed by a lexical category that is not a lexical case assigner. For example, direct objects are assigned accusative case structurally because the "transitive" verbs that govern them are not lexical case assigners (this analysis is based on the distribution of the genitive of negation (Babby 1980b)). N^m is assigned nominative case if it is simply not governed by a lexical category.

If a NP in Russian does not contain a quantifier phrase, the head noun and all its modifiers have the same case marking. We must turn to quantified NPs for unambiguous evidence that NP-internal case agreement is not controlled by the head noun.

2 Quantified Noun Phrases

Quantified NPs in Russian have a striking morphosyntactic property. When they are assigned oblique case, their internal case distribution is *homogeneous*; in (1), for example, all the modifiers and the head are instrumental. But when quantified NPs are nominative or accusative, their case distribution in the path of percolation is *heterogeneous* (see ACC vs. GEN in (2)). This section will be devoted to a principled explanation of this curious fact.

(1) a. s   [pjat'ju   bol'šimi   butylkami
         with   five.*INST* big.*INST*.PL bottles.*INST*.PL

         vina   ]$_{\text{NP.INST}}$
         wine.GEN

         'with five big bottles of wine'

    b. *s   [pjat'ju   bol'šix   butylok
        with   five.INST   big.GEN.PL bottles.GEN.PL

         vina   ]$_{\text{NP.INST}}$
         wine.GEN

(2) a. [pjat'   bol'šix   butylok   vina   ]$_{\text{NP.ACC}}$
         five.*ACC* big.*GEN*.PL bottles.*GEN*.PL wine.GEN

         'five big bottles of wine'

    b. *[pjat'   bol'šie   butylki   vina   ]$_{\text{NP.ACC}}$
        five.ACC   big.ACC.PL bottles.ACC.PL wine.GEN

The case distribution in (2a) is characterized as heterogeneous because
the head noun *butylok* is genitive while its modifier *pjat'* is accusative.
The internal structures of (1) and (2) can be represented in (3) and (4)
respectively (case on phrasal categories is indicated by a lower case letter
preceded by a colon).

(3)

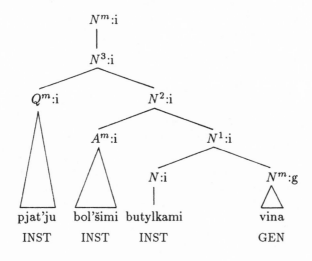

(4)

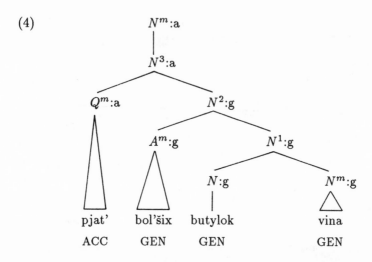

The heterogeneous case distribution in NOM/ACC quantified NPs like (2a/4) can be accounted for as follows: Q^m, the maximal projection of the quantifier, c-commands N^2 and all the categories it dominates, and assigns them the genitive case. C-command is a structural relation defined as follows:

(5)   Node A c-commands a node B if B is dominated by the first branching node dominating A, and A does not contain B; e.g.:

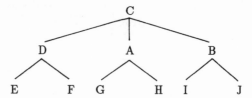

A c-commands B, I, J and D, E, F (but not G, H)

The accusative case assigned structurally to N^m in (4) percolates down to the quantifier *pjat'* 'five,' which is contained in the quantifier phrase and therefore not c-commanded by Q^m, but is prevented from percolating to N^2 (and the categories that it dominates) by the genitive case assigned to it by Q^m. This means that N^2 is the site of a *case conflict*: it is in the domain of accusative percolation from N^m and genitive, which is assigned by Q^m (hereafter GEN(Q^m)). The illformed structure in (2b) testifies to the fact that GEN(Q^m) takes precedence over NOM/ACC when they come into conflict. The resolution of this case conflict can be represented in (6).[1]

---

[1] See Babby (1984) for a more detailed discussion of case conflicts.

(6) $\text{GEN}(Q^m) > \text{NOM/ACC}$

Thus the heterogeneous case distribution in (2a/4) results from the interaction of percolation from N^m and c-command by Q^m, both of which are structural relations defined on X-bar structures.

The homogeneous case distribution in oblique quantified NPs like (1a) has the following explanation: N^2 in (3) is c-commanded by Q^m, just as it is in (4), but the illformedness of (1b) demonstrates that $\text{GEN}(Q^m)$ cannot be assigned to N^2 in oblique phrases; all the lexical and phrasal categories in the path of percolation must be marked with the same oblique case that is assigned to N^m. This homogeneous case distribution can be accounted for in terms of the resolution of another type of case conflict: N^2 in (3) is simultaneously in the domain of $\text{GEN}(Q^m)$ and INST, a *lexical case* assigned to N^m by the preposition s 'with' (see (1)). In other words, the N^2 node in (3) is c-commanded by both the phrasal category Q^m and the lexical category s. The wellformedness of (1a) vs. *(1b) demonstrates that lexical case takes precedence over $\text{GEN}(Q^m)$ when the two come into conflict, i.e.:

(7)   Lexical Case $> \text{GEN}(Q^m)$

Since (6) and (7) have a common term, they can be combined into a single set of principles for resolving syntactic case conflicts.[2]

(8)   Syntactic Case Hierarchy in Russian

Lexical Case $> \text{GEN}(Q^m) > \text{NOM/ACC}$

It appears to hold universally that lexical case takes precedence over all other types of case assignment, while structural case does not take precedence over any other type of case. The hierarchy in (8) therefore captures the traditional notion that nominative and accusative are "default" cases: they are assigned to N^m nodes that are *not* in the domain of a NP external case assigning category, and they are percolated to those lexical and phrasal categories dominated by N^m in the path of percolation that are *not* in the domain of a NP internal case assigner.[3]

---

[2] The Case Hierarchy in (8) can be viewed as a set of wellformedness conditions on the representation of a NP's internal case distribution.

[3] I have argued that quantified NPs like (1) and (2) have identical X-bar structures, and that the differences in their case distribution follow from the Case Hierarchy in (8). Note, however, that Government and Binding Case Theory (see Chomsky 1981) would have to claim that (1) and (2) have different X-bar structures since case in this theory is assigned exclusively in terms of "government" (which is defined as a structural relation) and the need for case hierarchies is not recognized.

3 The Case of Adjectives Preceding the Quantifier: Discontinuous Agreement

The first part of this paper was devoted to presenting the principles that determine the distribution of case in "core" quantified NPs; (9) is a schematic representation of a core quantified NP whose maximal projection is accusative.[4]

The homogeneous and heterogeneous case distribution patterns in (1) and (2) were explained in terms of the interaction of *percolation* from N^m and *c-command* by case assigning categories; the Case Hierarchy in (8) mediates this interaction. The following section will deal with the variable case marking on adjectives that *precede* the quantifier. We shall see that the small set of principles proposed in the first part to account for the case distribution in core quantified NPs also predicts the case agreement in these larger, more complex NPs. Thus the second part of this paper serves as independent motivation for the analyses and solutions proposed in the first part.

(9)

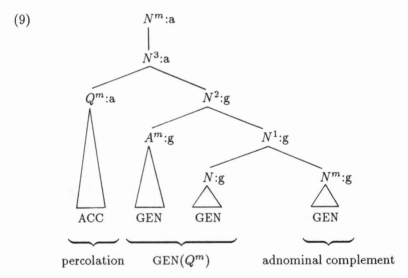

An adjectival modifier immediately preceding the quantifier in NPs that are NOM/ACC quantified can be either NOM/ACC—the same case as Q^m—or it can be genitive—the same case as the head noun. In the following examples, *vypil* 'drank' is a transitive verb and the accusative

---

[4] The rest of this paper is concerned with nominative and accusative NPs only because, as we saw above, the case distribution in NPs assigned lexical case must be homogeneous, and the heterogeneous case marking pattern on modifiers and the head that interests us does not therefore show up in oblique NPs.

marking on its object is therefore structural; the quantifier *pjat'* is declined for case only.

(10) Ja vypil (I drank):

a. *poslednie*   pjat'   bol'šix   butylok   vina
    last.*ACC*.PL   five.*ACC*   big.*GEN*.PL   bottles.*GEN*.PL   wine.GEN
    'I drank the last five big bottles of wine.'

b. *poslednix   pjat'   bol'šix   butylok   vina
    last.GEN.PL   five.ACC   big.GEN.PL   bottles.GEN.PL   wine.GEN

(11) Ja vypil (I drank):

a. *dobryx*   pjat'   bol'šix   butylok   vina
    good.*GEN*.PL   five.*ACC*   big.*GEN*.PL   bottles.*GEN*.PL   wine.GEN
    'I drank a good five big bottles of wine.'

b. *dobrye   pjat'   bol'šix   butylok   vina
    good.ACC.PL   five.ACC   big.GEN.PL   bottles.GEN.PL   wine.GEN

I will argue below that both these agreement patterns are entirely regular since they can be accounted for without adding any new rules or principles to those already proposed above. First we will look at the ACC-ACC-GEN contiguous pattern in (10), then the crucial GEN-ACC-GEN discontinuous case agreement pattern in (11).

Poslednie (ACC.PL) 'last' in (10a) belongs to a relatively large class of attributive modifiers that are normally used to modify the entire subconstituent dominated by N^3; the following are additional examples.

(12) $\left\{ \begin{array}{l} \text{ostal'nye} \\ \text{remaining.ACC.PL} \\ \text{vse} \\ \text{all.ACC.PL} \\ \text{pervye} \\ \text{first.ACC.PL} \\ \text{dannye} \\ \text{given.ACC.PL} \\ \text{predstojaščie} \\ \text{coming.ACC.PL} \end{array} \right\}$ pjat'   novyx   voprosov
                                                                      five.ACC   new.GEN.PL   questions.GEN.PL

294   Leonard H. Babby

Since *poslednie* modifies the N^3 subconstituent, it must itself be immediately dominated by the N^4 node since A^m is normally a sister to the maximal projection of the subconstituent that it modifies. The X-bar structure of the direct object NP in (10a) can accordingly be represented by (13).

(13)

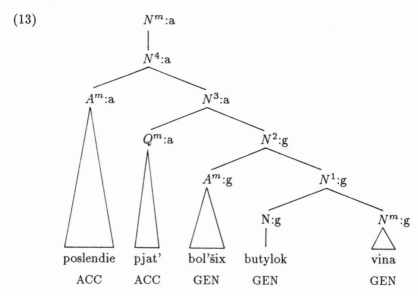

Notice now that the structure in (13) accounts for the phrase's case distribution. N^2 and all the categories it dominates are c-commanded by Q^m and assigned genitive case, just as in (2a/4). The adjective *poslednie*, however, is not assigned genitive because it is dominated by N^4 and, according to (5), not c-commanded by Q^m; it is therefore marked accusative by percolation from N^m. Since *pjat'* (ACC) is contained in the quantifier phrase, it is not c-commanded by Q^m (see (5)), and it also receives its case marking by percolation. The modifiers *poslednie* and *pjat'* in (10a/13) "agree in case" because they are both in the path of percolation of the same N^m and neither is c-commanded by a case assigning category.[5] Heterogeneous NPs like (10a/13) are crucial because they virtually rule out the possibility that a NP's internal case distribution is

---

[5] Since only determiners normally occur to the left of *poslednie*-type adjectives, we can conclude that NPs in Russian have five bar-levels above the head, i.e., N^m is N^5 in Russian. These determiners must also be NOM or ACC since, like *poslednie*-adjectives, they are not c-commanded by Q^m and therefore receive their case marking by percolation from N^m, e.g.:

èti   poslednie   pjat'   bol'šix   butylok

these.ACC.PL last.ACC.PL   five.ACC   big.GEN.PL   bottles.GEN.PL determined by the case marking on the head noun (cf. Chomsky 1965; Selkirk 1977): Since the two attributive adjectives *poslednie* (ACC) and *bol'šix* (GEN) have different case marking, the case agreement pattern in (10a) cannot be explained in terms of the head noun's case.

4 Prequantifiers and Discontinuous Case Agreement

Dobryx (GEN.PL) 'good' in (11a) belongs to a small class of adjectives that are normally marked genitive rather than NOM/ACC when they precede the quantifier in nominative and accusative NPs. The following are additional examples.

(14) a.   U   tebja   vperedi   [*celyx*   tridcat'
          at   you   ahead   whole.*GEN*.PL   thirty.*NOM*

          svobodnyx   dnej $]_{N^m:n}$
          free.*GEN*.PL days.*GEN*.PL

          'You have a whole thirty free days ahead of you.'

    b.   Luči   leteli   sjuda   [*dolgix*   pjat'
         rays   flew   here   long.*GEN*.PL   five.*ACC*

         let $]_{N^m:a}$
         years.*GEN*.PL

         'It took the rays a long five years to fly here.'

    c.   za   [*nepolnyx*   pjat'   mesjacev
         during   incomplete.*GEN*.PL   five.*ACC*   months.*GEN*.PL

         vojny $]_{N^m:a}$
         war.GEN.SG

         'during less than five months of the war'

The adjectives in this class, which I will call *prequantifiers*, have a clearly defined semantic function: they modify the quantifier only (see Crockett 1976:346) (in contrast, *poslednie*-type adjectives modify the entire N^3 constituent, which may contain a quantifier among its constituents). For example, *dobryx* in (11a) modifies the quantifier *pjat'*

---

vina $]_{N^m:a}$
wine.GEN

'these last five big bottles of wine'

'five'; it stipulates that the speaker considers the number of bottles consumed to be large, perhaps beyond the accepted norm (it can accordingly be glossed 'as many as'). *Dobryx* cannot be interpreted as modifying *vina* 'wine' or *butylok vina* 'bottles of wine.'

English too has a class of adjectives that can function as prequantifiers:

(15) a.   He drank a *good* five bottles of really bad red wine.

b.   Inflation increased this year by a *whopping* ten percent.

c.   Ronald ate a *phenomenal/unheard of/unbelievable* 25 burgers last night.

Phenomenal in (15c) refers to the excessively large number of burgers consumed (twenty-five), not to the quality of the burgers (cf. *Now that was a really phenomenal burger!*).

Prequantifiers form a natural class among adjectives that precede the quantifier phrase: they have a unique morphological property (genitive marking as opposed to NOM/ACC) and a unique semantic property (modification of the quantifier only). In the following sections we shall see that this pairing of morphological and semantic properties has a natural syntactic explanation.

It has been suggested that the genitive case marking on prequantifiers can be accounted for by simply generating them to the *right* of the quantifier under the domination of N^2, where they would be c-commanded by Q^m and assigned the genitive case along with the head noun, and then moving them to their surface position to the left of the quantifier phrase by means of a special transformational rule that operates on prequantifiers only, i.e.:

(16)   Prequantifier Fronting

$$[\ldots\, {}_{\blacktriangle}Q^m{:}a\ \ [\underline{A^m{:}g\ \ N^1{:}g}]_{N^2{:}g}\ \ \cdots]_{N^m{:}a}$$

The arrow represents the putative prequantifier fronting rule (see Corbett 1979).

The sole purpose of the derivation just outlined is to account for the genitive case marking on prequantifiers. It is, however, patently ad hoc and can be ruled out on both semantic and syntactic grounds. First, it requires a semantically unmotivated underlying structure (as we saw in the discussion of (11a), prequantifiers modify quantifiers, not the N^1 constituent or the head noun). Second, it requires an *obligatory* syntactic movement rule that has no purpose other than to map this illformed deep structure into a wellformed surface structure. I will argue in the next paragraph that in order to account for both their semantic interpretation and their morphological form, prequantifiers, like *poslednie*-type adjectives, must be "base generated" in their surface position to the left of the quantifier.

Since prequantifiers are adjectives that modify the quantifier phrase, they must be immediately dominated by the N^3 node; this is because, as we saw in the case of (10a/13), A^m is a sister to the maximal projection of the subconstituent it modifies. Thus the internal X-bar structure of the direct object NP in (11a) can be represented by (17), which captures the correlation between the adjective's scope in the NP, its linear position, and the bar projection that dominates it. Notice, however, that the X-bar structure in (17) also explains why prequantifiers in NOM/ACC NPs are genitive. Since the prequantifier $[dobryx]_{A^m}$ is immediately dominated by N^3, it is c-commanded by Q^m and, according to the Case Hierarchy (8), is assigned genitive case under precisely the same conditions under which it is assigned to N^2 and the categories it dominates. (Recall that c-command is defined in terms of *dominance* only; linear precedence plays no role, i.e., the node A in (5) c-commands B, I, J, which follow it, as well as D, E, F, which precede it.)

(17)

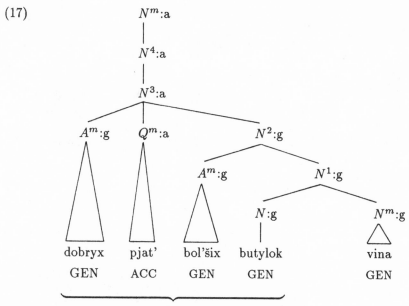

discontinuous agreement

The discontinuous case agreement found in nominative and accusative quantified NPs containing a prequantifier (GEN-ACC-GEN in (11a/17)) is the direct morphological reflection of the domain of c-command. The Q^m node in (17) assigns genitive to all the lexical and phrasal categories in the path of percolation that it c-commands, i.e., to the prequantifier $[dobryx]_{A^m:g}$, which *precedes* it, and to $[bol'šix\ butylok]_{N^2:g}$, which follows it. But the quantifier *pjat'* (ACC) is not assigned genitive because categories *contained* in the quantifier phrase are not c-commanded by Q^m (recall that the node A in (5) does not c-command G and H). Since *pjat'* is not c-commanded by Q^m or by a lexical case assigner, it is assigned the accusative case by percolation from N^m:a (see (8)). The schematic diagram in (18) represents case distribution in the path of percolation in a quantified NP containing a prequantifier.

(18)

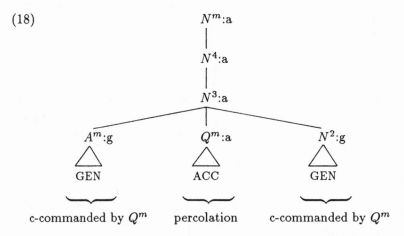

Contrast (18) with (19), which is a schematic representation of a quantified NP in which the quantifier phrase is preceded by a *poslednie*-type adjective; since these adjectives modify the N^3 subconstituent, they are immediately dominated by the N^4 node (cf. (10a/13)) and are assigned accusative case by percolation since they are not c-commanded by Q^m.

(19)

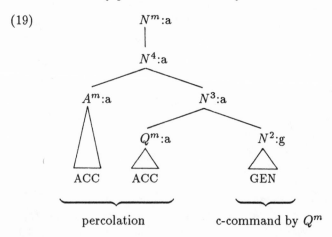

The principles of case distribution proposed in this paper allow for the possibility that a N^4-level modifier like *poslednie* 'last' and a prequantifier can occur in the same NP, and, furthermore, they correctly predict that such a phrase will have a *double* case agreement discontinuity in the path of percolation; e.g., see the ACC-GEN-ACC-GEN case agreement pattern in (20) and its X-bar structure in (21).

(20)   za   ostavšiesja   nepolnyx   pjat'
        for   remaining.*ACC*.PL   incomplete.GEN.PL   five.*ACC*

        let   (vojny)
        years.*GEN*.PL   war.GEN

        (lit.) 'for the remaining not quite five years (of the war)'

(21)

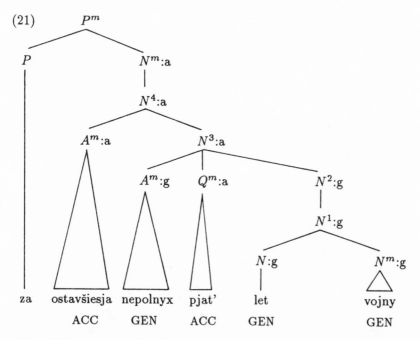

Q^m in (21) c-commands the prequantifier *nepolnyx* 'incomplete' and the head noun *let* 'years,' and assigns them the genitive case (cf. (11a/17)). *Ostavšiesja* 'remaining' and the quantifier *pjat'* 'five' though are not c-commanded by Q^m and are consequently assigned accusative by percolation from N^m, just as in (10a/13). The fact that we are able to account for the double case agreement discontinuity in phrases like (20) without adding any new rules or principles constitutes particularly strong evidence supporting the theory of case assignment and distribution that has been proposed in this paper.

It has been suggested that prequantifiers are not sisters of the entire quantifier phrase (see (17)), but are *contained in* the quantifier phrase as a modifier of its head Q. According to this hypothesis, the structure of (11a) would be:

(22)

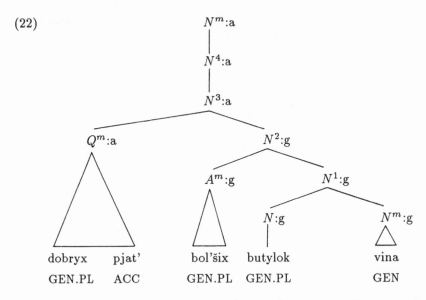

$$N^m\text{:a}$$
$$|$$
$$N^4\text{:a}$$
$$|$$
$$N^3\text{:a}$$

Q^m:a N^2:g

A^m:g N^1:g

N:g N^m:g

dobryx	pjat'	bol'šix	butylok	vina
GEN.PL	ACC	GEN.PL	GEN.PL	GEN

This suggestion is appealing because it involves a more direct match between the phrase's syntactic and semantic "bracketing": although the prequantifier $[dobryx]_{A^m}$ modifies the quantifier only, it is a sister to N^2 as well as Q^m in (17). The problem with this suggestion is: (i) if the pre-quantifier is contained in the quantifier phrase, it is not c-commanded by Q^m, and we cannot account for its genitive marking; (ii) adjectives agree in *number* with the head of the maximal projection in which they are contained. If prequantifiers were contained in the quantifier phrase, their plural marking would be a problem since quantifiers are not inflected for number (see *pjat'* in (10) and (11)).

If we assume, however, that any bar projection of the quantifier assigns genitive to the categories that it c-commands (as suggested by W. Harbert, personal communication), and, also, if we assume that quantifiers like *pjat'* are semantically plural and therefore induce plural agreement on adjectives that modify it (as suggested by J. Bowers), then there is no longer any reason to claim that prequantifiers stand outside the quantifier phrase as in (17). But a solution to this problem must be put off until we have a clearer picture of the internal structure of the quantifier phrase (see Babby, In Progress). It should be emphasized though that both of these analyses of the prequantifier's constituency are compatible with the theory of case distribution presented in this paper.

The case distribution in phrases like (1), (2), (10), (11), and (20) leaves no doubt that NP-internal case distribution is determined by dominance relations defined on X-bar structures, not by linear order, contiguity of constituents, or control by the head noun. Note, however, that these phrases also show that case and *number* distribution on attributive adjectives are determined independently, i.e., all the adjectives in a NP whose head is plural must themselves be marked plural, regardless of their case marking (e.g., in (20/21), *ostavšiesja* (ACC) and *nepolnyx* (GEN) are both plural, agreeing in number with the head noun *let* (GEN.PL)). Russian quantified NPs therefore demonstrate that the head noun controls its modifiers' number agreement, but not their case.

In addition to showing that discontinuous case agreement is regular and predictable, the analysis of NP-internal case distribution presented above also accounts automatically for the curious fact that discontinuous agreement is confined to nominative and accusative NPs only: If prequantifiers as well as N^2 and its constituents as assigned genitive under c-command by Q^m, as I am claiming, then the Case Hierarchy in (8) predicts that discontinuous agreement cannot occur in oblique cases (Lexical Case $>$ GEN(Q^m)), but can occur in NPs with nominative or accusative case marking (GEN(Q^m) $>$ NOM/ACC). In other words, this NOM/ACC vs. oblique case asymmetry is a necessary and natural consequence of the Case Hierarchy represented in (8) (cf. the heterogeneous vs. homogeneous case distribution asymmetry discussed in Section 3).

5 Case Marking on Postposed Modifiers

Until now we have focused our attention on case assignment to modifiers that *precede* the head noun. Since percolation and c-command, the two structural relations that account for case marking on preposed modifiers, are both *dominance* relations defined on X-bar structures, they should also account for case marking on modifiers that *follow* the head. In other words, if our hypothesis is correct and NP-internal case distribution is exhaustively determined by the interaction of percolation and c-command, then it should be the case that postposed modifiers in NOM/ACC NPs are assigned either NOM/ACC or genitive case (cf. heterogeneous vs. homogeneous case distribution in (1) and (2)). As the following examples demonstrate, this is precisely what we find.

(23) a. sem'   let,   *otdeljajuščie*   ix
         seven.NOM   years.GEN.PL   separating.*NOM*.PL   them

         drug ot druga
         from each other

         '(the) seven years separating them from each other'

    b. sem'   let,   *otdeljajuščix*   ix
        seven.NOM   years.GEN.PL   separating.*GEN*.PL   them

         drug ot druga
         from each other

302   Leonard H. Babby

(24) a. pjat'   priznakov,   *vvedennye*   vyše
         five.NOM   features.GEN.PL   introduced.*NOM*.PL   above

         '(the) five features introduced above'

     b. pjat'   priznakov,   *vvedennyx*   vyše
         five.NOM   features.GEN.PL   introduced.*GEN*.PL   above

The NOM/ACC vs. genitive case marking in postposition illustrated in
(23) and (24) has the following explanation. Postponed modifiers at
the N^3 level or below are assigned genitive case because they are c-
commanded by Q^m (see the schematic diagram in (25a)). But postposed
modifiers at the N^4 level or above are not c-commanded by Q^m, and,
therefore, they are assigned nominative or accusative by percolation from
N^m (see (25b)).

(25) a.

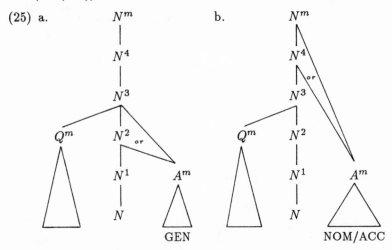

          GEN   NOM/ACC

    When a postposed modifier is genitive, it is felt by native speak-
ers to modify the head noun more directly than when it is marked
NOM/ACC (see Suprun 1964:83; Bulaxovsky 1953:298; Iomdin 1979;
Crockett 1976:345). This is because, according to the X-bar structures
in (25), postposed modifiers with NOM/ACC case marking are N^4 or
N^m level modifiers, and, therefore, have a *wider* scope (i.e., are sisters
to the maximal projection of a larger subconstituent) than postposed
modifiers with genitive marking, which are at the N^2 or N^3 level and,
consequently, have a *narrower* scope. Thus we see that this correlation between the case marking and scope interpretation of postposed
modifiers can be explained in terms of the NP's X-bar structure.
    Note finally that the structures proposed in (25) also explain why
discontinuous case agreement does not occur in postposition. As we
saw above in Section 5, the GEN-NOM-GEN and GEN-ACC-GEN "sand-
wich effect" that characterizes discontinuous agreement in Russian is

the direct morphological reflection of the domain of c-command. Q^m c-commands and assigns genitive to lexical categories that both precede and follow it, but it does not c-command and assign genitive to categories that it dominates (see (18)). Given the fact that in standard Russian the quantifier phrase's position is fixed to the left of the head noun, it follows automatically that discontinuous agreement is impossible in postposition: there are simply no lexical categories in postposition that are *contained* in a quantifier phrase and therefore shielded from c-command and genitive assignment by Q^m.

6 Summary

I have argued in this paper that NP-internal case agreement is the product of percolation from the head noun's maximal projection. The discontinuous case agreement pattern that characterizes Russian quantified NPs containing a prequantifier has provided crucial evidence that this hypothesis is correct (see especially (20/21)). While the Case Hierarchy, which forms the backbone of the theory of case distribution I have proposed, incorporates certain Russian-specific phenomena (e.g., GEN(Q^m)), I believe that the general principles on which it is based have universal validity and should therefore provide genuine insights into the complexities of case distribution in languages unrelated to Russian.

References

Anderson, S. R. 1982. Where's morphology? *Linguistic Inquiry* 13:571–612.

Babby, L. 1980a. The syntax of surface case marking. In W. Harbert and J. Herschensohn (Eds), *Cornell Working Papers in Linguistics* I. Ithaca: Department of Modern Languages and Linguistics, Cornell University.

Babby, L. 1980b. *Existential Sentences and Negation in Russian.* Ann Arbor: Karoma.

Babby, L. 1984. Case conflicts and their resolution: a contribution to EST case theory. In W. Harbert (Ed), *Cornell Working Papers in Linguistics* VI. Ithaca: Department of Modern Languages and Linguistics, Cornell University.

Babby, L. 1985. Prepositional quantifiers and the direct case condition in Russian. In M. Flier and R. Brecht (Eds), *Issues in Russian Morphosyntax.* Columbus, Ohio: Slavica Publishers.

Babby, L. 1986. The locus of case assignment and the direction of percolation: case theory and Russian. In R. Brecht and J. Levine (Eds), *Case in Slavic.* Columbus, Ohio: Slavica Publishers.

Babby, L. 1987. Case, prequantifiers, and discontinuous agreement in Russian. *Natural Language and Linguistic Theory* 5(1):91–138.

Babby, L. In progress. *The Syntax of Surface Case (Evidence from Russian)*.

Belletti, A. and L. Rizzi. 1981. The syntax of "ne": some theoretical implications. *The Linguistic Review* 1(2):117–154.

Bowers, J. 1984. On the autonomy of inflectional morphology. In W. Harbert (Ed), *Cornell Working Papers in Linguistics* VI. Ithaca: Department of Modern Languages and Linguistics, Cornell University.

Bulaxovskij, L. A. 1953. *Kurs Russkogo Literaturnogo Jazyka*, Tom II (Istoričeskij Komentarij). Kiev: Radians'ka shkola.

Chomsky, N. 1965. *Aspects of the Theory of Syntax*. Cambridge, Mass.: The MIT Press.

Chomsky, N. 1981. *Lectures on Government and Binding*. Dordrecht: Foris.

Corbett, G. G. 1979. Adjective movement. Nottingham Linguistic Circular 8(1):1–10.

Crockett, D. 1976. *Agreement in Contemporary Standard Russian*. Cambridge, Mass.: Slavica Publishers.

Iomdin, L. L. 1979. Fragment Modeli Russkogo Poverxnostnogo Sintaksisa: Opredelitel'nye konstrukcii. *Južnoslovenski Filolog XXXV*, 19–54.

Muysken, P. 1983. Parasitic trees. Ms. University of Amsterdam.

Selkirk, E. 1977. Some remarks on noun phrase structure. In P. Culicover, T. Wasow, and A. Akmajian (Eds), *Formal Syntax*. New York: Academic Press.

Suprun, A. E. 1964. Imja čislitel'noe i ego izučenie v škole. Moskva.

15 Noun Classes and Agreement in Sesotho Acquisition

KATHERINE A. DEMUTH

THIS PAPER EXAMINES the acquisition of agreement in a Bantu noun class system. It finds that nominal-modifier agreement is productive before the systematic marking of nouns. When nouns are finally marked with class prefixes, marking occurs without error. This suggests that the learning of both nominal class and agreement marking is highly dependent on a class feature associated with each noun, even though its overt marking surfaces only later. The paper concludes with a brief consideration of the learning of agreement in some Indo-European and Semitic languages and discusses how these phenomena differ from Bantu.

1 Bantu Noun Class and Agreement System (Sesotho)

Bantu noun classes typically consist of several singular/plural pairs. The number of these noun classes varies from one language to the next, but generally include 13-18 individual classes, from which 5 or 6 pairs are formed. Each noun class has its own set of phonologically similar agreement markers for subject-verb agreement, object clitic, adjectives,

Data for this paper was collected with support of Fulbright-Hays and Social Science Research Council doctoral dissertation grants. Preparation of this paper was conducted while being supported by NICHD Developmental Training Grant No. 5T32 HD07181, administered through the University of California at Berkeley. Material for this paper stems from discussion by Slobin and Demuth et al. during a seminar in the fall of 1983 and has subsequently benefited from discussion with Dorrit Billman, Moira Chimombo, Mike Connelly, Bill Foley, Zygmunt Frajzyngier, Mark Johnson, Ed Keenan, Ruth Miller, Tanya Renner, Susan Stucky, and Susan Suzman.

demonstrative pronouns, independent pronouns, possessive pronouns and relative pronouns. While the system was semantically based historically (cf. Hiene 1982), psychological studies indicate that little of this old semantic system remains productive today (Burton and Kirk 1976). Those classes which are still partially productive include a human class (class 1/2) and an "abstract/mass noun" class (class 14). New or borrowed terms which are not semantically related to these classes are assigned to classes on phonological grounds, or put into a "default" class (9/10 for Sesotho). Most Bantu nouns are marked by prefixes (but cf. Greenberg 1977). The noun class prefixes and agreement markers in Sesotho thus include the following:

Class	subj-V	obj-clit	adj	demonstr	PN	Poss	Rel
1	mǫ-	ǫ	mǫ-	e-mǫ	enǫ	eɛna	oa-	ea
1a	∅	ǫ	mǫ-	e-mǫ	enǫ	eɛna	oa-	ea
2	ba-	ba	ba-	ba-ba	banǫ	bɔna	ba-	baa
2a	bǫ-	ba	ba-	ba-ba	banǫ	bɔna	ba-	baa
3	mǫ-	ǫ	mǫ-	o-mǫ	onǫ	ɔɔna	oa-	oo
4	mę-	ę	mę-	e-mę	enǫ	eɔna	ea-	ee
5	lę-	lę	lę-	le-lę	lenǫ	lɔna	la-	laa
6	ma-	a	a-	a-ma	anǫ	ɔna	a-	aa
7	sę-	sę	sę-	se-sę	senǫ	sɔna	sa-	saa
8	li-	li	li-	tse	tsenǫ	tsɔna	tsa-	tsee
9	∅	e	e-	e-N	enǫ	eɔna	ea-	ee
10	li-	li	li-	tse-N	tsenǫ	tsɔna	tsa-	tsee
14	bǫ-	bǫ	bǫ-	bo-bǫ	bonǫ	bɔna	ba-	baa
15	hǫ-	hǫ	hǫ-	ho-hǫ	honǫ	hɔna	ha-	haa

	sg		pl
'person'	1	mǫ-thǫ	2	ba-thǫ
'aunt'	1a	rakháli	2a	bo-rakháli
'dress'	3	mǫ-sę́	4	mę-sę́
'day/sun'	5	lę-tsatsí	6	ma-tsatsí
'spring/well'	7	sę-liba	8	li-liba
'dog'	9	∅-ntjá	10	li-ntjá
'bread'	14	bǫ-hɔ́bɛ	6	ma-hɔ́bɛ
'to cook'	15	hǫ-phę́ha		

Table 1. Noun Class Prefixes and Agreement Markers in Sesotho

Notice (a) the phonological regularity of the agreement system, i.e., nominal markers have a high degree of phonological similarity with all their agreement markers, and (b) marking is for number and gender only—no case marking is involved on the noun. Thus, while the number of noun classes exceeds that of most gender or case agreement systems in other languages, this complexity may be manageable for learners due to its phonological regularity, its morphological transparency and the pervasive use of agreement throughout the language system. The use of these agreement markers is illustrated below:[1]

(1) a. mǫ-thǫ é-mǫ́-hǫlǫ ǫ-rata   Ø-ntjá ę́-ntlɛ   éa-haę̂
        1   1 1   1   9   9   9 1
        person big   he/she-like dog beautiful of-his/her
        '(The) old person likes his/her beautiful dog.'

    b. ba-thǫ bá-bá-hǫlǫ ba-rata   li-ntjá tsę́-ntlɛ   tsá-bɔna
        2   2 2   2   10   10   10 2
        people big   they-like dogs beautiful of-them
        '(The) old people like their beautiful dogs.'

Notice here that the possessives (at the end of each clause) are formed by markers which agree with both possessed and possessor, a case of "double" agreement.

2 The Data Base

The data upon which this study is based are drawn from a corpus of 93 hours of natural, spontaneous verbal interactions between 4 children, their peers, siblings and adult members of their families. The children were aged 2 to $4\frac{1}{2}$ years and were recorded over a 12 month period. The corpus includes an abundance of examples of both nominal and agreement marking at each stage of the children's linguistic development.

3 Noun Class Markers

3.1 Projected Problems for Bantu Noun Class Acquisition

Language acquisition research has led us to suppose that there are universal strategies which a child may employ during the language learning process, regardless of the language being acquired. Some of these strategies have been formalized as "operating principles" (Slobin 1985) which have been based on and continue to be refined by acquisition data from

---

[1] Transcription conventions used here generally follow Lesotho orthography, but include the marking of high tone (ó, é), high mid vowels (ǫ, ę), and open mid vowles (ɔ, ɛ).

a variety of languages from different language families. Using these principles, predictions have been made concerning the strategies one might expect to find in the acquisition of the Sesotho noun class system:[2]

(a) The learning of noun class prefixes might prove problematic as they carry little semantic content, are usually found in unlengthened/unstressed syllables, and bear low tone. The evaluation of this prediction will gradually evolve as we progress through this paper. Suffice it to say for the moment, however, that the use of full noun class prefixes is delayed till around $2\frac{1}{2}$ or 3 years of age. Once prefixes become productive, however, they appear with no overgeneralizations.

(b) In the process of linguistic development children tend to assign one phonological form to one grammatical function. Given the multiplicity of singular/plural forms in Bantu languages, one might expect children to collapse these distinctions, using only one plural marker for all nouns:

(2)   mę-sę́   >   *li-sę   'dresses'
         3   10
        ma-rú   >   *li-ru   'clouds'
         6   10
        li-ntjá >   li-ntjá   'dogs'
         10   10

This is apparently not a productive process in Sesotho acquisition.

(c) The stem plus singular prefix might be analyzed as the root form of the word, to which a plural marker would then be added:

(3)   sę-fate 'tree' > *sęfate 'tree' > *li-sęfate 'trees'
         7   10

Again, we find no such cases of erroneous segmentation, though this is precisely what has happened to plural formation in dialects of Kikongo (Stucky 1978).

(d) At another stage of development, children tend to regularize paradigms. So we might expect that, when singular/plural marking becomes productive, class 9 and class 1a nouns (that take Ø marking) will be assigned a singular marker of some sort, making them "fit the paradigm":

(4)   Ø-ntjá > *sę-ntja 'dog'
         9   7

---

[2] Predictions of agreement and noun class acquisition problems were generated during a seminar on Sesotho Acquisition at U. C. Berkeley during the fall of 1983, based on Slobin's Operating Principles as revised (1985). Comparative data from Sesotho, Chichewa (Chimombo) and Zulu (Suzman) was presented in a joint panel entitled "Problems in Bantu Acquisition," presented at the Stanford Child Language Research Forum, Stanford , March 1985.

Likewise, a few monosyllabic noun stems plus prefix might be mistakenly analyzed as more common CVCV nominal stems, being thought to belong to class 9 and prefixing a class 10 plural marker:

(5)   mǫ-sẹ 'dress' > *∅-mǫsẹ > *li-mǫsẹ 'dresses'
       3   9   10

Once again, data from the present corpus provide no evidence to suggest that either of these attempts to regularize a paradigm occurs, though again, such reanalyses have occurred in the history of Niger-Congo (Demuth, Faraclas and Marchese 1986). The following section provides examples of what *does* happen in the gradual learning and production of Sesotho noun class prefixes.

3.2 The Acquisition of Noun Class Markers

Before the age of 2 years, nouns of all classes frequently occur with ∅ prefix. Until the age of $2\frac{1}{2}$ years nouns continue to be used with ∅ or a "partial" prefix. Nasal classes 1, 3, 4 and 6 (*mǫ, mǫ, mẹ, ma*) are produced with N, or NV, earlier and with more consistency than non-nasal CV prefixes, which first appear with just a vowel. Phonological variation in the use of a single noun class prefix by one child during consecutive utterances is extremely common. Example (6) illustrates such a case, where ∅, -V and full CV forms are all used in one lengthy discourse sequence concerning green corn stalks. Judgements as to the singular or plural nature of the utterances are derived from discourse contextual information. Adult forms are provided in parentheses below.

(6)   (25.0 months):

sg	pl
pʰonko	phokɔ
a-pǝko	a-pokɔ
a-paka	ma-pǝnkǝ
(lẹ-phɔ́qɔ)	(ma-phɔ́qɔ)
'green corn stalk'	'green corn stalks'

Children progress through a stage of several months where a single lexical item may be rendered with no prefix, V- or full CV-, even in consecutive utterances in the same contextual environment. Connelly (1984) also reports similar findings.

After 3 years of age, when Sesotho speaking children exhibit correct productive use of all singular and plural prefixes, they occasionally omit prefixes of classes 5, 7, 8 and 10 (Sesotho *lẹ, sẹ, (N)li* and *(N)li*, containing [-grave] consonants) when an adjunct (demonstrative, possessive etc.) follows the noun:

(7)   (25.0 months)

ponko   láne

(lę-phɔqɔ   lá-ne)

green corn stalk that

'that green corn stalk'

Some monosyllabic nouns also occur with no prefix in the speech of 4 year old children when an adjunct follows (*li-jɔ* > *jɔ* 'food,' *sę-qǫ* > *qǫ* 'corn cob,' *lę-joɛ* > *joɛ* 'stone'). Omission of these particular class prefixes when the noun is used with an adjunct is a phenomenon also found in adult Sesotho speech, and may represent an initial stage of prefix loss in transition for Sesotho (cf. Demuth, Faraclas and Marchese 1986). Note that this strategy is also employed by Walpiri, where no agreement marking is needed when a modifier immediately follows its nominal head.

Table 2 below summarizes the developmental acquisition of noun class prefixes as used in spontaneous speech by the Sesotho speaking children in this study:

25-26 months: ∅, -V, CV

28 months: alternations between ∅, -V, N, C-, CV, but mostly NV with nasal classes (1, 3, 4, 6)

30 months: full appropriate prefix in the majority of cases. (classes 5, 7, 8, 10 occasionally omitted with adjunct)

36 months: all prefixes used in appropriate form

46 months: selective ∅ prefix with classes 5, 7, 8, 10 when used with adjunct

Table 2. Acquisition of Sesotho Noun Class Prefixes

Counter to the predictions, these data suggest that productive use of noun class marking occurs gradually and with no overgeneralizations. It would appear that the form of the current predictions do not adequately address the phenomena to which the Sesotho speaking child responds. This issue is pursued in the following sections.

3.3 Marking of Noun Classes in Experimental Conditions

The findings for spontaneous Sesotho data contrast with experimental results from closely related Siswati (Kunene 1979), where children of ages $4\frac{1}{2}$ to 6 *did* overgeneralize some prefixes. These children were given novel word forms and Siswati nouns out of context and asked to provide the corresponding singular or plural form of the noun. Table 3 below indicates the overgeneralizations which occurred:

Class	Siswati	Siswati Expt. *(overgeneralizations)*
1/2	umu/ba	umu/bo (2a)
1a/2a	Ø/bo	Ø/bo
3/4	umu/imi	umu/bo (2a)
5/6	li/ema	li/ema
7/8	si/ti	si/ti
		(i/ti)
9/10	in/tin	i/ti
11/10	lu/tin	li/ema (5/6)
		(i/ti)
14	bu	bu/bo-bu (+2a)
15	ku	ku/bo-ku (+2a)

Table 3. Siswati Noun Class Prefixes and Experimental Overgeneralization (E. C. L. Kunene 1979—$4\frac{1}{2}$ to 6 year olds)

Here we note (a) the use of 9/10-like class markings for classes 7/8 and 11/10, and (b) the overextension of class 2a to classes 2 and 4, and added to the liquid/mass class 14 and the infinitival class 15 (apparently analyzed only as stems, as they have no singular/plural alternations). There are also cases of class 11/10 being overgeneralized to classes 5/6, apparently due to phonological similarity. What is perhaps most striking, however, is that these same children did *not* make these or any other overgeneralizations in spontaneous speech. This would indicate a major difference in the linguistic nature of these productive contexts. In natural speech situations agreement information is available to help determine class affiliation, while in these experimental tasks it was not. Children in this experimental situation appear to have treated it as a "fit the paradigm" task. Many of our previous predictions for the acquisition of noun class prefixes are upheld in this case. It would be interesting if these same overgeneralizations occurred in an experimental task where the children were asked to use the given nouns in complete sentences.

3.4 Noun Class Acquisition in Zulu

According to Suzman (personal communication), Zulu speaking children spontaneously produce nouns with full prefix forms (although apparently with some overgeneralizations to the frequency and default classes) before the age of two, several months earlier than either Siswati or Sesotho speaking children. She notes that this may be due, in part, to the different nature of prefixes in these three languages. Zulu, as well as several other Bantu languages, is characterized by pre-prefixes, where the CV prefix has a copy (or near copy) of the prefix vowel prefixed to it, resulting in VCV prefix forms. Furthermore, these prefixes are never dropped in adult speech, as they optionally are in Sesotho. Suzman proposes that these prefix forms, with more consistent use and more phonetic information, may be more stable (both synchronically and historically) than those of Sesotho, and therefore easier for children to learn. Siswati, with only some pre-prefix forms, falls somewhere in between Zulu and Sesotho.

4 The Agreement System

4.1 Potential Problems for the Acquisition of Bantu Agreement Systems

As regards the Sesotho agreement system, one might expect a reduced number of distinctions to be made initially (one form, one function), with fully productive agreement developing only after the marking of nouns with their appropriate class marker. If the agreement system was originally represented by children as one set of singular/plural markers, one would predict that the "default" and most frequently used class 9/10 might be the one to be overgeneralized. Thus, there would be a collapsed agreement system where nouns of all classes would assume one agreement marker, as in the hypothetical case of possessives illustrated below:

(8) a. mǫ-sę   oa-ka ⎫
        3 dress   my   ⎪
                         ⎪
    b. sę-fate   sa-ka ⎬
        7 tree   my   ⎪   *ea-ka
                         ⎬   9 my
    c. Ø-ntja   ea-ka ⎪
        9 dog   my   ⎪
                         ⎪
    d. bǫ-hɔ bɛ   ba-ka ⎭
        13 bread   my

While such cases do occur in language contact situations and in historical change (Demuth, Faraclas and Marchese 1986), it is not entirely clear that this is the process which is involved in Sesotho acquisition.

4.2 The Acquisition of Agreement Markers

At two years subject concord, and sometimes focus marking, tense/aspect and object clitics (all pre-verbal morphology) are collapsed into a nonspecific pre-verbal intonational envelope which surfaces as an approximation of a:, e, or is entirely omitted.

(9)   (25.0 months)
        a   lahlíle
        (kę li   lahl-íle)
        I   them   throw-perf.

        'I threw them away.'

Occasionally at this time, but increasingly over the next few months, subject concord and tense/aspect marking become distinguishable and consistently present, if not always in their correct phonological shape. Object clitics become evident at the same time, 1st person *N*- being most phonologically prevalent, while other CV and V clitics begin to take consistent phonological shape by $2\frac{1}{2}$ years.

(10)   (25.0 months)

    a   ȩ shápa

    (oa   n-shápa)

    he/she me-lash

    'He/She is lashing me.'

Adjectives and demonstrative, possessive and independent pronouns are already in productive use by the age of two, surfacing frequently, but not always with appropriate concordial agreement. Here both of the forms (a) and (b) are found within several utterances of each other, while the form in parentheses represents the full adult form.

(11)   (25.2 months)

   (a) kolo   sáne

   (b) kolo   eáne

      (sekolo sá-ne)

      7   7

      school that

    'That school.'

While utterance (a) uses appropriate class 7 marking with the demonstrative pronoun, utterance (b) looks phonologically like a class 9 demonstrative. Many of the child's words at age 2 belong to class 9/10 and there is some tendency for what appears to be overgeneralization of class 9/10 agreement forms, as seen below in the case of noun-possessive-adjective. The line in parentheses again provides the appropriate adult prefix and agreement forms:

(12)   (25.2 months):

    Bɔ́ná   nto   ea-ka   é-nkɛ

             9?   9?   9?

             (lȩ-ǫtǫ lá-ka lȩ́-lȩ́-tlɛ)

             5   5   5- 5

    look-at foot   my   beautiful

    'Look at my pretty foot.'

Modifiers which appear not to agree with their nominal heads frequently occur when the prefix of the noun has not been specified, as seen in

Example (12) above (*nto* rather than *lǫ-ǫtǫ*, often *lento* in adult speech). There are, however, a few cases where the noun is clearly marked and the agreement marker still takes a different form:

(13)   (25.2 months)
       Lǫbese kǫ́ éo   é   pápa
       5   9?
       (lǫ-bese kǫ́ léo lé   pápa)
       5   5
       milk   is   here and   porridge

       'Here's some milk and porridge.'

Notice here that the /l/ is missing from the demonstrative pronoun *leo*, but also from the conjunction *le*. It is this kind of evidence which might support Chimombo's[3] suggestion that such errors may be due to inaccurate articulation at this stage. A much more in depth study of early Sesotho phonological development is needed to determine what phenomena can be attributed to articulatory problems and what to morphological overgeneralization. However, preliminary findings (Demuth 1986) show that both unstressed syllable deletion and initial consonant deletion are extremely productive phonological processes between 2 and $2\frac{1}{2}$ years.

As mentioned in Section 3.2, once the nominal prefix forms are produced with fair phonetic accuracy around $2\frac{1}{2}$ years, some prefixes are optionally omitted. There appears to be little problem in selecting the appropriate agreement forms in such cases. Thus, we find numerous examples of the following type, both in the speech of children under 3 years and with older children and adults. Here a noun is first used with no noun class marker, then postposed with full marking in the second sentence.

(14)   Two boys are looking at pictures of animals in a book. Mololo
       (5.2 yrs.) has just declared that they are pictures of mice.
       Hlobohang (36.2 months) retorts:

       -Talí   ha   lí-eɔ   ká   mɔna.
       ∅   10
       mouse NEG they-exist in   here

       'Mice, there aren't any in here.'

---

[3] Moira Chimombo (personal communication), in a study of Chichewa speaking children, suggests that apparent overgeneralization to the default class may in fact be a lack of young children's ability to produce phonologically distinct forms of agreement at this stage.

Ha   lí-eɔ   li-talí Bolólo! Ké̦ tšóene̦!

        10   10

NEG they-exist mice   Mololo   it's baboon

'There aren't any mice Mololo! It's a baboon!'

Even at this stage, where agreement appears to have been learned and applied correctly, we find the occasional example of apparent nonagreement such as the following:

(15)   H (36.2 months) and his grandmother are identifying different food types on a nutritional food category poster. Grandmother asks H where an egg is and he replies.

Ke̦ lé-ná le̦-hé̦

5   5

'It's here, the egg.'

Le̦ teng - a má-ngata

5   6 6

'It's here—a lot of them.'

(later, after discussion of other foods he says slowly ...)

le̦-hé̦ á   má-ngata

5   6   6

egg   many

'Egg—there are lots.'

It is not clear here if the noun is (a) being treated as a CVCV stem with no prefix, with plural marking specified only on the adjective, or (b) if the child started to say 'egg,' and then wanted to say 'a lot' without having to go back and say 'eggs' again. Alternatively, he may have been influenced by the grandmother's modeling of singular le̦he̦. Such cases do not appear to be productive and one could hypothesize that adult speakers might also produce such utterances on occasion. It is noteworthy, however, that in this case, where noun and adjective do not agree in number, they still agree in class pairing. In other words, random errors like those found in the experimental Siswati results and in bilingual Chichewa/English speakers (Chimombo p.c.) are not generally found in spontaneous Sesotho agreement forms.

In sum, the acquisition of concordial agreement, like that of nominal marking, is a gradual process which has already begun prior to 2 years of age, most notably with demonstratives and possessives. It continues until the age of 3 when most subject concords and object clitics, demonstrative, possessive and relative pronouns, adjectives and some numerals are used with agreement forms of the appropriate phonological shape.

The only overgeneralization which occurs between 2 and $2\frac{1}{2}$ years of age is a slight tendency for nouns of all classes to take class 9/10 agreement forms when the noun itself is not overtly marked, or at least many surface as such phonologically. This may be due to the large proportion of class 9/10 lexical items in the children's vocabulary at that time, or it may be due to the relative articulatory ease of the class 9 *e* agreement form over others. Comparative evidence from other Bantu languages may be of some assistance in determining which of these possibilities is most likely.

5 Discussion

If children were using semantic criteria as a means for learning Bantu noun class and agreement systems we would anticipate cases of overgeneralization, where a paired body part—say *tsɛbɛ/li-tsɛbɛ* 'ear, ears' (class 9/10) would be used with the class prefixes of other paired body parts— *lɛ-ihlɔ/ma-hlɔ* 'eye, eyes'; *lɛ-ǫtǫ/ma-ǫtǫ* 'foot, feet,' (class 5/6). We find no such cases in our corpus. As to the human and mass/abstract noun classes which are still productive, there is no apparent evidence that 2-3 year old children make these distinctions. If we were to find that *ngaka* 'doctor' (class 9/10) was used with human class prefixes or agreement markers (class 1/2), we would say that there seems to be some semantic influence in the learning of this agreement system. Again, such evidence is lacking from the present corpus. Bantu nouns having "derivative gender" (Greenberg 1978) can be assigned to different classes with a change in meaning. A 'person who sings' *mǫ-bini* (class 1/2) becomes a 'professional singer' *sɛ-bini* (class 7/8) with a shift in class. Again, there is no evidence to suggest that 2 and 3 year old children have control of or even access to this phenomenon as a productive part of their grammar at this stage.

How does one explain the discrepancies between the findings in this study and those of language contact and experimental situations? It would appear that processes of leveling and overgeneralization of agreement are accelerated in "non-natural" production environments. It is primarily in these cases that we find errors in nominal class assignment. Speakers in these situations appear to rely on extra-phonological criteria, such as phonological similarity to other noun class pairings, in their class assignment of unknown forms. In contrast, young first language learners appear to focus not simply on the nouns themselves, but on the entire nominal or verbal phrase where concordial agreement information is available. It is proposed for Sesotho that noun and modifier are attributed a class feature specification and are treated as some kind of prosodic, cognitive, or grammatical unit. Young language learners may adopt such a unit as a basic learning construct, using concord agreement productively while gradually coming to fine-tune the appropriate phonological marking for nouns. Once children become aware of this prosodic association feature, they then have access to tools necessary for learning and productively using the rest of the language. Comparative data from Chichewa and Zulu will help us to better understand this process.

5.1 Cross-Linguistic Agreement Acquisition

How does the learning of agreement develop in other languages? What kinds of mental constructs help in the learning of other agreement systems? It is difficult to know, in part because of the large range of different types of agreement found from one language family to the next, and in part due to the very different sources of data on which other studies are based, some drawn from natural speech and others experimental, some using 2-3 year olds and others using older children. A brief summary of some of the major cross-linguistic findings is found below.

In Romance languages (Clark 1985) there are early errors in article-noun agreement. In French, nouns are first used without articles. When articles start to be used there are numerous errors in appropriate gender assignment, but by the age of 3 most articles agree in gender with their nouns. A few problems persist in the appropriate gender marking of adjectives, and the masculine singular pronoun *il* is overgeneralized until 3 years or longer. Greenberg (1978) has demonstrated that Niger-Congo noun class markers are derived from demonstratives by much the same process that Romance articles were. We have noted that in both French and Sesotho nouns are first produced in simple root form with neither article nor noun class prefix. But here the similarity ends. Sesotho noun class prefixes do not function as definitizers (as pre-prefixes can in Zulu, Xhosa, etc.). Definiteness is achieved through the use of demonstrative and possessive pronouns. Sesotho nouns are "linked" with their definitizers at an earlier stage and with fewer errors than are French nouns with their articles.

In experimental conditions with older (6-8 years) French speaking children Karmiloff-Smith (1979) provided children with dolls and mismatched gender on corresponding articles and nouns which referred to the dolls. The 6 year olds changed the nouns or articles to agree with each other, rather than changing one of them to agree with the natural gender of the doll. Older children, in contrast, relied more on the sex gender of the doll in determining appropriate grammatical gender. Likewise, young Hebrew speaking children (Berman 1981, Levy 1983) use primarily phonological cues on the noun rather than contextual cues from adjectives or pronouns in their formation of plurals. In other words, erroneous plural marking occurs primarily in cases of phonologically irregular nominal endings. Levy (1983) notes that, in the period from 2-3 years, there was no use of sex gender knowledge in the early application of plural formation nor in adjectival agreement. On the other hand, it appears that the task of learning the plural forms probably helps in the learning of the gender agreement system. Thus, as in Sesotho, Hebrew speaking children rely on phonological rather than semantic cues to inform them of number and gender agreement, but unlike the Sesotho case, they appear not to use other grammatical agreement cues to help them in this task. This reliance on phonological cues as opposed to semantic natural gender cues also appears to hold for Russian (Popova 1973, Gvozdev 1961), German (Bohme and Levelt 1979, Mills 1985), Serbo-Croatian (Radulovic 1975), and Polish (Smoczyńska 1985). Only in a comprehension study of Icelandic pronoun gender (Mulford 1985), with children aged $4\frac{1}{2}$ to $8\frac{1}{2}$ years, are semantic criteria apparently used as a means for determining gender agreement. Icelandic nominal endings represent case, number and gender, nouns of one gender class have inconsistent phonological shapes and there is no phonological correspondence between nominal and pronominal forms. In such cases, then, where phonological cues to agreement are obscure, children (especially past 3 years of age) may begin to look for semantic cues to facilitate the learning of an agreement system.

5.2 Summary

In sum, only two of our original predictions were partially upheld: (a) that children might have problems learning prefixes and (b) that the agreement system might be collapsed to one form. With regard to the later, there appears to be a tendency around 2 years of age for agreement forms to surface with 9/10-like marking.

Whether this is due to poor phonological differentiation at this stage or actual misassigning of class marking is unclear. With regard to the former, the "difficulty" in the use of noun class markers is manifest not by the use of erroneous forms through overgeneralization, but rather by their relatively late productive use. When noun class markers do appear, however, they are used in correct form. The developmental process of noun class and agreement marking is outlined in Table 4.

Why were not more of the original predictions, based on studies of the acquisition of other languages, upheld for the acquisition of noun class marking and agreement in Sesotho? In part, perhaps, due to our inadequate understanding of how noun class marking and agreement function in this and other very different Bantu languages. Many of the predictions originally proposed here were founded on the understanding that the Bantu agreement system represents a paradigm problem like those found in Indo-European and Semitic languages. The phenomena exemplified in this study, however, indicate that this may not be the case. It appears that, unlike French, where children seem to learn nouns in isolation, and later learn what gender class they belong to, Sesotho nouns

2 years—Agreement marking is productive, especially with demonstratives and possessives. There appear to be some overgeneralizations to class 9/10, probably due to the fact that the majority of the nouns in the child's vocabulary belong to this class and that nouns are largely unmarked for class at this time. There may also, however, be phonological factors involved.

$2\frac{1}{2}$ years—Subject concord and object clitics are still frequently phonologically obscure, but most other agreement marking is distinct and often appropriate to specific classes. Nouns are usually marked with full and appropriate prefixes.

3 years—All agreement markers are phonologically distinct and appropriate to class. Nouns are all appropriately marked, though nouns of some classes optionally occur with no prefix when an agreement adjunct (most frequently a demonstrative, possessive, independent pronoun or adjective) is present, an attribute of adult speech as well.

Table 4.   Development of Noun Class and Agreement Marking in Sesotho

are learned in conjunction with their gender class features, even though the nouns themselves are not marked for these features until later. The Bantu agreement system is phonologically transparent and pervasive, suggesting the application of a class feature to phrases rather than to individual nouns. A much more in depth study of early phonology in these languages, the role of tone and other lexical and sentential prosodic features, a further understanding of the grammatical and discourse functions of the agreement system, as well as more complete evidence from different Bantu acquisition studies will help us to better understand the phenomena presented here.

References

Berman, R. 1981. Regularity vs. anomaly: the acquisition of Hebrew inflectional morphology. *Journal of Child Language* 8(2):265–282.

Bohme, L. and W. J. M. Levelt 1979. Children's use and awareness of natural and syntactic gender in possessive pronouns. Paper presented to Conference on Linguistic Awareness and Learning to Read, Victoria, B. C.

Burton, M. and L. Kirk 1976. Semantic reality of Bantu noun classes: the Kikuyu case. *Studies in African Linguistics* 7(2):157–174.

Clark, E. 1985. Acquisition of Romance, with special reference to French. In D. I. Slobin (Ed), *The Crosslinguistic Study of Language Acquisition.* Hillsdale, N. J.: Lawrence Erlbaum Associates.

Connelly, M. 1984. *Basotho Children's Acquisition of Noun Morphology.* Doctoral dissertation, University of Essex.

Demuth, K. 1983. *Aspects of Sesotho Language Acquisition.* Bloomington: Indiana University Linguistics Club.

Demuth, K. 1986. Phonological processes in Sesotho acquisition. Ms.

Demuth, K., N. Faraclas and L. Marchese 1986. Niger-Congo noun class and agreement systems in language acquisition and historical change. In C. Craig (Ed), *Noun Classes and Categorization.* Amsterdam: John Benjamins.

Greenberg, J. H. 1977. Niger-Congo noun class markers: prefixes, suffixes, both or neither. *Studies in African Linguistics, supplement 7,* 97–106. Papers from the Eighth Conference on African Linguistics.

Greenberg, J. H. 1978. How does a language acquire gender markers? In J. H. Greenberg (Ed), *Universals of Human Language 3,* 47–81. Stanford: Stanford University Press.

Gvozdev, A. N. 1961. Formirovanie u rebanka grammatic es kogo stroja russkogo jazyka. Izd-vo Akademii Pedegogiceskix Nauk RSFSR, 1949, Moscow.

Heine, B. 1982. African noun class systems. In H. Seiler and C. Lehmann (Eds), *Apprehension: das sprachliche Erfassen von Gegenständen.* Teil II. Tübingen: Gunter Narr.

Karmiloff-Smith, A. 1979. *A Functional Approach to Child Language: A Study of Determiners and Reference.* Cambridge, England: Cambridge University Press.

Kunene, E. C. L. 1979. *The Acquisition of Siswati as a First Language: A Morphological Study with Special Reference to Noun Prefixes, Noun Classes and Some Agreement Markers.* Doctoral dissertation, University of California, Los Angeles.

Levy, Y. 1983. The acquisition of Hebrew plurals: the case of the missing gender category. *Journal of Child Language* 10(1):107–122.

Mills, A. E. 1985. The acquisition of German. In D. I. Slobin (Ed), *The Crosslinguistic Study of Language Acquisition.* Hillsdale, N. J.: Lawrence Erlbaum Associates.

Mulford, R. 1985. Comprehension of Icelandic pronoun gender: semantic versus formal factors. *Journal of Child Language* 12(2):443–453.

Popova, M. F. 1973. Grammatical elements of language in the speech of pre-school children. In C. A. Ferguson and D. I. Slobin (Eds), *Studies of Child Language Development.* New York: Holt, Rinehart and Winston.

Radulovic, L. 1975. *Acquisition of Language: Studies of Dubrovnik Children*. Doctoral dissertation, University of California, Berkeley.

Slobin, D. I. (Ed) 1985. *The Crosslinguistic Study of Language Acquisition*. Hillsdale, N. J.: Lawrence Erlbaum Associates.

Smoczyńska, M. 1985. Acquisition of Polish. In D. I. Slobin (Ed), *The Crosslinguistic Study of Language Acquisition*. Hillsdale, N. J.: Lawrence Erlbaum Associates.

Stucky, S. 1978. How a noun class system may be lost: evidence from Kituba (Lingua Franca Kikongo). *Studies in the Linguistic Sciences* 8(1):216–233.

16 Noun Classes and Agreement Systems in Kru: a Historical Approach

LYNELL MARCHESE

THIS PAPER EXAMINES noun classes and agreement systems in the Kru language family from a historical perspective. In the first part of the paper, evidence is given for a proto-system consisting of at least four singular and three plural classes. The number of classes, however, as well as the noun class markers themselves have been reduced in virtually every language. Generally classes high in animacy are conserved. In an interesting twist, non-human classes in three languages have been reanalyzed as feminine, adding a new dimension to an otherwise genderless system. In the second part of the paper, agreement systems in Kru are surveyed. While anaphoric (or external) agreement is preserved in all cases, NP internal agreement is being lost in stages, with numbers losing agreement first and finally adjectives and demonstratives also giving way. Loss of agreement affects lexical items one at a time, a common phenomenon in language change. In the final section of this paper, I present a hypothesis on the origin of class suffixes and describe a present-day case of noun class suffix renewal.

Kru languages are spoken in southern Liberia and Ivory Coast and are presently considered to be an independent branch of the Niger-Kordofanian family. Kru languages derive, then, from a proto-language

Thanks to J. Singler, P. Saunders, and R. Thompson for discussions on Klao, Kouya, and Kuwaa.

with an extensive noun class system (Greenberg 1978; Cushingham, ms), which presumably had some form of agreement. The Kru language family is itself divided into two main branches: Eastern and Western, with the Western branch being further subdivided into the Grebo and Guere sub-complexes (Marchese 1979a). The languages mentioned in this study are classified roughly in the following way:

Isolate		Western		Eastern
	Grebo	Guere	other	
Kuwaa	Tepo	Guere	Dewoin	Godié
	Grebo	Nywabwa	Klao	Bété
		Wobe		Kouya
				Neyo
				Vata

Data in this paper come entirely from synchronic sources, there being very little historical documentation on this group. Though I consider forms from over ten Kru languages, the extent and reliability of the data on each language varies. I rely heavily on two comprehensive descriptions of Western Kru languages, Grebo (Innes 1966) and Wobe (Egner, ms), as well as on my own data from Godié, an Eastern Kru language. Part of the difficulty in untangling noun classes and agreement comes from the cyclic nature of the changes described. Noun class and agreement systems are often unstable, with markers emerging, reducing, and emerging again. Nevertheless, through a careful examination of the data, some reliable reconstructions and fairly likely scenarios can be proposed.

Most Kru languages have two vowel sets, retracted and unretracted. I have used the following symbols to signify vowels:

unretracted			retracted		
i	ɨ	u	ɪ	ʉ	ʊ
e	ə	o	ɛ	ə	ɔ
				a	

ɓ represents a voiced implosive bilabial stop, and n is a central nasalized vowel with limited distribution.

1 Noun Class Systems in Kru

1.1 The Proto-System

Though many Niger-Congo languages have between 12 and 24 noun classes with clearly segmentable prefixes or suffixes, Kru represents a fairly reduced system. First, while there is evidence for noun class suffixes, these have generally been worn down, lost, or rendered unrecognizable through coalescence with the final vowel of the noun stem.

The number of classes in Kru is also greatly reduced. The following chart gives the present-day subject pronouns of ten Kru languages.

(1)   Subject pronouns and reconstructed forms[1]

		HUMAN		NON-HUMAN	
		SG	PL	SG	PL
Eastern	Godié	ɔ	wa	ɛ,a,ʊ	ɩ
	Bété(Guiberoua)	ɔ	wa	ɛ,a,ʊ	ɩ
	Neyo	ɔ	a	ɛ,a,ʊ	ɩ,a
Western	Tepo	ɔ	ʊ	ɛ,ɔ,ʊ	ɩ,a,ɛ,ʊ
	Grebo	ɔ	ʊ	ɛ	ɩ
	Wobe	ɔ,ʊ	ʊ	ɛ	ɩ
	Nyabwa	ɔ,ʊ	ʊ	ɛ	ɩ
	Klao	ɔ	i	ɛ	i
	Dewoin	ɔ	ɛ		
Isolate	Kuwaa	ɔ	wo	e	wo/e
Proposed Proto forms		*ɔ	*ʊ	*ɛ,*a,*ʊ	*ɩ,*a

From the above chart, reconstructions have been made for four singular classes: *ɔ, *ɛ, *a, and *ʊ, and three plural classes: *ʊ, *ɩ, and *a. All of these classes are cognate with classes in other Niger-Congo languages, as will be made clear. With the convergence of both form and meaning across Africa, it is highly unlikely that any of these classes are innovative; they are clearly remnants of an earlier, probably more extensive class system.

The human singular *ɔ, found across the board in Kru, is cognate with Proto-Benue-Congo *u, which designates human singular. The human plural *ʊ has reflexes in most of Western Kru, as well as in the Kru isolate, Kuwaa. *ʊ is probably cognate with Proto-Benue-Congo *ɓʊ, the class used for plural kinship terms. This connection is supported by a *bo* human plural suffix marker found in Grebo (Innes 1966). The Eastern form *wa* is thought to be a coalescence of *ʊ + *a, an imperfective marker which no longer functions in most Eastern languages (Marchese 1982). Another possibility, of course, is that both *ʊ* and *wa* are cognate with Proto-Bantu βa, the human plural marker.

---

[1] Abbreviations used in this study include:

DEF	definite	N	noun	W	western Kru
DEM	demonstrative	NF	non-final	POSS	possessive
E	eastern Kru	NUM	numeral	SP	species
HUM	human	V	vowel		

326   Lynell Marchese

Evidence for the reconstruction of non-human singular *ε is clear in both Eastern and Western Kru. This class includes (though not exclusively) large and/or dangerous animals. Besides taking *ε anaphoric pronouns, many nouns in this class show traces of an earlier *-ε (or possibly *-lε suffix):

(2)   Godié nouns in the *ε class

mlε	'animal'	jε	'antelope' (SP)
luε	'elephant'	glε	'monkey' (SP)
kaɓε	'monkey' (SP)	tlε	'snake'
gbalε	'hippopotamus'	bɔlε	'monkey' (SP)
ɓlε	'buffalo'	gwε	'chimpanzee'
ɓaɓlε	'sheep'	ɓlε	'antelope' (SP)
kpəkε	'crocodile'	jι	'panther'
duduzuε	'anteater'	ɓlι	'cow'

This ε is clearly related to a front vowel prefix found throughout Niger-Kordofanian:

(3)   Forms for 'goat'

Yoruba	e–wúrέ	
Efik	e–bot	
Igbo	e–wu	
Proto-Bantu	ιN–boli	
Kordofanian	e–bonyi	
Kru (Godié)	wuli–ε	(definite form)

With its present plural pairing, *ε/*ι could be cognate with Proto-Bantu 9/10 and Proto-Benue-Congo i/í. Another possibility would be a correspondence with Proto-Benue-Congo *li/*a, typically used for animals. This idea will be discussed further shortly.

The reconstruction of singular *a and *u demands more explanation. Evidence for these reconstructions comes from Eastern Kru: Godié, Neyo, and Bété, and from Western Tepo (where a and ɔ are probably cognate). Confirmation of this reconstruction comes from two closely related Western languages, Wobe and Nyabwa, where an interesting reanalysis has taken place. In these languages, the proto chart has been redrawn along the the lines indicated in (4). Thus a masculine/feminine distinction has entered the family, an extremely rare phenomenon in Niger-Congo.[2] How did such a distinction arise? Egner points out that in Wobe, use of feminine forms is based on the name of the person in

---

[2] Ijo, spoken in Eastern Nigeria, also has a masculine/feminine distinction (Williamson, pc.). Along with Western Nyabwa and Wobe, Eastern Kouya has also acquired a masculine/feminine distinction, probably through contact with these neighboring languages.

question. Thus a man with a feminine name would be addressed with a feminine 'you' and a woman with a masculine name with a masculine form, so the system is still very much a noun-class system, with agreement being based on the noun, rather than on the sex of the addressee or referent. Nevertheless, according to researchers in the area, the distinction is clearly perceived as sex-based.

(4)

Proto-Kru			**Wobe and Nyabwa**		
	SG	PL		SG	PL

2nd PERS:			2nd PERS:		
			MASC	ɩ	
	ɩ	a	FEM	a	a(...)

⇒

3rd PERS:			3rd PERS:		
NON-HUM	a		NON-HUM		
	ɛ	ɩ		ɛ	ɩ
	ʊ				
HUMAN			HUMAN		
			FEM	ʊ	
	ɔ	ʊ	MASC	ɔ	ʊ

The innovative feminine forms in Nyabwa and Wobe strengthen the hypothesis that proto-Kru had *ʊ and *a. As far as class membership is concerned, *ʊ appears widely in liquids, non-solid masses, natural phenomena, and in some miscellaneous items. The following words from Godié take *ʊ pronouns and *ʊ agreement, and remnants of a back vowel suffix are clearly seen:

(5)

liquids

nyú	'water'
ɓlʊ	'milk'
dlù	'blood'
nʊ	'alcoholic drink'
zo	'soup'
bubu	'sweat'

non-solid masses

jlù	'fog'
vʊvɔlʊ	'wind'
gbaylʊ	'smoke'
ɓàɓù	'dust'
nyɔmʊ	'air'
zùzu	'spirit, shadow'

natural elements

kòsu	'fire'
lagɔ	'sky, God'
dʊdʊ	'earth'
glu	'soil'
ylʊ	'sun'
cʊ	'moon, month'

miscellaneous

wlú	'head'
lʊ	'song'
blɔ	'road'
ylʊ	'day'

The ʊ class suffix corresponds nicely to remnants of an *o-prefix in Yoruba, a Kwa language:

(6)   Yoruba

omi	'water'	ɔna	'road'	ɔbɛ	'soup'
ɔrun	'heaven'	ošu	'moon'	ori	'head'
orin	'song'				

Indeed it is quite surprising that despite the divergent development of lexical items, the membership of the ʊ class is quite stable. ʊ and its plural correspondent ι are cognate with Proto-Bantu 3/4 mu/mi, Proto-Benue-Congo u/(t)i, and Proto-Togo Remnant *o/*i.

In contrast to the ʊ class, the membership of the proto singular non-human *a class is more difficult to determine. It includes plants, plant products, small animals, birds, and insects, among others.

Turning to the non-human plural markers, evidence for plural *ι is clear from (1). A plural *a is reconstructed on the basis of singular/plural pairs ɛ/a found in both Eastern and Western Kru:

(7)   ɛ/a pairings in Eastern and Western Kru

	East			**West**		
	SG	PL		SG	PL	
'animal'	mlɛ	mla	(Godié)	nimi	nimia	(Grebo)
'antelope' (SP)	jɛ	ja	(Godié)	gɛ	ga	(Tepo)
'snake'	tlɛ	tla	(Neyo)	wɛsɛ	wɛsa	(Grebo)
'elephant'	lʊɛ	lɔɔ	(Godié)	dʊɛ	dʊa	(Tepo)
		[lʊ+a?]				
'lamp'	napɛ	napιə	(Godié)	nape	napa	(Grebo)

Membership in this class (animals) as well as the markers themselves suggest a relationship with *li/*a in Proto-Benue-Congo and Proto-Togo Remnant. Further confirmation for a proto plural *a comes from Neyo (Grah 1983) where a clear ɛ/a pairing is retained in the pronoun system.

The following system then is proposed for some stage of proto-Kru:

(8)

	SG	PL
HUMAN	ɔ	ʊ
NON-HUM	ɛ	a
	ʊ	ι
	a	

1.2 Reduction of the Proto-System

Comparing the system in (8) to the forms in (1), it is obvious that in many languages the number of classes has been greatly reduced. Eastern Kru is most conservative, with Neyo retaining all proto distinctions and Bété of Guiberoua and Godié losing the plural non-human marker *a*. In Western Kru, on the other hand, more reductions have taken place. As noted earlier, Nyabwa and Wobe have undergone a reanalysis in favor of a masculine/feminine distinction. In Grebo and the Kru isolate Kuwaa, only one non-human class remains.

(9)

Grebo		Kuwaa	
SG	PL	SG	PL
ɔ	o	ɔ	wo
ɛ	e	e	wo/e

In both cases, the semantics of the system have been somewhat skewed. In Grebo, proto human *ɔ has come to represent both humans and important or valuable items, while proto non-human *ɛ is restricted to small, unimportant or worthless things (reminiscent of the augmentative/diminutive classes in Bantu and Fula):

(10)

ɔ	ɛ
umbrella	toy umbrella
swollen lip	lip
person	terrible person

Reference to body parts follows similar lines. If a body part belongs to a human or large animal (sheep, goat, leopard), it will take the ɔ pronoun. If the animal is small (bird, mouse), its body parts will take ɛ. Interestingly, the plural forms are conservative, maintaining the proto Kru human/non-human distinction. Only humans take *o*, while everything else takes *e* (Innes 1966).

In Kuwaa, another semantic shift has occurred. According to R. Thompson (p.c.), the primary distinction between singular ɔ and *e* is one of animacy. In singular, all humans take ɔ, but words like 'fish' and even 'water' and 'tree' can take ɔ if they are animate (or as Thompson puts it "have spirit"). Inanimates, on the other hand (including 'fish' if it is dead and 'tree' if it is viewed as non-living), are designated by *e*. In the plural, the system is collapsing in favor of the human plural marker *wo*, with *e* used only for objects seen as collections or a group.

Both of these systems underline the role of animacy in determining which classes are preserved. Note that in both Grebo and Kuwaa it is the human *ɔ and large animal class *ɛ which have survived, while *ʊ and *a have been lost. The emergence of *wo* in Kuwaa as the general plural marker can also be seen as a case of the human winning out over the non-human (as well as an attempt to get around the ambiguity of *e*, a result of phonological neutralization).

Western Klao represents a further step in class reduction:

(11)   SG   PL

　　　HUM   ɔ
　　　　　　　　　　　　　　i
　　　NON-HUM   ε

Note that here again, in the singular, the human and large animal class markers have been preserved. Contrary to what might be expected, however, it is the non-human plural *i* which has been generalized to cover both human and non-human classes.

In Dewoin, the system has reduced even further. There apparently is only one singular third person pronoun (Mortvedt 1976) and not surprisingly, it is the human ɔ which is conserved. As in Klao, however, it would appear that a non-human form ε has been retained for the plural (probably representing a lowering of ɩ, though a possible reanalysis of singular ε as a plural marker cannot be ruled out).

Thus, overall, the general tendency is for the following hierarchy to govern the preservation of forms:[3]

human > large animal > everything else

We have seen, however, that this is a tendency and not an absolute, as the exceptions from Klao and Dewoin have shown.

As mentioned earlier, not only has the number of classes been reduced, but the noun class suffixes themselves have been continually worn down. Some suffixes have been preserved throughout the family, though most of these have been reinterpreted as part of the noun stem:

(12)   elephant *dʊ-ε   anteater *zʊ-ε

Godié (E)   lʊε   dʊdʊ-zʊε
Guere (W)   dʊε   zʊε
Wobe (W)   doε   soε
Tepo (W)   dʊε   hwε

---

[3] This parallels Comrie's (1981) hierarchy:

human > animate > inanimate

More evidence for this hierarchy comes from both Wobe and Godié, where the human pronoun is used as the "default" pronoun in relative, focus and interrogative constructions (Marchese 1978; Egner, MS)

Frequently, however, noun class suffixes are lost all together. In the word for 'water,' for example, *ʊ was retained in Godié, but lost elsewhere. On the other hand, in the word for 'saliva,' *ʊ was retained in Western Kru, but lost in Godié.

(13)

	water *ni-ʊ	saliva *dlɛ-ʊ
Godié (E)	nyú	dlɛ
Guere (W)	ni	seɛ ~ teo
Wobe (W)	ni	tɔ
Tepo (W)	ni	hɩjɔ

In other cases, the final vowel of the stem has been lost, having been replaced by the suffix vowel (making reconstruction of the stem very difficult indeed):

(14)

	tree ?*ti-ʊ	woman ?*ŋlV-ɔ
Godié(E)	su	ŋwlɔ
Guere(W)	tu	nynɔ (kpao)
Wobe(W)	tu	nynɔ (kpao)
Tepo(W)	tu (gbɛ)	nynɔ (gba)

The merging of noun class suffixes with the stem is strongest in the singular forms. In many cases, then, the singular form appears "unmarked," while the plural form appears to be marked by a plural marker (actually a remnant of the noun class suffix):

(15)

	SG	PL	
Bété	dɩba	dɩbawa	'father'
(Guiberoua)	da	dawa	'mother'
	tua	tuawa	'friend'
Tepo	pu	pui	'gun'
	bʊʊ	bʊɩ	'leg'
	toku	tokui	'tam-tam'
Grebo	ku	kui	'devil'
Wobe	jɔ	jɔe	'viper'

This is a common development in languages where class distinctions are being lost, as attested in Bantu (Stucky 1978) and Lower Cross (Demuth, Faraclas, and Marchese 1986). The forms in (15) are, however, exceptional. More commonly the forms pass through a stage of variation, presently attested in Kuwaa (Thompson, ms):

(16)   SG   PL

kùlù   kùlúí ~ kùlíí ~ kùlí   'day'

kolo   kolóé ~ koléé ~ kolé   'day'

fɔdɔ   fɔdɔɛ ~ fɔdɛɛ ~ fɔdɛ   'mud'

and eventually emerge, like the singulars, with the marker incorporated into the noun stem:

(17)   SG   PL

Bété   ɓle   ɓli   'place'
            glɔ   gwlι   'village'
            cʊ   cwι   'month, moon'

Tepo   plɛ   plι   'machete'
            kaa   kιι   'crab'
            to   te   'shop, store'

Godié   bəkə   bakʉ   'knife'
            li   lɨ   'spear'
            lʊ   lι   'thing'

Though no counts have been made, it is possible that human and/or animate nouns (15)may resist this change more than inanimate items (16), (17).

2 Agreement Systems in Kru

As has been seen in the preceding section, most noun class suffixes have been reanalyzed as part of the noun stem. As many linguists have noted, however (Moravcsik 1978:337; Greenberg 1978; Lehmann 1982), class marking does not need to be present on nouns for there to be a working agreement system. Indeed, this is the case in the Kru language family, where a variety of agreement systems are found.

In some languages like Godié, agreement seems to affect most of the clause. Anaphoric elements such as subject, object, possessive, and interrogative pronouns, as well as independent demonstratives and pronouns agree with their referent, irrespective of the distance or even the presence of the latter.[4] NP internal elements such as attributive demonstratives, definite markers, relative pronouns and most adjectives agree

---

[4] As noted by Corbett (1979:203): "... as syntactic distance increases... so does the likelihood of semantic (rather than syntactic) agreement." Thus, sometimes, in long stretches of discourse, semantic agreement may "outweigh" strict application of class agreement. In a story about a woodpecker, for example, a Godié speaker used an *a* pronoun (for the bird class), rather

in class and number with the governing head. In the following sentences, adjectives (a,c), demonstratives (a,c), definite markers (b,c), and relative pronouns (c) agree with their heads, while subject, relative, possessive and independent pronouns agree with their referents. Notice also the remnants of noun class suffixes on the noun stems themselves:

(18)   Examples from Godié

    a. nyʉkpɔ   kədɔ   nɔ   nii   mlɛ   kədɛ
        man   big   this   saw   animal   big

        'This big man saw a large animal.'

    b. mlɛ-ɛ   ɔ   niì   nə,   ɛmɛ   plʉ   lʊɛ
        animal-DEF   he   saw   NF   it   is   elephant

        'The animal he saw was an elephant.'

    c. nyʉkpɔ-ɔ   ɔ̀   nii   mlɛ   nɛ,   ɔ   kʊ̀   ɔ   ɓutʉ   kədʊ
        man-DEF   who   saw   animal   DEM   he   is   his   house   big

        'The man who saw that animal is in his big house.'

No other Kru languages I have examined have more extensive agreement than Godié, though Bété (from Guiberoua) and Neyo seem to exhibit almost identical systems. Many other languages, on the other hand, show varying degrees of agreement. What accounts for this synchronic variation? The answer must be a historical one: languages have either lost or gained agreement systems. Though the latter solution is not out of the question, I am assuming here that agreement systems are presently being lost. The reason for this is that both external (anaphoric) and NP internal agreement are widespread throughout Niger-Congo and probably existed prior to Kru's breaking off from the rest of the family.

In (19) I have plotted agreement in several Kru languages. Several observations can be made from this chart. First, we see that external agreement has been conserved across the board. Therefore we conclude that referential agreement is far more conservative than NP internal agreement. Secondly, we note that in no language is there number agreement, a common feature of many Niger-Congo noun class languages. Thus, numerals have only one form, irrespective of the class of the referent, as exemplified in (20). In all fairness, it is hard to determine whether numeral agreement was lost or simply never present. Evidence

---

than ʊ, which would have been warranted by the word 'woodpecker.' Some speakers also vary back and forth between pronominal forms, especially when they consider animals functioning as main participants to have human behavior.

from other language groups such as Lower Cross (Demuth, Faraclas, and Marchese 1986), however, shows that agreement on numerals is the first to disappear, suggesting a similar history in Kru.

(19)

Language	Anaphoric (External) Agreement					
	Subj	Obj	Poss	Ind	Ind	Interr
Godié	X	X	X	X	X	X
Bété (Guberoua)	X	X	X	X	X	X
Neyo	X	X	X	X	X	X
Wobe	X	X	X	X	X	X
Kouya	X	X	X	?	X	?
Grebo	X	X	X	X	X	NR
Kuwaa	X	X	X	?	X	NR
Klao	X	X	X	?	?	?
Dewoin	SG/PL	SG/PL	SG/PL	?	SG/PL	?

Language	NP Internal Agreement					
	Dem	Adj1	Def	Adj2	Rel	Num
Godié	X	X/10	X	X/8	X	O
Bété (Guberoua)	X	X	X	X	X	O
Neyo	X	X	X	X	X	O
Wobe	X	X/10	NR	X/1	X	O
Kouya	X	X	?	?	?	O
Grebo	X	X	?	O	X	O
Kuwaa	SG/PL	X/1	X	O	?	O
Klao	O	X	O	O	?	O
Dewoin	O	?	O	O	?	O

X   = agreement present   Adj1 agrees in number only
O   = agreement not present   Adj2 agrees in class and number
NR   = not relevant
SG/PL = singular/plural distinction only
?   = unknown

(20)   Godié

ɓìtì   kə́dì   nī   sɔ́
houses big   DEM   two
'Those two big houses'

nyū̄kpà kə́dʋà nūa   sɔ́
men   big   DEM   two
'Those two big men'

Third, we note that adjectives lose agreement in stages. There is evidence that class distinctions are lost first, with number agreement being lost later. For example, in Godié, all adjectives apparently agree in number, with eight out of ten also agreeing in class. In Wobe, at least ten adjectives agree in number, but only one *cɔɔ/cɛɛ* 'good' agrees in class (Egner, ms). In Kuwaa, the Kru isolate, no adjectives agree in class and only one agrees in number: *gbàà* (SG) *gbààvìì* (PL) 'big' (Thompson, p.c.). Such developments provide a nice illustration of change "working its way" through the lexicon, a quite common phenomenon (Stucky 1978; Lightfoot 1979; Marchese 1979b). Kouya, an Eastern language, provides another example of the role of variation; speakers presently alternate between two forms for 'good' and 'big,' one agreeing with the head noun in number and the other one not (Saunders, p.c.):

(21)   wee   [sakwala *nane*   ylukpa   *kade*   sɔ

~ wee   sakwala   *nanʊ*   ylukpa   *kadʊ*   sɔ

these   shoes   good   black   big   two

'These two big black beautiful shoes'

Note that *ylukpa* 'black' has apparently lost all agreement, since it does not vary. There may in fact be some kind of hierarchy of change affecting adjectives, since in all the cases cited here, both 'good' and 'big' seem particularly resistant to agreement loss.

Though all the evidence is not in, demonstratives seem more resistant to agreement loss than adjectives. In Wobe, Kouya, and Kuwaa, for example, demonstratives retain number and class agreement, while adjective agreement is clearly decreasing:

(22)   Examples from Wobe

ju   *nɔ*   'this man'
nynɔkpao   *nʊ*   'this woman'
tae   *nɛ*   'this cloth'

Exceptionally, Klao retains some number agreement on adjectives, but has no agreement on the demonstrative/definite marker *na*:

(23)   Klao

nyinɔ   *na*   'the woman'
sla   *na*   'the house'

What determines which elements will lose agreement first? Looking at the order of elements within the NP, it is evident that the element farthest from the head (i.e. the numeral) loses agreement first:

$$(\text{POSS}) \quad \text{N} \quad (\text{ADJ}) \quad \left\{ \begin{array}{c} (\text{DEM}) \\ (\text{DEF}) \end{array} \right\} \quad (\text{NUM})$$

However, it does not appear that distance is the only determining factor. We have already seen in (21) that agreement in Kouya "skips over" certain adjectives. Also, demonstratives, which are further from the head, appear to be more conservative than adjectives which are closer. A more likely hypothesis is that elements which are more tightly bound to the head will conserve agreement longest. In the case of numerals, there is good evidence that they are more independent that other elements within the NP. For example, in Godié, a tone lowering rule spreads through the NP, stopping short of the numeral (Gratrix 1976), suggesting the following possible structure:

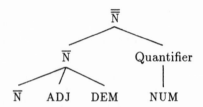

The reason for demonstratives and certain adjectives being more resistant to change, however, remains problematic.

There is one more observation that can be made in regard to agreement loss. A definite correlation exists between a decrease in class distinctions and a decrease in NP internal agreement. Turning again to the chart in (19), it can be seen that those languages with the most class distinction—for example, Godié, Bété, Neyo—have the most NP internal agreement. In Wobe, internal agreement is not as strong, with the removal of one distinction from the four singular proto classes. Those languages with less class distinctions, particularly Klao and Dewoin, show the least amount of NP internal agreement—at least to the extent that no head agrees with demonstrative, definite marker, or adjective in class.

3 The Future of Noun Class Systems

The present data have shown that class systems and class agreement are diminishing in most, if not all, Kru languages. If this is the case, what is the future of such systems? There appear to be several possible answers. First, languages may just accept their class-less nature as Dewoin seems to have done. Second, a language may lean toward a phonologically based system, and third, a language may try to "renew" its noun class suffixes and thus "revitalize" the system.

The first solution is rare. Despite the reduction of classes and agreement, most languages have held onto basic class distinctions and some form of agreement. Dewoin, a language with a small bilingual population, may have been "helped along" to classlessness by neighboring Vai, a Mande language with no class system.

The second solution is quite intriguing. In some languages where noun suffixes have replaced the final vowel of noun stems, what appears to be a phonological type of agreement has emerged. Indeed, in my first months of study of Godié, I was only able to figure out the pronominal system by appealing to a kind of phonological solution. I noticed I could never get the pronoun right unless I was referring to a human. Eventually, I formulated the following rule (Marchese 1975) to account for the non-human singular pronouns. If the word in question ends in a front vowel, then the front vowel pronoun ɛ is used. If the word ends in a central vowel, then the central pronoun a is used; likewise, if the word ends in a back vowel, the back pronoun ʊ is used:

(24)

i	ɨ	u
ɪ	ʉ	ʊ
e	ə	o
ɛ	ə	ɔ
	a	

ɛ   a   ʊ

Examples:

ɛ pronoun: mlɛ 'animal,'   lʊɛ 'elephant,'   li 'spear'
a pronoun: nɨmle 'bird,'   sʉka 'rice,'   nyidə 'cooking pot'
ʊ pronoun: nyú 'water,'   jlu 'fog,'   nʊ 'alcoholic drink'

Along these same lines, Tepo's large number of plural pronouns may be attributable to a system of phonological agreement. In fact, Kaye (1981) argues that Tepo and an Eastern language, Vata, have almost entirely phonologically based systems. Though I sympathize with the approach and intuitively felt this was the solution for Godié, I now must conclude that it does not, in fact, account for the Godié facts. Not only do we have to contend with the human/non-human distinction and the agreement system as a whole, we also have to deal with a good number of irregularities which can only be explained by the class system. For example, numerous words in Godié take ɔ agreement simply because they belong to this class; their agreement is not phonologically determined:

(25)   pɛpɛ   nɔ,   ɔmɔ n   nïi...
       little.thing DEM   it   I   saw

       'This little thing, it's this I saw...'

In the above example, pɛpɛ, 'little thing' shows both internal and external agreement based on its class membership—not on its phonological shape. Furthermore, many borrowed words "acquire" a proper vowel ending, allowing them to function normally in the class system:

(26) *mióko* 'milk' taking the back vowel *o*, triggering *ʋ*
pronouns and *ʋ* agreement (liquids)

jakásı 'jackass' taking the front vowel *ı*, triggering *ɛ*
pronouns and *ɛ* agreement (large animals)

Thus, though there is a tendency towards a phonologically based system, it is clear that Godié has maintained its noun class nature.

In fact, Godié, along with Neyo and Bété, appears to be in the process of reinforcing the noun class system. Along with all the other agreement described above, Godié has definite suffixes which share the same shape as the subject pronouns. Various morphophonological rules apply to these forms (including vowel harmony) as seen below:

(27) NOUN + DEF in Godié

nyʉkpɔ	+	ɔ	nyʉkpɔɔ	'the man'
6utu	+	ʋ	6ùtùu	'the house'
golʋ	+	ʋ	gɔlʋʋ	'the canoe'
li	+	ɛ	lie~liɛ	'the spear'
sʉka	+	a	sʉkáa	'the rice'
nyʉkpa	+	wa	nyʉkpùa	'the men'
6iti	+	ı	6itìi	'the houses'

Where did these definite markers in Kru come from? Greenberg (1977: 55, 75) has noted that commonly, demonstratives and/or pronouns give rise to definite markers, which can, themselves, develop into class markers. Godié has a demonstrative form *nV* (seen in (18a) and (18c)), which probably goes back to proto-Kru, making a demonstrative origin unlikely. However following Greenberg and many other scholars (Givón 1976; Childs 1982; Lehmann 1982), the origins of agreement can be traced in this case to other anaphoric elements. Givón, for example, suggests that subject pronouns give rise to subject agreement markers on the verb in Bantu. He suggests a topic-comment construction as the context for reanalysis:

Topic	Comment	
The man	he	come
	SUBJ PRO	VERB

The man	he-come
SUBJ	VERB

Interestingly, no Kru language has developed agreement markers on the verb, primarily because Kru languages are suffixing rather than prefixing. However, it seems very likely that a similar context permitted the reanalysis of subject pronouns as definite markers (i.e. the reanalysis went in the opposite direction):

Topic   Comment

man	he	come
	SUBJ PRO	VERB

man-he	come
SUBJ	VERB

Evidence for such a proposal is quite strong. First, topic-comment constructions such as (28) below from Godié are extremely common in Kru languages (Marchese 1979a). While definite markers were probably non-existent in proto-Kru, topics are inherently [+definite]. It would seem quite plausible, then, that the proposed pattern for reanalysis would be:

(28)   li   ε   kʊ̀   mɔ́
       spear it   is   over.there

       'The spear, it's over there'

The sentence-second element (i.e. the subject pronoun) would be cliticized onto the noun topic and eventually reanalyzed as a definite marker, as seen in the properly formed Godié sentence below:

(29)   li-ε   kʊ̀   mɔ́
       spear-DEF   is   over there

       'The spear is over there'

Once the reanalysis had taken place in this position, the definite suffix would eventually make its way onto other NPs in the clause. Similar reanalyses involving sentence-second particles are well attested in Kru. Both imperfective and negative pronoun sets have evolved in this way (Marchese 1979b). These facts may even explain why some languages have failed to renew their class suffix systems. In some languages like Wobe, innovative topic markers are present, which disrupt the environment needed for reanalysis, explaining why these languages currently have no definite suffixes.

Thus, the forms from Godié (and neighboring Bété and Neyo) provide good evidence on how class markers arose originally throughout the family. The development would be:

subject pronoun > definite marker > class marker

with the class marker eventually collapsing into the stem as described above.

This development parallels closely the formation of pre-prefixes in Bantu languages, where stems are doubly marked for class. In Godié, for example, one could claim that "post-suffixes" exist, a phenomenon only rarely attested in Sub-Saharan Africa (Greenberg 1977, 1978):

(30)   *ni   + ʊ   + ʊ   = [nyúū]
        water + CLASS   + DEFINITE   'the water'
                MARKER   MARKER

4 Concluding Remarks

This study leaves several unanswered questions, however. If we know how noun class suffixes emerge and are lost, we still do not know what motivated the original noun classification in the first place. It was certainly the distinction in anaphoric elements resulting from this classification which gave rise to the initial noun class suffixing system. Neither do we know how, once the suffixes arose as definite markers, agreement "spread" onto other elements in the NP. We do know, however, that despite the current tendency to lose both class suffixation and class agreement, such systems "die hard." Many Kru languages persist in retaining (and in some cases recreating) characteristics of true noun class systems.

References

Childs, G. Tucker 1982. *The Evolution of Noun Class Markers in the Southern West Atlantic Languages.* Master's thesis, University of California, Berkeley.

Comrie, B. 1981. *Language Universals and Linguistic Typology.* Chicago: The University of Chicago Press.

Corbett, G. G. 1979. The agreement hierarchy. *Journal of Linguistics* 15:203–224.

Cushingham, S. Undated. Outline of the noun class and concord system of Proto Niger-Kordofanian. Paper presented at the 11th Conference on African Linguistics.

Demuth, K., N. Faraclas, and L. Marchese 1986. Niger-Congo noun class and agreement systems in language acquisition and historical change. In C. Craig (Ed), *Noun Classes and Categorization.* Amsterdam: John Benjamins.

Dwyer, D. Undated. Evolutionary morphology. Ms.

Egner, I. Undated. *Précis de Grammaire Wobe.* Ms.

Givón, T. 1976. Topic, pronoun, and grammatical agreement. In C. N. Li (Ed), *Subject and Topic.* New York: Academic Press.

Grah, C. 1983. *Approche Systématique du N'wɔl.* Thèse de III cycle. Paris III.

Gratrix, C. 1975. Morphotonologie du Godié. *Annales de l'Université d'Abidjan,* Serie H. Abidjan: Institut de Linguistique Appliquée.

Greenberg, J. H. 1977. Niger-Congo noun class markers: prefixes, suffixes, both or neither. *Studies in African Linguistics, supplement 7*, 97–106. Papers from the Eighth Conference on African Linguistics.

Greenberg, J. H. 1978. How does a language acquire gender markers? In J. H. Greenberg (Ed), *Universals of Human Language* 3. Stanford: Stanford University Press.

Innes, G. 1966. *An Introduction to Grebo*. London: School of Oriental and African Studies.

Kaye, J. 1981. La selection des formes pronominales en Vata et en d'autres langues Krou orientales. *Cahiers Ivoriens de Recherche Linguistique* 9:5–24. Abidjan: University of Abidjan.

Lehmann, C. 1982. Universal and typological aspects of agreement. In H. Seiler and F. J. Stachowiak (Eds), *Apprehension: das sprachliche Erfassen von Gegenständen*. Teil II. Tübingen: Gunter Narr.

Lightfoot, D. 1979. *Diachronic Syntax*. Cambridge, England: Cambridge University Press.

Marchese, L. 1975. Morphonologie du verbe Godié. *Annales de l'Université d'Abidjan*, Serie H. Abidjan: Institut de Linguistique Appliquée.

Marchese, L. 1978. *Subordination en Godié*. Abidjan: University of Abidjan (Translated Master's thesis, University of California, Los Angeles. 1976).

Marchese, L. 1979a. *Atlas Linguistique des Langues Kru; Essai de Typologie*. Abidjan: Institut de Linguistique Appliquée.

Marchese, L. 1979b. *Tense/aspect and the Development of Auxiliaries in the Kru Language Family*. Doctoral dissertation, University of California, Los Angeles.

Marchese, L. 1982. Basic aspectual categories in Proto-Kru. *Journal of West African Languages* 12.

Moravcsik, E. 1978. Agreement. In J. H. Greenberg (Ed), *Universals of Human Language* 2. Stanford: Stanford University Press.

Mortvedt, 1976. Field Notes. Ms.

Stucky, S. 1978. How a noun class system may be lost: Evidence from Kituba. *Studies in the Linguistic Sciences* 8(1):216-233.

Thompson, R. Undated. Tentative Kuwaa Grammar. Ms.

Werle, H. M. and J. Gbaleyi. *Morphonologie du Bété de la region de Guiberoua*. Abidjan: Institut de Linguistique Appliquée.

Welmers, W. E. 1977. Mood in Dewoin. In P. Kotey and H. Der Honssikian (Eds), *Language and Linguistic Problems in Africa*. Columbia, S. C.: Hornbeam Press.

Language Index

Name Index

Subject Index

349